Globe-flower'
Boule d'or
May 28ᵗ
R SARENE

RANUNCULUS
JUNE 1927. RIVER SARENE

ELIZABETH DAVID
A Biography

ELIZABETH DAVID

A Biography

LISA CHANEY

MACMILLAN

First published 1998 by Macmillan

an imprint of Macmillan Publishers Ltd
25 Eccleston Place, London SW1W 9NF
and Basingstoke

Associated companies throughout the world

ISBN 0 333 65930 9

5 7 9 8 6

A CIP catalogue record for this book is available from
the British Library.

Typeset by SetSystems Ltd, Saffron Walden, Essex
Printed and bound in Great Britain by
Mackays of Chatham plc, Chatham, Kent

To Marcus and Keith
with gratitude and hope

Contents

Contents

Acknowledgements

SEVERAL OF Elizabeth's friends were most kind in lending me a number of her letters for lengthy periods of time. The task of describing her life was sometimes daunting, but I was frequently aware of being privileged to listen to an older generation of people recalling their lives, often remarkable in their own right and irrespective of their association with Elizabeth.

Mrs Priscilla Longland, Elizabeth's only surviving sister, always made me most welcome and allowed constant access to her papers at Wootton, for which I am very grateful. Her daughter, Sabrina Harcourt-Smith, worked tirelessly, cataloguing newly discovered letters and family papers with extraordinary persistence and exactitude, and making herself constantly available for discussion on many aspects of the family's history: this included Felicité, Elizabeth's younger sister. As god-daughter, Sabrina was here able to give me vital information. My thanks to her are, as Elizabeth said of Felicité, in a category of their own. Our efforts were on several occasions assisted by her son Will Harcourt-Smith, whose good-natured interventions and corrections were more than once decisive. To Charles Harcourt-Smith, Sabrina's husband, I am indebted for his remarkable forbearance. Julia Caffyn (née Longland) was also most helpful.

To family, friends, colleagues and associates of Elizabeth who so generously gave their time and hospitality, to whom I returned for more discussion and corroboration on numerous occasions, and who pointed me in the direction of others, sometimes proving to be of crucial importance, I owe a great debt of gratitude. Elizabeth's cousin, Lady Anne Brewis, patiently trawled through her remarkable memory for me on numerous occasions. Doreen Thornton was a lynchpin in the story and, with her husband Colin, has been most kind in her encouragement and support. Another to whose insights, humour and regular welcome I owe much, in particular one unforgettable midnight picnic, was Veronica Nicholson. Sybille Bedford's generosity and perception were most appreciated. Hugh and Judy Johnson, Viscount and Vicountess Ridley, Sir Terence Conran, Anne Scott-James, Audrey Withers, Dr Patrick Woodcock, Paul Bailey, Michael Day, Roger Eland, Ronald Latham, the late Joan O'Malley (née Warburton), Eve Durrell, Paul Gotch, Judith Lassalle, John Johnson, the late Peter Trier, his brother Stephen, Stephen's wife Caroline, Alix Coleman, the Earl and Countess of Selborne, Derek Hill, Lindsey Bareham, Frances Fedden, Sir Peter and Lady Wakefield, Peter Davidson and Priscilla Bain, were all extremely generous with their time and hospitality, often helping to disentangle much fact from fiction and clarify old misrepresentations with care and vigilance.

Others of considerable assistance were: Lady Daphne Maynard, Sir Bernard and the late Lady Burrows, Patrick Leigh Fermor, Lord Gowrie, Mrs Humphrey Brooke (née Benckendorff), Jane Blakemore, Peter Laing, Richard Morphet, Michael Helston, Mrs Dominic Morgan, the Hon. Harry Palmer, Sir Adam Ridley, Lady Laura Easthaugh, Margaretta Scott, Joan Hickson, her son, Nicholas Butler, Charles Pick, Susanah Plowright, Richard Leech, Major the Reverend J. A. Croft, MC (Royal Deccan Horse), Lieutenant-Colonel A. F. Harpur, DSO (Royal Deccan Horse), Irene Gilchrist, George Perry-Smith, Martin Lam, Simon Hopkinson, Pamela Pugh, Ann Barr, Diana Athill, Marjorie and Joan Lloyd, Cherry Ripe, Pippa Irwin, Victor Morrison, Mary Fedden, Claudia Roden, Chlöe Tyner (née Chant-Communal), Professor Edward Chaney (who first introduced me to the great significance of travel literature), Giela Goldstein (previously Gibson Cowan), David Conville, Alice Waters, Judy Rogers, Hugo Dunn-Meynell, Mary Abercrombie, Betsy Udall, John Ward, RA, Simon Blow, Patricia Moss, Bruce Purchase, Sam Beazley, Elizabeth Philips (née Good), Michael Bateman, Robin Weir, Diana Anderson (née Morgan), David Wheeler, Dr Lawrence Goldman, Anne Willan, Helen Langdon, Kitty Morris, Ivan Day and Margaret Willes, Clive Cookson and Malcolm Woolley of Cornfield Studios.

Institutions, their staff and those who have kindly given me advice and information include: Tim Moreton, Assistant Registrar, the National Portrait Gallery; Colin Randall, librarian to the *Bookseller*; Guildhall Library, Corporation of London; Lindsey Lardner, the Wellcome Institute; Sue Woods, Gosforth County Archives; Mary Wondrausch; Eastbourne Reference Library; Susan Santini, Phillips Auctioneers; Godstowe Preparatory School; Wycombe Abbey School; The National Trust Scotland; the Towner Art Gallery, Eastbourne; Frances Rankin, Prints and Drawings, the V & A Library; Condé Nast Publications library; Smallbone Kitchens; City of Westminster Reference Library and Archives; the British Library, the Newspaper Library, Colindale; Alex Warner, Museum of London; Will Ryan, the Librarian, Warburg Institute; Liz Seber, Books for Cooks; York University Library; Carol Whitehead, the Whitechapel Gallery; Liz-Anne Bawden, the Army Museum; and Mrs Brig Davies for Viscount Gage, Firle Place.

The completion of this work was made possible with the encouragement of my family who have my loving thanks. My father Keith's assistance, and inspiring and enlightening conversation, became central to the book, as did Marcus's perceptive commentary, infinite patience and wise counsel. Anna added to her sensitive and painstaking transcriptions of many hours of tapes, the same wit and humour with which she supported all my endeavours. Saul and Vanessa advised, corrected and amused with their habitual verve. My daughter Jessica's suggestions were always helpful, and on book design characteristically discerning, whilst her sister Olivia added her own constant and cheerful support. My mother Elizabeth taught me first to know good food. To the friends who read and patiently listened to on-going preoccupations I am deeply grateful. They include Alan and Jane Davidson, whose searching comments on the manuscript were decisive; Sira who was always welcoming, Harlan Walker, Janet Clarke (who also lent valuable books without hesitation), Laura Mason, Christianne Heal, Luis and Gloria Echarte, Matthew Fort, Jo and Richard Baker and Joe Roberts.

I thank my three editors who steered the book through to publication: Judith Hannam who commissioned it; George Morley whose positive editing of the first half (days before delivering her baby) gave encouragement to the second half, which she skilfully brought to its conclusion; and finally Catherine Whitaker, whose good humour and industry in editing and shepherding the book and its author through a plethora of problems were much appreciated. I must also thank Helen Dore, Becky Lindsay and Rupert Heath. To my agent, Caroline Davidson, who provided me with such consistent and effective stimulus and support, I am extremely grateful.

A work such as this will, inevitably, contain errors and omissions. The responsibility for these is mine and I appeal to the reader to draw them to my attention.

List of Illustrations

SECTION TWO

Introduction

ELIZABETH DAVID, OBE, CBE, is undoubtedly the greatest English writer on food this century. After her death it seemed possible that the full extent and breadth of her influence might be forgotten. This is not to say that she has 'gone out of favour', but precisely because her influence has been so pervasive (first in the home, then beyond it in food shops, kitchen shops and restaurants) some of us, now and in the future, will be unaware of its source. This biography began as a tribute. After three years, repeatedly making the mistake of trying to forge a life of consistency and coherence – perhaps particularly tempting with a subject as enigmatic as Elizabeth – the puzzle of her life is a little closer to elucidation. With it my belief in the merits and significance of Elizabeth's art is even greater than when I began.

English cookery writer *extraordinaire*, Elizabeth died in 1992 where she had lived for over forty years, in a discreet Chelsea house filled with the spoils of a lifetime spent hoarding and collecting, particularly books. Her following extended across the English-speaking world to America and Australia – over 1.2 million copies of her books have sold in Penguin alone – and they have been translated into several European languages. At her death the obituaries proclaimed her key role in the emancipation of the post-war British palate. Exercising her beneficial influence for more than a generation, she inspired not only thousands of domestic cooks, but influential chefs and food writers, to claim her as their chief muse.

Auberon Waugh maintains that 'she has brought about a greater change in English life than any other woman this century,' and his father Evelyn named her *Italian Food* his book of the year after its publication in 1954. Grey Gowrie, until recently Chairman of the Arts Council, used another of her books, *French Provincial Cooking*, in his classes for English literature students at Harvard University, for the quality of the writing, and it was as much for this that the novelist Paul Bailey wanted to know her. Her friend Lawrence Durrell wrote to her that a French devotee had told him she was the Jane Austen of cookery writers. Uniquely among cookery writers, Elizabeth was made a Fellow of the Society of Literature in recognition of these literary skills.

The essential appeal of her writing lies in its blend of escapism tempered with a sturdy realism. She was first a *writer*, then one whose subject was food, which she linked constantly to memories and to dreams, capturing the mind and imagination of her reader, altering perceptions and expectations of the everyday. With a steely intellect and mordant wit, her prose can be taut, acid and languidly descriptive, exuding an estimable good sense and a refined sensuality. She was gifted with a consummate ability to evoke time and place and – significantly for the English, enticed by it for centuries – this place was predominantly the Mediterranean. Her first five books are accordingly, as much evocative travelogues as they are illuminating manuals for the preparation of food.

Beginning her writing career in post-war Britain, Elizabeth was writing in reaction to both the bleak English culinary climate and a more profound legacy of repression and puritanism, represented for her and many of her travelled generation by the Protestant North. During the nineteenth century, an unsavoury alliance had taken place in England between the prevailing tenets of thrift and economy and the belief that only complicated food was good food. The result was that, as underlined by the complaint from the great French chef Escoffier, the English cared more for show than for the pleasure of eating. The Anglo-Saxon response in socially ambitious circles to simple and simply cooked food was largely one of conditioned snobbery.

Not alone among post-war cookery writers in denigrating English culinary travesties, perpetrated with an almost wilful zeal, the high literary quality and imaginative passion of Elizabeth's rejection of these tendencies, and her authoritative espousal of something better, brought her many supporters. In journalism and books she lovingly nurtured the British passion for the South and in time turned her readership away from some of their own culinary traditions, encouraging them instead to savour the food of the sun.

Having created the audience, in 1965 she began to supply her growing readership with the *batterie de cuisine* of France and the Mediterranean in her pioneering kitchen shop, Elizabeth David Ltd, opened in Pimlico, London. This commercial enterprise was no marketing ploy but an extension of an avowed passion; objects relating to the kitchen interested her as much as the food itself. A discerning eye for the beauty of functional objects and an appreciation of the social traditions of rooted cultures, still connected to their non-industrial past, were what drove Elizabeth's interest in the kitchen and its objects. Much of the appeal which France and the Mediterranean countries held for her lay in the certainty that they maintained strong links with their culinary past; Britain on the whole did not.

After the opening of her Pimlico shop similar ones quickly sprang up, and there is little doubt that Elizabeth's was the inspiration for them and the myriad others now catering for kitchens across the English-speaking world. Not only is her influence felt through the kitchen equipment so many of us presently use but, through the ethos of her writing, she helped to inspire the atmosphere we often set out to create in our own kitchen-dining-rooms. Kitchens are now rooms in which, more often than not, like Elizabeth, we not only cook but eat and entertain too.

Elizabeth's earlier Mediterranean books had successfully encouraged readers to react against the worst of their own culinary traditions. In her later works, at once stimulating recipe books and exemplary pieces of social and culinary history, Elizabeth described how English cooking could, at its best, hold its own with the Mediterranean. The more of an historian she became, the more she understood that the erosion of the English tradition had begun long ago, with the flowering of the industrial revolution. The final phase of her life was a response to this discovery and she proclaimed: 'We need to go back to the recipes of a century ago and further, when an authentic and still strong English cooking tradition flourished.'

Many of Elizabeth's devotees did not readily take her new 'English' message to heart. In the years since the Second World War Elizabeth's writing had played its part in the English embracement of 'abroad', eventually penetrating deeper into the English psyche than its reflection in the obligatory Mediterranean holiday and the production of Elizabeth's beautiful recipes for dinner parties. What England had witnessed was not simply the natural and invigorating assimilation of new ideas into its culinary repertoire through one region's contact with others. At another level Elizabeth's message had contributed towards a rejection of England's own culture, the Anglo-Saxon one, in a way which few Europeans would ever contemplate in relation to their own.

On a personal level, Elizabeth added a natural poise and elegance to her rather exotic beauty. She tried the stage when young, but was too cerebral and self-conscious to act with confidence. In keeping with a desire to reveal only part of herself, she was led to comment to the inquisitive that everything there was to know about her was written in her books. Photographs and public appearances were rare, and her notorious dislike of publicity led, in her later years, to a mistaken reputation for reclusiveness; this sprang as much from her privileged upbringing as from personal diffidence. Nevertheless, despite having no time for the cult of personality, there is ample evidence that Elizabeth regarded herself as superior to mere collectors of recipes, with a shrewd estimation of her own considerable literary worth.

It is strictly true that much of what there is to know about Elizabeth *is* in her books, but one must first possess the key. Most of the early part of her life passed in a state of rebellion against her widowed mother. In her youth she spent a crucial period in France. She later escaped from England and its constraints just before the outbreak of the Second World War. In the company of Charles Gibson Cowan, whom her family and most friends found intolerable, she met and befriended, with momentous consequences for herself, the writer Norman Douglas. There followed several months on a Greek island, concluding with evacuation to Egypt as Crete was being overrun by the invading German forces. Finally entering the war effort, Elizabeth worked first for the Admiralty, then for the Ministry of Information for the remainder of the hostilities. In Egypt she married, went reluctantly to India, and returned to a victorious but ration-blighted England in 1946. In 1950, at the age of thirty-six, she published her first book.

Many of these details of Elizabeth's life are already known more or less, but during the process of their investigation and scrutinization, determining episodes, hitherto concealed from all but her oldest and closest associates, began to emerge. Family, friends and colleagues helped immeasurably, sometimes through their conflicting views, in the process of unravelling and elucidation. The research path led, sometimes by remarkable coincidence, at others by dogged persistence, to two autobiographies written by the most obscure and perhaps most important of Elizabeth's several lovers, and to a cache of letters to her family, unread for almost half a century. This material proved to be of far-reaching significance and Elizabeth was, finally, more comprehensible. Through these discoveries it also became clear that her life determined and then permeated her work, revealing her as a most autobiographical writer.

Elizabeth emerges as a highly complex and driven artist, whose razor-sharp memory and concern for accuracy at times reached obsessive proportions. She could show breathtaking disregard for others' sensitivities, was passionate, emotional, forthright and abrasive to the point of rudeness. She was also diffident and, though not inclined towards self-reflection, was at times undecided and self-critical. To an almost classical, pre-Christian lack of *caritas* she sometimes added ruthlessness, a reluctance to forgive, and a tendency to judgment of others which was sometimes seriously blinkered. At the same time she was cultivated, witty and at times very funny. She could also be a most encouraging, generous and devoted friend, eliciting a touching and unswerving loyalty in those to whom she was close. In her work she demonstrated an unflagging concern for truth, coupled with a note of celebration which played throughout her lucid and masterful prose. Together these gave an authority and sureness to her work which has made of her readers thousands of grateful and devoted admirers.

CHAPTER ONE

Forefathers

CHALK-WHITE, a road cuts through the brow of the hill, brick chimneys and roofs emerging above its low summit. In fields close by wild mushrooms once grew and red Sussex cattle grazed with the rare black St Kilda sheep. Nearby is the bald northern scarp of the South Downs. To one side reaching away into a liquid blue distance is the Weald, to the other the sea skirted by its broad coastal plain, and further on still the sheer white coastal cliffs.

Since earliest times this downland landscape has harboured man, and everywhere are traces of ancient habitation. Just out of sight is the prehistoric Long Man of Wilmington, perhaps the oldest god of these islands, presenting his gigantic turf cut shape on the steep flat slop of Windover Hill and recalling Kipling's lines:

> *I will go out against the sun*
> *Where the rolled scarp retires,*
> *And the Long Man of Wilmington*
> *Looks naked towards the shires.*

One hundred feet above his great head, against the skyline the crest of Windover Hill merges with the downland ridge running on into the distance, since prehistory used as a high causeway reaching as far as Winchester Hill over 50 miles to the west. The Romans built fine villas hereabouts, the Normans castles and manors. Under their rule monastic orders raised new priories and abbeys, communications with the mother houses in France easy via the busy Sussex Channel ports. With Henry VIII's Dissolution of the Monasteries some of these, like

I

Battle Abbey and Michelham Priory, were turned over to private dwellings. Many of the county gentry – Howards, Fitzalans, the Bellinghams of Newtimber, the Shelleys of Michelgrove, the Gages of Firle – refused to convert and kept staunchly to the old (Roman Catholic) faith. A number of the oldest manor-houses, such as Glynde and Firle Place, are still lived in by the families who had them built during the prosperous fifteenth to seventeenth centuries.

Although the building of the railways made this coast popular in the nineteenth century as a metropolitan seaside playground, agricultural Sussex and its villages stayed remote from industrial England. In the nineteenth century the Downs were still covered in sheep and the shepherd was king of the agricultural labourers. Well into this century he could still be seen at dawn driving his animals high up on to the Downs, following their straggling course by day and bringing them down safely to the folds at dusk. Into this century, too, it remained customary to bury a shepherd with a tuft of wool to identify his occupation, to explain on Judgement Day why his attendance at church was so irregular.

Smoothed by melting Ice Age snows, the bold green chain of downland hills dominates the surrounding landscape and ends abruptly with the vertiginous chalk sea cliffs of Beachy Head. Divided into several separate massifs, the lower reaches of the Downs are sometimes densely wooded, elsewhere fields wave with billowing wheat. The upper reaches are rich in downland pasture, their majestic hilltops bared to sun and wind. In spring and early summer birds, wild flowers and herbs grow in profusion; grand beeches and ancient yews, holly and hornbeam flourish in the chalky soil. In the higher places ragwort and sometimes wild orchids grow, juniper and haw-thorn too – higher still the springy velvet turf alone.

Once over the brow of the hill, the chalky road drops steeply into a spacious courtyard set around with buildings: barns, stables, dairy, outhouses, all of soft red brick and gnarled grey flint. Through this courtyard and another, and the great rounded hipped-tiled arch leads on to the grassy oval forecourt flanked by a medieval chapel capped with a golden cockerel weathervane.

A few stone steps above the forecourt the patterned brickwork wing of the old house dictated the character of the two later adjoining ones. Kitchen offices, nursery and library lie to the south, another set of low buildings and a ballroom to the north. Everywhere the smooth mellowed brick and flint of Sussex are offset by the colour and texture of granite pavings, sea pebbles and greying oak beams. An inspired touch has every door about the forecourt painted a soft steely-blue. This imaginative use of materials fuses together the rambling assemblage in such a way that the pervading atmosphere is one of solidity, permanence – a unified, harmonious, and particularly English whole: Wootton Manor, childhood home of Elizabeth David.

The substantial manor-house was a fitting residence for Elizabeth's father Rupert Gwynne, the local Member of Parliament. Wootton was a typical seventeenth-century Sussex farmhouse, with gable-fronted entrance surveying the Downs and Folkington Hill towering up 630 feet to its summit. From the top floor of Wootton on a clear day you could look out over the Downs to Firle Beacon and beyond to Pevensey Bay where William the Norman first landed in 1066 and was met not far away at Battle by the brave and beleaguered English king, Harold. Around Wootton a series of outhouses, farm-workers' cottages, barns, stables and other buildings had proliferated over the years. Its origins are ancient, with mention of a small Saxon community there in the Domesday Book – Wootton means 'farm by the wood' – and came under the estate of William the Conquerer's half-brother, the Count of Mortain. (Windover Hill, on which is inscribed the Long Man of Wilmington, lies on the Wootton Estate.)

Changing hands and appearance over the centuries, Wootton Manor went through a gradual process of gentrification and was eventually sold to Elizabeth's grandfather, James E. Anderson Gwynne, in 1876. Simultaneously he bought Folkington Manor nearby, a grander family residence built not long before in ponderous Victorian-Tudor style. Here Rupert and his six brothers and sisters grew up. On Rupert's marriage to the Hon. Stella Ridley in 1905, James presented Wootton to the newly-weds. He gave his daughter-in-law a choice between Wootton and Michelham Priory a couple of miles away on the large Gwynne estate. Indulging his antiquarian interests, James had recently bought and restored this ruinously beautiful thirteenth-century Augustinian priory which had been extended at the Dissolution into a Tudor manor-house. Stella chose

Wootton, but the atmospheric photographs in her 1905 album indicate her indecision and Michelham's appeal. With stone-vaulted ceilings and delicate gothic windows, the house was reached through a towering ivy-clad gatehouse, its only approach still an old bridge spanning the wide, protective moat.

Ten years later, in March 1915, Rupert's father died. In old age he had become bitter and isolated, leaving a will of gothic proportions and relentlessly unforgiving content. Though not the eldest son, Rupert was principal beneficiary of his father's considerable estate, left in trust to him and any male heirs. Rupert decided to stay on at Wootton Manor and it was agreed that his unmarried brother Roland and his sister Dorothy should remain nearby in the family home at Folkington. The recent history of Rupert's family was fortunate in its members' gifts of self-possession, confidence and successful ambition, but it was often marred by bad temper and narrow-mindedness of sometimes outlandish proportions. This could result – notably with Rupert's father – in hyper-sensitivity to the smallest slight and a determined vindictiveness, displayed to the last in his will.

Rupert was sent to Shrewsbury and Cambridge, not Eton and Oxford, for it was feared they would corrupt. His oldest brother Reggie had attended both Eton and Oxford and disgraced himself by getting into debt, albeit on a small allowance: his father was wealthy but not generous. Reggie was a spendthrift. Enthusiastically munificent beyond his means at Eton, he was removed and dispatched to the recently founded Lancing. Later, after a short time up at Oxford, he was again in debt. Unable to face the fearful temper of his authoritarian father, he emigrated to Canada and aside from short visits never lived in England again. Poor Reggie's youthful inability to look after his money generated a train of events which led to the third son, Rupert, becoming the major inheritor of James Gwynne's estates.

The first event was the making of the will. Appalled by Reggie's conduct and in accord with his own relentless and unforgiving nature, James's will stated that Reginald, although his eldest son, was not eventually to have control over the family estate. He would receive an annual income, no more. Reggie's allowance was later much reduced.

James's final will is long, tortuous and full of codicils, the changes reflecting, with increasing age, a growing and wilful mistrustfulness and inability to communicate, especially with those apparently closest to him. Youthful resoluteness had hardened into inexorable implacability. Throughout, a desire to secure two main objectives is manifest: control of his adult children's lives (about his wife's he was already confident, not unusual for a man of his day) and the preservation of Folkington and his other properties intact, preferably via a son. This sad and vindictive document is the last testament of a man whose youthful will to succeed had initially conferred on him all the worldly prizes: a decorative and sensitive wife, daughters to indulge and be indulged by, and sons to enlarge the fruits of his labours and perpetuate his name.

Born in 1832, as a young man James Gwynne was full of vigour, tenacity and enthusiasm. His mother Agnes came from the respectable Scottish merchant classes, as did his father John. John produced Britain's first centrifugal pump, called the 'Gwynne Pump'. A technological advance, it eased the task of reclaiming flooded land and was to be invaluable for many years in the farthest reaches of the British Empire. With the financial assistance of a friend, the banker and tea trader Herbert Twining, John Gwynne set up a company of which James became a member at seventeen. The Great Exhibition of 1851 in the unique Crystal Palace in Hyde Park staged an exuberant demonstration of Victorian versatility, pragmatism and invention coupled with the early technologists' absolute belief in progress. The youthful James was responsible for the firm's stand. By 1855 his father was dead and James, the eldest of three brothers, was a managing partner in the firm.

At twenty-seven he had fallen in love with Mary (May) Purvis. James's mother Agnes was against the union and would consequently inflict suffering on him for many years to come. Having failed to prevent the marriage, Agnes subsequently strove to thwart her son's progress in business and never forgave him for acting against her wishes and according to the dictates of his heart. Although time now obscures Mrs Gwynne's reason for her antagonism, it probably sprang from the knowledge that her future daughter-in-law, May, was not pure Scottish, but part Dutch with exotic connections. May's beautiful mother Cornelia was the daughter of Theunis In'tveld, prosperous Dutch Resident of Padang of Sumatra and Anna Carels,

5

herself the daughter of a Dutch merchant and a Sumatran ranee. Thus, through Anna and Cornelia, May inherited both artistic talent and beguiling looks. In time these would re-emerge with particular originality in May's daughter Violet and her granddaughter Elizabeth.

In the tradition of successful entrepreneur–industrialist James completed the cycle of advancement by acquiring property. As the years passed he became less interested in his business and city life and spent most of his time in the country on his estate at Folkington, acquiring more and more land and socializing with his landed neighbours. Despite this James was neither a tranquil nor an easy man. His wife's gaiety continued for many years, but only in the company of the children. In order of seniority they were: Reginald, Evelyn, Neville, Violet, Rupert, Dorothy and Roland.

With this sketch of family background we turn again to Rupert. Down from Pembroke College, Cambridge, by 1895 he was reading for the Bar. During this period he launched himself on a steady round of enjoyment. In the country there was shooting, hunting, weekends with friends at Folkington and nearby estates such as Lord Gage's at Firle Place, or further afield. In London his was the life of the well-connected young man with prospects. A rich man's son, Rupert was bound by a set of constraints which were to determine the future course of his life.

After Cambridge he shared with his wealthy brother-in-law Gordon Woodhouse (married to Rupert's younger sister Violet) their large Georgian house near Hyde Park. James Gwynne kept all his children short of money and Rupert, though close to Violet, lived in her London house out of necessity as well as choice, from this time until his marriage several years later. Despite his shortage of money, his looks, demeanour and name were sufficient to provide him with a constant supply of invitations to some of the smarter houses in London. Violet and Gordon's London home had its full share of entertaining company, welcoming a colourful selection of the artistic élite of the time.

Violet was gifted, extraordinary to look at and about to become one of the most celebrated musicians of her day. Her mother May had recognized early her daughter's precocious keyboard abilities and nurtured them with intelligence and care. Indulging her own taste in music as well, she had always taken Violet to a wide variety of concerts and opera, making a large circle of musical friends *en route*, and the Gwynnes' London and country houses had always reflected May's love of music, with regular entertainments. By the turn of the century, Violet's musical salon had become one of the most celebrated in London, with invitations and friendship eagerly sought by some of the most influential contemporary musical and artistic figures. Among her admirers were Bernard Shaw, T. E. Lawrence, Delius, Pablo Casals, Diaghilev and the three Sitwells.

When already quite young Violet expected, and received, adulation. In spite of a reputation for generosity and warmth she could be icy when treatment did not accord with her estimation of herself. Her exertion of will pervaded her private and public life in what can either be excused as the mammoth ego thought necessary to an artist's survival, or seen as the scheming manipulation of a very selfish woman. Whichever it was, when Violet had her own way she was as charming and mesmerizing company as it was possible to be. Unconventional, even by the most bohemian conventions of the day, she lived in apparent harmony throughout her adult life with two adoring men, the Hon. William Barrington and Gordon Woodhouse, and for a time with four. Her husband Gordon Woodhouse was a retiring and pleasant facilitator who faithfully sought throughout their marriage to accommodate Violet's every wish. By whatever standards she is judged, Violet was a remarkable woman who inspired many and bore more than a passing resemblance in both character and looks to the niece, Elizabeth, who was to outstrip her in fame.

Whilst Rupert was now practising as a barrister, he was also socializing on a hectic scale. In 1902 a fellow-barrister and friend of his, the urbane Max Labouchère, joined the Woodhouse–Gwynne household. Unlike other members of the Gwynne family, Rupert seemed unperturbed by his sister's ménage, enjoying the company and sociable life-style it involved. Gordon Woodhouse, Bill Barrington and Max Labouchère had in fact all been introduced to Violet by Rupert himself.

Rupert, at thirty, was faced with some crucial decisions. A realist, he had undoubtedly admitted to himself that he did not have the makings of a first-class barrister. Perhaps it was with this same realism that he had chosen to embark on such a full and energetic life. While still at Shrewsbury School he was warned that a severe attack of rheumatic fever had left his heart severely weakened and that if he intended to live beyond middle age he must lead an abstemious life. He refused and continued to hunt, shoot and gather trophies for his equine and social prowess. His liaisons and flirtations with women had not so far turned up a girl to his father's liking or one that Rupert felt able to commit himself to. Following a terrible break between his father and his brother Neville, culminating by 1904 in Neville's banishment from the family home and disinheritance from his father's estate, Rupert was the next in line. Treated with circumspection, his father could now make him chief beneficiary of his estate, a potentially rich man and a highly eligible man.

In the following year Rupert at last made a most suitable and dignified match. His father's approval was absolute. Pressure had most likely been recently brought to bear on Rupert to abandon a concurrent liaison thought unsuitable, and James must have done more than hint at what the rewards of marriage to a 'suitable' girl would be.

The Hon. Stella Ridley came from a family long established as an important Northumberland dynasty. Wealthy and well connected, her family would certainly not have permitted the match with Rupert without some assurance of substantial financial support on a par with that to which Stella was accustomed. The earliest reference to the Ridleys, in 1154, records their ownership of extensive lands in the Tyne valley. Here they lived in a fortified manor-house called Willimotswick. From here they took part enthusiastically in the border wars and family feuds which dominated Northumberland life throughout the Middle Ages. It was in this house that one of England's more famous martyrs, Nicholas Ridley, Bishop of London, was born in about 1503. In 1555 his refusal to renounce the Protestant faith led Henry VIII's Catholic daughter, Mary Tudor, to have him tried and condemned for heresy, along with Cranmer and Latymer. His last letter was written from prison in Oxford to his

8

sister at Willimotswick Manor. The following day he was burnt at the stake.

When young, Stella Ridley was slight. A studio photograph at about fourteen shows her in riding habit, with pale skin and dark brown hair untied, then a fashion for unmarried girls. Still displaying the rounded contours of adolescence, her face nevertheless hints at the qualities which were to distinguish and sustain her. She looks determined, intelligent and stubborn, with little evidence of artfulness or guile. Thoughtful dark eyes resist inquisition. Her engagement photograph at twenty-one confirms these impressions.

In the year prior to her engagement Stella's father, Matthew White Ridley, fifth Baronet and first Viscount, had died. Her mother had predeceased him, dying in 1899 a month after Stella's fifteenth birthday. Stella may have been without parents at her marriage, but she came with self-assurance as to her pedigree and standing. Her mother, Mary Georgina (Polly), daughter of Dudley Coutts Marjoribanks, the first Lord Tweedmouth, spent much time with her children. Encouraged by their mother's enthusiasm and artistic flair, they frequently accompanied her on sketching trips, showing marked ability themselves. Stella continued painting all her life, exhibiting and maintaining important friendships with a number of painters.

Stella's father was Conservative MP for North Northumberland. In 1895 he was made Home Secretary under the new Conservative administration of Lord Salisbury. After the general election of 1900 he retired from political life and was made a peer (Viscount Ridley). He spent his last years in Northumberland at Blagdon, where he had always remained actively involved in the administration of the family estate. Throughout the north of England he was regarded as a man of considerable business acumen and wielded great influence.

When his wife Polly died in 1899, his son Matthew (since the eighteenth century the eldest Ridley boy was always given this name) had reached the age of majority, but the other three children were considerably younger. Grace and Jasper, only ten and twelve respectively, were still much in need of maternal anchorage, but Stella too, at fifteen, suffered from the loss of her mother. At Polly's death Sir Matthew still held the post of Home Secretary. As senior politician and landowner he was occupied with decision-making and public responsibility. This left him little time for the private role of mother-substitute to his three younger children.

Some time later the children's Aunt Ishbel, Lady Aberdeen, made it known to Sir Matthew that she thought the arrangements for them were unsatisfactory and Matthew asked her to take charge. Grace was a fairly biddable child but Stella never made things easy. She did everything in her power to disobey and antagonize the governess whose *modus vivendi* with her difficult charge was at times the stuff of farce. If, for instance, she wanted a window more open she would carefully ask Stella to close it, whereupon it would immediately be flung wider. Aunt Ishbel's plans underestimated the powerful personality of the eldest of her charges and the children were removed from Blagdon and taken back with their aunt to Haddo House in Scotland, seat of her husband's family, the Gordons, where before the nineteenth century they were established as a powerful landed Scottish family.

Lord Aberdeen's distinguished political career included appointments as Governor-General of Ireland, Governor-General of Canada (1893–8) and another Viceroyship of Ireland from 1905 to 1915. When Stella's mother died the Aberdeens had not long returned from Canada. Life at the House of Haddo was always conducted on a grand scale, the Aberdeens finding it impossible to behave otherwise. Stella, Jasper and Grace became familiar with their aunt and uncle's exalted circle, which included many of the oldest aristocratic families and the most powerful political figures of the day. Arthur Balfour had been uncle Aberdeen's best man, and the formidable Prime Minister Gladstone was a good friend.

Under her aunt's supervision at Haddo Stella was not to fare much better than at Blagdon. Her determination, intelligence and wilfulness, all qualities possessed by Ishbel herself, did not make for easy relations between the two. When Ishbel brought Stella out in London the episode was fraught with more than the normal share of irritations and tensions inherent in these occasions. Preparations involved endless fittings for a suitably beautiful, varied and becoming wardrobe, invitations given and received with anticipation of the impending event sharpening mounting nervous excitement. Dozens of girls, demurely sumptuous in white silks and satins, ostrich-feather headdresses and above-elbow gloves, queued for their curtsey and moment's audience with the King and Court. Filing their way out of the State Apartments at Buckingham Palace, the girls had to move crabwise so as not to turn their backs on the royal couple or fall flat on the carpet entangled in their trains. Great white tablecloths were frequently requisitioned to rehearse for this terrifying performance. Once the course had been successfully navigated, the débutantes and their chaperones went on to their first dance of the Season with mixed feelings of relief and elation.

Evenings usually began at ten o'clock, but Ishbel wished frequently, and rather inconsiderately, to leave these entertainments by about eleven. Stella was having none of it and unlike the more docile Grace would refuse to leave. Stella's dance-book was quickly full. She had no desire to be a wallflower and intended making the most of these occasions where it was finally permissible to meet and dance with so many new young men. Eventually Ishbel was forced to employ a woman to chaperone her wayward niece, sitting up late into the night long after Ishbel herself had retired to bed.

Through the heady weeks of the Season Stella did not discover any one young man particularly to her liking, the purpose of the Season being, after all, to find a husband. But her subsequent life was filled with independent social engagements and her brown suede commonplace book and photograph albums from this period read like a roll-call of many of the country houses of the day: Tatton Park, Raby Castle, Castle Howard, Meldon Park, Belsey Castle, Beaufort Castle, Beaumaris Castle, Penrhyn Castle. A busy round of house-parties, balls and shooting weekends are recorded with Stella's diminutive watercolour illustrations and signatures and *bons mots* from fellow-guests, including a revealing comment from her brother Jasper: 'Woman, I could brain you!' The sense of anticipation and excitement Stella must have felt at this new independence is palpable as one turns the crowded pages of her long-forgotten book.

The Ridley and Gordon cousins were similar ages and had lived together in Haddo House for much of the time since Polly Ridley's death. Dudley Gordon was the second of Aunt Ishbel and Uncle John's four children and a year older than Stella. He was later to become Elizabeth's godfather. Dudley and Stella had much in common and became very close. Realizing the strength of their attachment, Ishbel decided something must be done before the young pair made any formal announcement. Poor Dudley was dispatched abroad for a lengthy latter-day Grand Tour, Stella pined, and Ishbel resolved to divest herself of her difficult niece.

Some months later Stella met the eligible young barrister Rupert Gwynne. Not perhaps quite the social equal her parents might have wished for, he was nevertheless rich, Stella had recently been orphaned and Aunt Ishbel was in charge. Besides, this older man with such striking looks was a charming and stimulating companion whose attentions were flattering to a young girl. Her father's death in November 1904 had rendered obsolete Stella's occasional role as hostess for him at Blagdon. Another châtelaine, Rosie, now reigned there with Stella's brother, the new Lord Ridley, and in any case Stella was itching to be free of Haddo.

Rupert was invited to stay at Haddo and Blagdon and Stella came to Folkington. Family on both sides approved. Stella was very young, was falling in love and wanted to be happy. The 5th of May arrived and Society came to a grand wedding at St Margaret's, Westminster. By the summer Stella and Rupert were installed in Wootton Manor, with another pretty house in London, close by the Houses of Parliament, as Stella's dowry.

At the time of his father's death in 1915 Rupert was a fashionable gentleman-farmer, taking pride in the herd of red Sussex cattle he had inherited, in striking contrast to the flock of rare Black St Kilda sheep Stella brought with her from Blagdon. (Family folklore held that St Kildas were a breed descended from Spanish Armada spoils.) Rupert was a fine horseman, riding competitively – a photograph shows a table filled with his cups won at point-to-point meetings – for pleasure and with the local hunt. Stella too was a keen horsewoman, enjoying the hunt and riding the beautiful chalk Downs in sight of the sea. A popular Conservative MP for Eastbourne, with two small daughters, Priscilla and Elizabeth, and a busy political schedule, Rupert took advantage of his new inheritance and quickly set about enlarging Wootton to a standard more in keeping with his status. The services of a family friend, the architect Detmar Blow, were enlisted and Wootton was gradually transformed into the pleasing example of late Arts and Crafts architecture and design it remains today.

Blow added to Wootton a large staircase hall leading off which he created the south wing, providing kitchen and related rooms on the ground floor, nurseries on the second and a fine high-ceilinged library on the third. The library took up the entire floor and is beautifully lit by windows on all four walls with broad views out over the Downs and surrounding parkland. By 1920 Rupert asked Blow to return and make for him another addition to the house, a ballroom. Here, repeating his imaginative handling of traditional Sussex materials, Blow created a building which admirably complemented both the original Jacobean part of Wootton and his own earlier additions. By 1922, when these final additions were complete, Wootton was a substantial house, at once traditional and interestingly contemporary.

Among political friends and associates who were regular visitors to Wootton were a number of painters, designers, and the occasional actor. The painters included Cedric Morris, his companion Arthur Lett-Haines, and Allan Walton, eventually more esteemed for his influential textile designs than his painting. The society portraitist Ambrose McEvoy came too and in 1923–4 painted a portrait of each of the by now four Gwynne children – Priscilla, Elizabeth, Diana and Felicité. These are at once pleasing and observant paintings done in the thin, transparent glazes he favoured late in life. Delicate, slightly ethereal images reflect the sitter's social distinction. Through skilled and precise draughtsmanship the painter has caught something of the essential nature of each girl.

A trickle of distinguished writers also made its way to Wootton. Kipling lived nearby and when not entertaining the children loved to watch the red cattle and black sheep. Stella's brother Jasper (later director of the family bank, Coutts) was a favourite visitor and through him Walter de la Mare came too. De la Mare recorded the beauties of the garden in a poem which featured a diminutive boy statue under the trees by the water.

Under Stella's care the garden became a place of peaceful retreat. In reaction against the rigid formality of most contemporary gardens she planted mixed borders illuminated with colour, massed and spilling over the paths, whilst roses climbed and twined through pergolas and trees. Beyond the ballroom a pleached beech- and yew-lined brick path led away past lawns and vegetable garden to resolve itself in a great tree-lined paved circle, which still welcomes with its round Arts and Crafts oak table and heart-cut-out chairs. Beyond lie the sunken garden and a bluebell wood, and through a gate the open fields. Beside the stone circle Blow's round thatched summer-house provided shelter for Stella, who would spend hours absorbed in her painting.

William Robinson, the garden reformer, was a family friend and lived close by at the Elizabethan manor of Gravetye. Here he had pioneered romantically informal 'wild gardens', a pattern of their kind, and written his influential books. The fiery-tempered Robinson detested the formal Victorian style of gardening; in particular he loathed the practice of 'carpet bedding'. Stella's garden was not large or grand but with beneficial influences like that of Robinson it achieved that quintessentially English garden atmosphere of tranquillity underscored by a balance of discipline and chaos.

Such was Wootton.

CHAPTER TWO

A Rural Childhood
(1913–1924)

DURING THE CHRISTMAS season of 1909 Eastbourne was emblazoned with electioneering posters of Rupert Gwynne in grave yet becoming pose. A number of contemporary cartoons pay more than passing reference to the usefulness of his looks in gaining support from women. Interestingly enough this election coincided with the period when Women's Suffrage was an increasingly public issue, something of which Rupert was not in favour. After seeing out the last weeks of the old year with strenuous canvassing, his campaign was nearing its climax, election day being 29 January 1910. On 27 December, in the midst of the general excitement, Stella went into labour, and after almost five years of marriage was safely delivered of her first baby girl, Mary Priscilla. Only a month later Rupert was celebrating the winning of his seat with a good majority – Thomas, Liberal, 5249 votes; Gwynne, Conservative, 7553. Stella's photograph album shows crowds lining the streets of Eastbourne in celebration and Rupert on the balcony of the Town Hall, smiling and acknowledging the cheering sea of support. Priscilla (never called Mary) was christened in St Peter's Folkington shortly afterwards.

The next few years were filled with an escalating set of commitments for both Rupert and Stella. Rupert threw himself into the MP's life whilst Stella became an exemplary young political hostess. Wootton had its share of artistic visitors, but life for the Gwynnes revolved largely around politics. Stella's family background had primed her well for the role of politician's wife, which she entered on willingly and fulfilled with confidence. She also extended the call of duty to producing more children.

The house in London at Catherine Street proved a most useful and convenient address, sufficiently close to the House of Commons for a bell connected to it to be installed, so that Rupert was alerted as the Division Bell rang for proceedings to begin in the House. Popular in both his constituency and the House of Commons where his manner was calm, measured and purposeful, he was not adept at platform oratory but in time became known for his tenacious hold on a subject and strongly held beliefs. Opponents did not relish Gwynne rising to the attack, victims of his witty jibes and rapier thrusts. Rupert, in common with other high Tories of the time, regarded the young Gandhi as a dangerous political agitator and was in fierce opposition to his objective: independence for India.

On Boxing Day 1913, almost three years after the arrival of Stella's first daughter, she gave birth to another. The baby was named Elizabeth and, like Priscilla, was christened in St Peter's, the little Downland church nearby.

In the following year war was declared on Germany. As an MP Rupert was not expected to enlist, but during the four years of hostilities he was kept extraordinarily busy, for much of it his party was in coalition government. At the end of the war in 1918 ten million people had lost their lives and the social fabric of most of Central and Eastern Europe had disintegrated. Although England seemed less crushed by war, the country in which Rupert, Stella and their kind had grown up was in fact irreversibly changed. The general trend towards social equality had been speeded up by the war. As a consequence conditions for the poor and the lower-middle classes had improved, whilst the wealthy were constrained to limit the grandness of their style.

The war came at a time when women's improved status was being fought for by the Emancipationists, and women were called upon to work in factories so as to free more men to fight at the Front. Many of these girls would previously have entered the hard and often lonely life of domestic service, but now they discovered the attractions of easier work with better wages, and also more sociable working conditions. Although this did not initially affect those like the Gwynnes on country estates, the immediate consequences of the war for city dwellers of their class were seen in a paring down of life-styles, in greater difficulty in finding domestic help.

We saw earlier how after James's death in 1915 Rupert and Stella, as yet relatively untouched by these large social changes, had set about enlarging their scale of domestic arrangements with the extensions made by Detmar Blow. In this year, when Stella had her third child, another girl (Diana), the parents were yet again reminded of their lack of a son and heir. Stella's interests did not revolve exclusively around the political arena, but neither were they particularly maternal. Her own experiences of bereavement in childhood and youth had left her with a stoic resilience, an admirable ability to cope. She was a survivor who remained impatient with weakness and vulnerability and her forte was not small children. On completion, the nursery in Blow's new wing came into immediate operation and the little girls were removed there from the main body of the house.

In the furnishing and decoration of Wootton Stella had (with Rupert) become a confident and knowledgeable practitioner of a lighter style than the one then favoured by most of moneyed Edwardian Britain. Both informal and uncluttered, the atmosphere at Wootton was a successful merging of the simplicity of the Arts and Crafts Movement with elements of the more decorative Art Nouveau and another love of the Gwynnes, the eighteenth century. Stella and Rupert understood the stimulating juxtaposition of old and contemporary, so that each piece was enhanced by its surroundings. And however much the emotional tone might be set to darken at Wootton, for visitors the house retained a sympathetic atmosphere of artistry, comfort and elegance.

Inspired and innovatory gardeners like William Robinson at Gravetye and Laurence Johnson at Hidcote were family friends, and over the ten years at Wootton Stella's interest in the garden had grown and flourished. Although at times still vivacious, her youthful frivolity was now less in evidence and she was thought by some to be too serious-minded and reserved. As with many before and after her, Stella's involvement in the garden was not only an avenue for creativity but also a source of solace. It also provided a constant source of inspiration for her painting, carried on through the warmer months in the little summer-house overlooking Detmar Blow's circle and the bluebell wood beyond. The style of the charming but girlish water-colours from her premarital visitors' albums was becoming more worldly and full-bodied. Her favoured subject was now flowers, but the most cursory glance reveals in these pictures something quite other than the customary benign botanical tone. Set against mysteri-ous dark backgrounds, the kind so beloved of seventeenth-century Netherlandish and Italian still-life painters, Stella's flowers curl and twist to a more surreal rhythm. The colours and shapes are seductively intense; there is about them too a hint of the sinister.

With completion of the new nursery in 1916 and the installation of baby Diana with little Elizabeth and Priscilla, this was now the children's domain. By the following year a fourth and last daughter, Felicité, was born to Stella and Rupert. The little girls' lives revolved around the nursery and here they took their food, their lessons and their sleep. Nanny and a nursery-maid saw to their daily needs and as each girl reached the age of five so the governess introduced her to lessons in the adjoining schoolroom. Meals were sent up from the brick-floored kitchens in a small, hand-pulled lift, and until the girls reached the age of eleven they were invited to dine with both their parents only for lunch on Sundays. Unpredictable juvenile behaviour, unsettling to the smooth functioning of a busy household, was kept to a minimum. Detmar Blow's nursery was made accessible to the main body of the house, but also had its own quite separate entrance leading outside to the courtyard and garden beyond. Blow even saw to the needs of the canine incumbent with a brick-and-tile kennel in the children's entrance courtyard.

The practice of using nanny and nursery-maid to bring up the children was still followed by most families able to afford it in the years following the First World War. With that proviso, the amount of time parents spent with their children was variable. Fathers were normally rather distant figures. Little was expected of them regarding the intimacies of their children's lives until the latter reached young adulthood, if then. The upper-class mother's role was more negotiable. Labour in the country was still cheap and in larger houses a small army of servants was used to keep things running smoothly. At

Wootton this meant the butler Lavender with his gammy leg, the cook and at least two to help her, then the housemaids, the gardener, and the groom and stable-boy to keep the horses exercised and in readiness for use. As cars became more common after the war Rupert and Stella acquired one and with it a chauffeur.

The mistress of even small country establishments such as Wootton certainly never cooked, but her attitude to the cook and her kitchens influenced the quality of its creations. Some châtelaines of these houses were knowledgeably involved in keeping a good table. They knew and cared about food both for their family and their guests and regarded it as a reflection of their competence and success as women. They also knew the limitations and strengths of their cook and kitchen staff and went beyond the green baize door to consult on a regular basis. Discussions on what was available to hand from pantry, cellar and kitchen gardens, what could be ordered, who might be expected to visit that day and how this would affect dining arrangements, resulted in a daily menu plan. It was noticeable too that the mistress who was *au fait* with the organization of her kitchens, rather than leaving it up to the cook and housekeeper, usually presided over a better table than otherwise. But this degree of attention, with the resultant high standard of cooking, was rare in England at the end of the First World War.

Writers during the nineteenth century increasingly bemoaned the withdrawal of the mistress of the house from involvement in the kitchen offices. Recognized as a form of social aggrandizement, this was often derided in books on food and fictional works. In keeping with most well-off women at the turn of the century Stella was not interested in the kitchens and she seldom entered them. Mrs Arnold, the cook, was summoned to her bedroom on most days for particular requests, but menus and the maintenance of culinary standards were mostly left to the cook. In houses comparable to Wootton, if the children were fortunate the cook might be sympathetic and give them 'house room' in her kitchens. She might possibly be a woman large in spirit (and often physique) who welcomed the overlap between nurturing and nourishment. Going about each of these tasks with ease and generosity, these women bequeathed to those in their ambit memories of childhood overlaid with a Proustian reverence for the cook's reassuring earthiness and the warm mysteries of the kitchen. Not so at Wootton. Here the little girls were not welcomed. Nor were they recompensed by delicious food pulled up to their nursery and schoolroom from the kitchens down below. With few exceptions these were meals of little cheer.

However unwelcoming the kitchens were to the children they were a bustle of activity. Each day four separate sets of meals had to be prepared for the different members of the household: breakfast, lunch, tea and dinner for the dining room; breakfast, lunch, tea and supper for the servants' hall; added to that a variety of meals for the nursery and schoolroom. The comings and goings of stable boys, gardener, postman, telegram boy and delivery men bringing supplies of bread and meat from nearby Eastbourne were rewarded with tea made from the constantly seething black kettle on a great iron range, and usually accompanied by biscuits, cake or bread and cheese.

It was long ago concluded in English society that children must not only be largely segregated from adult company until they were civilized enough to enter it, but also required a different diet from their elders and betters. The child's régime entailed abstinence from all luxurious food and drink, as these were regarded as injurious to their moral and physical fibre. This strongly enforced set of taboos was lifted on reaching the exalted state of adulthood – permission to harm yourself was one of the perks of arrival.

What strikes us today is the degree to which children, until the recent past, were segregated from their elders. At the heart of the moral argument for this practice was the belief in Original Sin and its implication that children were born wicked, a belief already well articulated by the Middle Ages. In the seventeenth century J. Pechey could write in his *Treatise of the Diseases of Infants and Children* (1697) that 'Iniquity is connatural to Infants and they are more prone to Evil than to Good, we must not therefore indulge them too much.' About this same period also John Locke, usually considered one of our more sensible thinkers, states his belief in the value of a boy's having cold, wet feet. In *Some Thoughts Concerning Education*, §7, he writes: 'I will also advise his *Feet to be wash'd* every Day in cold Water, and to have his shoes so thin that they might leak and *let in Water* whenever he comes near it.' Mrs Gaskell tells of the half-starved Brontë daughters pleading for more to eat and being lectured by their clergyman father on the sin of caring for carnal things. No doubt those days are gone but the vestiges of this creed still linger on.

Reflecting these beliefs, earlier this century children's diet within families rich enough to confine them to the nursery was typically bland and unimaginative, and quite often downright unpleasant. Rupert and Stella's eldest, Priscilla, makes her complaint: 'The nursery food was not very nice. In fact it was disgusting.' An article in 1901 in *Queen* magazine describes the situation:

> In many households where the dining room cookery is of the most perfect kind, and the servants' hall ... leaves little ... to be desired in culinary ways, the nursery and the schoolroom often suffer from cooking that needs personal evidence to be credited. Many persons now a victim of dyspepsia might trace their trouble to those nursery meals, and of all the horrors of nursery fare, few can equal the disgust inspired by milky and other so-called wholesome puddings ... and the distaste thus acquired hardly yields in later life.

Along with this repellent puritanism in the nursery went the virtual ban on conversation about culinary matters at any 'polite' English dining table, a custom noted with such scornful frequency by foreigners. But the English thought it vulgar (some still do) to make more than passing reference to the merits of the repast. The gentlemen might discuss the wine, perhaps after dinner, but rarely the menu. By the end of the nineteenth century the enjoyment of good food in England was often confused with the old medieval sin of gluttony. Those who did pay proper attention to food were often stigmatized as decadent.

Rupert and Stella's daughters grew up in this climate and, of course, railed at the injustices of childhood. Like many before her, Elizabeth never managed to slough off her intense loathing for the culinary punishments meted out in her childhood. (Most food at Wootton, it should be said, was neither notably good nor bad for its day.) Unlike others before her, however, the inferior culinary quality of Elizabeth's childhood was to act as a gauge of avoidable defect against which she was to set her heart, her informed intelligence and her pen. Many years afterwards as a successful writer, with one or two beacon-like exceptions she was still unreconciled and unable to feel charity towards those long-dead perpetrators of her juvenile misery. The explanation is not sufficient, but she was not speaking idly when she told a friend, Veronica Nicholson, that she had been spurred on to write as much in reaction to this early unhappiness as to anything else. She wrote in reaction and with the passion of a reactionary. In one of her last pieces of writing, an autobiographical article for Smallbone Kitchen Designs, Elizabeth said:

> We ate a lot of mutton and beef plainly cooked, with plain vegetables. The boiled potatoes were usually put through a device called a ricer so that they came up to the nursery in dry, flakey mounds. Vegetable marrows were yellow, boiled and watery. There were green turnip tops, spinach, Jerusalem artichokes, parsnips. I hated them all. Puddings weren't much better. Junket was slippery and slimy, jam roly-poly greasy, something called ground rice pudding dry and stodgy, tapioca the most revolting of all, invented apparently solely to torment children. The obligatory mugs of milk at breakfast and teatime were a penance, although hardly one to be blamed on the cook or any of the kitchen staff. Presumably my mother, in league with Nanny, decreed those mugs of hated milk, and chose to ignore the odious puddings and vegetables dished up for her daughters . . .

Breakfast and tea were not made for the nursery by Mrs Arnold or the kitchen-maid; instead these were presided over by the nursery-maid and Nanny. Nanny Cheshire – a maiden lady of uncertain years and more sympathetic nature than the cook below stairs – held sway over the emotional life of her charges. It was with her cooking, surreptitiously carried on in the upper reaches of Wootton, that Elizabeth's first moments of occasional culinary pleasure lay.

Nanny had a small repertoire of sweet and savoury treats made over the little open fire in the nursery which never failed to please – no doubt due in part to the illicitness of their nature. A sticky fudgelike mass, called 'stuff' by the children, was concocted and doled out to them from spare soap dishes or saucers. Mushrooms, never again to taste so perfect, were gathered at dawn by expert girlish hands in the field beyond the bluebell wood and triumphantly carried back to Nanny to cook up for breakfast in the plentiful, thick cream from the home farm. Elizabeth's recipe for Mushrooms in Cream, by no accident found in *Summer Cooking*, at once springs to mind: 'To make a really good dish of mushrooms in cream very fresh little button mushrooms from the field are needed . . .'

And we are at once made party to those far-off days at Wootton lingering in her mind's eye. 'In high summer there was the best treat of all, big fat gooseberries, redcurrants and raspberries from the garden which Nanny used to throw into a saucepan with sugar, heat over the nursery fire and give to us then and there. This hot fruit salad somehow embodied the essence of summer, and as everyone knows the summers of childhood are longer and sunnier than those of later life.' Again *Summer Cooking* reveals these benign early memories of Wootton in the shortest and simplest of entries entitled 'Hot Fruit Salad'. 'This fashion of serving summer fruit has, to me, all the flavour and scent of a warm summer fruit garden . . . Stew the gooseberries, redcurrants and sugar together for 5 minutes (no water). Add the raspberries for 2 minutes only. Serve very hot, with thick fresh cream.'

There was much indeed to recommend Wootton as a place for the creation of idyllic childhood memories. A house of many levels and mellowed edges, of fine and curious collected things for feasting the eye and mind on, a library for more when you grew older, a garden of intimate views and corners and places to nestle and hide in, the air in spring and summer redolent with the scent of stocks, honeysuckle and rose. Outside beyond the garden, the wild-mushroom field; still further their father's lowing red cattle and their mother's black, black sheep. A short walk and, reaching the base of the wide open Downs, a quick breathless climb, and up high on Folkington Hill there you were alone in the stillness and quiet, with only skylarks calling and long, yellow summer grass rustling in a breeze from the sea.

Other children were brought to play, grown-ups came and went for lunches and dinners, in summer for tennis and picnics. Memories of these picnics are stored away, later, for *Summer Cooking*. The picnic – at heart a means of stepping outside the quotidian, for sharing food in pleasant company in a place highlighting the retreat from routine – has for centuries been a favoured pastime for rich and poor alike. Its well-documented history is replete with story and anecdote from the sublime to the ridiculous. Elizabeth records a number of picnics in her writing. Some in particular from Wootton days show her recalling the sublime *and* the ridiculous. In *Summer Cooking* she writes:

> then there was the hospitable family I remember in my child-
> hood; they owned a beautiful house and an elegant garden and
> were much given to out-of-door entertainments, pageants and
> picnics. On picnic days a large party of children and grown-ups
> would be assembled in the hall. Led by our host and hostess we
> proceeded through the exquisite formal Dutch garden, across the
> lane and over a fence into a coppice. Close on our heels followed
> the butler, the chauffeur and the footman, bearing fine china
> plates, the silver and tablecloths, and a number of vast dishes
> containing cold chicken, jellies and trifles. Arrived at the end of
> our journey, five minutes from the house, our hosts set about
> making a fire, with sticks which I suspect had been strategically
> placed by the gardener, over which we grilled quantities of
> sausages and bacon, which were devoured amidst the customary
> jokes and hilarity. The picnicker's honour thus satisfied, we took
> our places for an orderly meal, handed round by the footman,
> and in consumption resembling that of an Edwardian wedding
> breakfast.

Entertainments at Wootton were got up by all who were willing. Favourite stories were rehearsed with the governess in the schoolroom and performed in full stage gear; once a version of *Alice Through the Looking-Glass* with Priscilla as the Red Queen, Felicité as the Mouse in the teacup, and Elizabeth, appropriately, as the Duchess. The annual Pevensey Pageant was a great dramatic excitement when children and adults dressed the part. Palmer and Hogg cousins who lived nearby were regular companions and there were always the other three sisters for company, and animals too. A succession of puppies, a favourite the irreplaceable golden retriever who grew to be Old Crocus, and cats, always Elizabeth's favourites – in adulthood she was rarely to be without one, no matter how impractical the location. Among the cats was a huge marmalade Persian named Baghdad, which they, of course, called Baggy; there was also a black one with white paws known as Ally, short for Ali Baba.

Nanny and the governess might confine the girls more than they would have liked but they also had time to themselves. As the girls grew old enough they enthusiastically took up country pursuits, like their parents, and each was given a pony – all except Elizabeth, who was unwilling to overcome her dislike and fear of those sweating, snorting beasts and refused ever to ride. Nor was she a great walker. This aversion to physical exertion isolated her from an important aspect of life at Wootton, and from an early age she took to reading even more than was habitually required on Stella's insistence and schoolroom dictates. Stella herself, without the benefit of either formal education or any rigorous governess-led instruction, was a well-read, informed and cultivated woman, with strong opinions to boot. Elizabeth and Felicité, as the two who indulged an appetite for literature most, were later grateful for her example, Elizabeth noting: 'We had a haphazard education but mother always made us read.'

Idyllic in some respects, childhood at Wootton was increasingly pervaded by a sense of unease. After 1917 and the birth of their last child, Felicité, Stella and Rupert's relationship became more strained. Life was busy and their many friends and acquaintances were given much hospitality; however, in spite of their common passion for politics, collecting and gardens, the disparity between their temperaments was pushing them apart. Their strong inherited family traits were leading to increasing intransigence. With time they were unable to throw off differences and disappointments and were settling into a less flexible and forgiving mode.

Rupert remained for the most part an outgoing, warm and easy-mannered man who was rewarding company and delighted in that of others. He loved his daughters, was an indulgent father, and respected and admired his wife. Along with these qualities he had inherited his father's ability for long-sighted and sometimes ruthless persistence and determination. As he had grown to adulthood his father's abrasiveness, albeit with less bitterness, had become Rupert's hallmark too. When roused his temper was fierce, his tongue sharp, but his equally formidable charm was a fortunate and necessary counter to the well-known Gwynne pugnacity.

From infancy onward the Gwynne girls and their cousins, the Palmers, were often together. One of the Palmer children later became the zoologist Lady Anne Brewis, and with a clarity born of methodical scientific habits, recalls childhood days in the years following the First World War.

In 1910, the same year as Rupert was elected MP, Stella's younger sister Grace was married. Maintaining family tradition, she chose a political man. Her husband was Roundell Palmer, Viscount Wolmer, the future third Earl of Selborne. Roundell was elected (a very young) MP to a northern constituency. Stella and Grace always remained close, their relationship cemented by united suffering as children. The coincidence of marrying men with roots in neighbouring counties enabled regular family visiting. Although the Palmers found Rupert's argumentativeness and temper distasteful they liked him, appreciated his usual pleasantness, his taste, his generosity of spirit. Roundell also found him a good political ally.

The Palmers' London house was in Chester Gate, a superlative Nash terrace. Here Grace and Roundell's multiplying band of children (eventually six in all) grew up with a large complement of nannies and governesses. Over the years, at one time or another, these rooms were also to accommodate all the Gwynne girls. Out of London the Palmers often stayed at Blackmoor House in Hampshire, the estate belonging to Roundell's parents, the Earl and Countess of Selborne. During the 1920s and 1930s Blackmoor was handed over for Christmas to Roundell, Grace and the children, while the grandparent Selbornes sailed off on cruises in search of the sun. Elizabeth, Priscilla, Diana and Felicité visited during these periods, providing a lively mixture of age groups and interests for both sets of cousins. The wide oak staircase was polished to a brighter lustre as squawking children slid down head-first or sometimes commandeered baskets to fly down in. Grown-ups were gleefully spied on from behind a grille above the great hall fireplace. A game the children called 'hassock polo', using hassocks for hands and knees to emulate the horse and the *Illustrated London News* to hit the tennis ball, was battled out in the long shiny downstairs corridor, whilst other tournaments continued on the terraced lawns outside. In this imposing house, more likely to inspire fear than delight in a child, the effect was countered by parents and nannies alike untypically permitting children to be both seen *and* heard in whatever wild games they enjoyed. Aunt Grace wasn't interested in checking hands before meals or enforcing any rigid régime; her insistence lay instead in the enforcement of a strict consideration for one another – something the Gwynne girls had not always received.

Throughout childhood and youth the close relationship between Palmer and Gwynne cousins continued. Stella and Rupert frequently went away, leaving Grace in charge of their children and their nannies. Roundell and Grace would then gather up Elizabeth and her sisters to spend the summer with them at one or other of the houses they would take by the sea. The household moved *en masse*. With cook, maids and nannies, they travelled to Walcot on the Norfolk coast, other years to Hayling Island off Portsmouth. More than once the cousins were all taken on winter sports holidays to Adelboden in the Swiss Alps. At a lower altitude than some skiing resorts the snowfall at Adelboden was not always quite sufficient for skiing, so instead the cousins walked along snowy alpine paths, or skated on the ice-covered lake.

In later years the Palmers' house became a repository for family memorabilia and here albums of old postage stamp-sized photographs now recall those far-off holidays in the years following the First World War. Elizabeth with Palmers and Gwynnes plays 'Oranges and Lemons' on the seashore; Elizabeth holds hands in a line-up of cousins silhouetted against the brow of a hill; Elizabeth totters uncertainly over the ice on skates with Anne at Adelboden. In all the images these two stand conspicuously taller than the other children, their future height already apparent. Elizabeth was called Lizard by the others for her lithe length and slimness. Her dark hair frames delicate features, her dark eyes and pretty mouth rarely more than half smile. She is reticient, intelligent, wary. She holds something back. As she grew to young adulthood Gwynne photograph albums often reveal a look of suspicion and defiance, accompanied sometimes by a precocious and unsettling allure. Elizabeth now looks the camera straight in the eye, and something invites in her own.

In youthful letters to one another the three younger Gwynne girls approached life with a passionate intensity born of more than the passing pangs of adolescence. Interwoven with a girlishly breathless tone they lambast, dissect, ridicule; above all they *love* or they *hate*. Coupled with this intensity Elizabeth, at least, had inherited her father's forthrightness and ferocious temper. From an early age the other children learned that they crossed her at their peril. Lady Anne recounts a summer by the sea when they were about eight. The children were each given a pink paper-covered box for their respective collections of ephemera. There was one short, however, and Elizabeth was the loser. Anne felt sorry for Elizabeth and so gave her her own, which was to be used for shells. Later that day she regretted her magnanimous gesture when Elizabeth flew into a rage and whacked her repeatedly with a wooden spade.

Elizabeth was as impractical as Anne herself, who recalls an embarrassing occasion on the Serpentine in Hyde Park when her father had hired rowing boats with which the Palmer and Gwynne children were to entertain themselves. The other children managed the oars easily, and scooted about the water with much joking and general hilarity. Elizabeth and Anne, on the other hand, were so incompetent they proved incapable of doing anything more than rowing round and round the lake in ever more helpless circles. Finally, in desperation, Anne's father sent out a man to rescue them and bring them ashore.

With few exceptions Elizabeth's dislike of outdoor pursuits became more pronounced as she grew older and friends later describe her notorious reluctance to take so much as an after-lunch stroll, demanding a return almost as soon as the house was vacated. The rare occasions when Elizabeth would temporarily put aside her antipathy were notable.

Lady Anne had a precocious interest in all things zoological – her father and grandfather were both keen amateur botanists – and from an early age she enlisted Elizabeth's services. Hours were spent together scouring woodland and seashore, foraging, botanizing, collecting. Soon Anne began to sort and categorize and Elizabeth became a willing assistant. On their alpine holidays Anne would take advantage of inadequate skiing snow to tramp off in search of gentians. Elizabeth went too and much later in life she recalled such episodes to her cousin Anne as some of the happiest of her childhood. Certainly her subsequent interest in plants as food – herbs, fruits and vegetables – was, in her writing, as much in the order of categorizing as aesthetic. Growing up with her mother's example at Wootton, she imbibed a refined appreciation of the atmospheric and pictorial qualities inherent in landscape, but was never in the least interested in the practice of gardening herself. Any number of letters were sent through her later life in gratitude for offerings of herbs made by post or in person. Although Elizabeth's appreciation of the uses and appearance of herbs was intense, her interest in growing them herself was less than passionate.

Throughout Rupert's marriage a nagging and persistent disappointment for him was that Stella had not provided him with a male heir. Saddest of all for them both was the fact that before the birth of their first daughter Priscilla and their second, Elizabeth, Stella, seven months pregnant with another baby, had fallen from a dog-cart and lost the child – a boy, named Sackville and buried in the family churchyard at Folkington. She took considerable time to recover her health and the episode was never referred to by herself or Rupert. (Not until fifty years later, with that liberation from constraint which sometimes illumines old age, did Stella allow herself to confide the story to Priscilla.) After the loss of her son Stella's looks became more refined, her pale English skin set off the enquiring grey eyes to better effect and her tall, slim figure moved with a new grace.

Marriage to Stella seems not to have constrained Rupert's flirtatiousness with other women. He combined captivating looks with a similarly compelling manner. Urbane and pragmatic, engaging and agreeable, inevitably he was sympathetic to women. And, not unusually, he liked to be entertained and cheered. Society was as yet more lenient regarding this predilection and Stella was required to indulge it with patience and forbearance. Many women did so, with genuine understanding and tolerance, but probably as many became resentful if they suspected their husband had serious feelings for another. How tolerant Stella ever really felt towards Rupert is not known, but after a certain point her attitude hardened and she clearly became more reserved.

She may by now have regretted submitting to Aunt Ishbel's earlier manipulation of her own and her cousin Dudley Gordon's affections. She may also have realized that despite the fact that they had many mutual interests and commitments her love for Rupert was no longer what she had believed it to be – at any rate, family anecdote had it this way. This over-simplifies the matter but any doubts must have been exacerbated by Rupert's behaviour. He became attached to another woman and over the next few years this liaison was not concealed.

Rupert was seen on public occasions with his friend on his arm. She was beautiful, less serious-minded, intelligent or artistic than Stella, but less complex and easier company. She was brought regularly to lunch at Wootton, often after riding out with Rupert on the Downs. Rupert and Stella must have arrived at some kind of agreement over this relationship, initially perhaps amicably, either because Stella did not object or because she believed she could wait until Rupert grew out of his attachment. He did not. Over time the strain began to tell on all of them and Stella retreated more into the solace of her garden and her own friends. She took up the stance she had practised in her youth. Defiance once again became her practised defence, and Stella began to establish for herself a greater independence.

From about 1920 onwards Stella began to travel abroad in the summer without Rupert. It was said that an operation to remove one of her kidneys had left her more susceptible to the cold of an English winter, so sometimes she escaped that too. She could not or would not continue at Wootton. Her foreign journeys became more regular, sometimes taking her away for weeks at a time. Letters and photograph albums show her travelling the world at a furious pace: Strasbourg, Munich, Paris, Lisbon, Rio de Janeiro, New York, the West Indies. Whether aboard a train or ship, Stella took flight from Wootton. She rarely travelled alone, sometimes with a woman friend – a favourite was Princess Marie-Louise, last surviving daughter of Queen Victoria. Among new friendships she was discovering an affinity with intelligent and artistic homosexuals, and in her characteristically resolute fashion took little notice of the fact that Rupert could not abide them.

During these immediate post-war years many felt disillusionment with what they believed to be the cost of victory in terms of shattered lives and ideals. To some, England seemed overcome by exhaustion and lethargy and in a 'state of utter dithering deliquescence', as the poet Ezra Pound wrote. Even for the more optimistic there was less security in the established order of things, the predictability of the future. But the vicissitudes of war had also left people wanting to embrace life and thirsting for a more frivolous and less irksome existence. As if to bury the loss of conviction, a kind of hectic gaiety surfaced and flourished. By 1925 Flappers had cut off their skirts to knee length and their hair to a boyish bob; the Twenties were described as Roaring and everyone was dancing the quickstep, the foxtrot and the Charleston.

In spite of the fearful prognostications heaped upon Rupert on his youthful visit to the specialist and his subsequent refusal to be limited by the weakness brought on by rheumatic fever, his health had consistently held up. Now, modifying the intensity of his sporting activities, he never smoked and drank little. His hair had turned a snowy-white but this merely gave more authority to his fine appearance and appealing manner. His life was filled with engagements, both public and private (he had built the ballroom at Wootton in 1920), but by now he was socializing less than in the past, aware that his health needed care. Nevertheless, although there were always bottles of medicines beside him at each meal, he never complained. Stella's own stoicism and a growing tension between the two did not, however, make for an easy atmosphere.

Rupert was deeply attached to his daughters, but with the arrival of each new baby girl he was more keenly aware of his father's will inexorably hanging over them all. Having sired no male heir, at his death Wootton was willed to pass to the last of James's sons. This was Roland, still living nearby at Folkington with their sister Dorothy and aged mother May.

Though his capacity for unpleasantness was not fully developed until adulthood, Roland seems by all later family accounts to have matured into an ambitious, scheming and generally unlikeable man. As a child he was badly spoilt by his mother and learned young to play off one sibling against another to his own advantage. During the 1914–18 war his DSO for 'conspicuous gallantry and judgement' was not easily won, but his undoubted bravery did little to endear him to the hearts of his family.

May's death in 1922 heightened Rupert's concerns regarding his own position. Action seemed imperative. With no male heirs not only Wootton but Folkington and the other houses and huge estate would pass to Roland on Rupert's death. Rupert's daughters would have nothing except their annuity. He consulted one of his sister Violet's 'other men', his barrister friend Max Labouchère, who suggested that they should draw up a proposal in which each potential inheritor would renounce any claim they might have on the estate in return for a sum of money. All those with a vested interest must, however, agree to this plan. Roland would retain a life interest in Folkington whilst Dorothy was to remain at Folkington Home Farm. After May's death Dorothy had been unwillingly and unceremoniously deposited there by Roland to live on her small allowance, thereby exacerbating her propensity for intensity and despair. Uprooted and thrust from her childhood home and with no experience of housekeeping, Dorothy had for the first time to look after herself and manage with a single servant. Roland was a spendthrift and indulged in lavish and conspicuous entertaining. On his father's death he had immediately gone out and bought a Rolls-Royce. He and Dorothy agreed to Rupert's plan; they could both use the money.

Not long afterwards Dorothy asked Rupert to help her pay for the restoration of some of her farm buildings with money from the estate. Knowing that his own debts were mounting, Rupert refused, and Dorothy's thinly veiled resentment at her mistreatment by father and brothers boiled over. She announced that she had changed her mind and would no longer agree to sign away the rights to her inheritance. Without Dorothy's consent Rupert could do nothing more to ensure Wootton for his family – but he believed that given time he would convince her.

In spite of attempts to scale down the pace of his life Rupert had effectively ignored doctor's warnings, culminating the previous year in advice to take three months' rest. The strain of the 1924 election campaign – in which he was returned for Eastbourne with a resounding majority – and the extended responsibilities of his new post as Under-Secretary at the War Office were considerable. These were compounded by mounting personal unease apropos Stella's discontentment with his other relationship, and the unresolved issue of the Gwynne inheritance. He became ill and was forced to rest. The doctors informed the family that the situation was grave. It was rapidly clear that Rupert's heart was finally exhausted – his kidneys too were now failing. Contemporary medicine could do nothing, not even to alleviate the dreadful pain. So, with nurses in attendance, all everyone could do was wait for the end. He was fifty-three.

CHAPTER THREE

A Taste of Abroad
(1929–1932)

WITHOUT RUPERT IN command there was now a diminished
sense of purpose at Wootton (Uncle Top, the future Lord Selborne,
and Douglas Hogg, Viscount Hailsham, had been made the girls'
guardians) and energies were unfocused. His daughters had lost their
guiding spirit; they were bereft. As James's appalling will continued
to spin out its relentless course, Roland was now possessor of his
father's estates, leaving Stella and the girls with a tenuous hold on
Wootton – they were permitted to remain there only on condition
that Stella did not remarry. Roland's presence nearby at Folkington
was overbearing, Dorothy and Stella were hardly on speaking terms,
and Violet was too far away to be of much immediate help – Stella
and she had in any case never been close. After Rupert's death,
though, Violet – who was heartbroken – did make an attempt to
include his daughters in her orbit, and entertained them more than
previously, with the help of Gordon Woodhouse and Bill Barrington,
at their handsome house at Nether Lypiatt in Gloucestershire.
Although Violet had not wanted children of her own, and would
never have survived that daily round, the perennial child and per-
former in her understood how to make an occasion special for
Elizabeth and her sisters when they came over from Wootton. One
memorable visit was in the chauffeur-driven Rolls to the cinema in
Bath. Cinema was still a novelty in 1924 and the girls' aunt was as
mesmerized as the girls by Douglas Fairbanks silently playing out the
fantasy of *The Thief of Baghdad*.

These lighter interludes were interspersed with increasing
unpleasantness from Roland and progressive uncertainty and insecu-

34

rity for Stella and the children. The eventual outcome was acrimoni-
ous and bitter.

Life with Rupert at Wootton had sometimes proved difficult for
everyone. Without him, however, it was much more so. Though
bearing a full share of responsibility for the tensions between himself
and Stella, he was also a unifying presence vis-à-vis the girls and their
mother. This is borne out by the touching regularity of the letters
and cards he dispatched to his children at Wootton. In his absence he
was full of news and reassurance. Priscilla in particular, who was
fifteen years old when Rupert died, and by then most able of the four
to sustain a more adult relationship with him, occupied a special
place in her father's affections. She appeared slower than the younger
girls in recovering a sense of equilibrium and incorporating his death
into her life. Felicité and Diana's suffering was no less than Priscilla's
but their ages (seven and nine) rendered them almost mute on the
subject, less able to voice their loss. Elizabeth, four years younger
than Priscilla and equally older than Felicité, remained, as often,
somehow distinct from the rest. She was old enough to articulate her
grief but, having little opportunity for expressing it, set a precedent
for future behaviour; she withdrew.

Searching for explanation among the bundles of letters lying
hidden away for more than half a century, one can see Stella gradually
emerging as unwilling or unable to give any significant support to
her grieving daughters. In her own way she tried to maintain a
semblance of family life but she was unable to show great warmth
until age finally mellowed her. For now she effectively abnegated her
emotional responsibilities after Rupert's death, and in her place
Priscilla gradually took on the role of surrogate mother to her
bereaved younger sisters.

For nine years after Rupert's death in 1924, Stella continued
with Wootton as the main family home and Catherine Street as its
London base. In letters between the four girls during this period it is
amply clear that Stella was the scapegoat for most of their woes.
When apart, their letters to one another railed against the tedium of
their mother's friends, her changeable moods, severity of judgment,
unfairness, lack of warmth. Their feelings of anger and disappointment were at times extreme. They became well practised in unity

against their mother, referring to her with biting regularity as 'The Hon. Lady', and contrived strategies for withstanding her authority. With their sense of loyalty to one another sharpened by loss, the girls made increasingly formidable adversaries for Stella who, nevertheless, inspired a kind of awe in her daughters and seems to have ruled Wootton with an iron hand. A younger acquaintance recently described her as 'Severe, haughty, grand, remote'. An anecdote from Elizabeth in the article for Smallbone Kitchen Designs shows the child's point of view:

> On one unhappily memorable occasion the family's golden retriever [Old Crocus] found his way into the larder and was discovered gobbling down the remnants of what had been an entire chocolate cake, fresh from the oven. Who had left the larder door open? Recriminations and arguments raged for days, the younger children were, as always, suspected, and the kitchen regions were more strictly than ever out of bounds to us.

A rare light note is sounded in Elizabeth's memories of this period when in the same article she recalled her transition from the austerities of nursery food to adult fare in the dining room downstairs.

> Yet as each of us in turn grew old enough to be promoted to grown-up tea, we discovered a rather different world [from the nursery]. True to English country house usage at the time, tea at five o'clock was presided over by my mother sitting at the head of a long table, the silver hot water urn set over a spirit lamp and the silver teapot in front of her. There was a jug of milk, of course, but that was for visitors, because once we were out of the nursery my mother, who was nothing if not consistent, considered that it was wrong to put milk, not to mention sugar, into her fine China tea. Lemon, yes, but nothing else ... I at least was more than thankful for the release from the odious tea-time milk. Five o'clock tea was nice too. I don't remember anything spectacular, but there was always a spread of simple wholesome things like thin bread and butter, scones, home-made jelly – crab apple, quince or blackberry – cucumber sandwiches,

a sponge cake. For special visitors there was usually a cake with delicious orange-flavoured icing, one which must have been a house speciality, passed on from cook to cook. At any rate, I have memories of it all through my childhood and school holidays. Today it is still a source of wonderment to me that anyone contrived to cook such faultless and delicate cakes in the oven of that old coal range . . .

The little girls' letters to one another at this time are sad yet angry documents. They are also forcible reminders of Stella's own anguish and anger at her mother's death and its aftermath at Blagdon a quarter of a century earlier. Again in her daughters that same sense of juvenile frustration and powerlessness acted as a uniting force, with Stella this time the adversary. So too in Priscilla and Elizabeth's early letters an echo of Stella's youthful obduracy and disregard for opinion is apparent. A significant reason for the clashes between Stella and her elder daughters was that her own stubbornness had not mellowed but instead ripened into an autocratic and unselfconscious eccentricity. Accurate descriptions of family events and relationships are hazardous enough at the time they take place but, in the case of Stella and her daughters, the emotional accretions and distortions of vision over time make decipherment of their relationship near impossible. Whoever was to blame, Stella found her daughters too difficult to manage on her own. Within months of his death Rupert's belief in governess education for girls was abandoned and Priscilla and Elizabeth were sent away to school.

Although Stella kept up with a number of political friends – her own family was still in the thick of politics – Wootton was no longer a household where political matters were the dominant influence. With a wide circle of friends and relations ranged about the country, she comfortably maintained friendships with many of the more exalted members of local Sussex society too. Visits were also made to Wootton by her sister Grace and by her brother Jasper, now chairman of the family bank, Coutts, and married to Countess Benckendorff, daughter of the last Russian ambassador to England before the 1917 revolution. Stella's widowed cousin, the first Viscount Hailsham, Douglas Hogg – made Elizabeth's guardian on Rupert's death – lived nearby and was another Wootton habitué. His sons Quintin (the future Lord Chancellor) and Neil were of similar ages to Stella's girls and their paths were to overlap with one another on into adulthood.

During this period Stella also made or sustained a number of friendships with artistic figures whose lives and work were to support and influence her own, and so contributed substantially to the ambience in which her daughters were growing up. Prominent in this group of friends were the painters Arthur Lett Haines and Cedric Morris, Allan Walton, painter and textile designer, and Stanford Holme, the entrepreneurial actor-director who was later to play a part in Elizabeth's life. Stella had met Cedric and Arthur before Rupert's death, but his dislike of their life-style had not always made their visits to Wootton comfortable. Cedric and Arthur (always referred to as Lett) had lived together since their first meeting at a party on Armistice Night, 1918 (Lett was married at the time). Despite numbers of liaisons with other men and women, the stormy yet remarkably creative partnership of these two men continued for the remainder of their lives.

Lett Haines painted and sculpted but his profound belief in Cedric's abilities set him early on the path of evangelizing agent for his more retiring companion. Cedric's main subjects were people, birds and plants. Elizabeth came to possess several of his paintings and one of them, *The Eggs*, illustrated the cover of her penultimate book, *An Omelette and a Glass of Wine* (Robert Hale, 1984).

Through friendship with Cedric and familiarity with his work and ideas, Stella's own painting broadened in outlook and style. So also, through identification with friends such as this colourful and exuberant pair of outsiders, she was reassured in her own difference from others. As a widow she was also at greater liberty to explore a wider variety of friendships and with them the milieu at Wootton grew more varied, more unconventional. Stella was not only independent in her opinions but had no fear of voicing them. Years later a younger friend, Judith Lassalle, said, 'I have never come across a woman who was so much her own person as Stella.' That Stella's artistic associations were not always approved by agricultural, conservative Sussex was of less and less concern to her.

More than once in these years Stella set sail for Jamaica on a banana boat with her friend the eccentric Princess Marie-Louise, a talented painter who within the confines of her upbringing and heredity carried on the semblance of a normal life. As well as travelling incognito on banana boats with friends like Stella she was also in the habit of leaving Buckingham Palace and travelling around London on a double-decker bus.

Stella acquired her friend Allan Walton's work for her houses. At first a painter, his experience in textile and interior design led him to set up Allan Walton Textiles in 1931. One of his earliest design successes was for the colourful French writer and entrepreneur Marcel Boulestin's unique restaurant Boulestin's in 1925. Commissioning an article from Virginia Woolf, *Vogue*'s editor Dorothy Todd agreed with Boulestin that the details should be discussed over a lunch prepared by himself and his partner Robin Adair in their apartment. Allan Walton and a wealthy friend were invited, along with Virginia Woolf and Dorothy Todd. The lunch was so successful that Boulestin was asked why he did not start a restaurant where others could come and enjoy his delicious food. He agreed. The rich friend put up the money whilst designs by Walton created the perfect backdrop for Boulestin's authentic French food.

The litany of daughters' complaints against Stella took little account of the socially privileged and cultured climate to which she introduced them. They took it for granted, wanting warmth and security before interest and aesthetic education. Stella was no doubt unconcerned about the girls' opinions. Both Felicité and Elizabeth later recalled how as children they were rather intimidated by Lett's large presence and weren't interested in the conversations about art. But in just a few years Elizabeth's appreciation of and friendship with Cedric and Lett and their large circle at Benton End would grow. Lett's gossipy forthrightness and Cedric's concentration on the essence of a matter would early appeal to her own sensitivities.

Despite her daughters' adult lives strongly reflecting the legacy of Stella's taste, their appreciation – always grudging – only came much later in life. At the last Elizabeth finally had the good grace to admit this, writing to a friend, Maudie O'Malley (an ex-Benton End student), after Stella's death many years later. She conceded that her mother really had been a very remarkable person, although she could seem alarming, as her personality was so strong. Stella had not been a good mother in the conventional sense, but she had extraordinary qualities in other ways. None of her daughters had inherited her talent for gardening, but the furniture in all their houses, their very surroundings, came from her. Her influence on her children was great and would endure.

Stella's haughtiness kept many at a distance; she made no attempt to put others at their ease nor to subdue her own eccentricity. This same eccentricity extended to her dress which was at once deliberate and utterly unconscious in its very individual stylishness. Veronica Nicholson, in conversation with the author, said of the Gwynne style, 'Oh they were very "Greenery Yallery". Although superior about the Bloomsburys, they dressed in a way rather similarly. Colours, textures, they were always doing things with them which were interesting. And jewellery. When others of their kind were mostly still wearing precious stones they were forging ahead in semi-precious.' A later story, illustrating Stella's dress and blithe unawareness or insensitivity to opinion, is told of an occasion when she was in retreat from her second husband Major Hamilton (left, she hoped, for good in Jamaica because she had grown exhausted by his drinking). Met off the train by a relative at a country station, far from being inconspicuous Stella stepped out of the carriage, stately and resplendent in a huge brimmed hat hung all around with little tinkling bells.

Stella's own education by governesses, themselves badly educated, had been a failure. This was no great matter, since little more was expected of her than to take on the mantle of gentility and confine herself to the domestic sphere. But then she also had the conflicting precedent set by such formidable female members of her family as Aunt Ishbel. Ishbel had contributed to Stella's restlessness and dissatisfaction with the Victorian triad of responsibilities given to women from families with the slightest of social pretensions: produce as many children as possible, organize the servants, and look pleasantly decorative. Stella was not an intellectual, nor did she set out to destroy the traditional position of women, but she had considerable natural intelligence, which had led her to be more wide-ranging and better read than many of her social counterparts. She was unwilling to mask this forceful intelligence and at times was branded a blue-stocking, then as now generally disapproved of by men. She did not practise much the ancient female arts of subtlety, compromise and accommodation and her development (however unconscious) of the English habit of individuality did not always make her an easy woman to be with.

Although she remained conventional enough to put her daughters through the same social hoops as those through which she had jumped herself, with the concomitant expectation of good marriages, other factors were at work too in the decisions regarding her charges. To her credit, in sending the girls away to school Stella was not simply ridding herself of an irksome responsibility. She was reflecting both dissatisfaction with her own education and the rapidly changing expectations for women in the 1920s. It is also worth noting that having revoked Rupert's decision about education at home, the school to which Stella planned handing over her daughters, Wycombe Abbey in Buckinghamshire, was as much concerned with the academic training of a new generation of thinking women as with the training of young ladies in social accomplishments. Priscilla and Elizabeth, however, were aware of Rupert's views on their education and were reluctant to leave the home where they had spent their childhood. When ordered to pack their lives into the hard school trunks, they did so with resentment and foreboding. Diana and Felicité were only nine and seven and Stella decided to keep them at home under the tutelage of their governess Miss Spencer for a short while longer.

Priscilla was the first to leave Wootton, sent to Wycombe in January 1925, only four months after Rupert's death. Elizabeth was not yet old enough to enter the senior school and so in September 1925 she began her own life away from home at Godstowe, the preparatory school for Wycombe. Experiencing the pangs of first days at boarding school, Priscilla and Elizabeth felt thrust from home. However much their anger might be projected at Stella while at Wootton, away from it their sense of belonging drew them back. All four girls also felt the pull of separation from one another for the first time in their lives. Priscilla was not to last out long. Having completed only one term she was so unruly and unhappy that she was sent back home – in quarantine. The school was relieved by the excuse that she had contracted whooping cough, then more dangerous than today. Elizabeth, meanwhile, had not yet gone to Godstowe, for she too was ill, recovering from appendicitis. It was feared that in her weakened stage she would be more receptive to Priscilla's whooping cough, resulting in abortive attempts at Wootton to keep them apart.

Elizabeth spent the next two years at Godstowe, with journeys back and forth for school holidays at Wootton, or with the Palmer cousins if Stella was away travelling. Her reports of this time are mixed and sometimes contradictory; a postcard to Felicité at Wootton in July 1926 from Godstowe thanks her for the 'letter and silver paper. Exams are over. Have you been on any picnics? Isn't it lovely weather. Love from Elizabeth.' But she did, like most others, remain steadfast in her hatred of mealtimes at school. The food, she said, was atrocious, 'terrible boiled fish, awful meat'.

Ill and sent home early in the spring of 1927, she missed what should have been her last term. In the lazy warm days of May Elizabeth wrote to Felicité that her enforced absence from Wootton had kept her from savouring its beautiful gardens at that season for two years. She had forgotten how lovely, and how peaceful, they were.

After recovering from her whooping cough in 1925 Priscilla had never gone back to Wycombe. Her dislike of the school was intense and she had refused to return with such vehemence that Stella had relented and sent her daily with the chauffeur to school in Eastbourne. Under the same roof again, Stella and Priscilla found each other's company no easier than before, but this was soon relieved when Priscilla was sent off to Paris with her cousin Vivien Ridley.

By now Stella had decided not to make the mistake of having Elizabeth at home too. By 1926 Felicité had begun at Moira House in Eastbourne, and after Elizabeth's recovery from appendicitis, instead of going up to Wycombe Abbey she too was probably installed at school in Eastbourne, where it seems she remained for only one academic year. Family tradition has it that Elizabeth was so piqued at not being given a major part in the school play that Stella was obliged to remove her, sending her further away to board at St Clare's Ladies' Private School in Tunbridge Wells. The principal, Miss Despree Vickery, had extended and developed her own property as one of the many small private educational estabishments which flourished for only a few years earlier this century. After two terms, and just as Elizabeth was preparing to sit School Certificate exams at sixteen, Stella decided her daughter should leave the school. In later life Elizabeth seemed undecided as to whether or not she resented this move on Stella's part. Probably divided between resentment of Stella's prerogative and subsequent gratitude for its effect on her life, her reminiscences on the subject reflect this when she says at one time that she was 'torn willingly' from her school and at another, that, although she liked it, Stella thought she was 'becoming too hockey-stickish there and sent me off to France'.

Resentful or not, Elizabeth went to Paris, where she boarded out with two other English girls with a family called Robertot in the rue Eugène Delacroix while studying at the Sorbonne. One of her fellow-boarders was Marian Butterworth, an unassuming, sweet-natured girl with whom Elizabeth had made friends at Godstowe. Like Elizabeth she was intended for Wycombe and although she too had ended by going elsewhere, the two girls remained friends and were now to spend most of the next year-and-a-half in each other's company in Paris. Their friendship was cemented by this first youthful period abroad together and they remained close for much of the remainder of their lives. Elizabeth's more forceful and dogmatic nature found the perfect foil in Marian's unassuming and simpler one. Her acceptance of Elizabeth as the dominant partner set an early precedent for many of Elizabeth's female friendships – and to these relatively subservient friends, despite repeated lapses of sensitivity, she remained devoted and loyal.

The curriculum at the Sorbonne covered French language, literature and history. Study was hard and not very inspiring but gave Elizabeth a lifelong attachment to French literature and enabled her to become a fluent French speaker. While in Paris she led a fairly cloistered and hard-working existence, a sharp little flavour of which comes with a card to Felicité on Shrove Tuesday: 'I was going to write to you the other night but then I upset a bottle of ink all over my room and by the time I'd finished mopping it up with one piece of rather thin blotting paper and a hanky . . . it was time to go to bed. Did you have pancakes for lunch?'

Like most people Elizabeth was unaware of the artistic turmoil to which Paris was then subject and from which was being carved a new set of principles for the century. The latest in the hectic parade of artistic movements to emanate from the city was André Breton's inauguration of Surrealism in 1924. Elizabeth, however, followed a time-honoured Parisian route for the young foreigner and took more conventional painting lessons in a private studio. Influenced by the milieu in which she had grown up, she wanted to paint, always referring to it later as her 'first love'. Accordingly, after about eighteen months in Paris Stella sent her to Munich not only to learn German but also to further her painting studies. Veronica Nicholson says: '. . . she was far too realistic and honest with herself not to admit when she couldn't do something though . . . and she realized she couldn't paint. Elizabeth *had* to do something artistic, it was almost pre-ordained. If it was not to be painting then there were only so many other things she could try her hand at. She took time to find her *métier.*'

Music was not a possibility. Unlike her sister Priscilla Elizabeth had no ear, no real need for music. A friend of later years, Gerald Asher, recently wrote, 'She was bored by music.' She felt no affinity with her extraordinary Aunt Violet's musical craftsmanship. Ever alert to the merest trace of foolishness in others, Elizabeth would instead lampoon Aunt Violet's musical crusade in a series of comments and letters in latter days.

The discovery of a satisfactory form of self-expression for Elizabeth took time but the foundations, in both negative and positive senses, were laid down early. In years to come she would record a crucial part of this foundation in her retrospective tributes to the bourgeois Norman-French Robertot family with whom she boarded in Paris. Their great greed was refined by an overriding concern, amounting almost to reverence, for the quality of their table. After several years of writing and with her wide knowledge of French food synthesized into the magisterial *French Provincial Cooking* (Michael Joseph, 1960), Elizabeth was able to register her appreciation for the gift given her by the Robertots: a first taste of food which did more than simply fuel her body. Though not responsive at the time, she realized that through French cooking it was not only her body which had been nourished, stimulated and soothed, but her emotions and spirit too.

The rather stifling routine in this most proper of Parisian households reached its weekly climax on Thursday afternoons, when Madame presided over her 'At Home'. This comprised a gaggle of female relations and friends dressed always in funereal black. Accompanied by a recitation of the previous week's calamities – which befell the assembled company with unerring regularity – they ate the choicest selection of cakes and *petits fours* the gifted young cook Léontine was capable of providing. Obliged to attend these excruciating social occasions, the three English girls remained unmoved by their culinary merits. Elizabeth was restless and impatient and she and her fellow-boarders learned to devise other commitments to avoid the following day's lunch. Friday meant boiled salt cod and this the girls simply could not stomach. In her book *French Provincial Cooking* Elizabeth wonders at this aberration of otherwise impeccable culinary taste, which allowed the family to eat, with such regularity, the 'Grey, slimy, [fish] in great hideous flakes, it lay plonked on the dish without benefit of sauce or garnish of any kind.'

In reaction to Madame Robertot's slimy Friday lunches the philistine young English mesdemoiselles would treat themselves. The wicked bad taste of a minimal plate in a cheap student canteen, or ham or an orange disgorged from gleaming chrome self-service cabinets in a Latin Quarter restaurant, were as exciting, because forbidden, as any of the quiet masterpieces which emerged with such unfailing certainty from the patient Léontine's kitchen.

A few years later while on enforced stay in the South of France for several months, Elizabeth discovered what she believed were more enlightened Provençal ways with salt cod and recommended it to Priscilla in ration-blighted wartime Britain. She told her that it was impossible to buy haddock, which was annoying, but that they did have dried salt cod – she wasn't that keen on it, but, if soaked for about two days, it became quite all right to eat.

With too many unpleasant memories of unimaginative and bad fish cooking served up at Wootton and at school, even at the beginning of the war Elizabeth was still not keen on fish. Writing again to Priscilla from the South of France, and beginning to suffer the first inconveniences of living in a country at war, she said that she wished they had a South Seas island dependent on coconuts and fish, much as she hated these foods, to which she could escape. She saw the catching and killing of a large octopus in the harbour at Marseilles, a sight that made her feel quite ill. She outgrew this distaste and realized too, ten years on as a fledgling author, that her readers might not hold with such aversions. Thus, again on the subject of cod in her first book, *Mediterranean Food* (John Lehmann, 1950), she describes *brandade de morue* – garlicky, creamed cod – as 'a triumph'. She gives another way with salt cod when she describes its accompaniment *aïoli*, that Provençal garlic sauce of such earthy pungency.

Oddly enough, for someone who began with such an aversion to fish, one of Elizabeth's most affecting memories of food from the first months of war spent in France was associated with another variety. The Robertots owned a small farmhouse at Bieville, near Caen in the Calvados region of Normandy, and during Easter or summer holidays Elizabeth sometimes stayed a while there with them. Set amidst rich green pastures away from the roar of Paris and the French exodus from town to country *en vacance*, the family's pretty farmhouse exuded a reviving atmosphere of calm. A traditional kitchen garden gave them all the fresh vegetables they could use and the farm supplied perfect Normandy cream and butter – normally sent to Léontine in Paris for her delicate cakes and creams.

Away from Paris Madame Robertot let Léontine return for a spell with her own family in the country, while the Robertots were looked after by a young girl from the village, Marie, with the help of her very small brother. Marie herself was little more than Elizabeth's age yet she unfailingly produced meat and vegetables dishes of a refined delicacy and simplicity. Little could she have guessed that the plate of *moules à la crème* or *mouclade*, mussels in their creamy herb sauce, which she served up one day, were to be such a revelation to the young English mademoiselle.

Elizabeth had neither heard of nor tasted mussels before and in recollecting their effect on her she calls them 'mysterious and extra-ordinary'. The small black shells harbouring such curious, seductive contents send her into a rêverie on another fleshy food: Wootton field mushrooms cooked with nothing but cream and served up illicitly by Nanny in her nursery days. 'So those Norman mussels which reminded me, for whatever reason, of our secret childhood feasts, became forever endowed with the mystery of far off and almost unobtainable things.' In tracing the lineage of what was to become a personal rite she tells us that other mussel dishes eaten over the years are often good, some even perfect, but they are ultimately 'more evolved, less innocent', and in her obeisance to a memory and its habitual re-creation she describes how 'to this day' the first dish she tries to eat on arrival and the last before departure from France is a dish of those 'mussels, sweet small mussels'. In her innocence Elizabeth believed the mussels special to the Robertot family or Marie and was amazed to discover the same dish on the menu at the great Walterspiels restaurant in Munich not many months later.

After concluding her stint at her Eastbourne school Priscilla had been sent to Paris to learn French, to acquaint herself with a wider social circle – in other words, to be 'finished'. Stella's daughters were sent away to become gentlewomen. In practice in the 1920s this often meant little more than perfecting languages and acquiring a cosmopolitan gloss. Priscilla was sent to France with her cousin Vivien Ridley, after which they went on to spend some months in Vienna together. Elizabeth followed suit and after Paris her 'civilizing' was completed with a period in Munich, where she would also continue with painting studies. Between the two world wars Germany and Austria were still regarded as suitable for the 'finishing' process. The Ridley and Palmer families had connections in both countries. Later Diana and Felicité took their turn too.

Attractive, sophisticated, with money enough to indulge their passion for beautiful clothes, and connections with which to distract themselves, the Gwynne girls each spent an intensely social time in these two countries, entertained by wealthy and well-connected young men and their families. There was plenty of scope for forming attachments. Shortly after Elizabeth's stay Vivien Ridley married a Baron von Bebenburg. Felicité too fell in love – unsuitably as it turned out; he was married – and recovery was slow, perhaps never complete.

Elizabeth spent a hectic six months in Munich with an aristocratic German family, accompanying them in their progress from town to country. Following a strenuous round of house-parties, balls, opera (notable in the light of her increasingly pronounced 'deafness' to music), gallery visiting, clubs and restaurants, it is doubtful that Elizabeth spent much time with her paint-brushes. Certainly on returning to England she launched herself into an entirely different career and made no further reference to her 'first love' for some time.

Munich was a brief episode in Elizabeth's life and she wrote next to nothing about it, once saying, misleadingly, that the food not the place was enjoyable in Germany of the 1930s. She records that her host family's Austrian cook was particularly adept at those rich cakes and puddings so much loved by wealthy Germans and Austrians. Sunday breakfasts often meant a delicious 'sweet buttery bread' whilst evening meals might provide venison from the forests outside Munich with 'a mysterious wild red berry sauce'. The cakes and puddings delighted Elizabeth: rich, tempting, sophisticated and quite different from those more homely English offerings at grown-up Wootton teas and from the subtle and refined productions of young Léontine in Paris.

Wary of the unsympathetic post-war attitude to Germany, Elizabeth was circumspect in her later pronouncements, but her own experience of the place remained forever associated with her final emergence from adolescence into young adulthood. She needed little encouragement, and gave herself up to an orgy of distraction. Her forte was never to capture the crowd, but in more intimate social gatherings she began to test the power given her by the development of her sparkling wit and sinuous dark looks. In Munich her concerns, therefore, were more likely to be with whether the stuff and cut of a modish new dress fell to her advantage, rather than any considerations on a larger scale. Simultaneously, though, her sharp eye was vigilant and her prodigious memory was storing up the sights and sounds of the great European city which was Munich.

Elizabeth returned to Germany and Austria on a number of occasions. In the spring of 1934, for example, she travelled to Munich and met up with Felicité, Priscilla and her new husband Richard Longland, to spend a few days there together. The reunion was not an entirely successful one and Elizabeth realized that with the change in family dynamics she should not really have expected otherwise. When neither Felicité nor Richard appreciated Munich as she did, she became cross – she tended never to notice the disadvantages of the place, because for her it was 'almost sacred', permeated with a charm and a beauty so powerful that nothing could spoil it. She had been happy there two years ago, and it retained its magic, in spite of the fact that when she went back she found that everything had changed and all the people she knew were gone.

And a few weeks later when Felicité wanted to leave, unhappy with the von Stengel family she was staying with in Munich, Elizabeth wrote to her: 'I think you would be mad to go there [Innsbruck], when you can be in the most interesting and beautiful town in the whole world, when you can hear the most perfect operas and concerts, and see the most lovely pictures and meet the most charming people. Munich in the spring is simply too lovely for words – I would sell my soul to come back at Easter – only no one wants to buy it.'

Probably the last visit Elizabeth made to Munich was in August 1937, two years before England declared war on Germany.

CHAPTER FOUR

The Stage

(1932–1934)

AFTER HER SIX months in Germany in 1932 Elizabeth was back in England. Her freedom from the confines of Wootton, Stella and serious schooling had initiated her into the independent life she now intended to lead. But Stella was adamant that in June it would be Elizabeth's turn to go through the gruelling process of presentation at Court. Elizabeth was not sure enough of what she wanted and had neither the singlemindedness of conviction, nor a large enough allowance with which to reject Stella's plans. Elizabeth's coming-out dance was to be held at Aunt Grace and Uncle Top's No. 3 Chester Gate, shared with Karen Harris, a girl whose family were friends and neighbours of the Gwynnes in Catherine Street and Sussex. Lady Cara Harris's country house was on the Isle of Wight where Karen had grown up with her eccentric parents – her mother Cara quite remarkably so. (Karen was soon to marry Osbert Lancaster, who became one of the most influential cartoonists of his generation.)

In the midst of the Season Elizabeth had been sent down from London to Wootton – in quarantine with measles, still a feared disease – and writes to 'Dearest Pris' staying with Nathalie and Quintin Hogg at Middleton House in Oxfordshire. She complains that Stella has written to her 'to the effect that in her house people don't do things without her permission and that I've given measles to the whole of London'. And in her frustration she continues to characterize Stella with her typical volleys: 'Really you'd think she was a Queen Elizabeth for power and Helen of Troy for looks the way she goes on – actually she's more like Catherine of Medici for both looks and abuse of authority, although she's not got a tenth part of that lady's wits.'

Elizabeth lists some of the young men whom she has suggested Stella might invite for her dance: 'Eric Cudder, Hearty Henderson, Desmond, Rag Shackleton, Stephen Bull, Norman Molle, Clydesdale, Philip Chetwynde, Tommy Martin, the Tivertons, Ridgeways, Alec Pilkington.' This in the hope of forestalling Stella who might otherwise 'go and ask some bloody growth she is pleased to call Bohemian'. But then Elizabeth declares that 'You can't think how heavenly it is here – the garden looking too lovely, the first time I've seen it in May since '25 and not a soul to be seen and nothing to do except walk about and pick flowers and breathe in the perfect peace.'

Elizabeth had two pretty, adjoining beamed rooms as bedroom in the older part of the house overlooking flower borders spilling on to lawns and the great paved circle and bluebell wood beyond. 'Wootton devoid of Mummie is like Paradise . . .' And further on in the same letter she is wailing: 'I wish to goodness I could stay here in peace. I'd rather be here than going to all the parties in the world – I'd sell my soul to be able to give the 2nd a miss. The thought of all those people makes me sick and giddy. I've got about 14 more dances till the end of the Season. I can only pray I don't get asked to any more as long as I live . . .' She concludes with a revealing threat: 'And . . . very soon if she isn't jolly careful I shall become some man's mistress and live with him.'

Nevertheless, having survived her presentation at Court on 11 May 1932 and in spite of saying to friends in later years that she was a wallflower and loathed it all, she also survived the dances of the Season. With her delicately smouldering looks and her shyness shielded by a steely coolness and barbed tongue, she must have been a daunting prospect for many of the equally shy young men in need of as much reassurance as herself.

Meanwhile Elizabeth had made up her mind that with painting rejected as unrealistic she would become an actress. The stage was still not regarded as a reputable place for a girl of her background but, with Gwynne–Ridley wilfulness already a well-defined trait, the alarm it might cause was unlikely to affect her decision in the slightest. There were fierce and prolonged arguments back and forth with Stella, but at the end of it all Priscilla remembers Elizabeth walking down the drive with her suitcase. Although she didn't then know it, this was the last time Elizabeth would spend any length of time at Wootton.

Stanford Holme was a maverick actor-manager who already knew Stella from a period spent acting in Sussex. J. B. Fagan, founder of the enterprising Oxford Repertory Company, had recently handed over to Stanford and Elizabeth had turned to him for advice. This procured for her an invitation to come and work for the company as assistant stage-manager-cum-trainee-actress in Oxford. The Repertory Company was based at the Playhouse, then a small building in Banbury Road more reminiscent of a village hall than of a theatre with ambitious intent. Undeterred by their unprepossessing building and position off the city's centre, the players were full of enthusiasm, and several had a good measure of talent.

J. B. Fagan's reputation for good plays well staged – but not too demanding, and aimed to appeal to both an undergraduate audience and townspeople alike – was maintained and enlarged. Stanford drew his cast and stage managers from a wide range of promising actors, mostly professional but some too from the set of undergraduates keen to be involved in the theatre. One of these, George Devine, later founded the prestigious English Theatre Company. Meanwhile a high proportion of the professionals succeeded, many of their names later reading like a roll-call of the most sought-after actors of their time.

Stanford was one of those experienced actor-managers more common in the days before the profession was made softer and safer by the institution of Equity. Work was hard, insecure and yet carried on with the cheerfulness of the amateur. With a witty urbanity Stanford saw to it that his young cast kept up their relentless schedule of dramas. Here he was abetted by the public school system from which many of the company had sprung, schooling them in a similar ethos of discipline and intensity combined with a determined lightheartedness.

The Oxford Rep made up for lack of money with inventiveness, and everything was done at breakneck speed. Assistant stage managers like Elizabeth were regularly sent careering off round the town in search of props to augment the company's own meagre collection. A market scene was one day ordered by the director, resulting in a first-night stage aglow with bright yellow posters announcing 'Fyffes Bananas'. During Christmas Elizabeth was doing the publicity for the pantomime, tearing around Oxford with posters, handbills and programmes, and generally making it known that on Boxing Day, at the Playhouse, there would be 'glittering scenes, exquisite singing, gorgeous girls and lovely music – and the Cat (it's Dick Whittington)'.

She was finding the producer 'particularly difficult and annoying', and told Felicité she was having such an awful time doing the shows, and having so many rows with everyone, that she would never stage manage again.

She was invited over to Aunt Violet at Nether Lypiatt and in her Christmas letter to Priscilla was in 'a savage temper about it'. Violet had made a gothic set of arrangements for collecting Elizabeth from Oxford, involving out-of-date train timetables and an obscure collection point in the Rolls. Elizabeth said that Violet could come half-way to fetch her. Another series of convoluted suggestions from her aunt about exactly where to meet followed, and she agreed to be collected at Moreton-in-Marsh, which is about twenty minutes from Oxford.

After further complications Violet suggested yet another meeting place. Elizabeth, who had to work and didn't really want to spend a weekend with Aunt Violet and 'all her old men', delivers damning judgement. 'It makes me absolutely furious. That woman has never done anything in her life except drive about the country in a Rolls-Royce with Lalique mascots and filled with rugs and sweets and adoring men, and occasionally earn £1000 by Tinkling on a Toy instrument. It's never occurred to her that anybody could have anything better to do . . .' Then she relents a little. 'Really I'm very fond of her and I'm always enormously entertained when I go and see her but she will not realize that there are people in the world who have a spot of work to do now and then.'

Elizabeth's sharp characterization of her aunt is a good one, containing as it does kernels of truth, but equally it reveals her own self-absorption. She appears both oblivious to Violet's great diligence and application to her music and quite insensitive to its merits. Working at her first job, at times gruelling and not very glamorous,

Elizabeth's jealousy of her aunt's 'leisure' is clear; but the particular irritation she feels at her capriciousness, her demanding and imperious manner, hints that these were nascent qualities of her own.

Later she experienced a vindictive pleasure when seated at Violet's dining table, telling Priscilla: 'Poor Aunt V. had her work cut out preventing any of us talking to any of her men, except Gordon, for longer than 3 minutes – Laurence Johnson was there – he is a perfect angel. [Johnson owned Hidcote Manor and was a good friend of Violet and Bill Barrington.] He motored me half-way back to Oxford and showed me his house and perfectly lovely garden on the way. Aunt V. was rather annoyed with him because he said: "Good." when I said I was on the stage, and she said: "Oh no Johnnie it's not good."

'And Denis said: "It depends if she's good . . ." (general roar.)'

The Rep usually did each play for a fortnightly run and in that time lines for the following production had to be learnt, props and stage managed, and the cast rehearsed. It was customary for the company to share digs in houses run by landladies in various parts of the town. Among the first people Elizabeth shared digs with was a girl already launched into lead parts. She was a little older than Elizabeth; a cheerful, hard-working girl experienced at living in lodgings and fending for herself. Her name was Joan Hickson and she became a steady, reliable actress. Always in work, her career recently concluded on a high note when her elegant, wry and sympathetic interpretation of Agatha Christie's Miss Marple made her a family name.

Without any hint of malice Miss Hickson told the author how Elizabeth's ignorance of the kitchen in those first Oxford days was so extreme that 'I even had to teach her how to make a cup of tea.' Until then Elizabeth had always lived in houses with servants, where young ladies were not expected to come into the kitchen. Her first attempts at cooking are recounted to Felicité in a flat and slightly bemused tone, and although she seems to expect little of the food itself or of herself as cook, it is worthy of comment that she says anything at all.

'I cooked my own lunch today. I had sausages, and tomatoes and fried onions and green peas. Then loganberries and cream and then cheese and celery and then coffee. Only the onions were burnt and they stank the place out. I shan't be able to have onions often. Or fish.'

Post-rehearsal high teas, in one of the recently opened chain of Cadena Cafés, provide no evidence of gourmandise, with tinned fruit salad for a sweet.

On another occasion she told of the supper she had had in her digs – 3 sardines on 1½ bits of toast, 2 digestive biscuits, 2½ cups of tepid tea, and 9 cigarettes – just before drinking her tonic, putting her hair in curlers and going to bed.

With Elizabeth in Oxford, Priscilla now uneasily back at Wootton, and Diana and Felicité undergoing their final stages of schooling and 'finishing' in England and Austria, the four girls maintained a regular and affectionate flow of letters back and forth. Priscilla and Elizabeth's busy social calendars are interwoven between family and friends and, nurturing their close relationship, they keep each other constantly abreast of the latest concerns and fears about the Hon. Lady, family, friends and men.

At twenty-three 'Dearest Pris' continued in her role as chief confidante and advisor to her younger sisters, and both she and Elizabeth exercised considerable thought over the welfare of the young Bulgies or Bolsheviks as Diana and Felicité were tagged. Elizabeth and Felicité were forming a particular bond through their literary tastes and although all four girls sent each other books as presents, literary discussion between these two was more thoughtful. Christmas 1933, and Elizabeth was terribly pleased with some Shaw that Felicité have given her – she had wanted to read him for a very long time, and already possessed a volume of his criticism. A year later Felicité made her a rather more extravagant present of two Shaws, one of which was *Back to Methuselah*, which she had particularly wanted to read. 'My collection of Shaws is gradually getting longer . . . thank you a thousand times.'

Meanwhile, in January 1933 the Rep was about to put on Shaw's *Arms and the Man* in which Elizabeth thought she would not have a part, but she could not leave Oxford because caught up, as she says to Felicité: 'working on this paper we're supposed to be going to publish – you've probably heard about it from Diana – it's going to have her design on the cover.' (Diana, unlike Elizabeth, began and continued to paint.) And revealingly in the light of her own future Elizabeth says, 'I'm supposed to be sub-editor of *Repertory* I believe – *but I can't write at all* [author's italics] so other people will have to do all the articles, write the jokes etc.' She then asks if 'Wicked Uncle [Roland] has given us the usual £9 to be divided between the four . . .' She asks Felicité about her Christmas presents and rounds off on a wry note: 'I also had a very singular piece of clanking chain from Aunt Violet, did you get one too? What are they meant to be?'

By the following year Elizabeth was taking more parts and living in new yellow and blue digs in Banbury Road by the Playhouse. The Rep were doing *The Cathedral* and *The Taming of the Shrew*, in which she played Bianca; for once the notices were good, and she was relieved at her reviews. She considered herself quite lucky to have the part of Bianca, as it was the only other woman's part, and the other five girls in the company were furious because they weren't playing it.

Elizabeth's 'luck' may well have coincided with her relationship with the Playhouse's director, Stanford Holme. Stanford's wife Thea was a beautiful and respected actress who had long since learnt patience with her husband's liaisons. Some preferred Elizabeth's sister Diana's cooler grey-eyed English beauty, but Elizabeth's dark mercurial looks hinted at the exotic in her ancestry and were well suited to the drama of theatre life. She now carried herself with a poise which rarely deserted her, and a certain reserve – at times haughty – added to the allure. Although her sharp temper and wit were not modified by a desire to please, her humour often did. She was challenging, unbiddable, compelling, and not surprisingly Stanford Holme was struck by her. It was fortunate that Thea understood forbearance, because any objections would have made little difference to Elizabeth, whose cast of mind is clear when advising Felicité about a year later. Chafing at the frustrations of her attempts to holiday in Norway with her love of the moment, Felicité complained to her sister about her guardian Mrs Headlam's refusal to permit the journey. (Mrs Headlam was a family acquaintance with whom Felicité stayed in Durham for several months to learn secretarial skills and be introduced to local society.) Elizabeth wrote to her 'Dearest Bulge' (Felicité) and told her to go to Norway and be damned to everybody. Felicité must do what she wants to about these sorts of things, because if she doesn't now, then she never will. 'How do you think I shook off interfering people who wouldn't let me do what I wanted?' Elizabeth said that if she were in her place, she'd go, whether it was over Mrs Headlam's 'dead body or not'. If it had been Stella who had forbidden Felicité to go, it would have been different, because she was her legal guardian, but Mrs Headlam had 'nothing to do with it whatsoever'. Felicité had asked Elizabeth to come up to Durham to make peace between her and Mrs Headlam, a suggestion that Elizabeth unequivocally rejected: 'You might as well ask Hitler to marry a Jewess as me to make peace with Mrs. H.'

Prior to this episode, by the summer of 1933, Stella and her daughters' lives had been irrevocably altered. Stella felt so beleaguered by the wrangles with her brother-in-law Roland at Folkington following Rupert's death that at one point an inventory of everything she and Rupert had collected whilst at Wootton was given to Roland to ensure that if the day came when she must leave, at least it would not be without her possessions.

Roland had spent prodigiously on entertaining and maintaining a grand style at Folkington over the years, and by the early 1930s he was in debt. Letting Wootton would go some way towards remedying his problems, and as a consequence his unpleasantness and obstructiveness towards Stella had increased the more pressing his financial problems became. To add to her sense of insecurity she knew that recent developments in her own life could leave her in just the position Roland wanted.

Stella's visits to Jamaica had been sociable and productive and she found the brilliance and fertility of the island a stimulant for her painting. She felt at ease among the expatriates and old landed Jamaican families. Life was conducted at a leisurely pace. And, although she loved Wootton and its gardens, its memories combined with the difficulties presented by her daughters and Roland made for tensions which grew rather than diminished with time. Far away from Europe she felt freer, soothed by the languid balm of this beautiful tropical island.

Major John Hamilton, ADC to the Governor of Jamaica, owned a plantation and a large house and garden in need of care. On a recent visit to England Stella had invited him down to Wootton and in between the filial tirades Diana had written to Felicité recounting a light-hearted lunch spent with Stella and 'Ham' – his inevitable Gwynne nickname. Stella was in good spirits and amused Diana and 'Ham' with tales of childhood conspiracy and wickedness together with Grace and their brothers at Blagdon. Life once again held possibilities of a more creative kind and Stella was happier than she had been for a long time. Sadly, her own increased sense of well-being did little to make relations with the girls easier.

The crisis which had been looming for so long finally came to a head with Stella's announcement of her forthcoming marriage to Major Hamilton. Her decision must have been tinged with relief at the prospect of escape from a brother-in-law whose lack of sympathy and bullishness she now found intolerable. For Wootton she was substituting a Jamaican plantation, a house with no electricity or running water and a garden surrounded by bush. (Within a year she would impose her will on the landscape and transform it into one of the most impressive gardens in Jamaica.) The girls' awareness of their mother's weakening hold on Wootton had grown with her increasing attachment to 'Ham' and their animosity towards both Roland and 'Ham' escalated accordingly. But even more bitterness was reserved for Stella, whose marriage would lose them Wootton. Not only was she replacing their father, but as a consequence they were to be ejected from their childhood home. Added to this, Priscilla had announced her intention of marrying.

Elizabeth had already left home. In spite of feeling as rooted in Wootton as the others, she avoided too much involvement in the family's last fraught years there. Committed to her new life, after 1931 she no longer returned to Wootton for Christmas and wrote wit-spiked grumbling letters for several years about the dutiful periods spent with the Palmers or Aunt Violet during the festive season.

Before leaving England Stella asked her sister Grace and brother Jasper to act *in loco parentis* to her daughters. The arrangements were not ideal for anyone, but the feeling was that, as Grace told her daughter Anne, 'Stella has had little happiness; she deserves some now.' Priscilla and Elizabeth were to be based at Chester Gate with Grace and Uncle Top whilst the other two would spend more time with Jasper's wife Countess Benckendorff's brother and his family at their houses in London and Suffolk. By the summer of 1933 Wootton was packed up, Roland had moved in a Miss Hudson as tenant, and Stella had fled.

Felicité was sent to learn secretarial skills with Mrs Headlam in Durham and Diana went to the Benckendorffs at Marlborough House, Marble Hill. When the Rep had no work for her Elizabeth moved back and forth between Oxford and London, staying with the Palmers or sometimes Aunt Violet, whilst Priscilla now took on her role as surrogate mother in earnest.

In a letter to Felicité the following year the girls' old drawing mistress, Miss Harrison, wrote: 'Hated to hear of Wootton desecrated like that . . . I loved the place – it was all just perfect and in keeping. I always wondered what Elizabeth would do – for I thought she would branch out some time. I thought at one time she would take up painting, but not acting. I was amused at your remark, "Sometimes with a job but more generally without." What a scattering of family you are now.'

In the spring of 1933 Priscilla had, like her mother, been making choices and decided against the more forceful dynamic of one of her present suitors in favour of a pleasant young officer called Richard Longland. He was a passionate francophile and was knowledgeable about French food and devoted to its literature. He was particularly fond of Proust. Elizabeth tendered her congratulations from the Playhouse on Priscilla's somewhat staggering piece of news. She thought Priscilla would be very happy with Richard, and agreed that he was utterly charming. She added a rather world-weary caveat, to the effect that his mother should be dispensed with it at all possible – she undoubtedly worshipped her son. She asks after those whom Priscilla has rejected and says: 'We're going on right through the Vac . . . Do come down for a week-end – this week we're doing *The Faithful Heart*, next week *The Sign on the Door*, then a farce, *Almost a Honeymoon*. I'm appallingly busy – our stage manager has gone on holiday for a month so I've got all her work to do – it's appallingly nerve-racking – never have a second to do anything. Let me know when you're coming and I can get you a room in my digs. Unless I am sacked I don't suppose I shall get a holiday in months.'

The company travelled when Oxford students were down for vacation, and the following year Elizabeth was acting and stage managing for a month in Sussex at the Pavilion Theatre, Peacehaven, in a special holiday season. Here she played in Frederick Lonsdale's *On Approval* alongside Joan Hickson, Stanford Holme, Harald Norway, Prudence Khan and John Boxer.

Uncle Top gave Priscilla away from Chester Gate in November, with her sisters as bridesmaids and Ismay Crighton-Stuart and Nathalie Hogg as maids of honour in shimmering satin. Society came and afterwards Violet wrote to Roland saying how satisfied she thought Rupert would have been at his Pris's happiness, and 'Yes, I did notice Elizabeth's poise.' The bride and groom spent the first night of their honeymoon with Aunt Violet at Nether Lypiatt, then sailed from England bound for Malta and Dar Ida, the house Richard had bought in Guardamangia. Her sisters quickly missed Priscilla's companionship and mothering and within weeks Diana was writing a distraught letter saying she was so lonely without her that life was unbearable.

Elizabeth spent Christmas with Violet at Nether Lypiatt and complained beforehand to Pris in Malta in the same letter intoning Violet's gothic travel arrangements. She knew she would have to go, because, if she did not, there would be a terrific family row and a reconciliation brought about by Roland. She was most dissatisfied with his Christmas gift to her, a pair of sham diamond and glass earrings; she said she disliked jewellery, never wore earrings and, even if she did, they wouldn't be of that kind. She thought it time Roland learnt not to buy expensive jewellery that looked cheap.

She went on to say that she should like to put Roland, Aunt Violet and Dorothy 'into a Siberian prison camp picking oakum 18 hours a day and have them shaken up in a sack together for the remaining six. Even then I doubt if any sense could be drummed into them.' She ends her tirade against the Gwynnes with enough self-knowledge to add that next time she writes it might be the Palmers or the Ridleys who are out of favour with her.

Although Elizabeth was apprehensive at the prospect, Christmas with Violet and her 'old men' at Nether Lypiatt was better than expected. Laurence Johnson was there and the Blows came over on Christmas Day. 'Green Line Bus' (the Gwynne girls' name for Detmar's wife, Winifred, Elizabeth's godmother) asked a great many questions about Stella and was altogether far too 'cock a hoop'. Violet gave her a 'perfectly heavenly' turquoise jumper, and Denis and Bill an attractive scarf. They doled out presents to each other from Fortnum's and Spink's, and from the moment she set foot in Nether Lypiatt to the moment she left Elizabeth suffered from indigestion.

Stanford had rung asking Elizabeth to do the publicity for the pantomime, so on Boxing Day she rushed back to Oxford and was left exhausted by spending what seemed a fruitless day's work with a demanding producer, Leonard Gibson Cowan. By evening he had relented and asked her out to dinner – it was her twenty-first birthday. She tells Felicité that 'Uncle Top has given me £20 for my 21st! Isn't that incredibly sweet of him? . . . And they're so hard up too.' She reminds her sister that at least they will spend part of the Christmas period together, with the Palmers at Blackmoor. She was dreadfully tired and in need of a rest – and also a proper job.

Elizabeth was, as always, worried about her finances but still protested to Pris that the five pounds she had sent her for her birthday was too much. The following year Elizabeth told Pris that she must stop giving her money, especially as Pris was without a job. It seemed pathetic to Elizabeth that she was the only member of the family with a job and yet she practically lived on charity. But the precedent was set, and although not particularly well off herself, Priscilla continued contributing to Elizabeth's and her other sisters' finances for many years to come.

More significantly, Elizabeth was suffering from the intense and insecure nature of her relationship with Stanford and confided to Pris: 'Things seem fairly alright with Stanford again. You know I can never stay away from him or from Oxford for very long. It'll always be the same – I can't exist without him for long – I feel so lonely and miserable and bored, and the other men I meet mean less than a spit in the eye to me. I wish I could have married him – or perhaps if I had or did I should have a row and kill him with the frying pan or something sordid.'

During the last days of winter relations between herself and Stanford became more strained, and letters flew back and forth as the sisters negotiated a few days' holidays together with Richard in Munich in early spring. (Felicité was already there.) Having survived an 'excruciating' train journey in third class, Elizabeth spent a frantically social but not entirely happy week in Munich. In her next letter to Pris in Malta she reflected on her anger at others' perceptions not always coinciding with her own and her regret that her comforting elder sister would no longer be so readily available to her. She stayed on in Munich until Saturday, going to several more hectic parties where she continued 'baby-snatching'; she soon grew very tired of it all and wished Pris had stayed longer in Munich. Apologizing for going off somewhere before Priscilla left she added that it all seemed so different now her sister was with Richard. She had previously refused to accept that Pris belonged to him, and not to her family – 'except that when there are two or three Gwynnes gathered together, nobody else has much of a look in, much as they may try'.

One remembers that for Elizabeth Munich was 'almost sacred'. She continues: 'And I was cross because neither Richard nor Bulgie would appreciate Munich . . . You were in Vienna and Munich has probably some of the same atmosphere for you. But Richard laughed at everything and Bulgie didn't know whether to copy him or agree with me.' And yet she sympathized with Richard managing three Gwynne sisters at a time and in spite of everything was terribly glad Pris came.

Munich was only a brief respite from the complications of Elizabeth's peripatetic and emotionally tangled life and she complained that it was perfectly frightful when she got back to Chester Gate. Diana's perpetual absentmindedness and scattiness were annoying Elizabeth, and relations with Aunt Grace and the Ridleys were at a low point, their concern about her present life-style fuelling her irritation with them. She told Pris that the next morning at breakfast Grace was savage with her for taking the butter with the same knife that she was using to spread the marmalade. 'When I explained that I was used to economizing on washing up and that compared to the magnificence of her household I lived in comparative squalor, she snorted "Yes, Bohemian squalor" and turned me out of the dining room in order to say prayers. After that crowning insult I packed my things . . . and betook myself to Oxford.'

But Stanford was not welcoming; his coldness threw Elizabeth into confusion and she decided the best thing was to leave. She would finish it all at once and go away. But after she had packed up and was on her way to the station, Stanford suddenly said: 'Don't go.'

And she couldn't.

'It's the same old story. We want to get away from each other and can't.'

For the moment they were reunited, and Elizabeth was, to Pris, unselfconsciously delighted. Stanford gave her a good part at once and said she was to have roles in the rest of the plays that term. With this encouragement she moved into new digs and said she was coping with everything. But these brave words were hollow. Elizabeth was miserably aware in a letter to Priscilla that things were hopeless between them. The sympathy they had felt for one another was gone, and yet they could not get away from each other. Elizabeth could not foresee what would happen, and her only remedy for the situation was to work desperately hard.

Blunting the edge of emotion by burying herself in hard work was to become a self-preserving mechanism for Elizabeth. She did an hour's work before breakfast every morning and stained and polished her three attic-room floors in spare moments during the day. To replace the green which she 'loathed' she had ordered some undyed linen curtains and sofa cover to complement the pale blue sitting-room walls. And in the letter about Stanford, she gives Pris instructions to have some napkins made up and embroidered: 'And tell the hag to send them immediately or I shall have left here before I get them.' Elizabeth's imperious tone was already well established; if they felt any resentment, her sisters nevertheless always acquiesced.

Looking down from her attic rooms: 'A lot of drunken undergraduates have just gone by singing "Night and Day". Sometimes I do wish life was more peaceful.' But it was not to be. Work once again became intermittent and Elizabeth's pretty rooms brought only a temporary consolation. Her cousin Anne Palmer was up at Somerville (she was one of the first college students to read zoology): the college was exactly opposite the Playhouse and she saw Elizabeth on stage a number of times: 'No, she was not a good actress,' she told the author in a recent interview. Elizabeth never learned the actor's knack of flinging off self-consciousness at the stage door, of giving herself up to instinct and intuition, of temporarily suspending the rational self.

CHAPTER FIVE

London

(1934–1938)

ON HER TWENTY-FIRST birthday Roland had wished Elizabeth a very happy future, as she deserved it and he believed she would get it. Her acid comment to Pris reflected her low expectations: 'I cannot think how or why he should have been led to believe anything so improbable.' By late 1934 she was driven, through hopelessness, finally to extract herself from Stanford Holme, and left Oxford for London and a brief period with Aunt Grace and Uncle Top. She quickly found a flat not far away in Primrose Hill at 112 Regent's Park Road, and moved in with her old schoolfriend Marian Butterworth.

Their rooms were in one of the large houses in Primrose Hill, no longer as grand as they had been and now divided up for a more reduced life-style. In this area, however, reduced did not mean small and Elizabeth had an enormous, high-ceilinged living room with huge windows overlooking the garden, a bedroom and a bathroom, albeit with a kitchen space carved out of a landing. Here she 'installed a gas cooker, one of those old food safes with perforated metal sides which nowadays you see only in junk shops and eventually a biggish refrigerator'.

Although the great chef Alexis Soyer had installed gas cookers in the Reform Club as early as 1841, it was not really until after the First World War that most new London homes had one. There were, though, many more who hung on to their coal-fired ranges, and the gas industry worried away at this reticence by exploiting the desire to be up to date. With servants more difficult to come by and many more women working outside the home, tools for labour-saving were quickly taken up and contemporary cookery books sing the praises of recipes which are 'efficient and labour-saving'. If Elizabeth's gas cooker shows her desire for 'modern convenience' in the kitchen, her purchase of a refrigerator in place of the ubiquitous old wire-meshed meat safe was almost avant-garde in its forwardness; in the 1930s fridges were still the exception.

She may have told Aunt Grace she lived in 'comparative squalor', but Elizabeth's expectations were still such that even if there was no cook, there was a maid to come in from time to time to clean and keep order in her rooms, and a wardrobe chosen with a sharp and discerning eye to the higher reaches of fashion. (Letters between the four Gwynne sisters from various parts of the world, for many years to come, were filled with ideas, advice, requests and orders for 'stuffs' to be made up.) In a permanent state of 'just managing' at the upper limits of her allowance, Elizabeth was bolstered by regular handouts from Pris and the occasional one from older and richer relations.

In a small social gathering Elizabeth could shine, but on the larger scale of theatre life, where many ambitious, talented and pretty girls battled for position, she did not always make that instant impact necessary to catch the eye of a director. Still determined to act, she did what she could to get work, but continued to spend more time 'resting' than acting. If her particular allure was too subtle for the relatively exhibitionist methods of the theatre, pulling a few social strings was not something Elizabeth would balk at in order to get what she wanted.

In 1932 an impresario businessman, Sidney Carroll, had put up the money for an Open Air Theatre at the Inner Circle Gardens, Regent's Park. Initially the company simply acted on a slightly raised stage, with the audience perched on green deck-chairs on the grass. The plays were a success and stage managing grew more ambitious. With lighting by the young Carol Reed, the stage made grander, and actors dressed in costumes of striking brilliance, the Open Air Theatre drew some of the sought-after performers of the time.

A beautiful and promising young actress, Margaretta Scott, had recently played Ophelia to the legendary Henry Ainslie's Hamlet and was taken on straight from a season at Stratford. In interview with the author she remembered that the Open Air 'had a sylvan quality to it, a fresh spontaneity which was enthusiastically picked up on by the audience'. Miss Scott recalled how every performance was introduced by an elderly actor: 'And a little eight piece orchestra down right accompanied the performances. The situation demanded movement so, as well as other playwrights, much of Shakespeare was perfectly suited. *As You Like It, Twelfth Night, Midsummer Night's Dream* – many others. We changed costumes in a large tent, and if it rained we moved inside to a marquee, which the audience liked because they were closer to us.'

Each play ran for two or three weeks, with Robert Atkins the company's first producer. 'Matinées were always popular with school-children, and nannies and their charges. In the evenings there was a normal theatre-going audience. Quite large, several hundred people to a performance. As we got bigger we used microphones, but it lost some of its simple quality then.' The company was a large one. Sidney Carroll was noted for his ability to spot talented unknowns and to persuade established actors to play for him: John Laurie, Jack Hawkins, Leslie French, Agnes Lockwood, Greer Garson, Joan Hickson, Jack Carlton and many more.

Elizabeth asked her Uncle Jasper if he would say a word on her behalf to Sydney Carroll; she wanted an audition. Carroll said she could have a walk-on part. A girl called Doreen Brownlow was there at Elizabeth's first rehearsal: 'Sydney Carroll was mad keen on titles and knew her family were rather smart, so he let her in. I shall never in my life forget it. The rehearsal was taking place underneath somebody's vegetarian restaurant just off the Strand. We were all sitting there in jeans and sloppy clothes when in walked Elizabeth. She was wearing a *huge* black hat, and a black summer suit with white organdy cuffs and white here, and white there, and all of us just – *looked* at this apparition ... Anyway, she learnt how to dress, or how not to, after that.'

In spite of her connections Elizabeth never landed more than those walk-on parts and money remained continually short. Initially this did not stop her using her Selfridges account with abandon. The refrigerator she installed at No. 112 was bought with her twenty-first birthday money from Uncle Top and, as she still knew little about cooking, it was regularly filled with pre-cooked food ordered from

Selfridges Food Hall. In her article for Smallbone Kitchen Designs Elizabeth later wrote: 'I had only to pick up the telephone for roast chickens, smoked salmon, butter, fruit, cheese, cream, eggs, coffee to be delivered next day. It wasn't till the monthly accounts seemed to be adding up to much more than I could afford that it dawned on me that having a roast always handy in the fridge was rather an extravagant way to entertain friends.'

Since the bills from Selfridges were too much for her allowance and meagre earnings, she was obliged to take greater care. The two girls had to eat, and Elizabeth began to teach herself to cook. In about 1934 Stella had given her daughter a cookery book, one of her first, and instead of simply reading it she now began using it. In spite of her own complete lack of interest in cooking, Stella, with her sure artistic touch, had found a little book which could not have been better calculated to inspire a girl of Elizabeth's temperament and inclinations. *The Gentle Art of Cookery* (Chatto and Windus, 1925), by Mrs Hilda Leyel and Miss Olga Hartley, was a book to which Elizabeth, much later, devoted almost the entire introduction of her own *Spices, Salt and Aromatics in the English Kitchen* (Penguin, 1970), musing:

> Come to that, I wonder if I would ever have learned to cook at all had I been given a routine Mrs Beeton to learn from instead of the romantic Mrs Leyel, with her rather wild and imagination-catching recipes ... I am recalling ... the reactions ... of a young woman quite ignorant of cooking techniques but easily ... beguiled by the idea of food as unlike as could be to any produced by the conventional English cook of the time.

Elizabeth continues with the observation that she was uncritical of Mrs Leyel's vague attitude to quantities and paucity of technical instruction, because in her ignorance she didn't even notice the lack of them and would probably 'not have believed anybody had they tried to tell me'. She came to the conclusion that Mrs Leyel's 'greatest asset was her ability to appeal to the imagination of the young'. And that the young and the 'totally inexperienced will usually prefer a book which provides stimulus to one which goes into technical

details, makes strenuous efforts to keep the reader on the straight and
. . . the main roads of established cookery.'

Hilda Leyel was that extraordinarily dynamic woman who had
founded the Society of Herbalists and the Culpepper herb shops as
well as writing over half a dozen books and editing the encyclopaedic
A Modern Herbal (Jonathan Cape, 1932). Unlike most English cookery
books of the 1930s, which give instructions for economical, labour-
saving food – cookery as domestic science – *The Gentle Art of Cookery*
is indeed an alluring little book, which evokes with a quirky charm
the strange and the mysterious.

In her own introduction Mrs Leyel makes a bold claim: 'There
are seven different ways in which this cookery book differs from all
others.' Amongst these differences is a chapter containing 'a unique
collection of flower recipes' and another with recipes for the dishes
conjured up in the *One Thousand and One Nights*, and about which
Elizabeth writes, 'No doubt because of its vagueness and brevity [it]
contained the true essence of magic and mystery.' She recalled that:
'When I first had Mrs Leyel's book nothing and nobody on earth
could have sold me an English rice pudding, but a rice cream made
with lemon and almonds and served in a silver dish, well, that gave
one something to think about . . .'

In this same vein of rebellion against the prosaic, Elizabeth
lauded Mrs Leyel's separation of mushrooms and chestnuts from the
more ordinary potatoes, beans and sprouts, and approvingly recorded
her love of fruit, vegetables and salads. She described 'her treatment
of them almost as dishes to which meat and fish and poultry were
little more than incidental accompaniments, or scarcely necessary
adjuncts to a meal'.

The Gentle Art abides by traditional (French) culinary principles,
exactly those which Elizabeth had witnessed Madame Robertot practising daily when she returned from the Parisian markets, laden with
the produce of the day for her greedy family and those reluctant
young English lodgers. Thus another of Mrs Leyel's 'seven ways in
which this cookery book differs' is that the recipes 'are arranged under
their principal ingredients, because it is more economical to do as the
French do, shop first, then arrange the dinner according to what is
most plentiful in the market, than to go out and buy for a pre-

arranged menu'. In using this book Elizabeth, however unconsciously at first, began slowly to imbibe these same principles, and also Mrs Leyel's advice that *The Gentle Art* was 'not intended to be an elementary handbook on cookery, but has been written for those who appreciate the fact that good cooking is one of the obtainable amenities of life if extravagance is eliminated'.

Stimulus, the quality Elizabeth claimed so abundantly for Mrs Leyel, was also provided for her by another book published at about this time. In her Smallbone article she described seeing piled high in Selfridges' window copies of a Countess Morphy's *Recipes of All Nations*: 'At 2s 6d or 3s 6d. for a version with a thumb index. . . . The book seemed amazing value for money. One day I carried home a copy with me on the bus and began reading it. It was fascinating – it still is – but Countess Morphy . . . threw little light on such matters as quantities, timing, temperatures and other technical details.'

Unusually for the period, and in spite of her shortage on detail, Marcelle Morphy had a keen eye for good food. In the Thirties and Forties she put out a stream of cookery books for 'bright young things'. With books like *Lightning Cookery* and *Picnic Snacks*, she epitomized that conflict between the time-conscious kitchen sensibilities of the age and the (unresolved) problem of making what were often essentially grand dishes without the grand back-up to go with them. 'Still,' continued Elizabeth, 'with the help of Mrs Leyel . . . I began to teach myself to cook nice food.' And in *Spices, Salt and Aromatics in the English Kitchen* she says that *The Gentle Art* 'turned out to be almost the equivalent in cookery of [that old family friend] Walter de la Mare's unsurpassed poetry anthology *Come Hither* which had enlightened my childhood.'

This was all very much a beginning for Elizabeth, who simultaneously continued a liberal use of the plethora of tinned goods by then available. With methods improving during the nineteenth century, at its conclusion canning had been used mainly for luxury goods. Although more basic foods were flooding the market, inexperienced upper-class housewives and girls like Elizabeth – with a shortage of servants – were still turning to tins for much labour-saving and problem-free food. Fortnum and Mason, for instance, sold tinned Scotch salmon, mulligatawny soup and chicken gumbo, and it was to be some time before Elizabeth applied herself to anything more than uncoordinated and erratic essays in the kitchen.

Looking back in *Spices, Salt and Aromatics*, to her mind, however, Mrs Leyel's 'Arabian way of cooking red mullet . . . sounded irresistible, so much so that even if you barely knew whether a red mullet was a bird, a flower or a fish, you quickly set about finding out'. *The Gentle Art* 'certainly took one very far away indeed from the world of grapefruit and Scotch eggs to which a bed-sitter cook so easily succumbs.' And so far this had been Elizabeth's style. She was writing about Scotch eggs from experience, for they were one of her first [and abortive] attempts at cooking anything much more than 'fry-ups' and things on toast since moving into No. 112 Regent's Park Road.

Among the actors playing at the Open Air Theatre were several Elizabeth already knew from the Oxford Rep, including Joan Hickson. The Open Air players were a relatively amicable group and Elizabeth made friends with several of the other performers. One of those was the young Leslie French whose rendering of the part made him for many the quintessential Puck. Another new friend was a striking redhead, Doreen Brownhill, the girl who recalled with such vigour Elizabeth's melodramatic entrance to the 'vegetarian' rehearsal. A young woman of spirit and cheerfulness, Doreen was determined to have a good time. She put on no airs, knew her own mind, and was a match for Elizabeth. Although fascinated by her, Doreen was not going to be dominated. In conversation with the author she described Elizabeth: 'Oh, she was desperately intolerant. Always. Even from our youth. If people disagreed with her they were out. Yes, Liz and I fought.'

Disagreements failed to diminish the girls' youthful energy and they were imbued with a sense of *joie de vivre* which propelled them along. The intimate friendship which they quickly formed was to remain intact for the rest of their lives. Doreen recalled the dish to which, Elizabeth later wrote, 'a bedsitter cook so easily succumbs': 'One crazy day Liz decided we would make Scotch eggs. Don't imagine she was doing any *real* cooking then. We'd got this recipe and went to the butcher's and asked for a huge quantity of sausage-meat; we hadn't really an idea how much to get, or really what to do with it. I do remember her making broad beans in pasta sauce – that was lovely. And then there were those delicious things from the Selfridges account. She was hopeless about money, she'd be forever saying, "Oh, put that on my account."'

When they had a part, however small, work at the Open Air was hard work for the two girls: 'After a wretched day rehearsing at the theatre – from ten in the morning till eleven at night – or on other days when we weren't working, we'd go to the Lyons Corner House in the Strand, often with Dickie Kerr [Richard Kerr Carey] and Gar Greerson [the future star, Greer Garson].

'We'd sit around drinking coffee for hours and hours, because it was only 4d a cup. And *then*, when it was late, I'd say to Liz, "Oh, you come back" . . . and we'd listen to records and look at magazines and read the agony columns together in my flat [in Chelsea]. And by now, in the middle of the night she'd say, "Let's go back to *my* flat," and we'd walk through the night right across London from Chelsea to Camden Town. Can you *imagine* it, Liz walking those distances?'

The Open Air Theatre's Shakespeare seasons were popular, and one performance which unfailingly held the audience, until the last words had died away on the balmy evening air, was the romping pastoral comedy, *As You Like It*. In the play's outdoor setting the famous wrestling match was 'staged to such advantage that the audience were on the edge of their chairs until the very concluding moment', recalled Margaretta Scott. In the summer of 1935 the scene was fought with great panache between a young, and as yet unknown, Jack Hawkins and the fight's choreographer, Leonard Gibson Cowan . . . actor, producer, journalist, tramp, con-man, beggar, reprobate – a man who was to play a crucial part in Elizabeth's life.

Leonard preferred to be known as Charles Gibson Cowan, and under this name he was soon to write a book called *Loud Report* (Michael Joseph, 1938), in the idiom of W. H. Davies' *Autobiography of a Super-Tramp* (Jonathan Cape, 1921) and Orwell's *Down and Out in Paris and London* (Gollancz, 1933). In a disingenuously simple style, and under the Orwellian guise of candid observation, Charles also writes purposively, one aim being a demonstration of the appalling social conditions still experienced by those at the bottom. Like Orwell he is selective when something does not fulfil his purpose, and like many travellers before him his apparently documentary method allows for embroidery. 'Why not add a little later?' as a fellow travel writer, Norman Douglas, once said.

To the generation of the Twenties and Thirties travel (and its literature) had an aura of the sacred about it and some travelled unrelentingly, to the point of neurosis. Within this milieu the romantic figure of the wanderer, the vagabond, the gypsy was not a new one; George Borrow's *Lavengro* (John Murray, 1881) was popular, so too was W. H. Davies' book, never out of print since publication in 1908. (Lionized by literary salons, both sociable and retiring, W. H. Davies, whose poetry is now almost forgotten, was befriended by the Sitwells and Elizabeth's Aunt Violet – he lived near her in Gloucestershire until his death in 1940.) Between the wars the vagabond theme was given new life with books like Helen Waddell's *The Wandering Scholars* (Constable, 1927), about medieval itinerant clerks, Orwell's *The Road to Wigan Pier* (Gollancz, 1937) and, in the same year, Robert Byron's *The Road to Oxiana* (Macmillan). And in the same way, Charles Gibson Cowan's memoir reflects the roving, questing mentality of the inter-war generation. Charlie Chaplin's cinema tramp epitomized on screen the man Cowan sometimes depicts himself as having become: a past master of the shrewdness, cynical evasiveness, self-reliance and initiative necessary for the open road and, by implication, for life itself. However, it is clear from the book (and also from later events) that Charles is a far more complex character than this would suggest; there is a naïveté in him too. Often he is emotionally honest to his own detriment, trying to reconcile conflicting drives at just those times which most demanded the persona of a con-man.

A world of difference existed between Charles Gibson Cowan and George Orwell. Orwell's Eton education made him part of that class for whom the worker was still 'quite foreign'. He was seen as a specimen for anthropological study, as the subject of missionary zeal, or as one whose sufferings should be shared . . . sometimes all three perspectives together. (It was in the air. Across the Channel another gifted middle-class intellectual, Simone Weil, driven by similar forces, had gone to work for a while in the Renault car factory.) By contrast Cowan is at one with Davies in coming himself from that foreign land; he writes about territory with which he is totally familiar. However harrowing the 'down-and-out' life Orwell encountered, he had chosen it himself, just as Simone Weil had opted to endure what was for her the nightmare of a giant mass-production factory. However grim, it was still a kind of game, an experiment from which they could extract themselves at any time. For Charles it was not a game, it was a central reality. He *was* an Outsider, whereas George Orwell was playing at being one.

In his autobiography, *Loud Report*, Gibson Cowan wrote: 'My father was a Jew, my mother the daughter of an English mother and a Dutch father. We were lower-class. My father was the only man I have ever heard admit he was lower-class.' Charles's family were a ramshackle, feuding, cheerful and intense lot of Portuguese Jews. His great-grandfather was a rabbi, and of this detail the family were inordinately proud. Work, as coalmen, costermongers, booksellers' assistants, boot-clickers, tappers, fortune-tellers or itinerant musicians, was precarious and their lives were often lived close to the edge of wretchedness. Some Jews, like Charles's father, had married out of the faith, but more retained their Orthodox religion and sociable European ways in the midst of London's teeming, impoverished, raucous East End. Charles remembered his very Jewish grandmother who 'lived in Merchant Street and was a wizened little woman ... with a foreign lilt of phrase. When she was eighty she still went to the theatre, alone.

'She remembered all the great actors and actresses. Marie Lloyd, Vesta Tilley, Lottie Collins, Bernhardt, Duse, Irving, Tree, were all names to me; they meant nothing, but stuck in my memory. She went to the films once or twice before she died. She could not bear Chaplin. "Chaplin! Tch! He makes himself silly." '

Summoned to her bedside the doctor said she would probably die. She wanted to see *Ruddigore* at the theatre, but Charles's father would not let her get up. She nevertheless evaded their surveillance and was later found in the front row of the auditorium, where Charles's father and his brother watched her from the back of the gallery. They 'followed her home travelling on top of the same bus. That night she fell asleep quite normally. In the morning she was dead.'

Charles Gibson Cowan was born in a village outside Guildford.

His father had left London, and the trade of cobbler, in 1903 because his wife had seen a position advertised for a chauffeur. 'Very few owners could drive themselves ... and a gentleman had just bought a three and a half Benz ... My father said he knew nothing about cars.' But with her usual pluck his wife was not going to let such a small obstacle keep him from a good job. With the help of an uncle who had a cycle shop in Southend, they mugged up as much as they could and Charles's father managed to bluff his way into the job and the lodge house above the stables, and greater security than he or his wife had ever yet known.

When he was old enough Charles went to the local school where 'The boys were all snobs, the masters, if anything, worse than the boys. Anti-Semitic feeling was openly upheld and I had no means of redress. I was called Jew and Sheeny even by the masters, but I did not complain to my parents.'

After the outbreak of the First World War his father was asked by his employer to enlist, he refused and was dismissed, taking his wife and son back to live near Mile End in London to sit out the remainder of the war. At sixteen Charles left school. In spite of regular cribbing his examination results were poor in every subject except chemistry. He began as an underpaid junior with a Rachman-like estate agent who 'managed a great deal of slum property, and the job of rent-collecting was cordially disliked and fell to me'. In this invidious position he spent nine months familarizing himself with the extreme deprivations of London's low life. He got along, however, the tenants and himself having a common enemy in his employer.

Lying his way into his next job as interpreter for an import company, Charles was gaining experience with drink and girls. After the death of his first (French) love in a car accident, followed by a recuperation period spent working on fishing boats, he found solace with a girl on the stage, playing the amateur lead in Shaw's *Pygmalion*. The Rotherhithe Peace Players were ardent Shavian Socialists, torn between putting on the plays as 'propaganda or art'.

'At the end of the War and in the years following, the film was one of the chief influences in our lives.' But Charles's new love now gave him a contact 'which eclipsed even the close-ups of the screen'. He had read little, hardly ever been to the theatre. But the day after his first taste of amateur theatre he announced to his family that 'I did not intend finding another job but . . . proposed to spend the next twelve months writing a play.'

After a quarrel which lasted several weeks he found himself a room and a clerical job in a chemical works, at 2s 9d a week. For developing a method of calculation more efficient than the one already used by the company he was reprimanded for 'getting above himself' and was soon given the sack. Determined not to return home, he set off out of London along the Great North Road and began to live as a tramp, a down-and-out. He tells us: 'On the road consists of incidents, connected only by dreary walks through the rain, or sleeps under haystacks when the weather is warm enough to stop moving. It is difficult to estimate time . . . Once a goal, however futile, was in sight, each day gave the illusion of progress.'

Months later Charles settled down and spent part of the winter living off fish and the proceeds of begging in his dugout shelter of driftwood and sacks on the cliffs beyond Hastings, entertaining himself with a local servant girl. Months later still he had walked the 200 miles to Wales, his clothes falling apart, his shoes full of holes. With an orphan Chinese teenager encountered along the road he returned to London where he inhabited a series of insanitary, unsavoury lodging rooms, with actresses, prostitutes, pushers and hustlers for friends.

By now a consummate beggar, Charles also learned to pick pockets to supplement his earnings. He next found work as a confidence trickster's assistant, then took a job with a sideshow at a travelling fair, and eventually, a past master at brazen ruses, was asked to complete the play he had years ago left home for. It was called *Eastside Westside* and had a successful run in one of the smaller London theatres, with his current girlfriend as leading lady.

His grandmother's love of the theatre had eventually surfaced in Charles; he had found his *métier* and was soon producing avant-garde plays for the actor-playwright Miles Malleson at the Arts Theatre. His experiences over the last few years at the seamy edge of existence had fitted him well for the transient world of the theatre, where security is non-existent – you take what you can while you may – and where reality and illusion are only loosely distinguished. However much the tales of his exploits may have followed Norman Douglas's prescription for travel writing – 'one suppresses much' (what is boring or unprintable) – Charles's autobiography nevertheless gives us a definite flavour of the man and his times. Over the next few years he read, wrote and worked hard at establishing himself as playwright and producer, working in rep and for the Oxford and Cambridge Dramatic festivals and the prestigious Oxford University Dramatic Society, OUDS. Then, in 1933, he landed his first part, in *As You Like It* at the West End's Phoenix Theatre. He played Charles the Wrestler and made the part his own.

Elizabeth had met Charles on the occasion when he annoyed her so much producing for the Rep at Oxford in 1934, and after her move to London they met again. Here he had worked on his part in *As You Like It* for Sydney Carroll at the Open Air Theatre in the summer of '34. In the following year his and Elizabeth's paths once more coincided.

Years of living rough had toughened Charles mentally and physically, sharpening his resolve and teaching him the usefulness of a dark and (to some) alluring gypsy appearance. At thirty-two he was now a rakish and enigmatic figure whose slight aura of danger added, for Elizabeth, to the attraction – he was a type for whom she would retain a weakness. Charles's magnetism notwithstanding, Elizabeth's friend Doreen was not smitten and always kept him at a distance. Elizabeth, though, was intrigued. Exhilarated by his company, within a short time she was intimately involved with this man about whom not only her family but also her friends were alarmed. Whatever her own doubts may have been, Elizabeth acquiesced in Charles's 'open' life-style, which now included an actress wife and a baby. She ignored warnings and appeals and, faced with her usual self-willed determination, there was little anyone could do.

It is worth remarking here that the family did not object to Elizabeth's associating with Aunt Violet and her four men, did not fear contamination from her aunt's life-style, which was in effect more deviant than that of Charles. It was a matter of social class, race and money, rather than one of sexual morality.

Even when she was ostensibly setting out to help others Elizabeth's determination was not always appreciated. A case in point was her involvement with the proceedings for Diana's apprehensive visit to Stella in Jamaica. Felicité, in Durham with Mrs Headlam for six months, told Pris in Malta that she was appalled by Elizabeth's current behaviour, which had left herself and Diana wounded and exhausted. Elizabeth had attempted to organize Felicité seeing Diana off from Bristol, and a series of phone calls followed. Elizabeth found all concerned intolerable and Felicité wrote to Pris that she ended by 'ringing Diana up in one of her ghastly storms of rage ... and a fearful scene ensued' during which she abused Diana, and later Mrs Headlam, 'violently'. Eventually Aunt Grace felt obliged to intervene and rang Mrs Headlam to apologize for the 'ill-mannered' behaviour of her niece, while Felicité was left in Durham to live with the consequences: a very disgruntled landlady who had 'made everything so marvellous for me and now L has wrecked it for the time being'. She continued bitterly: 'Liza is making everything go wrong ... You know, Pris, much as I like Liza, I think she can make herself more unpleasant than anyone I know. It's desperately despairing.' Felicité noticed too that 'really she's quite changed. She looks such a sight, goes about with a face like a shiny ball of light, never particularly clean ... hair ... with no vestige of ever being combed ... And ... takes no notice of anyone. Besides she gives such a very slovenly impression, clothes creased, dirty shoes.'

Writing to Pris in Malta the following spring, 1935, Felicité felt more positive about her sister when describing the terrors she had recently encountered in her presentation at Court. 'The strain was altogether too much for me – and I'm relieved that the fans and feathers and trains are carefully laid away in their boxes again.' With a distinctive Gwynne gift for acerbity, Felicité nevertheless does not practise the same level of forthrightness or defiance as Elizabeth, revealing herself in her letters as more retiring and modest. She was 'highly surprised' when Viscount Hailsham – Quintin Hogg's father and at that time Lord High Chancellor – recognized her in the crowded and tense spectacular of a Court presentation and noted that he 'was very affable to me'. Overcome by the splendour of all the uniforms and the great numbers of people; 'when it came to my turn to curtsey I was rooted to the ground with terror and could hardly see the Royalties without my glasses.' Then afterwards she 'forgot to curtsey to the Duchess of York – I don't ever recognize her'.

Elizabeth was at the celebration dinner at the Savoy afterwards and Felicité was now pleased to tell Pris that 'Liza seems quite flourishing,' but added, 'though as far as I gathered with no prospects of a job at all – and she doesn't even seem to be looking for one.'

In fact Elizabeth was making more concerted efforts in other directions and thus by the end of the year she could tell Pris, after thanking her for a typically generous birthday cheque, that she hadn't bought a single item of clothing since her sister had left England. With her inexhaustible delight in clothes (in spite of her more artistic and 'slovenly appearance') this predicament was probably an exaggeration, especially when she later added that some blouses had been the exception, made up from 'bits of stuff' that she'd had for years. But the point underlying the sartorial comments was that for now she wanted to use Pris's cheque to finish doing up and making habitable the spare room and other things about the house. She says that any such house beautifying has been at a standstill for months, lack of money making basic necessities more pressing. She had been concentrating on how 'to obtain three meals a day for about four people for thirty bob a week'.

In the absence of Marian who was with her parents and of Diana and Felicité who were abroad, Elizabeth was again at Blackmoor for a 'pleasant Christmas', although bursting with indignation at both Stella and Uncle Top who seemed 'to absolutely loathe me these days. Either it's that people have been doing too much talking about me or else its that infernal H. L. [Stella] telling him I'd frittered away his £20 which was an absolutely malicious lie seeing that I spent it on the flat, and as that's the thing that it gives me most pleasure to spend it on I can't see that anyone should complain. Pesk them all!' The money [for her twenty-first] was that which had recently gone towards the purchase of the fridge.

She gave Aunt Violet a beautiful set of enamel buttons which she found in an antique shop. It broke Elizabeth's heart to have to give them to her, knowing well that they would only go into the bottomless pit of Violet's knick-knack box, but Lily [the maid] had instructions to retrieve them after a decent interval had elapsed. Elizabeth cooed with pleasure over a pair of long suede gloves from Fortnum's given her before Christmas by Violet, and then lambasted Uncle Roland for sending her yet another present quite different from the one she had hinted at. Instead she was given a tiny mirror on a stand with very dirty drawers and the mirror as black as her 'best hat, most probably turned out of her room by the under-housemaid at Folkington'. Diana and Felicité received the usual pink and green beads, which they immediately gave to the servants. None of the girls gave Roland anything. Elizabeth had sent a Christmas card, thinking even that too good for him. 'Dirty old bastard . . .'

'We had the usual Christmas Tree orgy, the stairs are as slippery as ever and the cover of the silver breakfast dish still comes to pieces in your hand, and there is as usual a spider in one's bath in the morning.' This was so unfailingly the case that the family called it 'the spider bathroom'.

Oblivious to the possibility of her sisters' disapproval, Elizabeth was excited by life in the shadow of such a colourful lover as Charles Gibson Cowan, whose friends included a mixture of figures from London's underworld and members of the left-wing avant-garde. He had engineered a contract to translate some Russian plays and was paid fifty pounds in advance, much to everyone's astonishment. Elizabeth and Marian earned 'a nice little windfall' by doing some 'shady business' with cut-price cigarettes for a friend of his just before Christmas. Elizabeth told Felicité that she'd be going to a party with him on New Year's Eve – 'what the H. L. would call a Bohemian Party' – where there wouldn't be many men with flowers in their hair, but quite a few with beads. As she hadn't been to a party for six months, she hoped it would be worthy of her. The party undoubtedly was.

Despite these defiant immersions in London's experimental avant-garde, symptoms of Elizabeth's reaction against her family and background, she was sufficiently bound by an ingrained sense of etiquette to be appalled at Aunt Violet's phone call on New Year's Day morning at dawn, when Elizabeth was completely 'blotto', asking her to lunch. She felt she 'had to go'. Having been entertained by Aunt Violet to that lady's satisfaction, Elizabeth was sent home in a

taxi when she proved too ill to remain any longer. She rang Violet
the next morning to thank her, when her aunt, much to her surprise,
proceeded to ask her to lunch *again*. So she again 'had to go'. The
following day she was lunching with Tony Hogg.

To Charles, Elizabeth's family and friends were, in theory,
anathema, but his liking for her money and fascination with her
exalted milieu prevailed over the promptings of his political convic-
tions. For Elizabeth, Charles was a vital and stimulating companion
and like him, she was happy for the moment to lead a double life.
Unwilling to relinquish the benefits her privileged background had
conferred upon her, her social values remained ultimately intact. She
was questioning art rather than politics, and in the process took on
certain mannerisms which her sisters found distasteful. Felicité,
writing to Pris of her distress about Elizabeth's 'fits of passion',
described how she now 'throws her hands about all over the place and
casts her eyes to heaven and ruffles her hair'. Felicité thought it
'altogether very stagey . . . it's silly and affected'.

Charles scraped a living together through a variety of sources.
He was producing and acting fairly regularly, had written a couple of
plays and found the odd commission for pieces of journalism.
Although hampered by a certain lack of application, he was increasingly determined to make his living as a writer. Elizabeth had made
no such serious decision, but her appetite for books was no less
voracious. Books, both classic and contemporary, are constantly
referred to in letters.

An important part of the attraction Charles held for Elizabeth
was that their talk ranged at length over literary ideas, and before the
year was out they were writing a book together. After a few months
Elizabeth told Pris that nothing had yet happened about it, and Charles
later wrote: 'The idea was a good one, but it was not a success.'

Elizabeth and Charles's lives gradually became firmly interwoven. Initially Charles's wife and the baby were in evidence. They
lived in a beautiful down-at-heel Georgian house Charles had discovered near the pierhead at Wapping. In the heart of the East End,
it had a view of Tower Bridge from the window, with the sirens of
steamers and the whistle of tugs in the air.

Unmoved by children, Elizabeth was certainly not interested in babies, and Doreen Brownhill remembers an isolated journey across London on the tube one day, with the baby unwell and in their care. 'I wasn't going to have anything to do with it, so Elizabeth had to carry it. She didn't want to.' At about this time Elizabeth writes to Pris that it is a good thing their cousin Anne is not yet having a baby because 'she and John seem extremely happy'. By implication, a baby would diminish rather than enhance their happiness.

Charles' ménage eventually disbanded, wife and baby drifted off the scene and he and Elizabeth spent the following three years, on and off, sharing a succession of London flats. Elizabeth made several trips abroad, including a final visit to Germany, but it was the journeys to warmer southern Europe which were now to affect her more and alter her perceptions of England.

Just before Christmas 1935 she excitedly told Felicité that Dorothy Goodwin had invited her to stay in Cairo, as soon as she liked for as long as she liked, with her cousin Kit, Neville Gwynne's daughter. They were to go on to Malta afterwards, and Elizabeth was thrilled. She intended to go at the beginning of March and to stay for about three months altogether. Dorothy and Teddy Goodwin were old friends of Stella's. He worked for a firm which had a post in Cairo.

Elizabeth soon informed Pris about her ideas for the trip and indicated her impatience with any form of restriction of plans. She thought that she would wander over to Malta 'on some old tub or other', remain a fortnight, and then take the first cargo boat that presented itself to Cairo or Port Said. She couldn't bear the idea of having her trip planned out weeks ahead – she wanted to go and come back when she chose, and avoid at all costs 'such abominations as P&O boats and changing for dinner on board'. Elizabeth's comments establish early her attitude to travelling. Though some were willing to do so, many women still felt uncomfortable travelling alone, but Elizabeth was well endowed with the independence required, unafraid of the solitude it might bring and relishing the prospect of encounters along the way. From youth onwards she demonstrated a consistent impatience with obstruction of any kind and, for many years, a tendency to be easily bored if situations and people did not adapt quickly enough for her.

Elizabeth did make the journey to Egypt with Kit, probably in 1936, and seems to have spent an energetically social time there with the hospitable Goodwins, who appear to have been in the thick of Cairo expatriate life. The trip did not, however, coincide with the prospective one to Malta.

Any restraint was irksome to Elizabeth at this time and, despite tacit agreement of 'freedom and openness' in the relationship between herself and Charles, there were often difficulties. She remained intrigued by him yet, always wary of being wounded, was reluctant to commit herself and at the same time was impatient if her demands were not quickly met. Meanwhile, Charles's regular infidelities neither deterred Elizabeth nor meant Charles had lost interest in her. Knowing that something was lacking, and propelled by her need to be in a state of either stasis or incessant movement, Elizabeth set off for Malta during the spring of 1936.

Felicité saw her off and Elizabeth's subsequent letter – 'still on this rotten old tub plodding through the Mediterranean' – barely contains her frustration. Her capacity for independence as a traveller never stretched to enjoyment of uncomfortable surroundings unless these were counterbalanced by a high degree of visual satisfaction. She complained that the boat was dirty and her cabin right over the engine room – for the first few days the noise almost drove her mad. She tells how she was sick, couldn't eat so much as a dry biscuit for days, the food was more or less uneatable when she could, and her cabin so uncomfortable that she managed almost no sleep. The weather through the Bay of Biscay was passable, but as soon as they got down the coast of Portugal there were gales with winds of over a hundred miles per hour, and seas so violent they washed right over the ship and smashed one of the life boats. Things improved, though, and as they moved south she began sunbathing on deck and ate with the officers who, although from Yorkshire and with 'terrific accents', were all 'charming'.

Wireless contact was lost for a time, and the ship eventually arrived two days late. Elizabeth was greeted by Priscilla and Richard and taken to their beautiful house, Dar Ida, overlooking the limpid, sparkling blue of the lapping Mediterranean Sea.

Pris and Richard spoiled and cosseted Elizabeth and she luxuriated in the straightforwardness of their cheerful and busy social round on this small but cosmopolitan island. Malta was a refreshing and stimulating retreat for her and she stayed for the full three months, leaving only reluctantly, in a flurry of flowers and telegrams from new friends and admirers. Pris as usual helped Elizabeth by organizing and paying for her berth on the ship back to England. The three months had done her an enormous amount of good, and she felt absolutely different from when she went out.

Unlike the backgrounds of Charles and his friends, those of her recent associates in Malta were on a par with her own. Malta being a major British naval base, with several regiments, such as the Rifle Brigade, stationed there, most of Pris and Richard's friends were in either the military or the navy. Pris herself had gone out because Richard was there with the Royal Engineers Corps, so some of her and Elizabeth's friends who had enlisted were also now stationed on the island. In contrast to Charles's political ambience, politics amongst these Malta friends did not lean to the left.

In the manner of expatriate communities, social life was hectic and sometimes intense. Far from home, with its perfect Mediterranean climate and sometimes spectacularly beautiful scenery, Malta made an idyllic backdrop for liaisons of all kinds, which developed quickly. However illicit some of these may have been, Elizabeth's time there was simpler than the complexities of her recent London life. Although she was defiant and quite open about her intention to do as she wished, family disapproval of Charles was undiminished and she had still to weather it constantly. So invigorated and cheered was she by her stay that the following year she returned to Malta for another long spell of entertainment under Pris and Richard's care.

Not only had Malta been a place of extended respite from the realities of London, its Mediterranean bounty had the effect of sending Elizabeth into Priscilla's kitchen in a spirit of enquiry which she had never previously displayed. Angela, Priscilla's cheerful, absent-minded and gifted cook, was the person responsible for Elizabeth's present interest in the cooking, and she gave her her first lessons. A Maltese who had always worked for military and naval families, Angela was unschooled yet instinctive, both inspired by the possibilities of the kitchen and at ease with its demands, serving up unfailingly delicious meals. Elizabeth more than once accompanied her on her forays to shop for food and was amused and impressed by her competence, in spite of the noise and scattiness. Once the cat managed to leave a dinner party for that evening short of a vital quail. 'Piercing wails rent the air . . . the council that followed was one of desperation.'

Years later, in 1951, shortly after her first book, *Mediterranean Food*, had come out, Elizabeth wrote an article without recipes, entitled 'Two Cooks', for the inimitable André Simon's quarterly, *Wine and Food*. In keeping with the style of this élite and influential journal, Elizabeth's essay was a true piece of gastronomic literature. For one so relatively inexperienced, her sense of concision and her sense of humour were already beautifully honed, and with these as tools she used the vehicle of her own experience of a small Mediterranean island to give the outlines of a philosophy of taste.

> In those days food was remarkably cheap in Malta, drink was untaxed and entertaining was easy, and immense fun. Marketing was carried on with an Oriental approach to the delights of haggling . . . In the market you could buy a variety of boned, dressed meat and game at ridiculously small prices . . . there was a prodigal supply of fruits and vegetables grown on the neighbouring island of Gozo; the local oranges were sweet and delicious; there were figs, grapes and exquisite wild strawberries.

In the summer of 1937, when Pris and Richard returned to England and a cottage on Salisbury Plain, they brought Angela with them. For a while she was 'blissfully happy in that damp and clammy atmosphere: she thought the little red bungalows on the road to Andover the most beautiful houses in the world and she continued to cook like an angel. On English mutton and most un-Mediterranean vegetables her talent thrived.' But Angela's Southern temperament and love of her little island got the better of her. 'You cannot [in England] haggle with a village grocer, and she began to pine for the shouting and the disorder of Valetta's market, the incessant gossip, and the fun of preparing immense quantities of food for the parties which had been an almost everyday occurrence in Malta.' Angela returned home, came back to Pris, and eventually went back for good to the island of her birth.

If a gastronome's message is about choice and discrimination, then in the short space of a page and a half 'Two Cooks' succeeds with admirable skill. Elizabeth inspires the wish to emulate the culinary style, the tenor of Mediterranean life, describes the minimum required to be a good cook, and hints that England would be the richer for a turn in this direction.

As the narrative unfolds, in the reflection of Angela's lovable personality Elizabeth conjures up the noise, warmth, vibrancy and sparkle of a bustling Mediterranean town. Here one has the impression that food, without necessarily being luxurious, is in 'prodigal' supply. The quality of fruit and vegetables is the best, whilst inexpensive cuts of meat are not considered drawbacks, because the cook is one for whom things like 'stringy birds' can be transformed into 'creamy soufflés and mousses'. Everything is cooked with a simplicity and sureness of touch which has at its heart the assumption that food is a matter for celebration. By contrast a picture of a grey and overcast England also emerges in the essay. It is judged a place ruled by an unbending obedience to order, where a sense of largesse is absent and where the natives fail to cook even their national dishes with any distinction.

Homeward bound from Malta, the thought of London appalled Elizabeth and on arrival her worst fears were confirmed for she found it 'simply awful'. And she was thrown into a depression. Lyrical in her praise of Pris and Richard, and of all the trouble they had taken, she surprises by recalling her huge enjoyment of one of Pris and Richard's favourite pastimes, sailing: 'The [sailing] and bathing were absolutely divine . . . all the parties and . . . your lovely house and all the flowers . . . and lovely food were miraculous.'

The state of No. 112 Regent's Park Road and the response it provoked in her now seemed symptomatic of her rejection of London, England and much of what it represented. She arrived back to find the flat filthy and untidy, and in exactly the same state in which she had left it – empty jars of face cream and bath salt jars everywhere, and a kitchen grimy with dirt. She was very annoyed with Marian's lack of domesticity in her absence and, as the maid was not always as readily available as she would have liked, Elizabeth began cleaning almost as soon as she arrived. Wishing she could go straight back to Malta, she decided that despite the unlikelihood of finding such grand rooms again, the only answer was to leave. She would find a smaller flat for which no one but herself was responsible and added that she would have to get somewhere with more modern conveniences. Elizabeth shared houses and spent much time in the sociable company of any number of people over the years, but her childhood habit of retreat, of hiding away with a book, remained a passion not to be thwarted. It was a restorative, a means by which she replenished herself, and this retreat always remained utterly essential for her.

For now, however, she wanted company in the awfulness of London. She needed to reinstate herself in the metropolis in order to justify returning there, but it was Whitsun and everyone she knew seemed to be out of town, frustrating her attempts. Doreen was not yet back from working with a rep company in Ireland. Marian was about to go up to her family in Kendal, Felicité was away at Folkington, Elizabeth couldn't find Diana, nor Arthur Watkins. One person who did prove to be around was Charles, and any hopes Pris and the others might have had of Elizabeth giving him up had quickly to be shelved.

The holiday in Malta had filled her with a new purposefulness, and she announced to Pris that she was full of energy, desperate to find a job and equal to facing 'a regiment of foul beastly Sydney Carrolls and film agents and pimply theatre managers and I have a feeling that perhaps I'll get a job this time'. Concurrently with these good intentions Elizabeth was pragmatically facing up to the fact that it was unlikely she would find any acting work that could be called a living and concluded that if she didn't within the next two months she would give it up altogether.

Pris would be back on several weeks' leave in the summer and Elizabeth promised to set about finding a cottage in Wales where the four sisters could spend some time together. The Welsh origins of their name seemed an inducement to indulge what became something of a fixation with this beautiful and still unspoilt part of Britain. Between 1935 and 1938 they took at least two or three houses together in Wales. One, Glys Andreas, was a cottage at Talybont, which Felicité described as a 'lovely lonely place' in the winding, leafy Usk river valley. Friends came to stay and Doreen remembers one year when 'Elizabeth threw herself into learning Welsh.' Although it can hardly be claimed typical of anything Welsh, during the Thirties Elizabeth also spent the first of several holidays at Portmeirion in North Wales, on that occasion with Stella, Cedric Morris and Arthur Lett Haines. The mix of sometimes diminutive, sometimes grand, ice cream-coloured baroque splendour set amidst a very un-Continental Welsh landscape appealed to the quirky and at heart metropolitan sophisticate in Elizabeth – as it had done to many other artistic figures since its opening in 1926 by the remarkable Clough Williams-Ellis, who was a friend of Cedric and Lett. Elizabeth's fascination with Wales took her back many times over the years to a succession of houses for holidays and work, and a restaurant near Abergavenny, The Walnut Tree, was eventually to become her favourite outside London.

During the war, abroad and worn out with it, she nostalgically recalled to Priscilla a little house they had seen near Machynlleth on their first Welsh holiday together. It was found along a path by a river, which ran through the garden, and nearby was an odd-looking sugar loaf hill. Elizabeth always regretted that she didn't take it, and longed for its beautiful rooms and the little pool in the garden.

Back in London and still finding only the odd acting assignment, Elizabeth took up a recommendation from Cedric Morris to his friend Madame Chant-Communal, the gifted chief designer for the influential fashion house, Worth. Worth prided itself on the social prestige of its clients, many of whose dresses were made for Court occasions. The girls who assisted clients with fittings were required to have not only something of Elizabeth's social clout but, for all her delight in clothes, considerably more knowledge of design and materials than she could then muster. Resulting from this meeting with Madame Chant-Communal was a brief new part for Elizabeth, as a Worth vendeuse in a very junior capacity.

After leaving No. 112 Regent's Park Road Elizabeth lived in a flat in John Street, most of the time with Charles and not doing very much. Doreen was out of work and her father insisted she took a

typing course at Pitmans, only a few streets away from Elizabeth and
Charles, but her resolve was not very fixed. 'I used to pop into
Pitmans for about half an hour then I'd abscond to their flat. We'd
lounge around, listen to records, spend the rest of the day there. We
didn't seem to *do* anything much.' But the inactivity did not bring
peacefulness. Charles and Elizabeth's life seems to have had little
tranquillity about it and when not 'lounging around' Elizabeth
continued with her incessant activity.

By July 1937 she had finally decided to quit Charles once and
for all and set off on a (last) visit to Germany to recuperate with
friends. Diana wrote to Felicité in the Tyrol on the eve of her
departure: 'Saw Liza last night – had supper with her and we went to
the flicks – she's looking very well now ... and C. [Charles] has
produced – in his usual way – a little black kitten from under the
wheels of a tram ... It's called Alexander and I think it makes her
feel much less lonely ... C. you will be glad to know is definitely off.
I think there is something new.'

In spite of her own and her family's attempts to extricate
Elizabeth, she was not as independent of Charles as she believed, and
his ability to reinstate himself with her was unnerving. Stella, now
returned from Jamaica, summoned Doreen to her house. During their
friendship Doreen recalls that she had 'got Elizabeth out of many
fixes' but this time, despite feeling intimidated by Stella's haughty
manner, when commanded to 'do something about Elizabeth and that
most *unsuitable* man', she was obliged to reply 'Mrs Hamilton, there
is *nothing* I can do.'

By August, when Elizabeth had returned from Germany, Diana
wrote again to Felicité from the Benckendorffs' house in St John's
Wood: 'I am rather worried about Eliza – she went off with Charles
on his bally boat for the weekend – said definitely she was going to
be back on Wednesday ... and now it's Thursday evening and she
still isn't back. I hate her going out on that rickety boat. Marnia
[Constantine Benckendorff's wife] says the engine is permanently
wrong.' Diana concludes by observing that Elizabeth 'seems very
restless'. On another occasion Diana had said to Felicité that Elizabeth
'has taken Selma's flat instead of her own – and is now choosing the
colours in which to have it done. I really think she's a bit mad – all

this money spent on moving house every year – and immediately it's completed and made liveable in – moved out of.'

The same restlessness had taken Elizabeth on trips to the South of France with Doreen, and once together with another friend, Diana Morgan (later Anderson). Their route usually took them down by the Blue Train to the South where they stayed in *pensions*, hotels or friends' houses. These were trips for sun-bathing, sea-bathing and assignations, with as much inebriation as their youthful constitutions would allow. Once they chanced on several of Diana Morgan's university friends (she had been up at Oxford) and the girls spent about a week in their company, during the day on the beach and in the evenings playing at casinos and dancing in clubs, or nude-bathing in the moonlight off secluded sandy beaches.

In the nineteenth century the South of France and Italy were usually visited in the winter but after the First World War a complete volte-face occurred and it became fashionable to travel during the season of sun. The nineteenth century had been obsessed with the implied wealth, privilege and 'refinement' of pale skin. Now, spurred on by a new generation of writers such as E. M. Forster with *Passage to India* and D. H. Lawrence with *Lady Chatterley's Lover* taking the power of the sun to incite and affect as one of their central themes, England succumbed to the heat. The notion that the sun made naturally hypocritical Englishmen and women from the cold North more passionate, sincere and true to their real, instinctive nature was always implied and often articulated. Typically, Evelyn Waugh reacted to the craze for sun-bathing and wrote an article hating it, entitled 'The Sun-bathing Business'. Friends like Peter Quennell up at Oxford had formed a Cicada Club, the sole purpose of which was for members to cook themselves on the beaches of the Riviera.

In the Twenties and Thirties the way to sun and South began at Victoria Station. Here, like Henry Green's South-bound *Party-Going* crowd, you boarded that magnificent Blue Train in the evening, enveloped yourself in its blue velvet upholstery, ate its exotic food – a tank full of writhing eels was exhibited in the dining car – bedded down in the luxurious cabins while the sleek blue and gold locomotive sped you, sleeping, or perhaps not, south to Marseilles, Toulon, Cannes, Nice, Monte Carlo and further afield. 'Sleep your way from the city's fogs to the Riviera Sunshine' ran the seductive advertising posters. The grey of London left behind, next morning you awoke 'to the sight of mimosa and orange trees . . . the red rocks of the Esterel on one side of the line, and the blue waters of the Mediterranean on the other', wrote Patrick Howarth. The Blue Train came to symbolize everything about holiday, freedom, frivolity. Diaghilev's *Le Train Bleu* enshrined it in a ballet with costumes by Coco Chanel and scenario by Jean Cocteau, Agatha Christie set a murder mystery on board it and any number of other writers used it in their fictions. This was the post-war world of international travellers for whom holidays that no longer proved attractive in remote places of stillness and quiet were now being replaced by urban glamour and ritz.

Elizabeth's attention, however, could be diverted from physical pleasures and direct itself to literary ones with knowledge, feeling and conviction. Her confident intelligence and energy reinforced her tendencies to impatience and fits of boredom but also endowed her with a prodigiously accurate memory, a sharp curiosity and an ability to leap nimbly from observation to judgment to characterization. In strong contrast she was often complacent, incurious and insensitive to others. She suffered also from an unwillingness to analyse her own motives, avoiding introspection; often she was hampered by a debilitating indecisiveness, aimlessness, lack of purpose.

In some ways Elizabeth now typified the non-political fast living of so many clever young Society people of the Twenties and Thirties. But by the close of 1938, after four years of living a life beyond her means and in busily pointless ease, this life-style was proving insufficiently rewarding and she began to tire of the demands it incurred. She was unable to convince herself any longer that success awaited her as an actress, nor had her joint efforts with Charles proved the written word to be appealingly easy. Charles too was struggling. Writing later (1946) in a second volume of autobiography, he regretted the eclipse of theatre by the ascendancy of the cinema. He believed that: 'Nobody stays in the theatre if they are good enough for the film', and continued with prophetic accuracy:

> Only a handful of stars stay in the theatre . . . It's the same story with the dramatists; make a list of the promising playwrights of

the 1920s and . . . you'll see the names of most of them . . . on the subtitle of some film. Soon the theatre will exist only as some museum piece. The Old Vic will be turned into a national theatre for Shakespeare . . . Already the film has all the brain and all the blood. Five years ago I would have had enough enthusiasm to start all over again in a new medium. Five years more and I'll be content to scrape a living where I am, but at the moment, what I want to do is get out.

Since his youth Charles had been fascinated by boats. He not only loved their endless physical variety but was seduced by their power of suggestion: places far away, mysterious and unknown. And for several years before his meeting with Elizabeth he had owned a succession of small boats, teaching himself how to sail and maintain them. Elizabeth's own experience of sailing had given her too a love of being out on the water where one experienced a feeling of freedom. So, as Charles put it: 'We decided to leave England. We decided to buy another boat. We decided to go to the Mediterranean: Marseilles, Nice, Naples, Piraeus, and the Isles of Greece.' A lack of purpose was the simplest and strongest motive spurring Charles and Elizabeth's exodus. They had found an answer to their present malaise: escape. Just when war in Europe had become almost inevitable.

CHAPTER SIX

Beautiful Evelyn Hope
(1938–1939)

BETWEEN THE TWO world wars in Britain a shift of emphasis occurred in the collective artistic and intellectual sensibility. Where previously the Englishman who had gone abroad was often enamoured of what he saw on his travels, few were driven on return to denigrate their homeland. But since the 1920s, when for some travel had become almost a cult, for many dislike of home had become the prime incentive to travel abroad. This dislike encompassed dissatisfaction with the political system (the Spanish Civil War of 1936 concentrated the minds of left-wing sympathizers), a perception of intellectual and artistic stagnation, and a general feeling that England was at best dismal, moribund, graceless and dull and at worst mean, joyless, desolate and sordid. For many, such as Elizabeth, foreign travel was also an escape from family censure about one's personal life-style.

The list of writers who fled the country is a long one, and several, like Robert Graves, 'resolved never to make England ... home again'. D. H. Lawrence, Norman Douglas, W. H. Auden, Aldous Huxley and Lawrence Durrell intended not to return; Graham Greene too. Cyril Connolly spoke for many when he wrote that he was 'tired of England ... I do feel it is a dying civilization – going stuffy and comatose instead of collapsing beautifully like France.'

On the physical plane, reiterated themes in the same vein were the appallingness of English food, the puritanism of the drink laws and the hellishness of the weather. The cold and badly fed English were enticed by images of trains and ships sailing and puffing their way into balmier sunsets. In *The Rock Pool* (Obelisk Press, 1936), Cyril Connolly talks of a 'scabby winter landscape that seemed to cover; a thin soup under a greasy tureen'. In *How About Europe?* (Secker and Warburg, 1930) Norman Douglas rants about the disgusting food, and in *Coming Up for Air* (Gollancz, 1939), Orwell has George Bowling say that when he found the frankfurter he ate was filled with fish 'it gave me the feeling that I'd bitten into the modern world and discovered what it was really made of . . . Rotten fish in a rubber skin.'

Despite criticisms like these, and however much they may have been confused about other issues, Orwell and most other literate English travellers went armed with a sure sense of who they were – British. With few exceptions (notably D. H. Lawrence, Gerald Brenan and Charles Gibson Cowan) their privileged backgrounds had made them secure in their values and sense of implicit superiority. (There is a striking inconsistency here with their denigration of their homeland.) This did not mean that these young travellers necessarily had much money, but abroad the Anglo-Saxon had the initiative and drive to make the most of journeys where one didn't really quite pass muster unless one had suffered discomfort and inconvenience. When seen in the context of contemporary attitudes such as these, Elizabeth and Charles's projected voyage falls squarely into place as a journey in accord with the zeitgeist.

After three months' searching, according to Charles they found a boat 'in a mud berth at Hamble [near Portsmouth on the river leading into the Solent and the sea] on a wet day. It cost just twice as much as we had decided to spend, and . . . needed extensive repairs, but it was what we were looking for. We stood in the mud, heedless of the rain, for the best part of an hour, and agreed that it was a ship . . .' They bought it; Elizabeth paid, and in the certainty of their disapproval refused ever quite to clarify this point for her family. 'We went back to London full of enthusiasm for the first time for months.' The ship was called the *Evelyn Hope* (undoubtedly a reference to Browning's poem about the young girl, 'Beautiful Evelyn Hope is Dead', and one whose significance would not have been lost on Charles and Elizabeth). On the third day of the New Year of 1939 Elizabeth wrote excitedly to Felicité that she had been down to see the boat, and that it would be very comfortable when finished. 'You will *have* to come . . . and stay on her sometime.'

Charles had worked for several weeks repairing the boat before he was one day appalled to discover dry rot hidden in the timbers. In desperation he called in a small firm of shipbuilders. 'They tried to pose as hard-bitten businessmen, but it was a sham; their sole interest was ships. They tore out planks with vicious enthusiasm and settled down to build me a new ship out of the remains.'

Months went by. Charles continued to work in the theatre as a producer and finally, when work on the *Evelyn Hope* was nearing completion, Elizabeth was unexpectedly asked to play a very small part in a GPO film. She couldn't now start on the boat until the beginning of July, as she would have to spend all of June in London. The flat would be given up altogether at the end of that month. And, with no apprehension of the magnitude of the journey she was about to undertake, she commented that she couldn't afford to keep it on all the time she was to be away.

Whilst preparing to move out of John Street Elizabeth and Charles went 'on an orgy of spending' for the voyage. Elizabeth found bed and table linen, materials for mattress covers, curtains and cushions. She searched out a medicine chest and cheap china (to be replaced in France) in the Caledonian Market; Charles bought compasses, a camera, tinned food, tools; they spent a day in Woolworths. Whatever her living conditions, Elizabeth was not satisfied until she had not only made the place habitable, but had stamped it with her own particular brand of easy elegance, usually involving significant expenditure. They found they had 'hopelessly overspent' and Elizabeth suggested paying guests. A girl whom Elizabeth in her letters and Charles in his book always referred to as 'the paying guest' was found. She wanted to make the journey as far as Marseilles and was willing to pay a cheque immediately for the full amount. With this, the rest of the work and provisioning could proceed.

With diagrams to assist her Elizabeth had enthusiastically given Felicité a profile of the little ship. Several years later, in 1946, Charles published the second volume of his autobiography, *The Voyage of the Evelyn Hope*, dedicated 'TO E. G. [Elizabeth Gwynne] WITH ALL MY LOVE'. And here he carefully records his own description of the ship. In combination their two accounts leave us with a vivid image of the little craft. Charles loved any excuse to 'talk ships', so he gave details of the Certificate of British Registry, including the information that it was 'built in 1906 ... that the number of decks is one, of masts two: that it is carvel built, rigged as a yawl ... and is described as a wood pleasure yacht.'

Elizabeth's description made it a 'black fishing boat-looking sort of craft, with a lot of teak and not too much brass; a small cockpit, a roomy saloon which, with a lot of alteration, could be made fit to live in; a cabin aft with washbasin, one single and one double bunk ... a toilet that you could at least stand up in; a forecastle, which ... would make a fairly decent galley; and an engine amidships which looked quite clean and seemed out of the way.' She told Felicité that much needed to be done, with the inclusion of sink, bookshelves, washbasin, primus stoves in the galley, hanging cupboards some-where, more bookshelves and a chart case.

Just into the New Year of 1939 Elizabeth is writing excitedly to Felicité from the 'Beautiful *Evelyn Hope*' then moored at Hamble. Her description of the boat is deftly conveyed in two sketches: one a bird's-eye plan from above and the other a profile. Typically she takes care with all details, showing her sister the exact position of bunks, washbasin, lavatory, bookshelves, cooking area and sink.

As the end of June approached, in the frenzy of last-minute activity Elizabeth had made a complete list of the things she was packing off to Pris for safe keeping. It amounted to a quantity of boxes, trunks and pieces of treasured furniture, rather more than she had described to her sister. And she appends instructions to hang up clothes and take out her precious silk paisley shawl. She gives Pris permission to use her lacquer tea chest if she would like to, but then in characteristically commanding tone gives strict orders that on no account is anything ever to be stood on top of it – 'I never allowed people even to put their hats on it.' Priscilla's favours must stretch to Richard taking a 'filthy' carpet to be cleaned in Bristol (where he was then working for the BBC). The removers had sent inadequate help, so she had to send them back to get more men. In the midst of this débâcle Diana and her new man Christopher arrived to see how things were progressing.

Elizabeth stayed just a few more days in London, finalizing preparations before her departure. She tells Pris that Diana Morgan had arranged quite a good impromptu leaving party, over which Elizabeth revealed an inclination which was later to become notorious established practice: the segregation of her friends. Intending to be away from England for several months, she asked only the friends she had in common with Diana, feeling that she really couldn't cope with more.

After the party they went with her sister Diana and Christopher to Smokey Joe's and didn't get home until five o'clock. Christopher was 'well away' by the end of the evening, in fine form and refusing to go home. Elizabeth though he drove like a maniac but was still 'quite safe'. Marian was due to spend the weekend on the *Evelyn Hope* with Charles and Elizabeth before they set sail for France, but a severe hangover on the morning following the party put off the moment and they were going at the break of dawn the next day.

Elizabeth eventually arrived at Hamble, as Charles described in *The Voyage of the Evelyn Hope*, 'with half a dozen suitcases and a trunk-full of clothes, a small packing case and two kit bags full of books, two cases of assorted dried and tinned provisions, several parcels containing curtains, mattress covers and various oddments and arm-fuls of . . . cushions; the result of an extra week's shopping and the paying guest's cheque'.

Her propensity for collecting books was well established and Elizabeth would not submit to their ejection from the ship by persuasion or argument, even when reminded that there were already about 400 on board and shelf space for about a third of that number. A place was found for them and they were stowed away. Charles gave a partial list of titles. It is long and tantalizing for what is omitted, and is clearly meant to impress the reader. Nevertheless it gives a remarkable impression of the breadth of Charles and Elizabeth's reading and implies that books are a basic requisite for (shipboard) life. There was no question in their minds that travelling was not an isolated event. A literate traveller set out with other men's (and women's) travels in mind. And undoubtedly some of the thrill was in transposing one's own present journey on to the experiences of other travellers, taking the same routes as those from the past.

The half-dozen desert island books had long ago been agreed upon, according to Charles, 'in the order named as: *Pears Cyclopaedia* [many years later Elizabeth's high opinion of Pears remained unaltered when, thanking Pris's younger daughter, Julia, for a new edition, she said how invaluable she had always found it], a Shakespeare, the Bible, one or two Alice books, a Marlowe or a Milton, and either the *Decline and Fall* or Boswell's *Johnson*, for bulk'. With these as a nucleus Charles had added: 'the *Oxford Book of Verse*; the poems of Rupert Brooke; a Byron, since we were going to Greece; *Dead Souls*; *The Enormous Room*, *War Birds* and *Le Feu*; Crane's *Red Badge of Courage*; *Love and Mr Lewisham*, *Kipps*, *First Men in the Moon* and two or three more early Wells; a complete O. Henry; Hardy's *Jude*; Huxley's *Antic Hay*; Rabelais, and a couple of dozen, mostly Greek, dramas, a few Shaws and some Anatole France. I took most of the Penguins . . . a few Everyman and a Hoyle.'

Elizabeth's selection included '*The Seven Pillars*; Doughty's *Arabia Deserta*; the entire works of Conrad; Flecker's *Poems* and *Hassan*; the plays of Jonson and Ford . . . a second Marlowe (in case mine was not complete); a *Golden Treasury*; Mather's *Arabian Nights*; a Tchekov; the remaining works of Anatole France; the *Odyssey* and the *Iliad*; several Baedeckers; *Robinson Crusoe*; some of the Barchester novels (because neither of us had read Trollope), Percy's *Reliques*; *A Short History of England*; two C. E. Montagues [a writer to whom Elizabeth remained singularly attached]; two Mark Twains; three odd volumes of Hakluyt; and about a hundred paper covered thrillers, which she said could be thrown over the side as soon as they were read.'

With her final words of farewell to Pris written on 8 July 1939, Elizabeth had thanked her again for the handsome present of a camera and the loan of her binoculars. She promised her a postcard as soon as they were across the Channel, hoping that it would not prove a long ordeal. Set to leave England, Elizabeth was twenty-five and Charles thirty-six.

A couple of days later they were at last under way. The sun shone through the clouds and it was warm. Passing out of Southampton Water, with the Isle of Wight to the leeward, they slipped out into the English Channel. Sitting along the bowsprit watching 'the stem cutting the sea', Charles mused over their final departure and the voyage to come, and was elated. By nightfall, with Elizabeth taking her turn at the tiller, the wind was freshening up and the ship began to make good headway. Charles sent Elizabeth and the 'paying guest' down below to sleep and kept watch for the rest of the night. By dawn they were in sight of the flashing Havre Lighthouse.

Anchored in the outer harbour, they intended leaving the following day but slept long and stayed on board until the evening when they went ashore and ate, appropriately, large soup bowls of *moules marinière*.

It rained the following day and they decided they would not be able to make it to Paris for the Bastille Day celebrations so stayed on in Le Havre. Elizabeth wrote her promised postcard to Pris saying that all was well, and on the 15th they weighed anchor and set off down the Seine estuary bound for Paris. At Rouen ocean navigation ceases and the Seine river technically begins. They moored, the *douaniers* came on board, and after a most cursory inspection handed them clearance to proceed. With the mast taken down and rolled they slowly manoeuvred the great river, sluggish and swirling by turn as they passed through the locks. It rained consistently for days and visibility was poor, but the novelty of the undertaking was still enough to keep fretting at bay.

On reaching Paris they shopped and did some sight-seeing. Unlike Elizabeth, who knew it well, Charles had not been to Paris before and was dazzled. He wandered through streets and museums, then went with Elizabeth to the Louvre. They met friends and found that all the talk was of war. It was nearly August. Unsurprisingly, Charles says he had foreseen the likelihood of war but had no intention of becoming personally involved; he describes himself as a conscientious objector. The day before leaving Paris Elizabeth and Charles 'took them [friends] for an evening on the river and everybody got drunk'.

In 1936 Germany had remilitarized the Rhineland; that same year the Spanish Civil War commenced; also the Italians had invaded Abyssinia. With the Japanese, German and Italian axis developing apace, in February 1938 Hitler had assumed supreme command of the armed forces. By March he had occupied Vienna and declared

Austria an annexe of the German Reich. By March 1939 Czecho-
slovakia was overrun by Germany. That month the fragmenting left
and centrist forces in Spain finally succumbed to the Fascist rebels. It
was a turbulent Europe, rapidly preparing for a gigantic orgy of self-
destruction, through which Elizabeth and Charles now began to make
their leisurely, escapist way.

Avoiding the great working Seine barges, they proceeded along
the river to Melun. It was cold and they spent half a day in a café
playing a trivial game on a pinball machine. At Montereau they
branched off the Seine along the Yonne to Sens where they passed a
day drinking *vin gris* at Tonnere. They entered the Canal de Bour-
gogne and followed its 150-mile length with over 200 locks, all kept
by women. These locks allow the canal to rise gradually until it passes
under the summit of the Côte d'Or, the line of hills running south to
Chalon-sur-Saône. Here, in this central part of Burgundy, which has
always been celebrated for the pleasures of its table, the food was
hearty and the wine full-bodied to match, and the travellers sampled
both with gusto.

Dropping down lock by lock, they reached the great medieval
city of Dijon, capital of the old dukedom of Burgundy, its splendour
amply reflecting the magnificence of its rulers. Later Charles and
Elizabeth would regret the brevity of the ten days spent *en route*
through the rich and fertile surrounding land. Charles recalled that
'We wished we had lingered where once, even at seventeen hundred
feet, we were among the clouds, where the red earth and dark forests
of Burgundy were spread out below us, and where we sailed on top of
the world.' At Dijon, revered as one of the greatest gastronomic
centres of France, they ate at the city's famed Trois Faisans, and
Charles concluded that the meal 'came as a climax to ten days of the
best food that France can produce'.

On 23 August the Soviet–German Non-Aggression Pact was
signed. This sinister alliance at once launched the British government
into preparations for war.

Along the river Saône at Lyon, Charles and Elizabeth were
irritated by French mechanics, bad weather and the 'paying guest',
and consequently did not bother to see much of this ancient town, its
Roman ruins or cathedral. After Lyon the Saône joins the great swift-

flowing Rhône and here they took on a pilot to help navigate them south. Passing Valence, they went on through the valley of the Rhône past Montélimar and into one of the earliest settled areas of France: the Midi, Imperial Roman Provence.

Here were the immense broken arches of the Pont d'Avignon, still reaching half-way across the river. The beautiful city of Avignon was long home to the exiled poet Petrarch and still holds the vast palace refuge of the schismatic Popes, for a hundred years rival to the throne of St Peter. They continued past Montélimar; past Beaucaire, the castle standing precipitously above the river, where Aucassin and Nicolette played out their tragedy; past Tarascon and finally to ancient Arles lying at the head of the Rhône delta and at the entrance to the great river valley along which the Romans had brought their domination and culture north.

At Arles they ate in a restaurant where, Charles wrote, 'we obtained an excellent five course dinner with wine and coffee for five francs'. But in this city of winding streets, the strangest of which is Les Alycamps, a straight 'miraculous' tree-edged avenue of marble tombs, they did little more than speed through the most famed sites. Even in a hurry these remain fabulous: the cathedral of St Trophime, a Romanesque beauty, one of the loveliest in Provence, and the Roman amphitheatre, comparable in size to the Colosseum. Elizabeth later told Felicité that she went to see only the Roman remains and the cathedral, which she thought marvellous. They were there one day, and were hampered by 'the awful paying guest', who walked about in shorts and sea boots, and carried several bottles of wine in a net slung over her shoulder.

They had navigated the 200 and more miles along the lower course of the Rhône valley from Lyon to the Mediterranean. The vegetation grew more Southern, grey-green and parched as they passed the tributary valleys, catching glimpses of the snow-clad Alps to the east and the lower volcanic hills to the west. The last stretch was along the Great Rhône to the sea. Here the river's broad eastern delta forms the mysterious, shimmering salt marshlands and lagoons of the Carmargue, whose pastures nourish beef and fighting bulls for the arenas of the South, the glistening waters harbouring wild ducks, egrets, ibis and flamingos. To the west lie the flatlands of Bouches-du-Rhône, bordered by Aix, once glorious, still beautiful; capital of Provence, site of a great university, seat of Count René and birthplace of Cézanne.

By early next morning the *Evelyn Hope* was at last out on the sea again. As the little black yacht crossed the Golf de Foy from St Louis to Port de Bouc, Charles wrote, 'It was our first taste of the Mediterranean, and it wasn't blue, it was brown with the muddy waters of the Bouches-du-Rhône.' By the afternoon they had crossed the edge of the vast salt lagoon, the Etang de Berre, and passed Martigue, the thriving little fishing port so favoured by the Impressionists, and still an artists' haunt. With fish-trap nets sinking to allow them passage, they left the Etang de Berre and entered the enormous, busy watery subterranean thoroughfare, the Tunel de Rove, final section of the Marseilles–Rhône Canal. Out of the lengthy cavern of muffled light, they passed Cap Janet and dropped anchor in the Vieux Port of Marseilles. One of the oldest and largest seaports of the Mediterranean, its influences and atmosphere have often been as much Levantine as French. Arriving in Marseilles, the *Evelyn Hope* had finished the first leg of her journey to those distant 'Isles of Greece'.

Elizabeth and the 'paying guest' went ashore and gathered food at the bustling Italian market, piled high with an abundance of glistening Southern vegetables, while Charles sat on board and marvelled. He had never before been South, and was enchanted. The 'painted fishing boats, with stumpy masts leaning forward to support the yards of lateen sails came alongside to sell their loads of black mussels, purple sea urchins, blue crayfish and green and white oysters. I watched them until it became dark.' Nearby was the broad Canebière, with its strolling promenaders and little bars and restaurants, the urbane yet explosive life of the South.

As night fell and Elizabeth returned through the Italian quarter laden with food, all lights were kept extinguished in the city in accordance with the new directives; and Charles wrote: 'The war scare had already overtaken us.' They ate that evening in a 'little Italian restaurant where in an open fire the chef turned strange vegetable pies with an immense baker's peel . . . and the embers filled the room with a steady red glow. We drank large quantities of Algerian wine.' In the Italian quarter of this often squalid, garish but always exhilarating port, with its ancient tradition of learning and commerce amongst a melting-pot of races from all quarters of the Mediterranean, the three travellers were indeed far from England and the concerns they hoped to have left behind.

CHAPTER SEVEN

By the Shores of the Mediterranean
(1939–1940)

AT DAWN ON 1 September Hitler attacked Poland and the mobilization of British forces was immediately ordered by the Prime Minister. Charles heard the news from a crowd as he walked the streets of Marseilles admiring the city. He made his way back to Elizabeth and the 'paying guest'. Although not a surprise, the actuality of war stunned them and for a short time Charles and Elizabeth were uncertain what to do.

The 'paying guest' rapidly decided to return to England; they helped her pack and saw her off at the station. On 2 September Elizabeth sat down and wrote to Pris in Chipping Sodbury, telling her that the Germans had marched into Danzig and bombed Warsaw. She was doing her best to remain calm, and to make arrangements; as far as she and Charles were concerned, everything depended on whether Italy came into the war – in that case they would go somewhere inland immediately. Meanwhile, Chamberlain was making last-minute efforts to preserve peace.

The boat was in need of repair and was now in dry dock at the Bassin de Carenge. When finished it would be in a condition fit to be left in the water for some time. Charles and Elizabeth had intended sailing to Spain in order to leave the boat in a neutral country, but this was now doubtful. Elizabeth felt that 'not a soul' in France was anxious for war, any more than in England, and that there was very little anti-German feeling. She told Pris to write to her at Cook's, 'as if I left here it would probably be in a hurry and I wouldn't know exactly where.' Letters would probably take a long time to arrive, so Pris should not be alarmed if she didn't hear from them. Elizabeth had a small suitcase already packed so that she could leave at a moment's notice. The reason she gave for not returning immediately was that, like everyone else, she hoped things might become more settled. On 3 September Chamberlain broadcast to the nation and said that Britain was at war with Germany. There was no longer any question of anything being 'settled'.

Elizabeth said to Pris that Charles had not tried to keep her there, but that she felt the boat to be in some sense her home, and that she would not like to leave Charles alone to deal with everything. She wanted to see things resolved, and their belongings taken ashore before she left France. A Danish ship's chandler would store their belongings and look after the boat. Meanwhile Elizabeth told Pris that if she needed any help Marian was a reliable person in 'times of stress' and would be at Melrose Place in Kendal where she was going to join her family.

By early October, after the initial uproar caused by the declaration of war, Poland's fall and France's entrance into hostilities, life in the South settled down into an edgy normality. Charles and Elizabeth swam in the dirty waters of the Vieux Port and fished for the little bony things ideal for practising *bouillabaisse* with. She wrote back to England saying that she was unable to return and be companion to Stella for a while because she couldn't afford it. (Having returned from Jamaica in the late 1930s, Stella had bought the Old Grammar School in Dedham, near Cedric Morris and Lett Haines, and here launched herself into the antiques trade with considerable success.) With the family's income growing smaller each year Elizabeth was desperately trying to pay off all her debts. She did intend to 'come back sometime', but refused to tie herself down to a particular date. Elizabeth was hedging here; she had little intention of coming back 'for the duration' and gave her habitual answer to requests for obligation: 'I don't want to tie myself down.' Romance escapes the ordered round of stability and structure. With Charles, Elizabeth had worked hard to achieve it, at least for an episode, and she was not about to abandon it because of the small matter of the declaration of a world war.

She grew to know Marseilles and its environs well, sometimes shopping for the pretty Provençal prints – she sent some home for

Pris, about to have her first baby, and her other sisters – and chafing at 'the unspeakable monotony' of staying in one place for so long. Elizabeth's friend Doreen had gone in 1938 to live in Rome with her new husband, working for a tourist firm, but at the outbreak of war they had returned to England. Her husband now had a commission in the Navy and Doreen was 'sitting at home again with her family right back where she started' whilst Pris had lost Richard to service back in the Royal Engineers Corps.

Charles and Elizabeth were suddenly given permission to move the ship out of Marseilles and spent a number of days sampling the beauties of the coastline between Cassis and Hyères. November came and the impending treacherous Mistral 'spelt certain disaster to a yacht'. They decided, without permission from the authorities, to make for Antibes where Elizabeth had friends and they could remain for the winter in the sheltered harbour. The journey was not a very long one but the nervousness of French officials, and the information that ships would be fired upon if they sailed at night, involved making short hops along this rocky, at times wild and lovely coastline. They stayed for a week at St Raphaël while Elizabeth made excursions into St Tropez to see friends and shop for pieces of the brightly coloured local pottery to replace their Woolworths china. As she later wrote for *The Times*, 'The charm of St Tropez is apparently indestructible.' The Mistral, as well as the war, was beginning to hold them up, but finally Mike Cumberlege was there on the quay to meet them as they sailed into the port of Antibes.

Elizabeth knew Mike and his wife Nan well. She had met them, like so many others, while holidaying on Malta with Pris and Richard. Mike wore an earring, was cheerfully high-spirited, the less conventional member of a distinguished naval family – his father was an admiral – and could not keep away from ships. His father kept a house near Antibes, where he and Nan were presently staying – Mike was captain of a 60-ton yacht, the *Landfall*, left at Venice at the outbreak of war. He had little to do and spent time on board the *Evelyn Hope* giving Charles tips and new ideas about boats. He was a member of the RNVR and hoped to be called up for the volunteer services' spying missions around the Mediterranean, being organized in part by his and Gwynne's mutual friend Henry Denham.

Pris's baby arrived on 10 November and Elizabeth described her name, Sabrina, as 'most beautiful'. She supposed Pris had been reading Milton's *Comus* and then – in case she hadn't – tells the story, and for a brief moment evokes a feeling of contemplation and ease, so rare in her letters. 'As you know . . . Sabrina was the nymph of the Severn, and as she was born in Bristol it's most appropriate. The Spirit in *Comus* sings the most exquisite song to Sabrina, summoning her from the cool translucent waves to come and save the lady who is under the spell of the wicked Comus. It's the most lovely bit in *Comus* which is one of my absolute favourite poems.'

Mike and Nan saw much of Elizabeth and Charles, introducing them to friends. This was the Riviera, the Côte d'Azur, where until late each year the skies remained intensely and cloudlessly blue, where a luxurious vegetation threw up flowers sometimes gaudy in their brilliance in gardens surrounding terracotta-roofed and white-walled towns, and luxury villas overlooking a sea hardly ever anything but warm. Since Lord Brougham popularized it in the nineteenth century, famed or notorious as the pleasure-ground of the rich, one came to see and be seen, a refuge from stern northern winters: with the resorts of Hyères, St Raphaël, Cannes, Antibes, Nice, Menton and more. The Riviera is bordered by the Alps: the Maritimes to the east rise at points to almost 7000 feet, snowy and magnificent. Provence to the west, sometimes parched grey-green and arid, was the land where olives, wine and garlic had been transformed over 2000 years into some of the best food in the world. Socializing was hectic and very bibulous.

In November there was talk of Mike and Charles making the journey by train to Venice and sailing back on Mike's boat. Elizabeth would spend the time while they were away on shore with Nan. Although Mike's changeability made the venture seem unlikely, the men had set off before the end of December. They were not well suited. Charles was assertively pacifist, a conscientious objector, whereas Mike, whatever the surface self-presentation, was essentially patriotic. Later in the war he was to distinguish himself in more than one episode of bravery and heroic endurance. Their differences of political opinion quickly surfaced and the rest of the journey was not particularly amicable, though Charles did retain his envy and admiration for Cumberlege's seamanship as he masterfully sailed the retrieved yacht back to Antibes.

The tension between the two was typical of Charles's relations with the men of Elizabeth's milieu. They belonged to the ruling class, whereas Charles was an outsider. They were the beneficiaries of the system and, for most of them, when it came to the test patriotism was both reasonable and instinctive. For Charles it was neither. He had nothing to be grateful for, no reason for loyalty, having been sneered at and maltreated too many times in his formative years. On balance Charles's attitude proved more his loss than gain: it made for limitations, and he would have led a happier life could he have transcended some of his resentments. He had educated himself to move among the more privileged classes, but in general the men he met there did not have the largeness of vision and imagination to reach out to him. He was always on the fringe, his presence tolerated, not welcomed.

Elizabeth was a rebel, not an outsider. She sometimes felt misplaced, but she was not a misfit. The problems of feeling oneself either misplaced or a misfit seem naturally to suggest the life of a nomad, a wanderer, or escape as a response. Before they met Charles and Elizabeth had both done their fair share of restless wandering and were at one in their plan of escape to the Isles of Greece. Their difficulty in living together was a social difficulty. They were united in their love of literature; there was no incompatibility of sensibility, but there was great incompatibility in social style and expectations. Charles's social malaise was effectively curable, whereas Elizabeth's was not social at all. Charles had spent years at the rump of society, unsure where the next meal was coming from, or where he would sleep that night. Elizabeth was Anglo-Saxon (still, in the 1930s, the world's dominant race) and at the upper end of the social scale. However much she went in for slumming she always assumed that in times of trouble she would be rescued. And she was, often.

In some fashion Elizabeth was aware of all this. Charles records her words as follows:

'Always live on a ship. Never wear anything but a blue jersey and an old pair of flannel trousers. Never wash the salt out of your hair.'

'Why?'

'Then perhaps I shall stay in love with you.'

In confining him to shipboard she was telling him that their liaison could only hold in a context outside the everyday, away from land – outside time.

While the two men were away Nan and Elizabeth had spent Christmas together and Elizabeth told Felicité that she hadn't had time for anything except drinking or sleeping – in fact, she hadn't been sober for ten days. If she thought she could get back, she would go home for a month or two, but knew she couldn't face England for the duration. 'God knows it's bloody enough here and I feel pretty well suicidal, but I should hate to cause the family the caper of a funeral in unconsecrated ground.' They had a party on New Year's Eve, 'which was quite fun, except that nothing now is fun', and she had to get drunk to find anything at all amusing.

The busy aimlessness of this socializing was interspersed with news of friends and their activities as the war progressed. Many from Malta had joined up or been promoted and Elizabeth wrote to Pris that she couldn't imagine Mike Edwards as a Major. What amused her more than anything else was 'old Hiles' joining a unit of the Rifle Brigade. 'Trust Hilary to get himself into good company.' (Hilary Magnus's friendship, initially with Felicité, extended to all the Gwynne girls.) Their cousin Quintin Hogg, a close friend of Hilary's, was also in the Brigade and Elizabeth says she thinks him less suitably placed there.

Leonard Watkins had offered his services to the army but had not yet been called upon: meanwhile his brother Arthur had become an ARP warden in Eastbourne. He had already practically killed a man by suffocation during a bandage test and set light to himself in the process of extinguishing a fire in a shed. He told Elizabeth that Stanford was a fireman in Oxford. 'After these two pieces of information nobody can say that the local authorities are devoid of a sense of humour.'

Mike Cumberlege had finally been called up and was now, Elizabeth wrote, second in command of the 'English Contraband doings at Marseilles'. He had in fact taken up spying for them: 'quietly seeking information on Italian defences in the Mediterranean', as Henry Denham later wrote in his book *Inside the Nazi Ring* (John Murray, 1981). Elizabeth said, 'He is a lucky devil.' Although she was annoyed at the nonchalance with which Mike seemed to fall on his feet in the most remarkable way, she had the good grace to add that he did work damned hard on board the *Landfall* when he was there.

Early in the spring of 1940, when Elizabeth and Charles had been in Antibes for several months, Elizabeth enthusiastically talked of meetings with a new friend, Norman Douglas. She had recently fallen under the spell of this elderly author, whose erudite travel-novel-writing of books like *Siren Land*, *Old Calabria*, *South Wind* (with their remarkable disquisitions and diatribes on food), had by this time achieved cult status with the travelled Englishman, and she was enthralled.

She introduced Norman and Charles, who recorded an evening spent together at the kind of place Douglas thrived in – a 'dirty' Italian restaurant. Norman was his inimitable self: gracious, his fine manners concealing a well-developed arrogance; witty, pragmatic, learned, following his gruff habit of *ex cathedra* utterances with 'It stands to reason', a favourite justification, then forestalling further argument with, 'Take or leave it.' In *The Voyage of the Evelyn Hope* Charles captures something of the Douglas style, but his account is noticeably less adulatory than Elizabeth's. Unsurprisingly, there appears to have been a mutual wariness and Douglas was ultimately disapproving of him. Any negative response Charles might in turn have had to Douglas was not going to deter Elizabeth, who told Felicité that she very much enjoyed the time she spent with the spry 72-year-old. She described him as full of fun and wit, not 'caring a hang' for anyone or anything. He had taken her up to some of the little towns and villages in the hills, and utterly charmed her. Elizabeth had read only two of his books, one of which, *South Wind*, she hadn't liked; she asked him to lend her some more, and she did manage to borrow one. It seemed to Elizabeth that he knew Europe 'from end to end', and almost everyone in it as well. Two years later, again writing to Felicité about Douglas, she said that she regretted ever having left him all alone in the South of France – she would have been quite happy to have stayed with him. He was such good company that hearing about places and things from him was as good as seeing them with one's own eyes.

The burgeoning friendship between this unlikely pair grew into a relationship which was to affect Elizabeth profoundly, maintaining its influence upon her long after Douglas's death on Capri in 1952. Although she didn't recognize until much later quite how momentous the occasion of her meeting with him was, at the time she certainly felt mentally revived and inspired by Douglas's company and now sought it out whenever possible.

She was relatively familiar with the Riviera from those recent holidays and the novelty of this visit for her had been as much in living there, and on a boat. After six months, though, she was exhausted and made restless by inactivity and the lightweight nature of most of those with whom she socialized. Her friendship with the Cumberleges, on whom she had been so dependent, was becoming strained too. Writing to Priscilla, she complained that Nan Cumberlege and her sister Nora were clothes snobs, and jealous of her because she had clothes from Worth and Maggy Rouff. They indignantly asked why she wasted money on them – and she felt her own indignant and justified reply might well have been to ask why they wasted their money drinking champagne all day in the most expensive bar on the coast. She also said that Nan had changed: 'always arrived late for dinner'. Despite her criticisms Elizabeth did add that Nan had been kind to her and that Priscilla must not breathe a word of these indiscretions to anyone.

She maintained that although the English community on the Riviera was 'peculiar anyhow', the worries engendered by the war and too much leisure are 'now making people odd'. This was the recognizable frustration of living in a provincial, albeit sophisticated, goldfish-bowl expatriate society and, accustomed to a larger stage, she recounted the minutiae with a sharp but weary eye. She told Pris that 'the gossip is something staggering here. Malta was *nothing* to it. One never has to tell anybody where you've been the day before because they always tell you *first* and if you forget what day someone has invited you out you've only to ask the first person you meet in the town and they'll be able to inform you.' She did not care what the gossips would try and invent about herself and Douglas. 'Probably that I'm his illegitimate daughter, or that we sacrifice goats up on the hills – anything for a story.'

When Elizabeth met Douglas in Antibes early in 1940 he was in rented rooms with little money, but enduring an enforced exile from Florence with the famous Douglas equanimity, bite and humour intact. He had spent many years living in Florence, maintaining friendships with most of the remarkable group of expatriate English who lived in and around the city. Atypically, for these self-imposed exiles, Douglas also befriended Italians. A number of these had always been young boys, for whom his predilection had necessitated his flight from England to Italy in 1917. In 1937, however, Douglas was again in trouble, this time for his alleged affair with a little girl. After seducing two brothers he had in fact bought their little sister a new set of clothes. When questioned as to their origin she revealed her patron, and Douglas was immediately ordered to leave Italy.

In Norman Douglas Elizabeth found a man of great charisma and charm who at the age of seventy-two was fascinating to her without representing any threat of sexual predatoriness. (Always attractive to women and retaining many as friends, Douglas no longer had physical relationships with them after the age of about fifty.) The novelist Sybille Bedford, who later became a close friend of Elizabeth's, had also fallen under the Douglas spell before the war and describes him as 'very masculine, very attractive . . . robust, but so gracious'. Intelligent and sensitive women were often drawn to Douglas, responding to his robust humour, his quirky, wayward, yet ultimately scholarly methods and beguiling way of dealing out his vast knowledge to those younger and less informed than himself.

Elizabeth's relationships more often than not involved something close to exploitation and her friend Doreen Thornton says, 'Oh, she always had slaves.' She wasn't often inclined towards anything in between, unless the other party stood up to her, and then Elizabeth frequently came off best. Usually charming about it, and often grateful, she nevertheless took it as her due to accept favours rather than to dispense them. In like manner she inflicted more pain than she received, and if she recognized her will to make others subservient to her she chose not to comment on it. In her relationship with

Douglas, for once there was no doubt who was master. For Elizabeth, Douglas clearly represented something of the father lost in childhood. She had found a kind of soul-mate. His effect on her was complex, but she was inspired, fascinated by his erudition and manner of presentation, and touched and flattered that so distinguished an author should find her acceptable company.

In cast of mind they were very compatible. They both respected, even worshipped the Fact – what *is*: a respect for what is simply *because* it is. This was a matter of temperament even more than doctrine, of unconscious presupposition rather than explicit theory. In Europe seen as peculiarly British, it is given the name of empiricism. And the predominance of this temperament accounts for the enduring talent of the people of these islands for natural science, engineering and the useful arts. Writings about Douglas usually claim that he was a scientist as well as a travel writer and novelist. This is misleading, for he was a natural historian, not a natural scientist. Like Elizabeth he had little feeling for the abstract, for explanation, for the poetry of analysis; was perhaps even contemptuous of such things. This is the key to both his strengths and his weaknesses.

In spite of being separated in age by almost half a century, the common elements in Elizabeth and Norman's lives helped to bind them in an unlikely friendship. Both were familiar with Austria and Germany (Douglas grew up in Austria and was one-quarter German, three-quarters Scottish, but German was his first language). They were social equals; each a part of that vast, intricate web of social and family ties which extended amongst the European upper classes, making it rare for one to meet a person to whom one was not either related, however distantly, or who at least knew someone who knew someone whom one knew oneself. Both Elizabeth and Douglas had reacted against their backgrounds, yet had a strong sense of social order; both were at heart diffident, but were also robustly individual and capable of ruthlessness and arrogance.

There is no doubt that Douglas – older, more experienced, learned without being in the least academic – was better able than Elizabeth herself to articulate what she was fumbling towards in her journey South away from England.

The educated British resonated to the cities, the ruins, the landscape; to the golden light and warmth of the South. It was all so familiar from history, literature and art – this was the classical world, the root of their civilization. Once South they were emancipated from the web of Northern constraints. More than one such visitor wrote that on his first visit to the Mediterranean it was all so familiar it was as if he had arrived home. Here, where man was seemingly more practised at harnessing and living in harmony with his surroundings than in any other part of Europe, the traveller was able to reconnect with what Norman Douglas called those '. . . elemental and perma-nent things . . . Casting off outworn weeds of thought they escaped to a world . . . removed from the wilderness of our ever-changing circumstances.' In *Siren Land* Douglas says, 'Many of us would do well to *mediterraneanize* ourselves for a season, to quicken those ethnic roots from which has sprung so much of what is best in our natures.'

Douglas's was a complex and refined aesthetic hedonism, based on a deeply felt antipathy to what he had experienced as Christianity, for which he substituted, with a real knowledge of the classical world, his own form of morality – some would call it amorality. His escape into exile from Northern Europe, and his rejection of much of what it represented, had not landed him by accident in the region which lay close to the centre of the ancient Greco-Roman world. His mode was nearer to a modern Hellenism than to anything from further north. The Hellenes were the first people to become intoxicated with ideas, to examine how we learn and to develop the concept of suspended judgement. If the Mediterranean had been no more than the region of empirical and temperate hedonism that Norman Doug-las depicts, it would never have served as the origin, the focus, of what has become the nearest to a world-culture that mankind has ever developed.

Without being as yet aware of it, Elizabeth too had within her a similar strain of anti-Christianity and warmed to the hedonistic spirit of the Mediterranean. (As well as the better qualities she was also to demonstrate some of the worse ones characteristic of the pagan mentality – most notably in her unwillingness to forgive.) In her erratic way she had tried to throw off 'outworn modes of thought' without sacrificing her deep feeling for truth. Here also Douglas was the right model for her, with his precise observation, empirical exactitude, his knowledge of literature and capacity for accurate scholarship. With minor differences they were at one, both in how they set about it, and to where they had chosen to escape. Underlying all this was the consistent theme of escape, which permeated both Elizabeth's and Douglas's vision.

For centuries the South had enticed and beckoned educated Englishmen, so much so that Dr Johnson could write: 'The grand object of travelling is to see the shores of the Mediterranean.' They had gone in the Middle Ages as pilgrims to holy sites, later in search of education, health, and finally in the eighteenth and nineteenth centuries as 'aesthetic escapists'. With the growth of the railways and the middle classes, the nineteenth century saw the Grand Tourism of the seventeenth and eighteenth centuries gradually eclipsed by mass tourism and the eager customers of Thomas Cook.

It is hard to find a Victorian poet, painter, novelist, philosopher or historian who didn't make the pilgrimage South at least once. So much had been written on Egypt, the Levant and the Mediterranean by the end of the century that some thought there was nothing left to say. By 1845 the traveller and collector Robert Curzon was already complaining that, for example, 'The public were overwhelmed by little volumes about palm trees and camels and reflections on the Pyramids.' But the allure of the South did not diminish with familiarity, nor did the voracious appetite for literature feeding every aspect of this allure. Apart from the great travellers of earlier centuries, during the nineteenth century and into this one there was a host of literary figures: Thackeray, Robert Louis Stevenson, Dickens, Henry James, George Eliot, the Trollopes, Samuel Butler, Gissing, Belloc, Ford Madox Ford, Forster, Lawrence, Osbert Sitwell, Robert Byron, Patrick Kinross, Cyril Connolly, Lawrence Durrell, Patrick Leigh Fermor . . . and the list continues.

Relations between Elizabeth and Charles had become strained since before Christmas and by now she was spending time away from him and the *Evelyn Hope*, either with friends such as Norman and the Cumberleges, or helping a rich American, Stanley, in a soup kitchen he had set up for the local poor, recently enlarged by the costly addition of a huge dining hall panelled in oak. One senses Charles's ultimate isolation from Elizabeth and her privileged friends when he succinctly conveys his scorn at the rich man's 'war effort'. He notes that the interior of Stanley's hall now has 'refectory tables, Jacobean chairs, and an assortment of china and cutlery which would have frightened away the poor had they not been too hungry to notice'.

Elizabeth wrote to Priscilla in early January of her work in the soup kitchen and said there were a great many very poor people there, mostly Italians with huge families. If a family had a soldier home on leave, they would be given extra food. She described how galling it was for the soldiers to come back from the trenches to be fed by charity. It is worth noting that Douglas, like Charles, would have been contemptuous of these efforts. Helpful and generous to friends and individuals in need, he had no time for organized welfare, for charity in the abstract, or away from home.

Into the New Year of 1940, and on the same theme of wartime deprivations, Elizabeth wondered what Pris's staple food now was — she supposed it to be bread and cheese without butter, and potatoes. In these enforced months on the Riviera she had now spent many hours wandering the markets on her own. More recently she had luxuriated in the company of Douglas, whose knowledge on the foods and traditions of the region was boundless. In spite of feeling some guilt, in her letters Elizabeth cannot hide an unceasing delight in the sumptuous variety and quality of produce available on this paradisia-cal coastline. Back in September she had already remarked to Priscilla on how impossible it was to believe in the war there, under sunshine and blue skies, and with piles of brilliant fruit, rainbow fish and straw-covered wine jugs in the markets. To Elizabeth on the Riviera, the whole idea of the war was like a Hollywood extravaganza by Cecil B. de Mille.

A few months later the list of foods Elizabeth recites to Priscilla is striking in the variety still obtainable compared with the sparsity in rationed Britain. She found meat and butter expensive, but said that cheese was cheap, and of a great variety. Vegetables cost little, and salads — lettuce, endives, etc. — were never more than about 1½d. There were ravioli, gnocchi, and ready-prepared food, all of which were inexpensive. She and Charles largely existed on stews, because they could be cooked on the coal stove that heated the cabin — a more effective way of cooking that also saved paraffin. Elizabeth recommended to Pris 'a very good dish' that she found in a French cookery book; cheap and nourishing, the recipe was later quoted with minimal alteration in *Mediterranean Food*:

> 1 lb liver (calves', or pigs' or ox, I use ox because it's the
> cheapest and quite as good done this way)
> 1½–2 lbs of carrots
> 4 onions
> about ½ pint of Espagnole Sauce

Cut the liver in the usual long slices, salt and pepper then wrap them up in the caul (like Angela used to do for beef loaf, or greaseproof paper I think would do), and fry lightly in margarine with the onions cut up. When they are golden take them out of the pan and make an Espagnole sauce (see recipe below).

Put the sauce through the sieve, put it in a big casserole, bring it to the boil; put in the liver wrapped up, the onions, and the carrots peeled and cut into rounds. Put in the herbs, salt, etc. and cook in a very slow oven or over a very low flame for about 2½ hours. When it's done take the liver out of its bag and serve it in the same dish.

*Espagnole Sauce   In the butter and gravy which is in the pan from frying the liver and onions, put some more butter (margarine I mean), add 1 teaspoon of flour, let it fry for a minute or two till it goes brown, add 1 small chopped onion and one small chopped carrot, let it fry two minutes more, add about ½ pint of stock if you have it, otherwise a cube of Bovril or Oxo melted in water (which is what I always use). Let it cook slowly for about 5 minutes adding salt, pepper, thyme, bayleaf, and water if it gets too thick, then stir in about a tablespoon of tomato pureé (Heinz Tomato Soup or ketchup would do) and when it's cooked about 3 more minutes strain it, put it into the casserole in which you're going to cook the liver.

Actually this is an excessively simple dish to make and is excellent . . .

The Espagnole Sauce should be a good dark brown, so I always put in some gravy salt, which is dark brown and colours it – I expect Connie [Priscilla's cook] uses it. In the ordinary way you have to cook Espagnole Sauce for about 30 or 40 minutes very slowly, then put in the tomato and put it through the strainer. I find it very handy for all kinds of things, and it's quite good with spaghetti as a change, or you can put in some blanched pieces of orange peel and orange juice with a little red currant jelly and it makes an orange sauce which is very good with escalope de veau or with chicken, duck, etc.

Another thing we have quite often is dried haricot beans soaked and then stewed with small pieces of gammon (what they call bacon here) and a few sausages. Of course you can't get smoked sausages in England except at a vast price ... If you add a spoonful of ginger to the beans it improves its taste enormously. [And here she makes a comment which in the future would become a dictum.] The secret of all these things is to cook them dead slow. You could put them at the side of the fire and let them cook for hours – the less they boil the better ... What makes even boring food like spaghetti eatable here is that there's such a variety of things to make sauces with – olives are very cheap, so are mushrooms, you can even buy a little tin of truffles for 6d. and of course you can always put wine into anything without being extravagant ...

Elizabeth described the variety of fish, and said a sort of Pilaff with mussels, pimentos and other shell fish made a wonderful dish. She complained that the coffee shortage was a great blow, the tea disgusting, and the olive oil exorbitantly priced, which was hard on the people there, as they cooked everything in oil.

This remarkable letter illuminates Elizabeth's level of knowledge and working practices at this time. In spite of the recommendation of 'Oxo cubes melted in water ... and Heinz Tomato Soup or ketchup', a change has taken place since those first tentative days at the stove in Regent's Park Road. The recipe may initially have been culled from a book, but more importantly it is the annotations and instructions to her sister which reflect her growing knowledge and confidence.

Apparently this was not Elizabeth's first offer of culinary advice.

Quite recently a little manuscript book in her hand was offered up for sale. While sharing the flat with Marian Butterworth in London, Elizabeth had written out a selection of recipes, for interest and use, as a present for her friend. In an attached note of authentication (1979) Elizabeth said that she had them from several sources, all but a few of which she could remember. Some came from the inspirational Angela, Pris's cheerful Maltese cook who had given Elizabeth those first instructions in cooking; next there was the Countess Morphy's *Recipes of All Nations*, Elizabeth's trophy from Selfridges; then others from *Farmhouse Fare* (a little book she recommended forty years on in a list of favourite cookery books) and finally, some from Mrs Leyel's *Gentle Art*.

These four books mentioned in her choice of recipes for Marian remained well used and were among those she took with her on board the *Evelyn Hope*. Fortunately we know that these made up the core of her little shipboard collection, because they and several others were subsequently lost, and Elizabeth later wrote in consternation asking Pris to find duplicates for her.

I'm terribly sorry to bother you with such details at such a time but one has to live all the same . . . All my cookery books are of course lost, including the ones I collected myself. Now could you ask Dillon or someone to order me the following, I will tell the bank to pay her bill [she refers here to Miss Dillon in the early days of the bookshop], and ask her to send them to you, to keep them for me until I come home or until after the war – I think it better to get them now because after the war these things might be out of print . . .

The Recipes of All Nations	(can only get at Selfridges)
The Finer Cooking	Marcel Boulestin
The Gentle Art of Cookery	Phoenix Library
The Farmhouse Cookery Book	(Published by the *Farmer's Weekly* I believe)
Good Savouries	Ambrose Heath
100 *Ways of Cooking Eggs*	Adair and Boulestin
Hors d'oeuvres and Savouries	Boulestin

French Wines	Paul de Caragnae. . .?
The Epicure's Companion	Edward Bunyard, Dent

Albeit a brief list, we can glean a fair idea of where her interests lay; with the likes of Boulestin. She was instinctively drawn to his crusade for fresh, subtle and simple food, what she later described in an article on him for the *Wine and Food* quarterly in 1965 as 'Boulestin's intelligence, sense and taste' and 'that feeling for authenticity which alone is true luxury'. Along with Marcelle Morphy and Hilda Leyel, Marcel Boulestin's delightful and approachable books do not stress the accuracy of quantities or the detail of instructions, but Elizabeth was already feeling confident (or as she later said, ignorant) enough to forgo the dry detail of more technical works in favour or inspiration and character. (Not that Elizabeth despises accuracy or detail – quite otherwise – but she expects her readers to be attuned to these necessities, and wants to avoid the dampening of individuality and the constraint attendant on over-specification.)

Although under straitened circumstances Elizabeth had by now ample time and opportunity to sample the foods of the South. As anyone will know who has experienced them, it is the markets of the South which first enthral, most extravagantly in the vast arenas of Marseilles, Nice or Naples, but any smaller town has its own and striking version. Here, with the animated bustling backdrop of clatter and chatter, Elizabeth had been enticed by the careless profusion of vegetables, many almost unheard of in England; marvelled at the glowing purples, pinks, scarlet reds, acid yellows of apricots and peaches, colours of the same intensity as the unfailing sun under which they flourished alongside myriad lettucy greens. The market air was heady with the musky, ripe scent from great bunches of glistening basil, silvery-grey wild thyme, marjoram and rosemary, brought down from the parched grey-green olive mountainsides. She had seen the fish, whose variety promised such possibilities: fresh sardines, spiky sea urchins, *poulpes*, tuna, red mullet, oysters and any number of shellfish; and other spiny little creatures ideal for the garlicky aromatic Provençal stews, blended with such skill and assurance after centuries of practice. In the cooler months there were still fruits and vegetables, and by now rabbits, game birds, and those tiny flying mouthfuls, figpeckers, and other wild birds, still sold by the trayful and so beloved of all the peoples of the South.

Elizabeth had eaten in the grand restaurants of the Riviera serving their lofty, emasculated menus. But she had also spent better hours in restaurants where the food served up was the true *cuisine à l'huile* – the cooking at whose heart is a refined blend of garlic and olive. She had eaten in expensive Provençal restaurants like Isnard's in Marseilles and Félix in Antibes, with reputations to keep up and Provençal wines like Chateauneau-du-Pape to match, where the much-abused *bouillabaisse* – the fish dish with garlic and olive oil – was prepared to perfection. She had eaten in many more modest establishments too, restaurants and cafés around the markets and quaysides where local specialities could often be had for very little.

But Elizabeth had also tried her own hand. And, with what she had seen and eaten in mind, although writing that they existed mainly on stews, she had also carried back the abundance of the markets to the galley of the *Evelyn Hope*, with other projects. Her cookery books were in regular use and new French finds were added too. Elizabeth did not spend her whole time bent over the galley stove, but she was experimenting and learning, picking up ideas and hints from those about her – a market stallholder, a fisherman cook, a friendly restaurant proprietor – taking down recipes and adding to her growing repertoire.

Most intriguing of all, in the letter requesting Pris to find duplicates of her lost books, was the brief and tantalizing reference to her misery at the loss of 'my precious cookery book'. From those earlier letters written in the mid-1930s when she was living with Charles, we know that Elizabeth had already begun to write, probably fiction. But here we have the earliest reference to her intentions. Although she may never have spoken about it to her friends, long before her first publication her future path was already half anticipated. At the time of its loss in 1940 the collection of recipes she had slowly put together had grown large enough for her to have been contemplating publication.

The stormy weather was nerve-racking and Charles remembered Douglas's advice: 'If you want to see Europe it is your last chance. There won't be any Europe left after the war. I envy you . . .' Charles wrote to the authorities in Nice for permission to move the *Evelyn Hope*. No reply came so he went in person. After a day spent waiting in corridors with worried Italians seeking repatriation he was told to put his application in writing. He wrote again and again received no reply. Finally he realized that although the French would not categorically deny permission to a British ship to move around their waters freely, by stalling they indicated that this was in effect their intention. He decided that when the time seemed right, they would have to leave in secret.

Meanwhile Elizabeth was profoundly apologetic for not having written to Pris for so long but she'd had flu and the boat was ashore being painted, and altogether she felt unable to do anything at all. Not doing anything does seem to have included regular meetings with friends, and she felt that she spent the entire day cooking, eating, washing up, marketing and meeting people for drinks.

She was enormously relieved that soon there would be money from an insurance company sorting out the aftermath of a previous theft at John Street, when many of hers and Charles's possessions had been stolen. She had written to Felicité in irritation and impatience at the procrastination of the insurance company's broker, Jewell, a friend of Stella's. Elizabeth's method of dealing with the situation highlights her expectation of sufficiently respectful treatment for herself, and her impatience with those who either didn't cooperate or wasted her time. Among other intended tactics was her intention to write a weekly postcard reminding the company of their obligations to her, the desired effect being to exasperate them into finishing the business with speed, to get rid of her as quickly as she wished to get rid of them.

This money had been so eagerly awaited that upon its arrival Elizabeth said to Felicité that she felt as if there was now no longer anthing left to look forward to. In view of the present state of relations between herself and Charles this statement was probably not an exaggerated description of her feelings. She didn't dwell on it, though, and was soon talking about sending pretty materials found in Cannes for Felicité and Pris (these were the Provençal prints that remained in vogue for years to come), with advice on lengths, possible styles and instructions to dressmakers. In an earlier letter she had bemoaned the fact that without the insurance money she was unable to buy any new clothes, which on the Riviera in the 1930s, just as now, was a serious drawback to fashionable self-respect. Everything she had left after the robbery was in such a 'disreputable' state from being constantly worn that she could hardly be seen out.

Descriptions of Elizabeth's appearance throughout her life usually reveal as much about the describer: there were some who were won by her dark, un-English prettiness, hinting at her exotic ancestry, and others who were not seduced, preferring instead the paler, less predatory, sometimes asexual English look with its implications of good breeding and refinement. Some found Elizabeth threatening at times in her seriousness and directness. Nevertheless, there was also genuine selfconsciousness and diffidence, as when she looks away from the camera in the fine studio photograph later taken of her in Egypt, for all the tart comments attached to the copy she sent her mother.

Having decided on escape from Antibes, Charles was advised by the Greek sailor Costa, who had returned with Mike and himself from Venice, that although they were still beset with heavy winter storms, the beginning of May would bring the Mistral. A herald to the light winds of summer, this stormy wind was exactly what was needed, and Charles now intended to harness its strength to get them across to Corsica. Elizabeth meanwhile was writing to Felicité on headed writing paper from one of the best Provençal restaurants, Grand Café-Restaurant chez Félix au Port Antibes; she was obliged to write on land because the gales of the past month made the boat 'rock like a shell'. Charles decided that they would sail on the third day of the first Mistral in May.

Later Costa helped him to pull the boat up out of the water on to the slip and scrape her down. In the six winter months she hadn't gathered much weed, so rubbing her down with coconut husks was not too arduous a task. They 'finished off with a coat of oil, and she shone'.

With the arrival of May Charles spent his days watching the mountains, waiting for the little puffs of cloud that would signal the coming of the wind. He wrote: 'Just before midday on 17 May it began to blow, gently at first, rippling the water of the bay, and then suddenly with gale force, bitterly cold, out of the north. The few fishing boats in the outer harbour doubled their mooring lines. It settled down to blow steadily from the north-west.'

On 10 May the Germans had finally begun their long-awaited attack on the Low Countries. Only the previous night Germany had professed its friendship, but now soldiers had crossed the Meuse and were pouring into Belgium and Holland, without pretext or warning. The Dutch had opened their dykes and were flooding their little country to stem the invading troops, but it would prove too late. By 15 May the Germans had swiftly crushed Belgium and Holland and would now break through French lines and move forward into France at terrifying speed. Official documents there were being destroyed, the evacuation of Paris had begun.

Charles said that Viscountess Astor epitomized their feelings about the war better than anyone when she declared that it was 'not only dangerous, it was dull'. He sums up how these feelings of monotony changed to bewilderment when the Russians invaded Finland and the initial incomprehension of most people regarding the significance and magnitude of this war. 'As far as we could see, to all intents and purposes we were at war with Russia, Russia was at war with Germany and Germany was at war with us; whilst somewhere to the East and somehow remotely connected to it all, the Chinese were fighting the Japanese. For the first time it became apparent that the war would last very long.'

CHAPTER EIGHT

Escape
(1940)

CHARLES WROTE that with the fear that something might stop them they 'told nobody that we were leaving but gave a cocktail party at five o'clock' on the eve of 19 May 1940. 'Even Norman overcame his dislike of boats and was on board.' Early the next morning, with the Mistral blowing strongly and no possibility of turning back, they weighed anchor and the *Evelyn Hope* slipped quietly out of the harbour. After a few miles under power they caught the full force of the wind in their sails and went full speed ahead, neither of them sleeping during that night. The next day they discovered that, 15 miles off course, they were nearing Corsica.

On 20 May Elizabeth wrote to Pris with the news that they had left Antibes and arrived in Corsica after twenty-six hours. She said it was terribly difficult to get permits and dangerous to tell anyone where you were going. She was careful not to give away any details of their plans; she didn't know how long they would stay or when they would leave. Should Italy enter the war, they would have plenty of warning and time to get back to France – an optimistic belief on Elizabeth's part, as the invasion of France was in progress. To Elizabeth, sheltered in that calm sea, it seemed impossible that the Germans were pounding into France and that an 'absolute battle of Armageddon' was going on.

Amongst these comments there were hints at what their real intentions were: perhaps to go to some other country. She couldn't think exactly where, but was finding it impossible to live in a boat in those regions. She had become so sickened by the war that the only way to retain a sense of proportion was to get away from it for a bit.

She told Pris that on her last visit to Corsica she didn't get to see Bastia and was now glad to be there. It was an attractive little place, dilapidated, like most Corsican towns. 'The last visit' refers to the journey down France with Doreen Brownhill and Diana Morgan during the mid-Thirties, when Elizabeth had come across on her own to Corsica. Doreen and Diana's parents would not give permission for their visit, but at the time Elizabeth's mother was in Jamaica and, according to Doreen, 'didn't have much say as to where she went, or appear to worry about it that much either'.

Elizabeth revealed that her only sadness at leaving the Riviera was in the loss of Norman Douglas, who had heaped innumerable kindnesses on her and was one of the most fascinating people she believed she could ever hope to meet. She then recommended Priscilla to look at *How about Europe?* by Douglas because it was very stimulating. In fact the book is a weakly argued diatribe, which has been called 'a sort of pink Nietzscheanism', against the awfulness of conditions in England; the puritanism of the licensing laws, the food, hotels, cooking, the misery of the climate. Douglas calls the British 'a pack of masochists' and maintains that they are weighed down by duty and sobriety. In his novel *South Wind* (Secker and Warburg, 1917) he has Count Caloveglia say that 'a plague has infected the whole world, a plague of repression'.

Elizabeth maintained that another Douglas book to be searched out was *Alone* (Secker and Warburg, 1921) – she preferred his travel books to his novels. And next she delivered a dream: that Priscilla could be with her in the beautiful sunshine. If the war were to end, they could all come out to the Mediterranean – none of them would have a farthing, but it would be better to be penniless in a warm climate than in England, and one could 'always line in fish, and [there is] maccaroni'.

Leaving Corsica after several days of regal treatment, they set sail for Greece. A storm forced them to shelter in the harbour of the tiny island of Giglio (now a major tourist resort, then little more than a rocky outcrop with a few people surviving by quarrying). Again they set out for the South and finally Elizabeth informed Priscilla that they had intended going straight from Corsica to Piraeus, but were held up by bad weather. She was still hoping to escape from the war on a 'paradise' island and maintain her exile from England, to which she felt little allegiance at the time.

'By the time you get this we shall probably have sailed. We shall go to Athens where I know one or two people and then possibly go to the islands. Our plan is to try and find some little house somewhere and keep it ready in case any of you want to come out. In any case when the war is over it will be impossible to live in England and I really feel I may be of some use to you all if you have somewhere to come to . . .' The boat was full of provisions, the engine working perfectly – 'with luck we should be in Greece a week or so from now'. Little could Elizabeth have imagined quite what was in store for them.

Weeks later Elizabeth wrote a long letter to Pris from Athens, outlining all that had befallen them, when she was, for the first time, forced to confront seriously difficult conditions of war. She did so with both an admirable resilience and a self-centredness that must at times have seemed quite breathtaking.

She began with their stop on the island of Giglio in Italy, where they put in during a fearful storm. The bad weather kept them there for five days – the people, even the officials, were more than friendly, giving them gifts, inviting them to meals, and seeing to all their needs. On the morning they were due to sail, one of them came down and told Elizabeth and Charles that the news was bad, and warned them to leave as soon as they could. By that time it was obvious that Elizabeth's over-optimistic hopes of going back to France could not be realized. Their only course was to stay completely out of territorial waters while at the same time keeping the coast of Italy in sight, watching to see if the lights were on at night – if they went out, they were to make a dash right round Sicily.

On the first day they had a very good wind, and in twenty-four hours were past Ostia. After that they encountered nothing but light winds and flat calms – perfect weather for sailing, but the situation caused too much anxiety to be enjoyable. They were also becoming weary, not 'heaving-to' much at night because of their desperate hurry. Off Ischia they were stopped by an Italian warship, which then followed them all night across the Bay of Naples and past Capri. Elizabeth wrote, 'That morning was the most beautiful dawn I ever saw in all my life', with Vesuvius in the distance and Capri behind them.

It took them five days to reach Stromboli, and at five o'clock in the morning on 10 June, with Stromboli in sight, an Italian cruiser passed them. They dipped the ensign, and the ship replied to the salute, giving Elizabeth and Charles the impression that England was not yet at war with Italy. They thought that later that day they would be through the Straits of Messina, and then into the open sea, with Greece the next land they would see. As they passed Stromboli, they stopped a fisherman and bought a lobster from him; Elizabeth called it 'exquisite, the last decent meal we were to have for weeks'.

At five o'clock that afternoon the wind stopped altogether, and they started up the engine in order to enter the Straits that night. A fast Italian coastal motor boat raced out from Messina, taking no notice of them. As they approached the entrance to the Straits, the signal station signalled them to hoist their colours but was unable to see the *Evelyn*'s ensign; Charles ran another one up the main mast. The station then asked for their name, and they signalled back *Evelyn*. They progressed into the Straits and saw a dozen large warships from Sicily to Italy. No one tried to stop them, so they carried on through the Straits. Suddenly the warships began to 'dash in every direction, signalling, hooting & simply hurtling past. Then we saw that the decks were all cleared for action, sandbags round the gun turrets and all the rest of it & realised that something serious was up'.

Soon after a patrol boat ordered them into Messina harbour, but without revealing what was afoot. When another ship came up and towed them in, they saw that there was a blackout in Messina. A young officer came on board once they were in the harbour, and Elizabeth asked him if Italy had declared war: he wouldn't answer. Then a captain came alongside on the quay and Elizabeth repeated the question. He asked if they had a radio on board, and, when she said no, told her that Italy had declared war on the allies at five o'clock that afternoon. 'That moment,' wrote Elizabeth to Pris, 'was the worst of my life, without any exception.' Many horrors passed through her mind, not least the idea that if they'd been twelve hours earlier they would have been all right. Two officers immediately came on board and took away every scrap of paper with writing on it: charts, log book, letters, Charles's manuscripts, address books. The officers, whom Elizabeth found unfailingly polite and considerate throughout, then allowed them to stay on board for the night.

The next morning the officers came to collect them to be questioned, and took them to the Admiral's office. The first thing they were asked was: 'Vous êtes de l'Intelligence Service, n'est ce pas?', to which Elizabeth giggled in reply. They could hardly have been spies, 'cavorting into Messina & not even knowing they'd declared war'. They were told to go back on board to pack their things, for they were to be taken to the police. They were given two hours to do this. Thinking that any minute they might be sent straight to a concentration camp, they threw together clothes, books and bits and pieces, tying them into bundles because there were only two old suitcases on board. Charles just had time to take down the sails and stow them below. When the naval officers returned, they told them to leave the luggage and come back for it afterwards. While they had been waiting, Charles and Elizabeth had polished off a new bottle of apricot brandy.

They were kept waiting at the police station for three hours, during which time, they discovered afterwards, the chief of police had been fighting with other authorities to prevent them from being thrown into prison. Finally, 'after writing down when our grand-mothers were born & all the addresses we had had in England for the past 10 years', they were informed that they would be sent to a hotel, to be paid for by the Italian government, as they had no Italian currency. They were now told there was no question of them returning to the boat to collect their things; someone would be sent to fetch them. Someone did, and left behind half of what Elizabeth had requested, including two pairs of her spectacles. Someone was dispatched once again, and this time returned with nearly all of their books and 'a mass of perfectly useless clothes including C's dinner jacket, but without the things we really wanted, such as the type-writer, the coffee, the wine, brandy, etc. And they absolutely refused to go back again.'

The 'so-called' hotel to which they were sent was crawling with insects of every description, including 'cockroaches as big as mice, I am not exaggerating, so you can imagine how big the mice were in proportion'. It was full of Italians who had fled from Egypt, Tunis and other French and English colonies, and who were equally displeased to be in Italy. The proprietor's wife was Austrian, 'the meanest dirtiest harridan ever I saw'. They had a very small room, with a bed and a chair but no window, and a partition dividing it from the kitchen. The washing and sanitary arrangements were beneath Elizabeth's contempt. With the exception of the proprietor and his wife, everyone was kind and generous to them, even though Charles and Elizabeth had not a penny. The food was appalling, and of such a small quantity that they felt hungry all the time. The evening meal consisted of bread, half a dozen black olives, and very little else – no butter and no coffee (Elizabeth longingly recalled all the marvellous French coffee left on the boat). She then kicked up such a 'shindy' that they also gave them soup (pasta and water).

During the day Elizabeth found a secluded corner of the roof and spent all day sun-bathing, in the midst of the beginnings of war. Whenever she wanted anything she staged a 'fortissimo scene of hysteria' in English, German, French and Italian, in order to ensure that she was understood by everyone. She discovered that the Italians crumpled up 'astonishingly' when confronted by a screaming woman.

After two weeks in the hotel the police told them they were not regarded as suspicious and were free to travel on to Greece, but without the boat. Elizabeth and Charles then made every effort to retrieve their papers – 'the log book and Charles' half written novel, my address book, full of addresses and notes for Greece given me by Norman and others, & my precious cookery book & the typewriter'. There wasn't the slightest possibility of this, they informed them, but added that the war would surely be over in two weeks, when they could return to Messina and retrieve their boat, along with everything on it. This was, in fact, the attitude of all the Italians to whom Elizabeth spoke: 'they were so pulled up by the French débacle 3 days after Italy entered the war that they thought England was going to capitulate at the first sight of an Italian warship'.

The detainees were told they would be taken to Venice, where they would be put on a ship for Greece; this was the first of a long series of lies that nearly drove Elizabeth mad. Two guards arrived to escort them to Venice and promptly informed them that they were allowed to take only one bundle each – Charles and Elizabeth had eight bundles between them. Elizabeth categorically refused to leave without her luggage. Unless Charles and Elizabeth could get together the money for a taxi to the station, they would not be allowed to take their possessions – and that was that.

Charles threw himself upon the generosity of three destitute Greek sailors and asked them to carry the bags to the station. The sailors were so shocked by the behaviour of the Italians that they lent them eight lire for a taxi; the maid in the hotel gave them ten lire to buy cigarettes. They were now finally on their way, but Elizabeth was still distressed because they had had to leave behind her large packing case of books to an unknown fate.

Messina to Venice was a journey of two days, and on the way they spent five hours in the waiting room at Rome. They were given very little to eat and asked to be taken to the American Counsul; the reply was that there was no American Consul in Rome.

In Venice they were taken to a hotel for the night. The next day, after countless questions, Charles was thrown into a cell at the police station and Elizabeth was left in the gaoler's room all day. By this time they'd had nothing to eat for two days.

At three o'clock she made a 'scene' and they were given some macaroni. Elizabeth found out later that Charles had been told she had been sent to Yugoslavia, and that he would be kept in prison for another week or two and then sent to a concentration camp. She again asked to see the American Consul and was told he had gone. They were to leave for Trieste that night, so were given permission to see a yacht agent Charles had met in Venice when he was there with Mike Cumberlege. They had only a moment to speak with him, but he managed to give them fifty lire.

At the station they bought wine, but ran out of time before they could get any food. Upon arrival in Trieste they were given bread and a cup of coffee, in spite of the fact that they had the money for food and a hotel – and then they were both thrown into police cells. These were crawling with bugs, and stank. Everything was taken away from them except some cigarettes and matches. During the night two well-dressed young prostitutes, caught in a street brawl, were thrown into Elizabeth's cell. The only place to sleep was a sort of sloping shelf with filthy blankets, and Elizabeth found it impossible; she talked to the girls instead, and was grateful for the company. The police and gaolers were polite and not unfriendly. Charles and Elizabeth heard subsequently that Trieste had been bombed by the English, which undoubtedly accounted for their treatment, which was so much worse than that which they had received at Messina.

The next morning they were told they were to be taken to the Yugoslavian Consul to get a visa. Elizabeth asked the guard who went with them if their fare would be paid into Yugoslavia or just to the frontier; he said as far as Ljubljana, the first town in Yugoslavia where there was a British Consul. Elizabeth explained the situation in German to the Yugoslavian Consul when they arrived there; the man 'knew exactly what was what' and told the Italian guard to take them to the American Consul, because he wouldn't give them a visa unless they had some money. The guard was furious, but didn't dare to say anything, so they were at last taken to the American Consul.

Elizabeth thought the American Consul charming and the consulate a haven of peace. He said he would get their tickets to Zagreb; there was an English Consul at Ljubljana; they would be given some money before they left and they were to return to the American consulate at five o'clock. The American Consul gave them their tickets and some money, and went out with them to buy them food and wine. At nine o'clock they got the train for Posthonia, a frontier town. Arriving at midnight, they were told there was no train for Yugoslavia until six thirty the next morning. The night was spent in the waiting room with about thirty Italian soldiers, with all the doors and windows locked. By this time Elizabeth felt she hadn't really slept for at least three weeks; her stomach was also in a 'fearful state'.

The next morning they were in the train 'like a flash' and over the border in ten minutes, much to Elizabeth's relief. In Zagreb they saw the British Consul, who paid their hotel bill for three days and their fares ('second class') to Athens. Yugoslavia seemed 'excessively Germanic' to her after the Latin countries they'd been in, with 'thin sausages & beer & enormous meals & Ruritanian uniforms. Zagreb is a dull new & very teuton town.'

Writing her long letter to Pris, Elizabeth felt stuck in Athens with very little money, no boat, no 'suitable' clothes, and having to live in hotels and restaurants in the boiling heat. Luckily, she still had the address of a friend of Norman, Jimmy Roan, an amusing homosexual concerned, according to Charles, that under the financial constraints of war he might become too conventional; Elizabeth described him as a 'godsend'.

Elizabeth was shocked by her first sight of Athens: despite ample forewarning the noise, the trams, the crowds overpowered her. She was unable to do any sight-seeing owing to the lack of proper shoes and the discomfort of walking on city pavements 'after a whole year of espadrilles'. The food she pronounced 'unspeakable', 'although if one did one's own cooking one could live like a millionaire on £1 a week'. The system she described as prevailing in all the restaurants was to cook large quantities of rice, spaghetti, stuffed aubergines, stuffed tomatoes, fried fish and potatoes, and to 'leave them in large pans soaking in oil for the next 8 days'. It was only with the greatest difficulty that she could persuade them to heat the food up. 'And when you cannot even read the language, let alone speak one solitary word of it, hope of survival is small.'

She wrote that there was some chance of Charles getting a job with the British Council in Athens, because their 'boys' were sent to Cyprus but never got further than Alexandria as a result of the Italian declaration of war, and would now probably not come back. Without a job, the Consul would have to keep them — the probability of getting money out of England was slight. As was the probability of them getting back the boat. Elizabeth thought that even if it had not been blown to bits, it would undoubtedly be in a terrible state, with rotting ropes, peeling paint, a ruined engine and water flooding in. Elizabeth *had* said that she was getting sick of living on board, but she 'didn't intend getting rid of the boat in quite that way'.

She fantasized to Pris about taking themselves off to a small cheap island and living in a hut or tent and eating octopus: 'it can be delicious, although a year ago I should have fainted at the idea'. She was resigned to taking a flat in Athens if it turned out that they had to stay, but was finding a large city 'hell' after living on the sea for a year.

'*How I regret France*,' she wrote to her sister, knowing full well that if they had remained they would have been in much the same predicament that they found themselves in now, as they would have been forced to flee the Germans and leave the boat. She realized they were extremely lucky to get out of Italy at all – if they had been imprisoned there she believed they might very well have died of starvation or gone quite mad.

Elizabeth detailed to Pris what she considered their most serious losses to be: the typewriter, Charles's manuscripts and her cookery book, 'which was getting to be such a good collection that I was thinking of writing it up properly and trying to get it published in America'.

Worrying about her family, Elizabeth asked Pris to send a wire, if she could afford it, to say that they were all right. Her letter was to be passed round and then given to Marian, who would give it to Diana to read. She asked after Stella, saying that she hoped she had left Dedham, as it seemed a bad place to be – acknowledging that no place was particularly good. Her letter is full of advice to Pris about how best to survive: always have money ready, and buy jewellery; 'if I'd had even so much as one little diamond ring I'd have been in a better situation than I am now'. It is also full of requests for her clothes to be sent out to her: her blue coat, red flannel dress, black woollen dress, two blouses, red velvet coat for the winter. She apologized for bringing up such trivial matters, but then went on to say that there were no 'good shops' in Athens, and that all she had for the winter was her black suit, red jacket and old clothes from the boat. She was perfectly serious about this need for her wardrobe, and pointed out her clothes could be sent care of Cook's by way of India and Turkey. 'If by the time you get this England is not in chaos & you have time & courage would you consider the matter?'

She expressed concern about her friends in France, especially Norman. Two letters from him awaited her, but they had of course been sent before the outbreak of the war. She fretted about how little news they received, no English newspapers despite the presence of quite a few English people, who had been very kind to them.

Desperate for money, she had wired to her bank from Zagreb to send a hundred pounds, to break her trust if possible and sell the shares, regardless of how much could be got for them. It was better to get what one could rather than lose it all when the crash came, as it must, whether they won or lost the war.

Elizabeth includes few political reflections in her letter but does express disgust with 'the whole bloodstained business'. She believed the Italians were going to be very sorry that they had ever got into the war – there was little to eat, with the coffee ration at about two ounces a month and sugar half a pound a month; there was no soap for washing clothes and only the rich could get butter. The Italians, she said, would be 'done out of' all the colonies they hoped to acquire. And if they got Corsica, then 'God help them . . . the Corsicans hate their guts & there'll be wholesale murder of them if they ever set foot on the island'. They would soon see that things were not to be as easy as they thought; they were so frightened of each other to start with that she couldn't imagine what would happen to them if ever they came into contact with the British Fleet. The Italian newspapers had been full of the damage they had done in Malta, but she knew this was an exaggeration – Malta would have been under the sea if it had been bombed as much as they claimed. As for the names of the important bases in Malta allegedly wiped out, she had never heard of one of them, and was certain that they had simply been invented by the newspapers.

The letter concludes by asking for news of friends and family, and for the first time perhaps, there is a hint of genuine alarm, genuine concern: 'I am thinking about you all the whole time.'

Far away in Greece which seemed so alien after Southern France, Elizabeth's concerns for those at home were edged with new sentiment for she was feeling cut off and tired. Still set in her determination to stay away from England, her recent experiences through Italy and Yugoslavia had brought about a change in her. She remained confirmed in her intention to stay outside any involvement with the war effort, but some of the realities of this war were no longer avoidable. The tone of her request for news of friends' movements – she had heard nothing from anyone since the middle of May – has a note of fear not previously evident. Her loss of papers, books and home – as the *Evelyn Hope* had become – now began to extend to human loss in this war which gradually encroached.

Elizabeth inquires after 'Chan' in the Athens letter – this was Chandos Hoskyns, one of the Gwynne sisters' greatest devotees on Malta during the Thirties, and himself universally admired. A Lieutenant-Colonel in the Rifle Brigade, he was a sparkling figure of humour and wit who charmed all he met and was often at Priscilla and Richard's dinners. In keeping with all who met him Elizabeth liked Chan, and it was he whom she enshrined in her first piece of non-recipe-based writing, 'Two Cooks'. Chan was the 'honoured . . . guest coming for dinner' to eat 'one of his favourite dishes . . . Angela's way of doing quails, boned and stuffed with sweet corn and wrapped in bacon', the quail which Angela so endearingly and carelessly lost to the cat. Back in May, as the Germans relentlessly pushed forward towards the French coast, with the British army before them, Chan was killed in action while commanding the 2nd Rifle Brigade – part of the crucial and sacrificial defence of Calais, without which Dunkirk would certainly have fallen and the great exodus of men could never have taken place.

At first Elizabeth and Charles found themselves ill at ease in the Levantine atmosphere of Athens. As Elizabeth complained to Pris, after so long on a boat wearing espadrilles (and sea clothes) the noise and crowds and pavements of the city were almost too much to endure. But, despite saying she loathed Athens – the English colony were just Malta all over again – she maintained that now she simply couldn't return to England. Now that Italy had joined in the war and Mediterranean sea routes had been cut off, the journey back home was a mammoth undertaking. One had to go to Turkey and from there to Karachi and 'practically around the world', or to Egypt, Syria and Palestine, plane to Durban and boat from there. Elizabeth had had enough of being stranded in strange countries without money, and captured by enemies. She recounts the story of the British Consul in

Athens who informed a girl intending to make the journey back to Britain that, if she had been his daughter, he would have locked her up in the gaol rather than let her make the trip alone. The physical results of war were now a legitimate excuse for Elizabeth not to return to England. Equally important, she was not yet sufficiently moved to make that journey, she wasn't ready to return.

It was in this letter that Elizabeth asked Pris to try to replace her lost cookery books at Miss Dillon's. She bemoaned the loss of all her other books but said it was useless to think about them, they couldn't be ordered again. Many were irreplaceable because she'd had them all her life. Her most treasured ones had been left in England – she wondered if their fate would be very different. Letters from friends and family were beginning to get through to her and she wrote that she had had news from Norman, who remained in Antibes. She thought he must be wretched and lonely, as everyone had gone. The Cumberleges, he told her, had left in their car, and been heard of in Gibraltar. She presumed Mike had left in a battleship. (Mike Cumberlege was in fact continuing his spying missions around the Mediterranean and beyond.)

Athens was a Mecca of sorts, however, and Elizabeth and Charles decided, as he put it, 'as we had left England with the express purpose of seeing Greece . . . to make the most of it'. Before using Norman Douglas's introductions, however, they thought it best to familiarize themselves with the city. They made valiant attempts: searched almost in vain for a route up to the Acropolis, hindered by knowing not a word of Greek; were surprised at the dirt, the dust, the mess, the neglect of the past out of ignorant disregard or a ramshackle grasping for the future: and decided that Greece was the salvage dump of Europe, with everything – including ships, trams, anything mechanical – apparently made from the discards of other countries. Elizabeth described the clothes shops as provincial and overpriced, and shopping generally as one long pain in the neck. She could never get anything that she wanted, and had to bargain for everything, down to the smallest packet of pins.

The days spent reluctantly in Athens did not pass with complete awfulness. They could sit with all the foreign newspapers on the terrace of the grand King George Hotel looking out, Charles wrote, 'watching the changing light on Hymettos . . . We sat in the tavernas at Phaliron, eating grilled fish – slightly burned, over-salted and covered in cold oil – while the boats with acetylene lamps to attract the fish to the nets, moved like fireflies on the Bay of Salamis'. They explored the ancient silver mines at Lavrion and spent nights in the Turkish quarter at the base of the Acropolis . . . exquisite against the garish architecture of modern Athens. 'We visited (finally) the Parthenon.' They saw 'the Theatre of Dyonisios, and the Temple of Poseidon at Sunion, where we searched in vain for initials of Byron carved on the stone; we visited Eleusis and Daphne'.

In fine form, Elizabeth described the rituals of food in Athens to Priscilla. Having grumbled that kitchen utensils were colossally expensive, and that when she got a flat of her own it would cost a small fortune, she berated the Greeks for their inability to make utensils with lids, which may have accounted for the food in restaurants being stone cold. Her next statement was uncompromising. 'In a hundred years I could never get used to Greek food.' She told Pris that she had eaten the food of almost every country in Europe, but that in Greece she had met her Waterloo.

Pris, Elizabeth thought, must be glad of her vegetable garden now. She continued her letter, gradually more withering as she warmed to the task: she found it difficult to get sugar, there was only brown bread, meat only two days a week. Vegetables were plentiful, but they consisted of tomatoes, aubergines, small marrows, potatoes, ochra, cucumbers and pimentos. There was no green salad, or anything remotely like it. 'There is a kind of spinach muck which they boil to shreds, chew up and then spit out into an enormous pan full of oil where it stands for a fortnight and is served under the name of green salad.'

'They say one gets to love Athens in time but the report is exaggerated . . . the islands and the Peloponnese are different . . .' It was difficult to get around without boat or car and Elizabeth clearly dissociated herself from the contemporary traveller into unknown regions à la Robert Byron in Persia, or Peter Fleming in China and Brazil, and neatly characterized that style with her usual touch of irony. 'I never was one for packing ten days' supplies in a basket, hanging it on the back of a mule and tramping off into the wilds.'

Matthew White (1842–1904),
5th Baronet and 1st Viscount Ridley,
Stella's father

Mary Georgina (Polly), d. 1899,
Viscountess Ridley, Stella's mother.

Blagdon Hall in Northumberland, Stella's birthplace. The lake was designed by
the celebrated architect Edwin Lutyens. His daughter Ursula married the
3rd Viscount, Elizabeth David's cousin.

Wootton Manor, Elizabeth's childhood home. Detmar Blow's library and kitchen wing are to the right, the ballroom to the left.

A meet at Folkington Manor where Rupert grew up. Stella is far left, beside her stands the architect Detmar Blow. Centre left are Dorothy (Rupert's sister) and Grace (Stella's sister). Far right is Rupert.

Rupert's parents May and James (Stick)
Gwynne shortly after their marriage
in 1862.

James Gwynne in old age.

The Hon. Stella Gwynne
(1884–1973), Elizabeth's mother.

Rupert Sackville Gwynne
(1873–1924), Elizabeth's father.

Pre-election Gwynne family photograph, 1923.
Rupert was to live only a year longer. Back: Priscilla and Rupert.
Front (left to right): Felicité, Stella, Elizabeth and Diana.

The four Gwynne sisters at Wootton c. 1923–4.
Left to right: Priscilla, Diana, Felicité and Elizabeth.

In the garden at Wootton, c. 1923–4.
Back (left to right): Elizabeth,
Aunt Grace and Uncle
Top: Lord and Lady Selbourne.
Front (left to right): Felicité and Diana.

A rare photograph of Elizabeth (left)
caught smiling for the camera.
With Priscilla (centre) and
Stella at Wootton, c. 1930.

At Wootton in 1931. Back (left to right): a friend of Stella's, Priscilla, Stella,
Felicité. Front (left to right): the Gwynne girls' cousin, Neil Hogg, and Diana.

Doreen Thornton, Elizabeth's spirited friend from Regent's Park Theatre days, in the 1940s.

Richard Longland and Priscilla at Guadamangia, their house on Malta where Elizabeth spent several idyllic holidays in the mid-1930s.

Elizabeth said of this blouse in which she posed for the society photographer Dorothy Wilding: 'It looks terribly nice with my black suit and the maid (the only person who has gazed upon my beauty today) said, "It looks sweetly pretty."'

Above: Charles Gibson Cowan, the pacifist with whom Elizabeth escaped England.

Above right: Felicité, Elizabeth's youngest sister, at about seventeen. They were to share a house for over thirty years.

Right: The writer Norman Douglas at Capri in 1951, the year before his death. His outlandish style and quirky scholarship influenced Elizabeth and her writing, though she ignored his advice to leave Cowan.

Nonetheless she saw things for what they were and added, 'This method is the only way to see Greece.'

Charles and Elizabeth preferred the islands to the mainland and Elizabeth told Pris that they had been taken to several. The Greeks were frightfully hospitable and they had been asked aboard practically every yacht in Greece. She described the extrordinary luxury exhibited by these wealthy Greek sailors and laughed at their meekness and Mediterranean *sprezzatura*. She thought the people who owned yachts there a 'perfect scream' – with 80 and 100 ft yachts they sat all year in the harbour, venturing out occasionally in the summer to the nearest island five miles away. They gaped when told how big the *Evelyn Hope* was, and thought Elizabeth and Charles were like Christopher Columbus. In spite of cynicism about the Greek yachtsmen's showy use of their wealth, they took advantage of the snobbish collecting of English friends, accepted the unsophisticated generosity of the newly rich and the occasionally stifling but boundless hospitality of the Greeks. One of their hosts, Embiricos, was the owner of a shipping line whose bounty included the island of Andros, where he was happy for them to borrow a house.

Elizabeth had a chance to observe customary Greek behaviour. Although, as we have just seen, her vision could be limited – she did not tend to look inward – her outward eye was exceedingly sharp, especially for any signs of pretentiousness or absurdity. In one of her letters to Priscilla she describes a custom rigorously maintained in Greece, what she calls 'the jam and water party; an ordeal one sometimes has to go through'. The piece is such a fine example of Elizabeth's style and the high level of writing she has already attained when on her mettle that it is quoted here almost verbatim. She already succeeds at something her mentor Douglas was a past master at, namely description with an eye for accuracy, for objective truth yet at the same time making the description personal, letting the reader know – mostly by implication – her own opinion, all set down with most effective understatement.

> Among all the less Europeanized Greeks of all classes, at whatever time you call on them, or even if invited to a party you will find a number of people sitting in a circle right round the room.

After you have been introduced and given a chair you sit bolt upright and don't speak to anyone until you're spoken to. Presently a maid arrives with a tray on which is a small dish of jam (very sweet and syrupy) and a large glass of water for each guest. On top of each glass is poised a spoon. The technique, which it takes some time to master, is as follows: you take the spoon, dip it in the jam, take a mouthful, put the spoon in the glass, take the glass off the tray and drink the water, trying to avoid knocking your teeth out with the spoon. If you stay a long time and if you're lucky you may get a tiny cup of coffee and a piece of Turkish Delight . . . (the Turkish Delight is excellent here but now they have stopped making it for lack of sugar.)

She then appends to the story another example of Greek hospitality, with timing and variations.

Just before I left Athens I went to a party – 10.30 I took my place in the circle, round an immense room with parquet floor, marble statues and 18thc. furniture (the sign of enormous wealth in Greece) and we had coffee, jam, water and little sweet cakes. At 12 o'clock I had not moved off my chair, and nor had anybody else . . . and then a lot of cocktail party food was handed around, little bits of ham on bread, little clams (delicious shell fish) nuts and so on. At 1.30 we were offered a whisky or brandy and soda and at 2 o'clock the party broke up – voted by everyone a riotous evening.

Their money became desperately low, eaten up by hotels and restaurants. Charles was attempting to get work in Athens, preferably at the newly founded British Institute – Elizabeth comments wryly, 'Institute for teaching English culture (!) to Greeks' – but, in spite of promises, neither Charles's obligatory work permit nor the job materialized. They now went out as little as possible to avoid spending money. Throughout the whole period in the South of France Pris had, whenever possible, sent Elizabeth sums of money. Each was gratefully accepted, and spent. Now finances were worse than ever before and Elizabeth had written asking for a loan and the release of her trust fund. Richard was away and Priscilla was on her own with the baby, Sabrina – intermittently with Felicité or Diana – in the Old Vicarage, Chipping Sodbury.

In straitened circumstances herself by now, Priscilla must have asked her mother for advice. This elicited a revealing outburst giving vent to Stella's exasperation with Elizabeth. It is a harsh and also a wounded letter and gives a valuable insight into the way Elizabeth was perceived by Stella. It was written in July 1940 from Dedham where Stella, with the hazard of regular air raids, was continuing with her antiques shop. The Old Grammar School was very large and here she was alone except for a maid whom she wished would leave (but felt unable to throw out) so that she could save the money. A student from Cedric and Lett's school, Maudie O'Malley, remembers Stella 'working away there all on her own. She stripped pine before anyone else did, all those things she did on her own.' Stella said she no longer took any notice of the raids, that she refused to hide in the cellar with her furniture; felt encouraged by 'our own Fighters overhead' and 'existed'. Cedric Morris and Lett Haines were nearby and they also doggedly kept on with work. Stella writes:

> My dear Priscilla,
> I am answering at once, tho I do *not* know what to say re E. My own experience is that she does her best to flout and annoy me, always has. She is still owing me £250; the arrangement made by the bank that she was to repay me £20 a month having come to nothing. Remember she has no morals re money – like Eva and Violet & will roll you till your last [farthing] . . . without any feeling or gratitude – So whatever you do you will be the loser. & she is I imagine keeping that Pacifist and the £100 is probably for him too. I never realized the implication when she decamped like that before the War – jolly clever . . . to find a person like Elizabeth to support him – I shd let the Bank do whatever they think best.

Stella asked Pris if she could not persuade Elizabeth to return, and 'could you tie her down to a furnished room and a job? What does Richard say?' Stella is sure that Athens must be cheaper than London.

'and I feel sure she only asked for the £100 to keep the party [Charles], so that if getting her home wd get her away from him, I shd be in favour – because the more you help her the quicker will you have nothing left. I'm sorry to appear so hard but I have bitter experience of Gwynne morals . . .

'I think E. ought to come home and live in a British place – but one can't do anything and it is so involved with that awful worm – one can't call him a man . . . I'm thankful Daddy is not alive I cannot imagine what he'd say to E. going off with a Pacifist.'

This was not the first letter Stella had written about Elizabeth's present activities. Pris had sent on to the family the long letter from Athens describing Charles and Elizabeth's capture and their eventual journey to Greece, and this elicited a fiery response from her mother regarding Elizabeth's war effort. 'She's alright, but how *can she* sit there idling when the Athens hospitals are shrieking for helpers of all kinds. And if ever she returns to England what sort of reception will she get from everyone who is working in every possible way. She'll *never never* get a job. However – nothing can be done. Love Mummie.'

Meanwhile, after three months in Athens a more serious proposition than hanging around waiting on the British Institute was made to Charles: teaching English on one of the Cyclades islands. He went ahead to look. There were complications but it seemed that he might manage to muster a few students – better than nothing in Athens. Within a fortnight Elizabeth was packed up and on her way to meet him. Charles had rented a small cottage on the island of Syros. Under circumstances quite other than planned they were at last to come to a halt for a time on a small island in the midst of this sea of which Elizabeth's future friend, Lawrence Durrell, wrote: 'The Mediterranean is an absurdly small sea; the length and greatness of its history make us dream it larger than it is.'

CHAPTER NINE

A Kind of Idyll
(1940–1941)

SYROS (Syra is the name of the principal town) is one of that strung-out group of seductive, harshly beautiful islands in the Central Aegean, forming a chaplet around Delos – from whence comes their name, the Cyclades. Long inhabited, their rounded forms burnt by the searing Greek sun, each island is quite distinct in character: Syros, Andros, Tinos, Paros, Naxos, Kynthos, and more, their names ring out back beyond Homer into prehistory. Most are rocky, at times spectacular; several are arid and waterless. Some, like Naxos, were famed in antiquity for their wines and fertility. Delos, really no more than a great granite rock, was the birthplace of the god Apollo, and the vast sanctuary which grew up there became one of the holiest and most revered sites of the ancient world. At the maritime crossroads between Greece and Asia and the Northern Aegean and Egypt, this tiny island also became one of the great commercial ports of the Mediterranean.

Syros was not illustrious but, until its displacement by Piraeus at the end of the nineteenth century, Hermoupolis (or Syra as it was renamed), was the first port of Greece. Approaching by steamer through the indigo sea, two hills rise steeply to the left and right of the town, each terraced with the brilliant white houses so characteristic of these islands. The hill to the left holds the Roman Catholic community, the cathedral of St George at its summit, whilst the hill to the right is the Greek Orthodox quarter. The entire town of Syra was built of marble, glistening a sparkling pure white, from the gleaming waterfront upwards along the winding stairways to the Old Town on top of the Catholic hill. The shipyard was famous for its building of caiques, the brightly painted fishing boats seen across the Eastern Mediterranean.

Beyond the town the vine and the olive grew well on this arid little island; there were also vegetables and some orange groves in the valley. The low, winding stone walls were marble — stones cleared from the fields — and led towards the sea. Charles found a place for them to live in the tiny hamlet of Vari, a few miles out of Syra. Charles describes the hamlet and the house they were to live in for many months thus: 'A cluster of cottages overlooked the bay, narrowing between high broken cliffs to seaward . . . It widened to a stretch of shingle, upon which, side by side, were built two small tavernas. Beyond them a strip of flat, white sand led from a shallow side of the bay to a pink rock at the foot of a thorn-covered hill. In the angle between the rock and the hillside, overhung by a willow tree, was a white marble cottage.'

After they had settled themselves into the cottage on the edge of Vari, Elizabeth wrote home, but in the knowledge that her letter might take months to get there. She now comprehended the magnitude and the implications of this war, the truth of Douglas's prophecy that Europe would be ineradicably altered, and her lines are weary with a sense of endurance when she says to Pris that what will happen to them all is no longer a matter that they can decide for themselves. Elizabeth is becoming resigned to the idea that for many years to come life will be little more than just a dreary scrabble for a bare existence. The less one thinks about the future the better, she tells Pris, because for their generation there is none. She recalls Bryan's words at the famous party in Malta, after which they had dinner on *The Delhi*: 'I b-b-believe that our g-generation is g-going to be b-blown to p-pieces.'

They were, for the present, on the island of Syros — not the most interesting or beautiful of the Greek islands, but the one where there were likely to be more people wishing to learn English. And because they were exhausted with life in hotels and restaurants. Elizabeth told Pris that their failure to rent another house 'absolutely new and fully equipped with everything, including a small sailing boat' had led them to their small furnished cottage in the village of Vari, five miles from the town, on a lovely bay. There were no communications with the town, and they had to walk in or borrow a donkey or horse from one of the peasants. They were, however, when not cut off by the tide, only five minutes' walk from the tiny hamlet with its tavernas.

In *The Voyage of the Evelyn Hope* Elizabeth is identified as Caroline. Charles describes their first night in the cottage:

Tootosi took us out to Vari in his car. We managed to find an excuse to get him to leave us at the road, and the two of us went together across the shingle to the house. Unasked, the fisher-woman and her son followed us, carrying our bags. She placed them just inside the doorway and slipped timidly away. Caroline ran after and shook her hands. I undid the padlock of the inner door. The house was barely furnished; a chair and a bed in each of the bedrooms, four broken cane chairs, a small table and a kind of settee in the living-room and in the kitchen, besides the small charcoal brazier stove, a large table and four bentwood chairs. I walked out on to the large stone balcony and waited. Caroline came up behind me and put her arm on my shoulder. We looked at the nine little houses, washed pink or yellow, each with its flat square roof of mud, and the small walled balcony leading down three or four steps to ground level.

'I like it,' she said.

'The lavatory is outside, and is just a hole.'

'I've seen it. It's luxurious, it's got a roof.'

'It's not going to be too terribly comfortable.'

'It's all marble, even if it's whitewashed. There are not many people who can boast a lavatory in marble.'

'You haven't seen the best of it, the view. Now is really the time to see it, or are you too tired to climb the hill?'

'No,' she said. 'I'm not too tired to climb the hill.'

I helped her up the rough ground, jagged with marble outcrops, and covered with clumps of thorn.

'That is what you use to light the fires. They burn charcoal, and they are good to cook on, once you get used to them. You have to keep them going with a fan. I've had an idea to get a girl here to help you, who speaks French. The *papa* says that there is an Italian woman about half a mile away, she speaks French, too. I'm afraid she'll be your only intellectual neighbour.'

'I liked the fisherwoman.'

We stood on the top; around us was the purple circle of the Cyclades, lifted slightly from the sea: Kythnos, Seriphos, Siphinos, Paros, Mykinos.

That night we slept together, without proper sheets, and with a lumpy mattress, in a shaky iron bed.

In the morning we were awakened by a soft tapping at the door. Outside stood the fisherwoman, timidly holding a plate of fresh fish.

Caroline spent the day cutting some cheap material she had bought in Athens into covers for the chairs and for curtains. I walked into Syra and came back with a few necessary pots and pans. At dusk we had our first visitor, a short, cheery-faced peasant with an almost Chaplin moustache and a twinkling eye. He introduced himself.

Kala Speras! Josipi.'

We offered him a chair. I had brought a bottle of cognac from the town, and I poured three glasses, while Caroline cut some small pieces of bread, and a little cheese; the conventional offering of food and drink to a guest. He raised his glass and clinked it against ours

'*Issigean!*'

It seemed that something was required of us. We repeated it after him.

'*Issigean!*'

He laughed, a soft musical laugh. A few minutes later he pointed to the large hooked briar pipe which I was smoking. I handed it to him. He put it to his lips and puffed before handing it back.

'*Sibouki*'.

'*Sibouki.*'

We began our first lesson in Greek.

The next day I arranged with the girl to help in the house for one thousand drachmas a month. In the evening Josipi arrived again, with a bundle of sheets, blankets, cushions, and a collection of cutlery, china and glasses. He had quietly noticed what was missing and had supplied all the deficiencies. We attempted to refuse the gift, the girl interpreting.

'But he says that you have no sheets, and that you must have sheets, also you have not sufficient knives and forks. If friends come to stay with you, you will need knives and forks. If he does not give them to you, where else will you obtain them?'

Josipi laughed away our protests, refused a second glass of cognac, and settled down to our second lesson. He turned up punctually every evening at the same time.

Here, for once, Charles and Elizabeth's different social backgrounds were forgotten. They were accepted hospitably and judged only by the most ancient and elemental criteria, that simple moral code which scarcely varies throughout the Western world. As far as one can judge, from Charles's writings and Elizabeth's letters, they seem to have stood up quite well. Syros brought out the best in each of them, and for a few months they were mostly happy, probably happier, the evidence suggests, than either was ever to be again.

Elizabeth's description of her life on Syros – the house, the neighbours, her daily round – is confirmation of a change taking place in her over the last few months. The arena of war was initially in Northern Europe, which meant that staying South, on the Mediterranean coast, one was left reasonably unaffected. As Italy entered the combat and the German forces pushed down through France, Elizabeth and Charles had fairly inevitably become involved. Their retreat further South on to this little island allowed them to settle down for a time.

Undoubtedly it was the most uncomplicated milieu Elizabeth had ever experienced, in both a physical and an intellectual sense, and at times her 'civilized' irritation at the simplicity and lack of sophistication of most of those she now encountered was palpable. Before leaving France she and Charles had been subjected to no more than the 'dullness' of war, as Lady Astor puts it; after Italy and Yugoslavia they understood better the fear and danger. Athens was ultimately a period of anxious and deteriorating tediousness. In combination, these experiences wrought a change in Elizabeth's writing. The first Athens letter describing their capture by the Italians nis a narrative of concision, sharpness, coherence made out of chaos; but her present pared-down existence completed the sacrifice of her old life, and this is reflected in her letters. They become noticeably less effusive, less sprinkled with the gushing hyperbole of a 'bright young thing', and are a more accurate reflection of that self which was at heart motivated by the austerity of truth.

In several letters to her sisters and mother from Syros a vivid picture of Elizabeth's island life emerges which complements Charles's descriptions. The house was rather dilapidated, badly in need of painting, with holes in the floor. The roof, thankfully, was sound. Furniture was of the scantiest: one bed, one mattress, five wicker chairs, two tables and a charcoal cooking stove. The sea was at their door. She had two blankets from the boat and a hot-water bottle; Elizabeth always found it difficult to live without one. Water was brought from a distance of a hundred yards.

The cooking stove was a 'sort of brazier', then common to most country houses in Greece, and Elizabeth was thankful that as far as food went they were pretty well off. Compared to heavily rationed Britain the level of choice was luxurious. They had stores of rice, macaroni, flour (brown, mixed with some bran) and small quantities of sugar, coffee and dried beans. Everything else was obtained locally. In spite of butter being very expensive, it was almost inedible – 'margarine would be a treat after it', Greek cheese was 'impossible', coffee, sugar and tea almost unobtainable, 'olive oil so bad that it ruins the taste of anything cooked in it'. No spices were obtainable, but there were compensations.

Every morning they had fresh milk and newly laid eggs from a local peasant, the Josipi of Charles's book; he also brought them the fresh things that he grew for market: tomatoes, onions, potatoes, aubergines, turnips; and fruit, including pomegranates, oranges and lemons. Although prices had risen she said that the two days a week when meat was sold, it was cheap. The fishing was not very good, but she was not particularly worried by this – occasionally they had an octopus, which she found delicious when properly cooked. Chickens could be had from their market gardener although Elizabeth baulked at killing them herself. After three months of hotels and terrible restaurant food it was a great relief to have her own dwelling, however modest.

We are made party to the routine of her 'existence' as she called it with a résumé of her day, sufficiently predictable to be written as an hourly timetable: '7.30 a.m. get up and go for a swim, 8 o'clock breakfast, 8.30–10 cleaning up, getting dressed etc., 10–12 out in the garden reading, endeavouring to knock a few Greek verbs or sentences into my head, writing letters etc., 12–1 cook lunch, 1 o'clock lunch – 2.30 go for a swim, walk or row in borrowed dinghy, general pootle around, 5 o'clock cup of excessively weak tea and piece of toast, 5 to 7 more reading, or local café for a glass of wine or oozoo, the national Greek drink, or call on our local Catholic priest Père Pedro who speaks French, 8pm supper, 9.30 bed. A somewhat aimless life – but better than swanning around Athens drinking and spending money I haven't got – and as I said before one merely exists nowadays.'

She bemoaned her inability to travel around exploring the other islands of the Cyclades visible in the distance because of lack of funds, but commented that two years ago if she had found herself in such a hovel without electric light, bath, water, carpets, armchairs, and in a kitchen without gas or electricity, coffee, butter or tea, she wouldn't have remained there two minutes – now she took what she could get, ate what there was, and considered herself lucky to have it.

Elizabeth and Charles's home comforts extended to a tiny flea-infested white kitten brought to Elizabeth by the 'crazy one', the village simpleton, and named Asphodel after the lily-like flower of the underworld in Greek legend so hated by Norman Douglas. In fact there were fleas everywhere, and the locals thought Charles and Elizabeth quite touched in their persistent battle to be rid of them. Clothes of any description besides the utterly basic were impossible to buy and Elizabeth regretted her oilskin lost with the *Evelyn Hope*. She told Pris that the lack of rain in Greece was a myth and that when the South Wind blew the sea came right up to the door of their cottage, cutting it off completely from the village.

This she did not at first entirely regret because it gave them some respite from the inquisitive eyes of the local peasants. Quite unabashed, they would walk right into the house or simply stand in the doorway, watching. They didn't expect to be spoken to or entertained, but would simply sit down and 'gape for an hour at a time'. Elizabeth and Charles grew accustomed to these visits, however, and when they made Sunday suet pudding their neighbours continued to drop in as if by accident and now brought gifts of their own food specialities in return for their hospitality. An old horse pulled round the windlass for their neighbour Josipi to irrigate his fields; the fisherwoman, whom Charles sometimes helped, continued to throw her nets; and the two foreigners became accepted and welcomed and invited to the little feasts commemorating a child's birth or the killing of a pig.

On 28 October, after they had been on the island for about a month, Mussolini invaded Greece, using his best divisions. A few days later Elizabeth wrote to England and said that she did not now know what would happen, or for how long they would be able to remain on Syros, or what they would do. She knew she might have to get out of there pretty damn quick. They had heard no further news after the bombing of Patras, nothing certain except that everyone had been called up. This was the third time she had been in a country at the moment war started – the men mobilized, the women weeping, the lights all out. As usual there were requests from Elizabeth to Pris to negotiate with the bank on her behalf and also immense thanks for money given. 'I can't thank you enough for this ... with all the expenses and worries you have on your own account and I owe you so much already I wonder if I shall ever be able to pay it back.' Coutts had telegraphed Elizabeth the money to Athens and asked her her intentions, saying that her family would prefer her to return. 'Please give all my news to Marian, Di, Doreen, Arthur – Mummie, D & F. No news of Richard in D's telegram. Where is he?'

She realized that it was unlikely any more letters would now get through and worried about Norman, from whom she had received several missives; he was still in Antibes and trying to get to Portugal. France was now in a bad way – very close to famine conditions. Elizabeth had written to their cousin Neil Hogg, Under-Secretary at the Embassy in Lisbon at the time, asking him to help, and he had responded generously with an invitation to Douglas to stay. This

Douglas eventually did and spent almost a year in Neil's apartment with him before finally returning to England (with great reluctance) for the remainder of the war. Elizabeth ended her letter to Priscilla days after the Italian invasion of the mainland of Greece with the news that for the moment they were still peacefully there.

But men of military age had already gone off to the war and Charles chronicled the melancholy occasion:

> Barely distinguishable in the half light, the village gathered outside Jorgos' before dawn. We watched from the balcony. Slowly they dispersed. A small group remained standing on the shingle. Against the white road the figures were clearer; twenty men walked slowly towards the town.
>
> I took a footpath through the canes, and met them at the bottom of the hill.
>
> 'Josipi, for you! The English pipe to bring you luck in the war.'
>
> His eyes were already wet. He held me in an embrace for a moment, and kissed me on both cheeks. I bade him the traditional Greek farewell:
>
> '*Kalo molivi.*'
>
> Without speaking he thrust the pipe in his mouth at a jaunty angle, and swaggered after the retreating men.

Elizabeth wrote that they were very out of touch with things there, and were living almost like hermits. They did nevertheless give a Christmas party for their neighbours who were left, including the young village priest. In the town and their little hamlet of Vari the bells and fireworks were absent except on days of great victories. It was still cold there, but not exceptionally so by English standards. The fields were full of narcissus and wild anemones, oranges and mandarins were plentiful, and they managed quite well for food.

Most of the islands were casually bombed. News of the progression of war began to filter through to Syros. The Greek army, often under severe winter conditions, was holding back the Italians in a series of victories; the capture of Koritza, the annihilation of an Italian division, the Italian retreat from the Kalamas river; for months the

Greeks kept twenty-seven divisions hemmed into Albania with only sixteen of their own. This impressive Greek resistance kept the Balkan countries in optimistic mood. Meanwhile Churchill and his War Cabinet had acted on their immediate realization (following the Italian invasion) that at all costs Crete must be in British hands: as a strategic airfield and naval refuelling base it would be invaluable in the defence of Malta and Egypt. On 31 October the best harbour in Crete, Suda Bay, was occupied by British forces at the invitation of the Greek government.

By the end of January General Metaxas, the Greek dictator, had died after an unsuccessful operation and although he was replaced immediately, Greece felt itself effectively without a leader. Steamers no longer visited the islands and sailing boats were once again used to ferry food secretly at night from island to island. British, Australian and New Zealand forces had been sent into Greece to prevent German invasion, but they were heavily outnumbered. On 6 April German armies invaded both Yugoslavia and Greece from the north and south. Newspapers ceased to arrive from the mainland; what news Elizabeth and Charles received on Syros was from brief radio reports broadcast from loudspeakers in the square in Syra. Salonika was lost, the Allied armies were fighting a rearguard action; they began a retreat. Korysis, the new Greek Prime Minister, committed suicide, unable to bear the stain of failure to save his country.

Greece surrendered on 24 April; the King and his family retreated to Crete, the last foothold for the government and a brief haven for evacuated troops. Under appalling conditions of attack over 50,000 men had immediately to be evacuated, by night, from mainland Greece. A huge operation was set in motion and, aided by the Greeks, many thousands were saved. On 28 April Charles and Elizabeth watched from the hillside as Syra was bombed. The island was in chaos, and surrendered. Having refused offers of protection in the hills from the villagers, Elizabeth and Charles packed and left for Syra in Josipi's cart, to search out a boat to get them off the island and away to Crete. Now they were fleeing a pursuing enemy and at times this escape made their experience of Italy seem almost trivial by comparison.

A Palestinian soldier who had a 40-foot caique hidden on the other side of the island invited them to take passage with him to Crete; they would leave that night. The company grew and by nightfall there were six or seven, including Charles and Elizabeth. The *Agios Marco* left as darkness fell; Charles wrote that 'The plan was to make it to Crete in three hops, travelling at night, and stopping during the day at lonely island anchorages where . . . we ourselves would scatter against possible machine-gunning from the air.' First halt, just before first light, revealed that the navigator was not an expert after all. They discovered they were now mistakenly on Mykonos, 25 miles due east of Syra – Crete lies due south. In the ensuing debate, heightened by anger and fear, it transpired that the boat was stolen. Eventually a Greek army sergeant, a Cretan soldier and Charles took command of the *Agios Marco*; Charles was now at the tiller.

In the pre-dawn light of the following day the boat crept in along the shores of Ios and the company on board quickly disembarked to hide for the day – they were still 90 miles from Crete. Walking inland, they were soon met by weeping village women who told them that all the men, except for one old one, had gone and they must not stay outside, because enemy planes flew over every day searching out retreating boats and any figures they could see. Divided up between the village houses, they were fed and despairingly requested news of the war.

The old man who had remained advised them on a possible route to Crete: very dangerous but they had little choice. After an intensely nerve-racking voyage in a ship whose motor was failing and whose sails were falling apart they finally entered Heraklion harbour in broad daylight, with three German dive-bombers attacking the town. A British naval officer swore at them from the quay and ordered them to drop anchor immediately and get ashore under cover. It was Mike Cumberlege, not seen for almost a year since Charles and Elizabeth had sailed out of Antibes harbour determined to reach Greece.

Elizabeth took up the story of their flight from Syra in her subsequent letter to Pris from Egypt, saying that those at home must have been dreadfully worried about her, but it had been quite impossible to communicate with them. The escape to Crete had taken four days and they'd had a 'perfectly wonderful' view of the Cyclades. They stopped at Ios, and as they passed Santorini flames came out of the volcano. Elizabeth said that Santorini was where she wanted to live when 'this foul business' was over. She thought Crete beautiful. In contrast to the aridness of Syra she responded to the fertility of Crete, its vines, its fruit trees, 'real' rivers and snow-covered mountains.

Having encountered Mike Cumberlege in the midst of the bombing raid on Heraklion, they heard his latest news. It is here, for the first time, that Elizabeth and Charles's descriptions of events markedly diverge. Either Charles's story is blatant fabrication, or Elizabeth is aware that her letters may be opened, and in her wish to protect Cumberlege, acting as a Navy spy, gives a very edited version of events. From the safety of Alexandria her desription of the next few days is tantalizing brief and to the point. '*We were there about 10 days. They had already started heavyish night bombing when we left – in a comfortable and uneventful convoy*'. Later she adds: 'While wandering around the port of a certain town in Crete who do we see . . . on the battered deck of a . . . ship but Mike – *he has done wonderful work I believe*.' 'We were just that minute going off to the other end of the island in an Army lorry which couldn't be kept waiting so we only had about ten minutes conversation.' (I incline towards Charles's story. His chronicle of events is entirely credible, whereas that of Elizabeth makes little sense, in the light of what other survivors of Crete had written.)

Charles's version, written after the end of the war and with no concern for censorship, filled the last twenty pages of the *Voyage of the Evelyn Hope* with a remarkable and terrifying escape story which began by stating, contrary to Elizabeth, that they spent *two* days with Mike Cumberlege, who 'left us liberally supplied with cash'. The 'cash' was certainly a fact although it became confused in family myth. Trying to piece together this escape, it does appear to coincide with the known events of the battle for Crete, one of the great disasters of the war, which began with the terrible German bombardment on 20 May. Whitehall and Middle East command between them had realized the possibilities for months but were quite unprepared. As a consequence of changing commanders too many times, lax forward-planning and unimplemented directives, the force of the onslaught was so overwhelming that many more lives were lost than might otherwise have been the case. As the soldier-poet John Manifold later put it, in laconic Australian style: 'Muddle tall as treachery.'

According to Charles, he and Elizabeth spent time sightseeing at the recently excavated palace of Knossos (near Heraklion). Here they wandered through the Minotaur's labyrinth, where two Australian soldiers good-naturedly cleared sandbags for an hour, enabling them to see the famed king's throne. As well as the troops recently sent in, Crete was already awash with the remnants of units of different nationalities fleeing from the mainland; one of these sheltered Charles and Elizabeth and a café nearby cooked basic food for them.

One night, with bombs falling unceasingly around them, the Cretan captain walked with them 2 miles out of the chaos into the hills to eat their first proper meal for days at a taverna hidden in a ravine: roast chicken, a dish of stuffed peppers, tomatoes, eggs and a quantity of retsina. From these extraordinary Cretan days Elizabeth later drew – with remarkable sangfroid and the sure touch of the true artist's ability to synthesize experience into art – some of the recipes for *Mediterranean Food*. To the innocent reader they are already redolent with the smell and taste of the wildly beautiful mountains of Crete; knowing more of their provenance, one almost begins to believe that, like so many others in the book, these short and to-the-point recipes have such a weight of experience and history behind them that part of the spell they work upon us is at the level of the subliminal.

ARNÍ SOUVLÁKIA (lamb on skewers)

Cut a piece of lamb from the leg into inch cubes. Season with salt, pepper, lemon juice, and marjoram.* Thread the meat on to skewers and grill them. Serve them on a thick bed of parsley on the skewers, with quarters of lemon.

Eaten on the terrace of a primitive Cretan *taverna*, flavoured with wood smoke and mountain herbs, accompanied by the strong red wine of Crete, these kebabs can be the most poetic of foods . . .

*In Greece wild marjoram is used . . . *Origanum* means in Greek 'the joy of the mountains'.

Before the conclusion of the ferocious German assault and the last desperate evacuation of Allied troops by the Navy twelve days later, the largest-scale airborne attack ever mounted had been directed at Crete by the German Air Corps. Utterly regardless of heavy losses to their own forces soon after landing, and almost unopposed from the air, thousands upon thousands of highly trained German troops, in wave after wave, were relentlessly parachuted on to the island. In spite of gallant and sustained back-up from the Navy and the outstandingly valiant and continued defence of this beleaguered little island by New Zealand, Australian, Greek, Polish and British troops, accompanied by a Cretan population mostly unarmed, but bitter and ruthless in their island's defence, the task finally proved hopeless. The Allied and Greek losses were huge in a battle which had been from the start, through lack of information and communication difficulties, confusing, quickly disheartening and ultimately in vain. Those remaining, nonetheless, could congratulate themselves that they had inflicted enormous (almost equivalent) losses and practically destroyed 7th Airborne Division, one of Hitler's elite fighting forces.

According to Charles he and Elizabeth were caught on the edge of this terrible battle. For days they tried to make their way towards Suda, then retreated, informed that the last civilians had left ten days ago and evacuation from there was now impossible. Constantly caught up in enemy gunfire, with bombs dropping incessantly, men dead and dying all around them, they gradually made their way with exhausted, retreating and wounded troops, towards Sphakia where boats and ships were desperately evacuating thousands to naval vessels waiting offshore. Here they were finally hauled on to one of the ships and sailed away from the battered island in the last days of its defence to safety in Egypt. If Charles's story is true, in only a few more days they would have been among the thousands reluctantly left to the mercy of the crippled but victorious German forces now occupying Crete.

According to Charles, he and Elizabeth acknowledged the end of their romance just before they waded out to the boats.

'It hasn't worked, has it?'

'No,' she said. 'It hasn't worked.'

'I know, it went wrong in Antibes, but it came back again. It would have survived Italy, but it went wrong again in Athens. I thought we had found it again in Vari, but if we get out of this, it will go wrong again. You can't live in a world of your own, you have to live in other people's world.' Charles' description is essentially true, but a précis of events; their final separation was neither immediate nor painless.

CHAPTER TEN

War and the Levant
(1941–1946)

ELIZABETH AND CHARLES, without knowing it, were in a state of shock. They were disoriented, bemused and found the teeming, ancient Egyptian capital city of Cairo, now the centre of Middle Eastern Operations for the British and Allied forces, almost unmanageable. The contrast between their present conditions and the life they had so recently relinquished was extreme. Elizabeth bitterly regretted her island, saying to Pris that she was broken-hearted to leave; for six weeks it had been 'brilliant Spring', with breakfast on the verandah and all-day bathing. It was all the more lovely for the knowledge that it couldn't last. They had lost more books and clothes but above all their peace and quiet. Elizabeth had become so used to leaving places at a moment's notice that possessions 'now meant nothing to me'. One was lucky to get out with one's life. She was writing in June 1941, two weeks after the fall of Crete.

Complaining of only 'one cotton frock' in Cairo's boiling heat, it appears that Elizabeth was finally about to enter the war effort. She begged for communications from home and huffed that they wanted to evacuate her to India, but she absolutely refused. One thing she had learnt after being a refugee for a year was to put her foot down and keep it down, a trait already rather well developed.

As a result of her determination to stay put she was sent to work as a cypherene for the Navy in the Ministry of War Transport in Alexandria, leaving Charles job-hunting in Cairo. Her job was not particularly exciting, but it wasn't very hard, although the hours inconvenient. Some of those with whom she worked could hardly read or write. The salary was not good. Not being a member of one of the forces, Elizabeth was always paid on a civil servant's scale, in other words less than those in the army. Lodgings were in a pension with an air-raid shelter, so Pris was not to worry about bombs, and anyway Elizabeth told her that she didn't yet venture out far at night. Her talk was of the 'fantastic' life of Cairo, where little appeared to have changed since her previous visits back in the Thirties when her sister Diana said Elizabeth had written home with 'some incredibly funny stories about the Goodwins and cousin Kit, and all her expeditions across deserts with pashas in Shell cars . . .'

'Except for the hordes of officers in Shepherds', one would hardly know there was a war on – no food shortages, people out dancing, gossiping, as if nothing had changed. Elizabeth visited her mother's old friends the Goodwins, her hosts of her previous visits to Egypt, both frantically doing war work. Some of her other friends were also there, and she was grateful for the sight of so many friendly faces after so long. She had also come across several mutual (Malta) friends of hers and Priscilla's, now stationed in Egypt, and gave news of their positions and advancements. Charles in Cairo told her that one of those from Malta, Mike Cumberlege, had just arrived slightly wounded. Elizabeth was not troubled about his safety, 'even after the Crete business', as Mike was the sort of person who would get 'into and out of anywhere and everywhere'. The Gwynne girls' friend from London days, Hilary Magnus, now a Lieutenant-Colonel, was around but Elizabeth couldn't track him down. She asked Pris to try to find out where he was, as she would be glad to see him. She continued in ambivalent mood, saying that it was in many ways a relief to be back in civilization, with coffee for breakfast, and hot baths, and able to buy what she wanted but that she missed her island. She felt it a mockery to look at the sea and not be able to bathe; there was no beach near the town and she could bathe only 'if taken out by someone who has a cabin'. When she first arrived in Cairo, she would go into the food shops just to look at the array of provisions – the last few weeks in Greece they had been unable to get anything at all. This letter concluded with instructions to 'take care of yourself and little Sabrina and Little Stranger no. 2'. Pris had recently had her second baby girl, named Julia, and was still trying to manage in her

vicarage in Chipping Sodbury, with little help and regular war work
– she drove an ambulance.

Elizabeth later described how on her arrival in Egypt, for the
first time since leaving home ten years earlier, a vision of Wootton as
a rare oasis of calm sprang into her mind, and for a short space of
time gave her a kind of succour. During the last few weeks, in
surviving the ordeal of escape from Syros and then Crete and the
'general ghastly misery of everything' in the present frenetic and tense
climate of war, her childhood had begun to reassert itself as a place
symptomatic not only of anger and sorrow, but also of isolated pools
of light and hope. 'When I arrived in Cairo and just couldn't think
what I was going to do I suddenly had a conviction for about three
days that if only I could find myself for a few moments in the bluebell
wood at the end of the garden I should find the answer.' This
conviction was accompanied by 'visions of the daffodils round the
summer-house, a wooden seat in the little hole where the hops grew,
a summer evening on the grass by the snapdragon borders, and I
came in to find a party in progress in the Ball Room – the memorable
party of Edward [Hogg (Marjoribanks), the favourite cousin who had
died] and Basil Taylor and "Mind the Step".'

For over a year Elizabeth was to live in Alexandria, a place of
such ancient memory and experience that by the time of the doomed
Antony and Cleopatra it was already well established as one of the
most cosmopolitan cities on all the Mediterranean. Alexandria is a
maze, lying low against the shoreline, a city without hills, at the
mouth of the Nile's great green delta with flatness stretching out
beyond, the Libyan Desert to the west and the Arabian Desert to the
east. The city, built by Alexander the Great 300 and more years
before Christ, quickly attracted scholars and artists of the highest
rank, and shortly after Alexander's death the greatest library in the
world was gathered together there.

'Five races, five languages, a dozen creeds . . .' wrote Lawrence
Durrell in *Justine*, one of the *Alexandria Quartet* novels set in the city;
at once a kind of microcosmic Durrell vision of the Middle Eastern
world and the seamier aspects of the psyche; one version of the East.
Later, in *Balthazar*, Durrell's narrator tells us that these parallel
Alexandrian communities 'still live and communicate – Turks with

Jews, Arabs and Copts and Syrians with Armenians and Italians and Greeks . . . ceremonies, marriages and pacts join and divide them . . . it is a great sprawling jellyfish.' From its founding Alexandria was a polyglot city whose culture and atmosphere were nevertheless above all Greek since its founding by Alexander the Great.

The Second Secretary at the British Embassy in Cairo was then Bernard Burrows (later Sir Bernard), and in conversation with the author he recalls being stirred by the knowledge that 'In the Middle East one was surrounded not only by the war but also by the Classical world. This evidence of that past world, it brought it home . . . very much. Before the war I travelled in the Eastern and Western Deserts. In a remote oasis you might find a long Greek inscription on a great stone lying there. And then in the Eastern Desert, going on in time you found the place where the Romans quarried granite for columns and floated them down the Nile, and then a broken one left there before they got it out. This continuity with the Classical tradition should not be underestimated . . . Egypt was such a puzzle; a great melting pot, culturally and politically . . . In the first war we in Britain had a greater empathy with Egypt, it was an Arab-European war with people like T. E. Lawrence and Gertrude Bell fostering that alliance. In the second war this had gone. We had written them [the Arabs] off, let them down really; it was an inter-European war. In the First War we had sought to build up the Arab States to use them against the Turks; in the Second War SOE [Special Operations Executive] was building up the Greeks, the Albanians, to use them against the Germans.'

Sir Bernard continued: 'As well as the soldiers and the diplomats, during the war there was this great inrush of intellectuals into Cairo and Alexandria, a number of whom were not really much interested in Egypt as such, but rather the literary life of London, of Paris. With the English, they were either at the Egyptian University or they'd been with the British Council in Greece. All intellectuals or at least semi-academics of one kind or another. These different strands all added to make a very potent mix. A good part of one's conversation was attempting to unravel that, to relate one part to another. But one thing which one shared with many of these people was an acquaintance with the Classical World.'

With his future wife Ines (née Walter), Sir Bernard later became part of that group of officers, diplomats and writers from whom Elizabeth was to derive stimulation and support. Many of them, like her, felt in some sense marooned by the war in a land where their European education made them more familiar with its Greco-Roman past than either the ancient Egypt of the Pharoahs or the fast developing modern country, which since the early nineteenth century had become prosperous again through a commerical revival – the cultivation of cotton.

Elizabeth's job in cypher was initially dull, hard work, and necessitated 'the most ghastly hours, all-night watches and suchlike antics'. It also made her terribly tired and hurt her eyes. (She had appalling sight, possibly brought on by the attack of measles she suffered as a girl, and always needed glasses.) But after several months, by March 1942, she had changed her job for the better, although she was still working for the Navy in the Ministry of Transport. She was relieved to report to her sister Diana that the work was more interesting, no longer requiring sitting out night watches, and her hours were now civilized. She worked from 8.45 until one o'clock, and 3.45 until 6.30 in theory, but rarely got away before 7.30. She had two free afternoons a week but worked Saturday and Sunday. Her eyes improved and she was feeling 'in fine form and walk backwards and forwards to the office and am also frequently known nowadays to walk even when I don't need to. This country does most queer things to people.'

Elizabeth remained only a short time in the 'ghastly *pension*' after her arrival in Alexandria, moving out to share a flat with Mike Cumberlege, now based in the city. Apart from its cooler climate and the possibility of sometimes getting to the sea for bathing and sailing, she thought 'Alex in every other way a shocking dump'. Nevertheless the re-affirmation of her friendship with the more grounded Cumberlege was to prove a soothing period and encouraged her re-establishment in society. She afterwards wrote to Pris that he helped her, probably without knowing it, over the first few agonizing weeks of war and town and office life, after she had lived in a remote place for so long without contact with civilization. Even to wear shoes was painful to her at that time, and she was convinced she could never again exist 'without the sound of the sea in my ears as I went to sleep'.

Cumberlege himself was in a dreadful state owing to his cousin's recent death in battle and his own experiences in Crete; he couldn't be left alone and needed the society of women. Elizabeth supplied this for him without any complications, which he did his best to avoid, feeling as he did about his wife, Nan. Elizabeth, with some relief, said that they succeeded in living in the same apartment for six months without 'sex rearing its ugly head'. In this mutually supportive atmosphere she began to 'feel connected up again' and to take her part in the hectic gaiety of Alexandria and Cairo.

Already exotic to those from the West, under conditions of war Alexandria and Cairo became, for Europeans, something like Western frontier towns in the Gold Rush years. Men would return there from terms of duty in the Eastern or Western Deserts having lived for weeks on end on bully beef and tea rations cooked up in the dreadful sand-filled jerrycans; in gruelling, parched-dry alien landscapes where the engulfing sands relentlessly infiltrated every possible secret part of the body and the convoys could travel for mile after mile over sands with as few landmarks as the waves of an ocean, finally to encounter minefields or the enemy, in the air or on the shifting, mirage-ridden land. Those fortunates who survived returned to the cities for respite with pay in their pockets and a desperate will to enjoy themselves if it was the last thing they did before returning to the desert and a good chance of maiming or death.

As Elizabeth told Pris, the bars, cabarets and restaurants were always full, everyone had plenty of money, and any girl who was at all presentable could go out every single night if she chose.

To her old friends and relations passing through or based in Cairo or Alex (among them cousins Bill Palmer and Quintin Hogg, 'covering himself in glory', and whom Elizabeth now found 'easier to talk to and . . . an extremely nice individual', she added a growing collection of new friends and admirers. The apartment she shared 'thanks to the kindness of Mike' was large, cool and comfortable and ideal for entertaining. They employed Kyriakou as a cook, a sympathetic and poignant figure who eight years later was to be enshrined, like Priscilla's Angela, in Elizabeth's beautiful essay for

Wine and Food entitled 'Two Cooks'. With minimum fuss, in evocative and disingenuous prose, the piece captures something of the essential nature of both herself, her cook and his homeland. The reader's imagination is swiftly captured, and we pause for a moment to listen as Elizabeth draws us into her cameo vision of another, far-off world. In the first part of the essay, Priscilla's cook Angela is open, enthusiastic, noisy, comprehensible out there in the clear bright sunlight; whereas this gentle man, though quite as vivid and passionate, has an aura of contemplation, mystery; the Mediterranean sun which is his natural element is of a mellower, more melancholy kind.

> Kyriakou was a Greek from the Dodecanese island of Simi. He was a sponge fisher and he had escaped twice from the Italians, for whom he had a boundless contempt. When they declared war he had sailed his boat to Mersa Matruh, and when Mersa Matruh was captured he sank his boat in the harbour rather than let the Italians get it, and escaped with the British Navy, carrying with him a sack of electrical equipment he had looted from an Italian store. How he came to be a cook-general in our absurdly grandiose Alexandrian flat is no longer very clear, and, devoted and charming as he was, a dedicated cook I cannot claim him to have been. He was not entirely of this world, perhaps it was being so much under the sea that made him so dreamy when he was on land. He would sweep the carpet with his gaze fixed on the ceiling, as if he expected any minute to swim to the surface.
>
> The Greeks are the most democratic people in the world and a Greek servant is in every sense a member of the family . . . every detail of expenditure is discussed with the same passion as politics. Together, conversing in unlikely French and fantastic Greek, Kyriakou and I went shopping.
>
> Kyriakou's grief as the cost of a bottle of olive oil crept up . . . was tragic to watch, and he often had to be consoled with a stiff drink of *ouzo* in the market after spending my money in this reckless fashion. The rising cost of living was considerably augmented by the alarming quantity of breakages in our hideous

but lavishly appointed flat. This turned out to be due to the fact
that poor Kyriakou, already affected by the disease which finally
gets all deep sea divers, would sometimes have a spasm of
terrible pain ... most often when he was carrying a laden
tray ...

Even this did not account for the number of teapots which
he managed to get through in a few weeks; going into the
kitchen one day at tea time I found him in the act of putting
the tea pot, in which there was half a pound of tea and a little
cold water, straight on to the gas.

Kyriakou took some of the responsibility of entertaining into his
own hands and sometimes organized those of Elizabeth's and Mike's
friends he preferred around a dinner he thought fitting. 'Not unnaturally the people he favoured [the garrulous, passionate Lawrence
Durrell was one of them] were usually Greek-speaking or connected
in some way with the Greek cause, so it happened that now and again
the chromium and mirror bar, the road-house splendour of our flat,
took on the atmosphere of a taverna. Kyriakou would sit and drink
with us, pouring out the drinks and fetching clean glasses with the
grace of a host which is instinctive to every Greek ever born.'

When Kyriakou heard one day that his wife and children had
escaped from their island to Palestine, his jubliation was such that a
celebration was called for: a party for Elizabeth and her friends.
'Nothing would stop him and we were not allowed to buy a single
bottle of wine or contribute in any way to the expense. When a Greek
sets out to give a party there is no cheese-paring.'

Elizabeth was unable to discover from where her 'cook-cum-
lady's-maid' Kyriakou procured his booty for the celebratory dinner.
But he 'returned home with a bucket of shellfish the like of which
had never before been seen in Alexandria; from this he concocted
a pilaff which would have made a Spanish *paella* seem positively
penny plain. It was a fish dinner, for as well as the pilaff there were
mountains of fried fish (in Greece they like fried fish cold)'. There
was a shift of emphasis here – previously Elizabeth had wailed and
railed at the Greek taste for cold food. Kyriakou produced 'a great
basin of skordalia, the Greek garlic sauce, and the masterpiece of the

evening was an octopus stew. With passionate concentration he prepared it, and I watched him build up in a deep pot a bed of branches of thyme on which he laid a huge quantity of onions, tomatoes, garlic, bay leaves and olives, and then the octopus. Gently he poured red wine over his carefully constructed edifice, stirring in the ink from the fish, and left his pot to simmer the rest of the afternoon.'

Although by early 1942 Elizabeth told Pris that she was preparing for limitations with the 'appalling goings-on' in the Far East, she had never ceased to be amazed by the quantity and variety of food available. The corner shops and vegetable stalls were piled high with fat shining aubergines, scarlet peppers, ridged courgettes, huge cauliflowers and other greenery; varieties of onions, tomatoes, acid yellow lemons, oranges, baskets of dates and figs; garlic, parsley, the beloved mint, yoghurt, simple and complex cheeses, butter, olives and their oil, eggs, fish, fresh and dried, rice and mountains of pulses and beans, and more besides. There was no rationing – although they were without meat for three days running, and without white bread, these were the only inconveniences she noticed. In Greece they were only able to buy meat once a week, the bread was as black, and as hard, as coal, and towards the end it was virtually impossible to get butter, cheese, chocolate, rice, tea, coffee, sugar or anything except vegetables. In Alexandria one could get almost anything if one had the money – 'even TCP!'

She told Diana that she was almost 'sickened' at the amount of food available and was disdainful of those, like Hilary Magnus, who complained because they couldn't get Camembert or pâté de foie gras, although Elizabeth was later to concede that a spell in the desert on army rations had made Hilary less decadent and better company. Her disdain was forcibly projected at her indolent maid, given short shrift by Elizabeth when she complained of eggs and macaroni three days running. The maid was somewhat chastened when Elizabeth asked her if she'd prefer to go to England, where she would be allowed one egg a month and no macaroni at all, and would have to really work instead of doing a bit of dusting, cooking and ironing, for which Elizabeth had to pay the 'colossal' sum of four pounds a week.

Elizabeth's published writing often presents the reader with a set of descriptive images arresting in their delineation. And often too, we remain conscious that she omits; never so much that we cannot follow the story, but enough to leave us intrigued, wanting that little bit more. Practising this latter quality – never revealing all – with such consistency in her own life, Elizabeth instinctively understood its virtues, and the methods by which one goes about it in writing. Her letters, although frequently long and full of news and events, are (aided by her persistent resistance to introspection) consummate examples of the partially revealed self. A consequence of this same trait made Elizabeth choose with a well-honed instinct the friends to whom she revealed those different aspects of herself, maintaining her habit of compartmentalizing these friendships.

After six months in Alexandria Elizabeth's friendships were as varied as they were many and included a wide spectrum of those then in Egypt, both foreign and native. As to herself and Charles Gibson Cowan, she told those at home, entirely without comment, that he had left Egypt in October 1941, bound for America, a country resorted to by many who had been caught as refugees in Egypt and had no wish to return to England and censure for their unwillingness to fight. The episode of Charles's departure is, as with many situations in which he is associated, not without contradictions. Some light is thrown on this by a series of related events.

A young man called Paul Gotch had made his own remarkable pre-war journey South with his wife Billy (on bicycles) on their pilgrim way to Greece. Paul took up employment with the infant British Council in Athens in 1940, on the same day as the writer Lawrence Durrell. Although they were both sent to different outposts, when the Germans invaded Greece Paul Gotch, Billy, Durrell and his then wife Nancy were amongst the English exiles who escaped to Egypt. Paul taught English to wealthy Egyptians for one of the Council's Institutes at Tanta on the Delta and together with Billy – and sometimes others – from 1943 shared their large villa apartment with Durrell.

Recently separated from his wife Nancy, Lawrence Durrell had been loaned by the British Council as one of the Press and Information Officers to the Ministry of Information. At first in Cairo, he was transferred to Alexandria in 1943. Here he utilized his remarkable grasp of Levantine languages, in combination with his garrulousness, to consort both with those of rank and to infiltrate any low dive; thereby gaining insight into the underbelly of the Middle East, to the advantage of the British government.

Durrell soon told Paul that he had met an interesting fellow whom he also wanted him to meet; this was Charles Gibson Cowan. It seems that after separating from Elizabeth and leaving Alexandria, Charles did indeed cross the Atlantic, possibly never reaching America. For a time he was in Jamaica, where he managed to get himself installed in an editorial position on *The Gleaner*, a well-known local paper.

An American millionaire, MacFadden, had bought cheap in Mombasa, East Africa, a large luxury yacht, the *Samothrace*. Charles had engineered himself the job of sailing the ship up to Alexandria on MacFadden's behalf and he probably arrived in mid-1943. The aim of the voyage was to try to sell the yacht to King Farouk. After the Flap, the *Samothrace* like many other ships was confined to harbour in Alexandria and Charles was at a loose end, with a luxury ship at his disposal.

Paul recollects an outrageous incident which occurred at this time. With the intention of giving some assistance regarding employment, he told the author that he had invited Charles to give a public lecture on the English theatre at the British Institute in Alexandria. Public lectures at the Institute were events attended by some of the more prestigious members of Alexandrian society. True actor that he was, Charles waited in the wings until the 200 or so members of the audience had arrived, before mounting the stage and seating himself casually on the edge of the table. For the space of several minutes, and in complete silence, he proceeded to give a thorough demonstration of the art of picking one's nose, after which he began his lecture.

Paul was horrified but also amused. Later, taxing Charles with his behaviour, he was given the reply: 'Well, they didn't give me a job, did they? (He was referring to the refusal of the British Council in Athens to give him a job prior to his and Elizabeth's months on the island of Syra.) Paul described Charles as: 'an East Ender, a wide boy; a very bright, tough courageous fellow but, let's face it, to those who were, he was simply not quite a gentleman.'

Another member of the Villa Ambron household was Eve Cohen, who married Lawrence Durrell. She had recently escaped from her repressive background into what at the time she felt was the luminescence of Durrell's vision. Eve's mother was proud Spanish–Jewish and her father an impoverished Egyptian–Jewish moneylender. Eve may have been untutored and clung to Durrell's superior knowledge, but there was no doubt regarding her natural intelligence and qualities of perception. She had an instinctive understanding of the languid decadence of her city, where, she told the author, 'You can do anything, be anything you want. Everything is too easy. Once you are out in the streets and breathe the exquisite air you are in an atmosphere of sensuality, and live for the moment, and tomorrow is another day. It is a city of the mind, but it is a sensual intellectuality. People become either self-indulgent and slothful – or ascetics. There is no middle path.' But Eve's own integrity mitigated against these extremes and she was gradually to reject the city of her childhood. This questioning of a Middle Eastern essence, combined with her beauty, Durrell found irresistible.

Elizabeth sometimes came out to Alexandria to see Durrell on Ministry of Information business and he would ask her to stay overnight at the villa. As to Eve, Elizabeth did not regard her as existing in the same social orbit as herself. She may have apparently rejected England, but her preconceptions remained for all that patrician English, amounting at times to a failure of imagination and an intellectual and social complacency. Not untypically, her interest in a less exalted class than her own extended only to a few, like Charles, with whom she felt she had a cultural bond; and Eve was conventionally unlettered. Durrell's 'Gypsy' remained quiet: 'At this time I hardly spoke,' but she observed more than Elizabeth was aware.

Charles became friendly with the members of the Villa Ambron household. He asked for Durrell's comments on his writing, but Durrell was not particularly enthusiastic. Paul believes Durrell was sometimes irritated by Charles, Eve believes he was sometimes jealous of his undeniable charisma. She says, 'Oh, Charles always took centre stage; Larry was – half of him – keen to torture Charles, and envious of him.' With a luxury ship at Charles's disposal, Eve and Paul remember extended parties on board at which he excelled himself at the stove. 'Charles was a very good, confident, and completely slapdash cook,' says Eve. (Apropos this when Paul was on a British Council posting to the island of Majorca after the war, his wife Billy started a hotel. One day Charles appeared from nowhere, and in recognition of his skills as a cook Billy gave him the job of chef. Charles was a success except that, as Paul remembers, 'He would come into the restaurant dressed only in shorts and tell the clients with some force what they should choose from the menu.' Years later and back in England, Paul came across Charles running a restaurant in Kent called High Rocks.)

Eve Durrell says she found Charles at times histrionic, a buffoon with an endlessly mobile face: 'He had the flavour of the East End about him. He was enigmatic, a loner; a man always performing – well – and never revealed all. But he was not a shallow man. He dared to trust people; unlike Larry. Sometimes Charles made me cringe.'

Whilst Charles made it clear that he did not want his own visits to the Villa Ambron to overlap with Elizabeth's, it seems that his reappearance provoked feelings of regret in her about their earlier separation, which she confided to Durrell with Eve present. Despite her flat, non-committal announcement to Priscilla about Charles's departure for America two years earlier in 1941, and her subsequent negative comments about him, Elizabeth seems to have hidden from her family, most friends and ultimately herself, the significance of her experiences and emotions in relation to the man whom her family had censured for so many years.

These experiences and emotions are more convincingly captured in the letter from herself to Charles, written some time after they had separated and quoted by him (anonymously) on the dedicatory page of *The Voyage of the Evelyn Hope*:

> We'll both think often of the things we have done together; of the canals, and the wine, and the red rocks of my beloved France; of the sea white with nautilus off the coast of Corsica; of dawn in the Bay of Naples; of a certain lobster mayonnaise we ate between one life and another; of mountains of golden oranges in Josipi's garden, and those purple islands lying all around us from the top of the hill behind our house. Thank you for the lovely

experiences you have given me, and remember that you made the Isles of Greece more than just a beautiful name for both of us . . .

Whatever the tangled sequence of events (and the vexed question of who had left whom), Charles and Elizabeth never lived together again. A postscript highlights the inconclusiveness of both their feelings. Eve Durrell and Paul Gotch remember that on several occasions at the Villa Ambron Charles would speak about Elizabeth and say, 'She was the woman of my life and that is why I left her.'

Years later, back in England, Elizabeth went to stay with her friend Doreen Thornton, who quickly regretted her misguidedness in putting a copy of *The Voyage of the Evelyn Hope* in Elizabeth's room. She was enraged, in tears, and tore up the book.

In Alexandria Charles found an Israeli girl called Giela with whom he went to live in Cyprus (they eventually married). Charles appears to have spent the remainder of the war in Cyprus, and while there wrote the elegy to his and Elizabeth's affair: *The Voyage of the Evelyn Hope*.

Returning to October 1941, the month in which Charles and Elizabeth had separated, Elizabeth was writing from Alexandria about her pleasure at receiving letters from Norman Douglas again. She was relieved at his present safety with her cousin Neil in Lisbon, and announced her approval of her sister Diana's August marriage to the young doctor Christopher Grey. By December Elizabeth and Mike Cumberlege had amicably decided it was time to move on and find themselves separate accommodation – he was frequently out of Egypt on secret Naval missions – and Elizabeth had found a tiny flat of her own. She gave Felicité a bitingly funny characterization of that ponderous aspect of Middle Eastern taste and conjured up a whole world. The flat was covered with brown wallpaper and filled with aspidistras, plush curtains and huge mirrored sideboards. She threw them all away and painted the flat cream, keeping only a few pieces of furniture. She described her bedroom furniture as 'Tottenham Court Rd modern', of a 'hideosity' rarely seen, but said the bed was comfortable and the wardrobe large with a long mirror. There was a minute bathroom and a fairly good kitchen.

And, although she was immensely grateful for the companionship and support that Mike Cumberlege had given her and the highly sociable life of their flat, she said, 'I'm really happier living on my own.'

Elizabeth was a little self-conscious about the burdens and the impoverishment of life at home in England while she was sitting there with an abundance of things to eat and drink and smoke, and continuously going out and enjoying herself, but she explained that if she didn't occupy her mind with other things, the war and Egypt would get her down completely. For a good part of the time Elizabeth's need to retreat from her own thoughts or unresolved emotions had been kept at bay with a very full social life, and the insecurity of war made this frenetic life-style even more seductive. She said, 'I feel I simply have to go out to parties and fall madly in and out of love and beat up the town from time to time.' Surprisingly, she added that she was no longer able to read, she lacked concentration and was always too tired after leaving her office. She then referred Pris to the perpetually worrying question of money and succinctly described what always seemed to be her position: 'I am extremely sorry to be such a pestering nuisance with my finances – I keep trying not to spend money & it just goes like mad.'

References to her social life, sometimes exhausting, and emotionally precarious, grew more and more frequent as the months passed and her circle widened. Amongst new friends she met old ones from London and Malta. She joined Hilary Magnus, now a Major in the Rifle Brigade, one evening in one of the grandest hotels, aptly described as the Shepherds of Alex. On the subject of Magnus Elizabeth was in fine form; irritated by his habits and tastes, she produced a good vignette for Felicité. She found him in the bar of the Cecil, 'consuming champagne cocktails at about 30/- a time', red in the face and looking quite extraordinary in what seemed to be a floor-length captured German overcoat. She had dinner with him, and for once had the money to pay the bill without having to borrow it, but he made her promise to buy him five pounds' worth of marmalade, which he would return to collect in a week's time. Fortunately

Elizabeth ignored this, because when Magnus came back he announced that he'd bought it himself. He annoyed her so much she made up her mind not to go out with him that evening. She gave him an excuse but Magnus outdid her, saying he'd had no intention of asking her anyway, he felt too liverish. 'In spite of this I'm always pleased to see him.' On another occasion he was 'the old wretch . . . had a new pose . . .' and was evocatively described as 'like a breath of Lincoln's Inn, the Ecu de France, The Café Royal and No. 16 John St' (Elizabeth's last flat before leaving London).

She was not unusual in her sensuous responses to the glimpse of a face, a curve outlined, an arresting ensnaring movement, a colour, a scent; the taste of another time and place. Where Elizabeth differed from many, aiming at Proustian effects, was in her wish to describe these sensuous responses and in her ability to achieve it. She was not to begin writing professionally for several years, but in her war letters all her faculties and sensitivities are at work: collecting, sifting, rejecting, criticizing, discerning. She also displays an endearing lack of punctuation, reinforcing one's impression of her in private: smoky silences, or thoughts and feelings spilling over one another so quickly her pen cannot keep up. These early characteristics are ironic in the light of her subsequent grammatical punctiliousness as a writer – so extreme that she once tried to have a young sub-editor on a magazine sacked for 'mis-editing my work'.

Her sensuous delight in clothes was a constant theme of her letters. A friend from Malta, Lindsey Jackson (later an admiral), had brought back with him from a recent trip to England a magnificent parcel of favourite clothes, jewellery, photographs and letters, collected together by Priscilla for Elizabeth and delivered to her office. Elizabeth thanked Priscilla ecstatically for everything, including the organization of letters from everyone she cared about in England. As soon as Elizabeth got home she tore open the parcel, to find clothes 'reeking' of John St and the existence they now thought of as 'before the war'. The first item to emerge was her blue coat: she remembered trudging through the snow with Pris, in woollen stockings and snowboots, on the way to her first fitting for it; and sitting in the flat during that dreadful winter, the pipes frozen, two enormous fires blazing, cutting out Penny Plain Twopence coloured prints for

Christmas cards. Next out was a little black taffeta jacket, new when Elizabeth first went to Malta; it reminded her of Pris's sitting room, pale blue armchairs, striped curtains, bowls of freesias, Angela in a panic about a quail that the cat had eaten. A blouse threaded with coloured ribbons, worn at the party for Felicité's twenty-first birthday: the flat pandemonium, people running up and down the stairs with food and champagne, while Elizabeth frantically made asparagus rolls. Twenty-five people came to dinner that night instead of the ten who had been expected, including a Romanian whom no one had invited. Evarts had carved turkey like one possessed, and Elizabeth was still painting her nails as the first guests arrived. With a 'wild yell of joy' she seized her scarlet woollen dress, and felt she could almost 'live through again two years' of her life, so often had she worn it. And then the black dress she wore the winter she worked at Worth, and a studded belt. And finally, 'in the midst of all this . . . past', some mysterious little parcels with exquisite bracelets, brooches, and beautiful old buttons that she had never seen before.

Elizabeth's friend from schooldays, Marian Butterworth, had recently married and Elizabeth hoped she would be happy. Felicité was working as a secretary in the Admiralty (organized by Uncle Top) and Pris struggled on in Chipping Sodbury, mother to two small children as well as continuing in that surrogate role to her three younger sisters.

By March 1942 Norman Douglas's welfare was again concerning Elizabeth. He had returned to England. She was immensely grateful to Neil Hogg for having looked after him so well in Portugal: 'One couldn't help being of course [grateful] . . . he is the world's darling and my life's love, but it is so nice of Neil all the same.' Felicité was thanked for writing to him, but Elizabeth was really concerned about him because he hadn't been in England since 1917, hated the climate and was bound to be very miserable. She asked her sister to look him up in London and told her that she would find him most interesting. Elizabeth next asked Felicité if she had read his *Old Calabria*. Elizabeth preferred it to *South Wind*, and thought it first-class writing; although *South Wind* was 'good fun to read', first-class writing it was not.

Although Elizabeth had now held down a job more consistently than ever before, her habitual emotional pathways were not easily altered. Her need to blot out the insecurity produced by war or her own unwanted thoughts – this was not conducive to an emotional state of greater equilibrium. She was hard on herself, hard in that she abused her body with too much alcohol and her emotions with relationships with men who were likely to hurt her. She was self-destructive, and at a profound level was untrusting, but she often leapt into the more existential levels of experience and took the consequences of her own actions. This pattern was already well established, and would remain more or less unchanged for the rest of her life.

Elizabeth's judgement of others was equally severe. But her severity sprang from self-centredness combined with a vein of austerity rather than the austerity of a moral vision. She was a realist and a pragmatist, yet endlessly hopeful and passionate; she was not a romantic but nurtured intense likes and dislikes regarding people and ideas. A friend of many years, Patrick Woodcock, recently said of her, 'I think she always liked pleasing men. But I don't think they ever came up to scratch for her. I don't think she was very perceptive about them. She had passionate friendships. What she really wanted was friendship.' This comment is instructive in the light of Elizabeth's romantic attachments. There are many factors at work here, but the most significant relate to her limited ability to accept men for what they were.

Meanwhile Elizabeth wrote to Pris that she had 'an occasional racket around the town when a particular friend turns up out of the blue', and then had the usual reaction: going home from the office, resorting to her old habit of unhooking the telephone, refusing to answer the door bell, ignoring dinner engagements, and behaving rudely to all her friends. In this mood she never emerged until she felt human again. She even went for long walks at strange hours of the day and strode along the Corniche Road in the heat of the afternoon, gaping at the sun and oblivious of passers-by – behaving, in fact, rather like her Aunt Dorothy, her maiden aunt still living on the home farm at Folkington.

She sometimes wondered if she wouldn't end up in similar circumstances. She told Pris that there might be many worse fates, and reminded her that she never could abide the idea of marriage. She never liked any man sufficiently to want him hanging around her all the time; and when she did 'lose her head' in that respect, six months was always more than enough time to cure her. Elizabeth knew this, she said, when she left England; Charles knew it; they had a good life all the same, though she had no intention of it ever becoming permanent. If she were to marry now, it would be for money, and only to someone extremely rich. She was perspicacious enough, however, to realize that hers was not the type that appeals to millionaires. She thought she would probably continue to exist in her current state. Pris was told that their childhood had completely put Elizabeth off having children of her own. Of course she never knew what she might do in a 'moment of aberration', because one of the 'main conditions of continued existence is that life should always be full of changes and surprises'. It certainly always had been for Elizabeth.

Of the numerous new friends Elizabeth acquired in Egypt only some were mentioned in letters to her family and old friends. In part this was because her instinct for a good story led her, in letters back home, to refer to those whom they could recognize and identify. But, of great significance for the future, this was the old inclination, now habitual, of keeping the elements of her life separate.

One of Elizabeth's new friends whom she did mention was a young woman she had met not long after her arrival in Alexandria, Renée Catsaflis. Renée was half Italian and half Greek, from an old and wealthy family of Alexandrian lawyers, and moved amongst that cosmopolitan upper echelon of Alexandrian and Cairene society where Jews, Copts, other Christians and Muslims tolerantly overlapped. These were people for whom French was the first language and who were perfectly familiar with Europe, often wintering in Switzerland or Paris or on the Riviera. Beautiful, intelligent, cultivated, Renée had been sent to school in France. She was at times both enigmatic and outrageous, reticent and forthcoming. She was devoted to her twin brother. Renée and Elizabeth became close friends and spent many of Elizabeth's days off together, in the summer months often spending the whole day by the sea, or going 'for some sort of totter around in the winter – one can't call it going out to the country because there isn't any sort of country here'.

By May of '42 Renée's company was helping to lighten the load represented for Elizabeth by her present job. Working every day, always distasteful to her, had become a daily burden, and she counted the hours until her day off. Without that weekly break she felt she would sink into 'sheer robotism'. Through friends like Renée Elizabeth got to know some of the more exalted members of Egyptian society, including Baron Georges de Menasce, a Jewish financier and one of those whom Elizabeth eventually regarded as the kindest to her during her years in the Middle East.

She told Felicité she was bored and frustrated by her work in cypher at the Admiralty, 'Being harried about by jumped up shipping clerks, forever typing out lists, cyphering a lot of rubbish, sitting in an office with a lot of clods smoking stinking pipes and having practically to ask permission to go to the lavatory.' This was soon to come to an end. She was too intelligent, self-willed and independent to flourish under any kind of mindless, bureaucratic discipline; however, the war would once again be responsible for a sudden change in her circumstances.

On 20 June 1942, when Rommel had relentlessly pushed the Allied Forces forward along the coast and in the Desert, after enormous bombardment and desperate resistance from the troops, Tobruk fell. In Egypt and Britain the loss was regarded as a disaster. The Eighth Army was in retreat from Rommel, but at El Alamein Rommel's exhausted forces stopped, only 60 miles from Alexandria. This terrifying proximity, combined with what was mistakenly interpreted as the withdrawal of part of the Allied Fleet from Alex, led to a general panic and a grand exodus of civilians from both Alexandria and Cairo. This was known as 'the Flap'. Rommel was in fact driven back and Alexandria and Cairo were never occupied. But Churchill changed his Commander in Chief in the Middle East, Auchinleck, who was unceremoniously dumped back in India, and Montgomery began his leadership of the Desert War which would make him a national hero.

On 1 July when the British Embassy and GHQ in Cairo began

burning documents, Elizabeth and her colleagues had already been evacuated to Suez from where she wrote to Pris telling her not to worry. She had become accustomed to speedy evacuations and said that by this time her sister ought to have confidence in her ability to extract herself from these tiresome situations.

In due course the office was returned to Alexandria. Elizabeth had to stay in a makeshift hostel, which she referred to as 'the Haggery', with numbers of other women about whom she was, of course, scathing, saying that they were all 'flapping like crows'. At the time she was suffering from a severe skin infection on her foot, picked up at the beach, and was almost unable to walk, both feet done up in yards of bandages. In fine acerbic form, she gave a revealing picture of her self-awareness and her ability to manipulate. Surrounded by battered cases, 'waiting for someone to come and help me or lean heavily on someone's arm looking as brave and splendid as any wounded hero while four or five other people follow carrying my fantastic pieces of baggage – the system has its advantages'.

After two months of encampment and borrowing (for three weeks) a house outside the city right on the edge of the sea, where a continuous wild party was in progress, Elizabeth was moved to Cairo. She was reluctant to go. Most of her friends were in Alex; Cairo was noisy, full of people, hot and sticky, and she could never find her way about and spent a fortune on taxis. A friend, Kit Ayling's husband, Alan, had recently said to her that she would soon be fed up with 'racketing around', but she thought England a difficult proposition and felt fatalistic about her own destiny. Making plans, she believed, was an utterly futile pastime, one she indulged in only when in reckless mood.

In Cairo she was at first in lodgings, bed and breakfast with a 'ghastly landlady in the centre of town' although it was clean and well furnished. Having overcome her distaste for landladies, she was relieved not to have dealings with 'beastly servants, the everlasting meals . . . the marketing which although I love, doing it takes a fearful time – and all the rest of the business . . . I know that . . . whoever I share a flat with it's always me who does the housekeeping. As you know I love entertaining and so am led into fantastic expense . . . I really cannot bear to share a flat with droves of people and that's the only way one can afford to exist . . . as living conditions in Cairo are so absolutely impossible . . . one considers oneself lucky to have anywhere to live at all.'

Naturally Elizabeth could not survive for long in the despised lodgings and so found herself a flat. It was small and like a little oven in summer but it was her own and she could luxuriate in the knowledge that when she was too tired to speak she could indulge in her favourite and indescribable pleasure of coming home, locking the door behind her and settling down in bed with a pile of books. She quickly made a great many friends in Cairo and for the first time in years actually had a job that she liked doing.

Elizabeth was now working as Reference Librarian for the busy office of the Ministry of Information, part of GHQ Middle East. J. M. Richards, since 1931 the influential and ambitious editor of the *Architectural Review*, was about to take over as Director of Publications and he and Elizabeth soon became friends. The MOI was a department of the Ministry of State in Britain and was set up as an information and propaganda machine with three sections: Publications, Library and Reference. The Ministry had any number of Press Attachés and Information Officers situated throughout the Middle East at embassies or high commissions, constantly feeding in information which might be useful in the exercise to persuade the Middle East that it was better off with the British than the Germans. These Press and Information Officers were an enormously varied bunch, recruited from all types of peacetime occupation; several were academics or writers of one kind or another. Amongst this particular group were a number who became good friends of Elizabeth's.

Reference librarianship was probably not a job Elizabeth would have sustained well for a lengthy period, but for a while, with her natural curiosity and formidable memory, it suited her perfectly, teaching her a considerable amount about gathering material, about precision and concision in writing, and giving her first-hand know-ledge of the workings of a library. Her job was to read newspapers, books and magazines, write summaries of the comments, and pass the important issues on to the people who could best use them. After her boredom in the Navy the job seemed wonderful, although what she had to read was not what she would have chosen for herself.

She also revealed her relative lack of interest, or certainly lack of sophistication, in the workings of politics. She had scarcely read any papers since the outbreak of war; her present job was a far cry from the days when the only newspaper she ever opened was the *Sunday Express*. The outpourings of journalists and propaganda writers were not her idea of mental stimulus, but it was another matter when she was paid to read them. Her office took all the daily papers and most of the weeklies, and she had to read them all. Speeches, battles, figures and statistics of losses, production, notes on well-known personalities, activities in occupied countries – all had to be carded up and distributed. Added to this, Elizabeth had to deal with people dropping into the office all day long asking for articles, cuttings, books: 'what Eden said at Anapolis, how many planes the Germans lost last month'. She had an unerring nose for anything with a whiff of the absurd: 'what date the Germans first took so and so, when the Russians retook it and when the Germans took it again'.

Two further references are good indications of her future self and what would become her established methods of working. 'I can never see over the pile of stuff waiting to be read ... I go nearly mad sometimes, and as I can't bear to appear inefficient I sometimes spend whole mornings looking for some footling date or other – to be quite honest *I really love the job* and wouldn't change it for anything.' Later she wrote with relish to Felicité that as far as books were concerned she was in a better position than most people, because one of her jobs was ordering them for the library in her office. This suited her down to the ground, because, although she couldn't order exactly what she would have liked, the library consisting mainly of reference books and propaganda, she was still able to buy most of the new Penguins and all the books reviewed in the English papers.

One of Elizabeth's old friends who regularly turned up at the library was a tall, dusky young man, with lustrous eyes as brown as her own and an equal attention to self-presentation. George Lassalle and Elizabeth had met in 1932 or thereabouts while he was up at Oxford and she was acting at the Playhouse. George was sent to Oxford by his father to read Forestry, changed to Law and ended by taking a degree in Modern Languages, in which he excelled. Strict

Catholics, the Lassalle family appear to have recently arrived from
Trinidad, where George and his father had both been born. His
mother was an eccentric from the Southern United States. After
Oxford, having been given an allowance for France, instead George
went off to the Greek islands where he perfected his fishing technique,
refined his wit, collected eccentric friends, got himself in and out of
dramas and a marriage, and returned to run a jazz music business in
Soho. Having remarried, he was called up, entered the Royal Sussex
Regiment and was sent out to Egypt. Here, as a result of his French
and what became fluent German and Greek, George eventually picked
up a job in Intelligence in the Greek section; ideal for someone to
whom subterfuge was second nature.

Always charming, dedicated almost as obsessively as Lawrence
Durrell to his conquest of women, the world's supreme liar (perhaps
he was matched here by Charles Gibson Cowan), George had long
since begun an affair with Elizabeth. Knowing each other well, they
had few illusions about one another, but remained friends – and
sometimes lovers – for the rest of their lives.

All those whom one should know – those, that is, who graced
the bar at Shepherds, Groppis and the parties at Zmalek and Bulaq
Dacrour – also often passed through the doors of the Ministry of
Information Library to give and receive information and gossip. Two
of Elizabeth's closest friends in Egypt were the aforementioned
Lawrence Durrell and Robin Fedden. A conscientious objector, Fedden had followed the course often suggested by pacifist beliefs,
working as an ambulance driver, before taking a lectureship in the
English department of Cairo's Fuad El Awad University. Fedden was
soon to marry Elizabeth's friend Renée Catsaflis and lived with her
and several others in a large, cool house in Bulaq Dacrour across the
river, to the west of Gezira Island and the Sporting Club. During
their stay, for the summer months the house became a favourite venue
for the literate and stylish to gather, and parties there made it one of
the most sought-after places at which to be 'seen'. John Brinton
(American Military Attaché) and his wife, Bernard Burrows and his
future wife, the beautiful Ines Walter, David Abercrombie (later
Professor of Linguistics at Edinburgh University) who also taught at

Cairo University, and his wife Mary made up the household. Elizabeth came there to escape the heat of the city, and after the drinking and the dancing one could always cool off in the welcoming pool.

Elizabeth had met Robin Fedden before the war in Egypt when she had first visited the Middle East and Fedden was already living there. In 1939 he had published *The Land of Egypt* in which he gives due credit to the classic works on Egypt and adds some resonant descriptions of the country and its classical remains. Fedden was an open-minded and cultivated man, a true European, who mixed with both the wealthy and more scholarly of Egyptian society; yet, despite cautious hopes for a future, emancipated non-fundamentalist Egypt, he was unable to disguise his distaste for aspects of the country, and a clear preference for the land, the culture and climate of Greece shines through *The Land of Egypt*.

The regret and nostalgia of exile are palpable through Robin Fedden's description and rejection of modern Egypt in his introduction to the literary quarterly, *Personal Landscape* (privately printed 1942–5, then by Editions Poetry London, 1945), which he founded with his friends Lawrence Durrell and the poet Bernard Spencer. For those who contributed to the magazine the identification was the same. They were, however, like Fedden referring in their lamentations of exile not to England but to an adopted country – Greece. And, like religious converts, those who adopt another country often do so with a fervour never accorded to their native land. In the case of Greece it was what most Europeans between the wars still felt was their cultural Mecca. Even for devotees of Italy, Greece was the source of Western civilization, still accessible enough for those who had the cultural resources to understand how to summon up its past.

Robin Fedden and Lawrence Durrell were both men for whom the ideal of Greece was very real. Elizabeth might not have benefited from the rigorous classical education of Spencer or Fedden, but like Durrell she identified entirely with their sense of exile, and was party to many late-night conversations emanating from the same principles inspiring *Personal Landscape* . . . (Burrows recalls that some believed Durrell's lack of a classical education made him not quite 'pukka'.)

Overlapping socially with this diplomatic and literary group of Elizabeth's friends was another set who fought their war with arms. Several afterwards wrote books, but, like the best-known of them, Patrick Leigh Fermor, a good friend of Elizabeth's, they were men of action as much as writers. That Leigh Fermor became one of the most revered of post-war travel writers is no coincidence. With his friend 'Pint Pot' Xan Fielding, Leigh Fermor was in and out of Cairo on one mission or another. With others of their circle they had taken a house of grand Italianate proportions and ageing elegance at the northern end of Cairo's Gezira Island.

In February 1943 Elizabeth was writing to Pris about her worries of the moment. Back to her old habits of regular entertaining, she fussed over arranging the flowers, sewing buttons on her clothes and her servant–cook who was giving concern. She found it impossible to explain to a cook who could not read or 'speak any known language', and who 'couldn't cook anyway', what she wanted for dinner.

For this cook, Suleiman, Elizabeth came to feel great affection and, as with those other cooks, Angela and Kyriakou, she recorded his sympathetic nature and abilities for posterity at regular intervals for the rest of her life. In *Mediterranean Food* Suleiman's Rice Pilaff became famous; in 'Fast and Fresh', an article for the *Spectator* in 1960, she characterized his talents and charm; again, ten years on, when Elizabeth launched her rediscovery of the East, in *Spices, Salt and Aromatics in the English Kitchen* and in the article she wrote for Smallbone Kitchen Designs, one of her last, he was lovingly remembered. The following extracts give brilliant, swift evocations of the food of the Levant. Most cooks working for the English were convinced that the only proper food for them was nursery fare with Middle Eastern overtones. In 'Fast and Fresh' she wrote:

> My own cook, Suleiman, was a Sudanese who had previously only worked for Italian and Jewish families. He was erratic and forgetful, but singularly sweet in nature, devoted to his cooking pots and above all knew absolutely nothing of good clean, English schoolroom food.

The description of Suleiman and his cooking was refined for the Smallbone article and as the story develops we are charmed and amused as he:

> performed minor miracles with two primus stoves and an oven which was little more than a tin box perched on top of them. His soufflés were never less than successful, and with the aid of a portable charcoal grill carried across the road to the Nile bank opposite (the kitchen was so small it didn't even have a window, and if he had used charcoal he'd have been asphyxiated) he produced perfectly good lamb kebabs. The rice pilaff I named after him . . . became part of quite a few people's lives at that time.

And: 'From an old hand-cranked churn on loan for the evening . . . it would have been hard to beat Suleiman's home made mish mash or apricot ice cream.'

Besides entertaining Elizabeth was, above all, preoccupied and tense about her present lover, an ex-Oxford student from North America, at present in the 9th Queen's Royal Lancers and lying wounded in a hospital outside Cairo. She told Pris in April 1945 he had been in the thick of battle and terribly wounded at Mersa Matruh in November. For the past five months she had gone out twice a week to the most 'god awful' hospital she ever saw, which was forty minutes outside Cairo. 'All the worst things that could have happened to him have happened to him and he never uttered a murmur of pain or discouragement.' She was thankful she was in Cairo, and able to attend to him.

She was terribly grateful to a friend, Guy Charvet (head of Shell), for lending his car twice a week for the purpose. 'The whole business has been very heartbreaking – I haven't mentioned it before because we've all got our own hells to cope with . . . I have been so glad to have had my flat and he has been able to come out of the hospital and have meals with me.' At about this time her cousin Neil Hogg, who had recently looked after Norman Douglas so well, dashed through Cairo on his reluctant way up to the Embassy at Baghdad.

He wrote from there to Priscilla, and the similar style explains something of his and Elizabeth's attachment to one another: 'Isn't it hell being sent away like this? I was bundled off in a flying cattle truck and just contrived to reach here alive a week ago. Now I shall roast and rot here for two years at least . . . Liza was in pretty good form, looking rather Persian I thought . . . We had dinner on the roof of an Arab restaurant – kebabs and rice and eggfruit – and talked of you and ourselves and the family . . .'

This Oriental touch in Elizabeth's appearance is also noted by her friend Leigh Fermor who told the author: 'She wore caftans of rather nice material, with many buttons down the front. But then it didn't look affected to dress up, we all did.' He noted too her 'beautiful voice'. But this only hints at that feline quality of Elizabeth's, so striking to some. Her voice has been described by some friends as 'quiet', by others 'breathy', still others 'actressy'. But perhaps the most evocative description is given by Alix Coleman, a journalist who later became a friend of Elizabeth's, and who told the author: 'She had an expiring voice. Very femme fatale . . . She could without doing anything make a man feel good. She used to turn her nose up or give a little gasp – or the way she put a cigarette out – she did it in a sexy way. Once there were some workmen across the way at Halsey Street, one look from Elizabeth and they would have been right over and through the door.'

In the same letter Elizabeth wrote to Pris about her wounded lover she mentioned having written to Aunt Grace and Uncle Top about their son Bill's recent death. Another cousin, Jasper Ridley, son of her Uncle Jasper, was killed in 1943. 'Not that there is anything to say under the circumstances. Tragedy is part of one's everyday existence and one thinks less of it than what one is going to order for lunch – it sounds callous but that's the way it is.' Perhaps these are truisms of the brutalizing consequence of war, but this was not the only response of survivors and reflects Elizabeth's capacity for insensitivity. In contrast to the solace she gave Mike Cumberlege after his cousin's death, on these other occasions her unwillingness to reach out emotionally and soothe those facing the starkness of this reality is striking. With no belief in an afterlife, death for her was complete oblivion – utter finality and nothing less. Its immensity was such that for the moment Elizabeth saw no point in wasting time over it once it had happened.

By July she was writing that her lover 'P.L.' was much recovered and had gone back to North America. Some of her oldest friends consider him the man whom Elizabeth loved above all others. Certainly at the time she believed herself much in love with him and was bitter a year later when she said that he had forgotten her. (He was extremely attractive and women were apparently smitten with unerring regularity.) In spite of the fact that many years later in her will Elizabeth described herself as relieved at his return home, for all her directness about some issues this appears to be a case of deliberately muddying the waters of her own history. This man hurt her and probably continued to do so for a number of years, when he picked up the liaison again after the war. In not marrying her he presumably recognized (no matter if unconsciously) what Elizabeth never properly faced: that she would have been unable to sustain the relationship.

As well as her very full working day, combined with entertaining friends and going out, Elizabeth had somehow fitted in 'a little acting for ENSA', the organization which produced entertainment for the troops. But she was feeling worn out and was missing friends no longer in Egypt. One of these was Mike Cumberlege, gone missing on one of his secret missions in the Mediterranean. It was subsequently discovered that he had been captured by the Germans, refused to talk under torture, and was incarcerated (sometimes in solitary confinement) for twenty-one months in one of the worst German prisoner-of-war camps, Saxonhausen, then taken out and shot just as the Russians moved into Berlin in 1945. Cumberlege was posthumously awarded two DSOs, 'a rare honour' as his wife wrote to Pris when asking her to pass on the final confirmation of his death to Elizabeth.

Elizabeth found some solace in her work. It was a pleasure to immerse herself in it instead of 'spitting' at everyone, which was how she felt in the old office. This repeated and very evident sense of fulfilment in her work reflects a subtle, but extremely important, shift in her attitudes and sensibilities. Here in Cairo she was for the first time doing a job which she cared about enough to do consistently well. Also her regular and increasing familiarity with the unpleasant details of war now made her own war effort (namely her job) more a matter of commitment than, as previously, mere necessity.

Time passed and a year later, on 5 July 1944, Elizabeth wrote in weary tones to Pris, and later her mother, with a startling piece of news. 'In fact what with one thing and another Cairo has so worn down my spirit that I am thinking of getting married.' She asked Pris's absolute confidence over this, not yet having decided whether she could face giving up her liberty, and continued in the same mode. 'The man in question is not at all the man I intended to marry, but he seems to love me very much and is apparently able to provide for me in modest comfort.' Her astoundingly practical and imperious tone throughout this letter and a subsequent one to her mother was tinged with the usual tongue in cheek. 'He has been in the Indian Army, poor man, most of his life and as a result is practically illiterate . . . He likes dancing and drinking. I rather suspect he is given to riding, and reading P. G. Wodehouse, but one can hardly expect anyone in the Indian Army to do anything else . . . However as all my intelligent and more irresponsible boyfriends are always penniless it would seem wiser to keep them as friends and marry someone who can look after me.' (Owing to Tony's tendency to do things 'in style' Elizabeth mistakenly believed her future husband to be richer than he was.) She again insisted on no presents, saying that Tony was very generous and would give her whatever she wanted, 'barring mink coats and Packard motor cars'. One of the most revealing aspects of this letter is Elizabeth's consistently objective tone. In her determination to protect herself from being hurt again she is choosing a relationship over which she believes she will have more control; possible with Tony because she is not captivated. Elizabeth has not yet learnt, however (perhaps she never did) that this control will only be partially effective, because those aspects of herself she refuses to address will always manage to surface in unexpected ways.

To her mother she said, 'I am beginning to feel the need of a prop'; and told her that although she would probably be horrified to hear he was in the Indian Army, 'I think he has spent most of his career dancing attendance on Governors and Viceroys rather than flogging the natives . . . I have told him that I don't see myself sitting in some compound or other watching people play polo for the rest of my life, and I think he wants to get out of it anyway.'

Elizabeth instructed her mother and Pris to tell only Diana and Felicité. Friends and family were not to make a fuss or spend money on presents. However, neither did she want anyone at home to be offended at her secrecy, but said that it would all be over quickly and, with a revealing piece of self-knowledge, that anyway they knew her well enough to expect anything she did to take place in a 'shady' manner. On Tony's return from a term of duty in the Allied advance taking place up through Italy, she would make her decision. They planned to marry at the Consulate and Elizabeth insisted that her dislike of formal weddings was so great that, as her large number of friends would 'insist on a demonstration of some kind', she had decided to tell almost no one in Cairo until after the event. She had threatened Tony with calling the wedding off if he disobeyed her instructions. However, as he was apparently friendly with John Brinton, American Military Attaché, and Sir Miles Lampson, Britain's Ambassador to Egypt, she supposed they would have to have a small party. Elizabeth said she would keep on her flat and her job after the wedding.

Aware that her announcement sounded as weary as it did, she explained herself. 'The glamour boy I was so attached to . . . has apparently forgotten my existence and at my age . . . I have no intention of being led a dance by anybody, I simply don't care enough. I'm afraid this letter doesn't sound a very happy one, but don't get a wrong impression. I like the man very much and get on well with him . . .' She added that he was kind, competent and intelligent enough to accept her as she was and not try and make her into something different, and that she would probably be able to lead quite a reasonable life with him. Her final comment admirably sums up her attitude: 'It is only the realization that I am so tired of living this haphazard life, never having enough money and never being able to do what I want and that marriage is the only answer has depressed me somewhat.' Elizabeth's desire for a protector is understandable, but her calculation is more startling.

An only child, Ivor Anthony David was born in Bristol in 1911. His father, Ivor Edward, became Inspector General of Police in

Ceylon, but was now dead, and his mother, Beatrice, lived in Llandaff in Wales. Following British tradition, Tony had been sent back 'home' to school in England; his public school was Bradfield College in Berkshire. The voyage out to India in the Twenties still meant weeks on board ship, so Tony became one of those small boys who was sent to relations or friends for the holidays, and rarely saw his parents. Initially this meant staying with two maiden aunts in Wales, but Tony was soon taken pity on by his friend Owen Llewellyn's mother, and for several years his holidays were spent in the hospitable Llewellyn household. Owen's mother was not only beautiful, she was also a woman of character and fun; Tony became devoted to her, and obviously found with his friends some of the sense of home otherwise missing from his life. According to Owen's sister Daphne (now Lady Maynard), Owen and their elder sister Hermione were as dynamic as their mother, and provided Tony with a permanent source of enjoyment and stimulation.

According to Lady Maynard he was 'a slightly lonely character, a loner, but always a very comforting person all the same'. Even as a boy it was clear that he was a follower rather than a leader. 'He tended perhaps to attach himself to "stars", and both my brother and sister Hermione were this.' In 1933 Owen was killed in an air crash and Daphne Maynard remembers Tony's solicitous visits when she and Hermione were sent away in that rather merciless Victorian style, to 'recover' by the sea. Hermione, later the Countess of Ranfurly, was to become a highly experienced and discreet personal assistant, whose social connections and determination to stay on in the Middle East during the war kept her in the thick of its highest-level politics. The Countess of Ranfurly recently wrote her memoirs of this period, entitled *To War with Whitaker* (Mandarin, 1995). Her sister Daphne meanwhile had come out to Cairo as a cypherene for Special Operations Executive, became Fitzroy Maclean's secretary and met up with Tony again in 1943. Regarding this she makes another pertinent comment about the man Elizabeth was soon to marry. 'My means of transport to work every day was on the back of a truck and Tony had a car. It was out of his way but he insisted on collecting me every morning. He was the kindest possible person at doing those most boring things.'

Anthony David was commissioned in February 1934 into the Royal Deccan Horse, a distinguished cavalry regiment of the Indian Army. According to Lieutenant-Colonel Harper who served together with him, 'Tony joined us because he was some kind of relation to our 2nd in Command, later Commanding Officer, Frank Tinley. He came from Oxford and Cambridge, not Sandhurst.'

Originating as a body of cavalry maintained by the Nizim of Hyderabad on behalf of the East India company, by 1903, with a confirmed reputation for bravery and fine horsemanship, the Royal Deccan Horse was incorporated into the Indian Army. In 1940 Tony was made Captain, for a time was ADC to the Governor of the Punjab and in 1941 transferred to the Indian Ordinance Corps and became a Lieutenant-Colonel. By early 1942 he was in Cairo, probably in a military policing capacity.

He was by all accounts a gifted horseman and belonged to Cairo's magnificent Gezira Sporting Club. The club owned a vast acreage of landscaped gardens, croquet lawns, tennis courts, golf and race courses and polo fields engulfing the southern end of the Nile's Gezira Island situated, effectively, in the midst of the city. In the welcoming cool of a newly built club-house heat and dust were left behind; here British officers, rich Egyptians and their female companions came to play. Although devoted to polo, according to Lieutenant-Colonel Harper, 'Tony David's main interest was racing and he was an accomplished amateur jockey.'

Most of Elizabeth's friends who met Tony thought them most unsuitably matched. Some believed Tony to be a fool, others, more astute, realized he was not. When he was brought out to Alexandria to visit Durrell, never mind his undoubted good looks, Lawrence and Eve found Tony 'wooden' beside Elizabeth. It was simply that he was unable to keep up with her knowledge and appreciation of literature, her restless curiosity about those things which interested her, her particular intellectual vigour. But at present Elizabeth found him soothing and entertaining. 'They had this rather annoying habit of giggling together,' says a friend. And anyway, Elizabeth was never given to taking advice.

Shortly before Tony's return to Cairo, and Elizabeth's decision to marry him, she was taken to meet the elderly Bishop Gwynne, a long-time resident in the Middle East. Although she found him 'a sweet old thing', she didn't relish his lecture on the 'sad moral tone of Cairo. He's heard rumours about me I expect.' (No doubt correct.)

In his autobiography, *A Sparrow's Flight* (Collins, 1990), Quintin Hogg recalls the Bishop:

> One of the curious features of Cairo at this time was the enormous attendance in the English Cathedral at Evening Service every Sunday. I always went . . . You had to be there at least half an hour in advance to get a seat, and there was a very large standing congregation of all ranks. The Cathedral was big, and when it was constructed under the auspices of old Bishop Gwynne it was already treated as a sort of *folie de grandeur*. Now the old Bishop's vision was fully justified and filled a great spiritual need, both for those on leave from the theatres of war and for those in residence in the capital. We were all far from home, and on these occasions all ranks worshipped together with an immense sense of purpose. The Cathedral is now no more, having been bombed by fanatics after the war in an outburst of anti-British and anti-Christian feeling. I have not seen its successor, but Gwynne's great church had already justified its existence.

Tony returned to Cairo from his stint in Italy and, despite having written to Pris three weeks earlier that she thought marriage 'perfectly ridiculous', Elizabeth said that 'as it's one of the things I've never done I might as well try it for a time'. She added, 'Poor Mummie, her daughters marrying regular soldiers *and* Indian Army.' Accordingly, amidst 'tremendous speculation here about the end of the war', Elizabeth signed away her 'liberty' at the Consulate on 30 August 1944, sending a telegram to Priscilla that afternoon. It read:

> Married Tony David today. I am very happy.
> My dearest Love to you Elizabeth David.

Elizabeth wrote to her friend Doreen in England saying, 'I have married an English Colonel.' Doreen remembers her first thought was: 'Oh *no*.'

By November 1944 'Tony has gone off again to the war and Cairo goes on.' She heard from him 'nearly every day – he is cold and uncomfortable' and longing to return to his bewitching bride and proudly walk out with her on his arm. Félicité was hoping to go to Europe to carry out relief work and Elizabeth said that if she hadn't had to wait on Tony's next posting she would have applied too. 'If there is a chance of him going to the Balkans I shall be there pretty quickly, otherwise I shall stay in Cairo, where I now live a life of comparative comfort. My work is still very agreeable and plenty of it.'

Elizabeth's friend Renée, now married to Robin Fedden, had come to work in the Ministry of Information and so the two saw each other with more ease. Renée's cool, patrician sophistication was in strong contrast to another lifelong woman friend Elizabeth made at this time. Lesley Pares was the daughter of an academic, Professor Pares, and began the war as a semi-trained nurse before being recruited to Bletchley Park, the seat of British Intelligence Operations during the war, by the art historian Cecil Gould. Lesley went through a brief training and was then sent out to Cairo to work in the Ministry of Information as a cypherene. With dark hair, milky skin and a beautiful figure, Lesley was pretty, dressed elegantly in clothes she made herself with skill and, as Sir Bernard Burrows says of her, 'She gave the impression of being delicate, a little fragile.' In combination with her utterly feminine manner this of course made her extraordinarily attractive to men. But Lesley's attraction lay as much in her gentle personality as in her looks, her 'great capacity for friendship,' as Sir Bernard and Lady Ines Burrows and all who recently recalled her wished to stress. 'She wasn't fundamentally an intellectual in the academic sense, though very well read; or perhaps particularly creative', says Sir Bernard. 'She was essentially receptive.' These qualities were a perfect foil to Elizabeth's more demanding and forthright intensity. They soon became close friends.

During the latter stages of the war the fighting moved north-wards and Cairo became less important as an active centre, but Elizabeth remained there for many more months.

Tony's posting was finally decided; it was not, as Elizabeth had hoped, to the Balkans (her friend Durrell *was* posted there) but instead back to New Delhi, GHQ in India. Contrary to her vows that she would never set foot in India, Elizabeth was persuaded to relent and early in 1946 having packed up several years of life in Egypt Elizabeth was in India. She wrote to England in February that she was harassed in her last few weeks, moving, handing over her job and wrangling with the movers, who were determined to get her on a ship while she was equally determined to get an air passage. Elizabeth won of course, and she flew to India, stopping in Baghdad for a 'hilarious evening with Neil' (Hogg) on the way.

Shortly before leaving Cairo she had also managed to get sent to Greece for a week on a mission for the MOI. To her delight she ended by spending almost two weeks there and reaffirmed her love of the country. In Athens she met up with old friends and, in contrast to her previous opinion, now decided it was the best capital in the world in which to find one's self in spite of present difficulties. 'The people are alive, it's a lovely city and the countryside of such indescribable beauty. I shall go back again.'

CHAPTER ELEVEN

India and a Marriage
(1946)

ON ARRIVAL IN India's vast and confusing subcontinent Elizabeth reacted in her customary manner – with passion. She loathed it. And here a point made by Robin Fedden is relevant, in his illuminating introduction to the magazine *Personal Landscape*. He reminds the reader that there is above all a cultural isolation for the European in Egypt.

> It is possible to travel almost anywhere in Europe without quite getting off a familiar cultural beat: whatever the country, Christianity – whether the inhabitants like it or not – is at the back of the way they think and act. Once you cross to Islamic Africa . . . the current of thought sets towards Mecca and the European is inevitably swimming all the time against the stream . . . he cannot hope to find his own life and . . . efforts seconded and strengthened by unconscious community with . . . the life and efforts of people around him.

She may have felt herself cut off from Europe in Egypt, but Elizabeth at least had the Mediterranean Sea on Alexandria's shores, the resonance of the Classical past if one chose to look, and friends, exiled like herself from Greece, for whom that past mattered. But India was so much worse. And here Robin Fedden's comments on Egypt are effectively underlined by E. M. Forster's Cyril Fielding in *A Passage to India*. Returning home via Venice, for centuries one of the centres of Mediterranean life and thought, Fielding is struck by 'the harmony between the works of man and the earth that upholds them, the civilization that has escaped muddle, the spirit in a reasonable form, with flesh and blood subsisting'. Fielding's vision proclaims 'the Mediterranean as the human norm. When men leave that exquisite lake ... they approach the monstrous and extraordinary.' And for Elizabeth, there is no doubt, India was monstrous, utterly removed from the Mediterranean arena, where the old conflicts between Christianity and the Classical world, Apollo and Dionysius, the spirit and the flesh, had inspired scrutiny and struggle for the last 2000 years and out of which had arisen some of the greatest works of man.

In 1911 the British government concluded (King George V himself announced the decision) that the British Raj was to move its seat of Empire from Calcutta and set up in the ancient city of Delhi. Built, fought over, destroyed, rebuilt; there had been no fewer than eight New Delhis over the centuries before this last and lavish display was completed in 1931. Under the auspices of two English architects, Herbert Baker and Edwin Lutyens, there arose beside the medieval forts, mosques and bazaars of Old Delhi a set of vast administrative buildings, a viceregal residence, and other noble monuments all set along enormous avenues and surrounded by huge planned gardens. There are many who regard New Delhi as a pompous, cumbersome piece of blind folly, whilst others believe parts of it Lutyens' masterpiece. It remained the Imperial seat of government for only fifteen years; India was granted independence in September 1947.

Robert Byron, whose highly praised travel book *The Road to Oxiana* had been in many ways a plea for the virtues of Islamic art, thought the new city flawed but magnificent. (Asked after his death why, as someone who was friend to so many homosexuals, she had not taken up with him, Elizabeth's response was that 'He was just too queer for me.') Her opinion of the new city was far more negative. As usual a reaction like this spurred her to some of her most pointed and witty writing and her letters from India are a discriminating howl of horror.

She spoke little of it after her return to England, but one anecdote stands out as exemplifying her experience. On her arrival in India she had to wait for Tony and booked into a hotel for the night, not realizing that the large room she was shown to was the only one. Exhausted from her journey, Elizabeth fell soundly asleep but was awoken some time later by disturbances in the room. She sat up and, peering about the darkened space, discovered that she was not alone. Her room was filled with 'a *massive*' number of people asleep or settling in, all over the floor. She was horrified and said she had never been so frightened in all her life. In India the concept of privacy has almost no meaning, and for Elizabeth lack of privacy was the ultimate deprivation.

Tony had done his best to find suitable quarters for his new wife, but in writing to Felicité she found Delhi terrible beyond all expectations and description. She slated the vast and stagelike conceptions of Lutyens and Baker, saying they had 'large ideas and a pretty good idea that they were supposed to put up something imposing and triumphantly Imperialistic but were evidently unaware that you can't have a city comprised entirely of palaces and parliament houses with the result that you have to drive for hours up and down processional avenues, interspersed . . . with the very charming domed tombs of Moghul Emperors and . . . with the less charming monuments to the glory of The Great White Queen and her successors, and when you get to the centre of the town what do you find? A great circus called Connaught Place round which are arranged the whole of the Delhi shops, round and round you go, incapable of differentiating one . . . street from another because they all look exactly alike in their sterility and hideousness.' This was the notorious centre, designed as the regal hub of the city, from where roads radiate out like the spokes of a wheel, and where getting lost is almost inevitable.

Elizabeth railed that after you had finally located the place you were looking for and couldn't buy what you wanted, 'Do you think you can drop into a café or bar to revive yourself with a drink? No. Because in *all* New Delhi there are no cafés and no bars and because for all their grandiose visions those two ridiculous architects could think of nothing better than to model the capital of a great continent on the town of Cheltenham . . . and nothing has ever been done about it because the British were all brought up there and the Indians wouldn't think of making the place more attractive because they're praying for the day when we'll bloody well get out anyway – so am I.'

Elizabeth and Tony were living in one of six newly completed blocks of flats near one of the main avenues, Kingsway, which Elizabeth told Felicité were as inefficient as they were ugly: 'a livid crimson'. But at least their flat was comfortable, chiefly owing to Tony's industry in getting it into a habitable state. Although the building was new, the flat had no bath until Tony installed one and with it a hot-water heater. This was unusable, however, because the building didn't yet have any power. Elizabeth described how the 'hordes of servants heat up buckets of water and pour them into the bath'. And any deviation from this custom, practised all over India would cause the most terrible unemployment.

As an officer's wife she was not expected to work and in fact did nothing about finding any, being unwilling to start again as a dogsbody, and as a consequence was burdened with more time than she had been accustomed to for years. In spite of her unerring ability to find willing hands to run errands for her, the numbers of servants in India disturbed and irritated her. Unable also to accept that the memsahib did not enter kitchen activities, she was indignant at the resentment this caused and told Felicité she had sacked two cooks within a couple of months of arrival. Her attempt at introducing her primus stove from Cairo had caused such panic amongst the staff that she had given in to the Indian habit of cooking entirely on charcoal fires. This didn't overly worry Elizabeth because she had become accustomed to this method of cooking on her Greek island where conditions were much the same as in the Indian capital. 'If only my God the compensations were as good. There are in fact *no* compensations in Delhi.'

She waged battle with her Indian cooks over their refusal to understand that she did *not* want the 'nice clean English nanny food' they were accustomed to providing for their English employers. She wrote years later in *Spices, Salt and Aromatics in the English Kitchen* that they produced 'cakes festooned in spectacular spun sugar work, attempts at French dishes savagely flavoured with hot green chillies ("I make a French a-stew as good as you," one of my Indian cooks remarked defiantly, and untruthfully) and, oddest of all, Edwardian fantasies of the school which liked to present food in any form except its own (mashed potatoes got up to represent a roast chicken, mushrooms made out of meringue and the like).' How could they, poor men, possibly know that this was part of the very reason Elizabeth had finally ended up in India – she was trying to stay away from that very England which the Raj was concerned to uphold, more desperately with each passing year. The food served up by Indians to their British masters was a fundamental reflection of this Raj ethos and, as despising a large proportion of the customary elements of Britishness had long ago become an integral part of Elizabeth's life, she was not likely to thank anyone trying to thrust them down her neck.

There was nonetheless, as she later told Judith Lassalle, fascination and amazement at the capacity of her Indian cooks to produce 'incredible food out of what were really no more than tin cans' (for cooking pots). In an obvious sense the exotic food of India appealed to her, but again she was disappointed. This was of course inevitable; not only because Elizabeth did not remain in India long enough to discover the enormous variety, complexity and subtlety which exist in the cooking of that remarkable country, but because she was unwilling to make the intellectual change of attitude necessary to its discovery. Having said this, with typical honesty she was aware that there *might* have been an India other than the one of her own experience. Her comments are, as always, etched with deadpan wit. 'Indian food is perfectly frightful, or at least what I have seen of it. The curries always look simply delicious, and one is presented with dozens of different little dishes, but when you come to taste them you find they're all so drenched in chilli peppers that you can't taste anything else for three weeks.'

Many years later, when writing *Spices, Salt and Aromatics in the English Kitchen*, Elizabeth knew more about Indian food but hadn't changed her mind about curries. Later still she would arrive at a stage where one of her favourite types of restaurant was the Indian. Her interest became sufficiently pronounced that on being asked to propose a venue for the launch of her friend Richard Olney's cookery book, *Simple French Food*, she suggested an Indian restaurant!

With her intense curiosity, in a new town Elizabeth would normally have set about discovering those areas which for her were particularly interesting, the markets. But here she complained that the teeming hordes of people were frightening and 'The ugliness and death-like barrenness of everything to be seen strikes horror and despair into anybody accustomed to European civilization, however degraded.' After a time she did of course venture from their 'livid crimson' flat and, with some trepidation, explored both the markets and bazaars of the city, more especially the old city. But she did not often go alone.

Although Elizabeth said Tony had 'wisely kept away from . . . local society, the majority of which is as dreary as you would expect', there was probably a certain amount of wishful thinking on Elizabeth's part here; it appears that Tony did socialize with friends in his regiment and rode often at polo and horse-racing. They did occasionally go together to watch the races, a favourite pastime of many in Delhi. 'But Elizabeth thought it *absurd* to go to the races, and *stand up* and eat and drink there, but of course there were many hands to do it for you,' says Veronica Nicholson (then Meagher), a woman of humour and charm who came into Elizabeth's life soon after the first shock of her arrival in 'this desert of a place'. Veronica described to the author how, having given up her job on *Vogue* to enter the war effort, she had come out to India some months before Elizabeth on a secretarial posting with the War Office. 'It was a kind of Renaissance to go to India – the black hole that was England in those days – and come by way of boat which took a month from London via Scotland.'

Unlike Elizabeth, Veronica 'had never been outside England before and the difference was dazzling. It was lovely . . . I never did anything really. I was a terrible Flapper of the Thirties – was awfully unserious. My department became rather fed up with me.' This may have been true but Veronica was also more than simply a Flapper. With the background of a large, close and comfortably off family she was less intense and endowed perhaps with less wit but more humour than Elizabeth. Not uncritical of British life in India and quite capable of mocking its pomposity, Veronica was of a more open nature, more willing to find a place for herself in this new milieu. She was soon sharing a house with the charismatic Biddy Carlisle and enjoyed socializing with the Commander in Chief of Indian forces Auchinleck and his entourage, which included Tony, relegated there from Cairo. It was a group similar to the 'suave and sprightly ADCs who helped to conjure up the atmosphere of a court' which in his

More Memoirs of an Aesthete (Methuen 1970) Harold Acton refers to surrounding the more austere Viceroy, Wavell. Veronica was immensely feminine, beautifully dressed, well read, funny, and light-hearted; as a consequence her social life was very full.

'Oh, but it was so unlike Elizabeth. She wouldn't have *lent* herself to it all – she was totally uninterested in that kind of man [Auchinleck]. And the Army wives, she was so much more greenery yallery than they. Hers was not in the least like a military family . . . She made it pretty clear that she found them boring . . . She was so much more intellectual than most people at GHQ at the time. I think she did keep herself to herself. Not that she didn't adore conversation more than anyone I have ever known. But it had to be *good* conversation or else she would do without. She wasn't doing what we were doing.' Veronica added that the commanding Biddy Carlisle and Elizabeth did not become friends. 'They were each too prima donna-ish for that.'

No less thoughtful than Elizabeth, Veronica was probably more perceptive, certainly more sensitive to others' feelings. She was fascinated, though, by Elizabeth's biting wit, her observations, her very literate company; saw her difference, realized it was quite unlike anything she had known before. She found Elizabeth retiring, prickly, disdainful. But Veronica also made it clear from the outset that although Elizabeth's wish for her friendship was mutual, she would not be dominated.

The two shared the same Italo-Indian hairdresser. At the hairdresser's expense, of course, Elizabeth was hilarious. 'He gave her the most marvellous hairstyle, Apollo-like with tight curls, for a particular outing. Very fashionable. At first I wasn't impressed by her looks. She had very pale coffee-coloured skin, brown eyes and very nice regular features and, as she remarked herself once, pretty hands.'

Veronica and Elizabeth visited the markets and bazaars together, watched Tony and other officers at their games of polo, and sometimes, with him, joined a party of two or three other army and War Office friends for dinner at one of the beautiful colonial hotels such as Maidens, set amongst elegant acres of lawns in the old city. 'Tony brought people into her life here, but I was sorry for him. It wasn't that he was unintelligent, he simply wasn't her weight intellectually at all.'

There was a certain coolness about Elizabeth; she was quite capable of maintaining a haughty distance, remaining reserved to the point of iciness. And yet behind the ice lay an intense and passionate nature. Increasingly too she reflected her mother's disregard for some of the niceties of social convention. She certainly didn't bother much with its more onerous aspects and felt no compunction about showing her boredom or irritation in public. Her preference at a dinner table was for the more intense, intimate and therefore isolating Anglo-Saxon dialogue between couples, rather than the French regard for more general conversation. This tendency was to become more developed. Veronica adds: 'But she was very good at being a friend too. Elizabeth was much more evolved than most people one met.'

Tony David was one of the few to have a car, and although rationing of petrol meant that a profligate use of vehicles was impossible, occasional excursions out of the city were still possible. Picnics were a favoured excuse for leaving town and one such event was famously recorded by Elizabeth (one of the few personal references she ever makes to India in her writing) in her book *Summer Cooking* (Museum Press, 1955), ten or so years later. This was to be a night-time picnic beside one of the marvels of India, the Qutb Minar. About 10 miles south of Delhi, this soaring round tower of sandstone and marble rose as a victory monument to celebrate the Moslem defeat of the last Hindu king as long ago as the twelfth century. Its five beautifully balconied storeys, set amongst scrubby land, are awash with Koranic inscriptions (the traveller Robert Byron thought them – in stone rather than stucco – too Indian and painstaking). Nearby stands the very earliest Indian mosque.

The party had driven out late, in the cooler air of evening, and Veronica remembers that 'We had settled ourselves down. The moon came out and we were all engaged in conversation when we were quite surrounded by Pi dogs.' Elizabeth takes up the story in *Summer Cooking*. She gives no recipe. Her piece is simply one of those at which she excelled, perfectly conjuring a small drama and its setting, leaving the reader anticipating the rest, always building enough tension to keep him just on edge, the ensemble carried along by the drive of Elizabeth's wit.

> There was nothing wrong with the transport, the food, or the moonlight; we had merely reckoned without the hordes of half wild dogs which are a familiar feature of Indian outdoor life. Scarcely had we had time to draw the cork of a bottle of . . . Australian hock . . . than we were surrounded; literally surrounded. They did not apparently want food, or at any rate not our food; they simply formed a circle round us at a respectful distance and stared and howled.
>
> First we pretended not to notice, then we shoo-ed them away several times. They returned immediately, with reinforcements, re-formed their dreadful circle, and howled and stared and sniffed again, until they forced us to get into our cars and return to the city.'

Although on a reduced scale, social life for British society in these last days of the Raj was still in full swing, but Elizabeth found it resonant with a sad gaiety. There was, she told Felicité, plenty of food and drink but parties were mostly formal and dull, and there appeared to be no spontaneous entertaining. To her amazement one was expected here to change for *drinks*. Neither was was there any theatre and the only films available were of the order of propaganda exercises such as *The Way Forward*; others, more attuned to her tastes, were occasionally put on in someone's house. She regretted Cairo and her 'hundreds of friends', where 'not a week ever passed without some old friend turning up. People were continuously arriving with introductions from England, from Greece, or other parts of the M.E.,' and she bemoaned the loss of her job where there was 'contact with a great many interesting people. So obviously Delhi is deathly dull after all that and I know nobody.' Attempting to console herself, she acquired two cats, having been without one for all her years in Egypt.

'Elizabeth didn't work, she was a wife,' recalls Veronica. 'That meant you could stay in bed all day if you wanted to – which

Elizabeth might well have done, but she'd be up all night instead if she had. Yes, she always kept odd hours.'

After a short time Elizabeth's lack of friends weighed heavily on her and Tony's charm and pleasantness were insufficient recompense. She was never a romantic and as her letters to her mother and sisters made abundantly clear, was highly dubious about the whole conjugal enterprise. Albeit with a combination of cool-headed pragmatism and weary disappointment, Elizabeth had nonetheless made a marriage. But she was not ultimately prepared to follow through her decision with the hard work necessary to sustain any marriage, let alone one made with such apparent calculation. Initially Elizabeth's instinct was to make herself attractive to men, and she was, but her relationships with them were usually uneven. She was so often more intelligent than her male companion that the rather mysterious and alluring woman who was also undoubtedly part of her seemed after a time almost to have been a disguise. When the relationship was more serious than a casual fling – on such occasions she was capable of fairly ruthless usage – her intelligence would gradually displace her emotional attachment.

She was passionate and feline, with a force of intellect and personality which could not content itself with feminine compliance for long. 'It was impossible to sit on Elizabeth,' says Doreen Thornton. She hungered for an equivalent force to counteract and complement her own, but for all her sophistication and intelligence, didn't really know how to nurture it when it presented itself. Tony was an attempt to convince herself that she could manage with a man who would make things work by *his* compliance and willingness to serve. For all her realism it was as if for a time she were wilfully suspending her beliefs. As she said to Veronica Nicholson: 'Well, everyone else was marrying.' It was as if Elizabeth was half hoping that by marrying, the future would see to itself. This was hardly destined to make a successful marriage, besides which she had reckoned without her own impatience and capacity for boredom with people who didn't stimulate her. Ultimately she needed a subtle yet authoritative man but went about acquiring one in the wrong way. A string of them had already retreated, but most hurtful was probably the rich 'glamour boy' officer wounded so badly at the battle of El Alamein. As much through her own behaviour as the inadequacy of the men she met, Elizabeth found 'they rarely came up to scratch for her'.

Idle in India, Elizabeth's old restlessness, for years in Egypt kept at bay with hard work, now had no outlet and she was 'praying I shan't have to stay'. Books were a vital part of her life; they were almost unavailable in Delhi and certainly one could only with difficulty get any packages, let alone the latest books, from England. But for the moment she had a stash brought with her from Cairo and wrote to Felicité (working for the Allied Commission in Vienna) that as long as they lasted she would be all right. After that she could not say.

She had read a few Trollope novels in Cairo, but her main escape in India was Henry James. She also read Proust, twice, Osbert Sitwell and the Greeks. In this same letter, in sharp contrast to what she felt was the intellectual stultification of her present life, she recalled her recent visit to Greece where she had sat in a café with a friend 'over a bad bottle of Cypriot wine talking Balkan politics, Greek literature, Shakespeare, and other gossip'.

Elizabeth's present choice of reading was revealing, in its appreciation of those writers at the turn of the century, and Sitwell into this one, whose work did not reflect the more destructively experimental aspects of Modernism. Elizabeth identified with that artistic vein of thought which was nevertheless intent on reflecting the effects of the modern age and with those writers for whom, paradoxically, this was achieved by an uninterrupted avenue of communication with the values of the past. Although Elizabeth doesn't mention writers like Eliot or Joyce – for whom this endeavour was their *raison d'être* – her great appreciation of another modern, Proust, is confirmation of where her sympathies lay. These writers were all committed to the present and lived it to the full, but were also firm traditionalists in that they were constantly aware of the past. This attitude was at the heart of Elizabeth's essentially high Tory stance. It is exemplified in T. S. Eliot's essay 'Tradition and the Individual Talent' (reprinted in *Selected Essays*, 1952): 'The historical sense involves a perception, not only of the pastness of the past, but of its presence; the historical sense compels a man to write not merely with his own generation in his bones, but with a feeling that the whole of the literature of Europe from Homer . . . has a simultaneous existence.'

Elizabeth's 'main escape', Henry James, was disdainful of the vapidity, the determined anti-intellectualism of the English country-house set whose mentality Elizabeth was familiar with and had herself largely rejected. But central to James's observations was something which concerned her too: civilization and its manifestations.

Veronica eventually left India to work in Rome. 'After six months of friendship, then I went on to Italy.' Having written earlier to Felicité from India that 'the majority of English here treat their employees in the manner one always supposed to have been invented for the stage', Elizabeth added that everything her sister had ever read about life in India appeared to be true. Elizabeth wondered how much longer it would all last. Meanwhile the country was preparing 'for the hottest summer and the most disastrous famine for hundreds of years . . . Everyone is running around getting fans, mosquito nets and loose muslin dresses.' Elizabeth concluded: 'I hate the Orient.'

But she stuck it out for a while, writing letters of frustration and boredom to friends and family. But having persuaded Tony that he did indeed wish to leave the Army and that they should return to England, she was struck down with a bad case of sinusitis, was advised that the climate was exacerbating the problem, and was given the excuse she needed. She must leave. Now. Tony would have to follow later when he had managed to extract himself from the Army. After years living away from England, but less than a year in India, Elizabeth was finally to return home. She was almost thirty-four.

Much to her sadness, only weeks before this Norman Douglas had finally managed to flee from London, 'this benighted hole', and his memories of penury and misery suffered during the last years of the war. He told his young friend Harold Acton, just back from India, that, but for a small circle, including loyal friends like Nancy Cunard, Faith Mackenzie and Viva King (wife of Willie, curator at the Victoria and Albert Museum), the last couple of years in England had been the unhappiest of his life. He had written to the Italian authorities asking permission to return to his beloved Italy. His request was unexpectedly granted because an official was moved by his statement that he wanted to return, not to live in Italy but to die there.

CHAPTER TWELVE

No More Talked of than Love or Heaven
(1946–1949)

IN AUGUST 1946 Elizabeth David came back to England, the land of her birth. She had been away continuously for seven years. And although she was to live abroad again for shorter periods, these were mostly a natural outcome of her work. For the rest of her life, then, England was Elizabeth's home. In 1939 she had escaped from her homeland with an appropriately disreputable character, Charles Gibson Cowan. This time she would not escape, she would, sometimes disgruntledly and with the application of all her barbed wit, make a stand. Instead of a wild, distraught departure away from the inadequacies of her own culture she was to use her remarkable gifts to remedy these inadequacies by showing how we can learn from those abroad.

With Stafford Cripps's rationing still very much in force the following year, ration books even had to be presented at restaurants and hotels – provisions for meals were nothing like the relative plenty which Elizabeth had known in war time. There are many examples and records of life under rationing – one in particular, in Vere Hodgson's *Few Eggs and No Oranges* (1976), demonstrates the types of meal being eaten by the average family in 1944; in 1947 things were no different.

> Meat ration lasts only for three evenings. Cannot be made to go further, that is, Saturday, Sunday, and Monday. Tuesday and Wednesday I cook a handful of rice, dodged up in some way with curry or cheese. But the cheese ration is so small there is little left. Thursday I have an order with the dairy for a pound

of sausage. These make do for Thursday, Friday and part of Saturday. Don't taste much of sausage, but [they] are of soyabean flour. We just pretend they are the real thing ... All rather monotonous, but we are not hungry.

This is really the operative phrase for the condition of England's diet in 1947: food was monotonous but people were not hungry. It is ironic, but strictly correct, that the British population as a whole were better fed during the war than before it. (Better, that is, from the viewpoint of nutritional science.) The failures of the First World War had taught subsequent politicians important lessons about the management and supply of food, so that by the Second World War a coherent plan was evolved focusing on the nourishment of the nation as a whole. The Minister for Food, Sir Fred Marquis (Lord Woolton), a successful businessman and natural communicator, and his chief adviser, the biochemist Jack Drummond, had between them set up a national system based on sound nutritional principles, including the development of allotments and the re-introduction of brown bread to a nation of white-bread consumers. The success of their policies meant that many people understood more about basic nutrition at the end of the war than they had at its commencement.

Preparations were put in hand for rationing well before the 1939–45 hostilities and by August of 1939 – a month before war was even declared – ration books had been printed and deposited at depots around the country. Implementation of the measures for conserving the nation's food supplies were avoided until January 1940, when Elizabeth was forced to remain in Antibes but suffering no hardships.

At this time bacon and ham, butter and sugar were put on ration in England. By March meat was added to the list and in July cooking fats, margarine and even tea – indispensable to the working of the English nation. Tinned foods, already used by the English in vast quantities, were more relied upon than ever and during the war dehydrated foods, loathed by most people, became much more common. Writing to Felicité in Vienna in early 1947, Elizabeth asked her when she was 'coming back to dried egg land'. Eggs had been rationed for years – a blow to any self-respecting cook, forming as they do such a vital part of most Western cooking. And, although their dried substitute was used for all the normal egg recipes, it was unsatisfactory and universally disliked. Many of those who had the space, even in the cities, kept hens in their back gardens. A sad anecdote forcefully illustrates the situation.

Judith Richardson's mother followed this practice in Onslow Square, an elegant South Kensington haven. Judith, who was later married to Elizabeth's friend George Lassalle and whose brother John became the noted art historian and biographer of Picasso, was then about seventeen. She told the author how the artist John Minton, who lived nearby, came round one day. 'He looked so sad, awfully thin and half-stoned, and said, "Do you think you could spare me a couple of eggs if I give you this sandwich for your chickens?" He was holding an envelope and inside was a dried up old sandwich.'

Judith's brother said, 'Don't give Minton anything.'

'But I boiled a couple of eggs and gave them to Johnny anyway.'

For those like Elizabeth who could afford it, an important dehydrated substitute for rationed tea was instant coffee, first manufactured by Nestlé as Nescafé in Britain in 1939. Elizabeth was never a tea lover and, interestingly, in Egypt before her return home she had already tried Nescafé and been converted. Eve Durrell remembers Renée Fedden offering it to her there and thinking it delicious, 'But after the war it was never so good.' Nevertheless, in a remarkable and enduring lapse of taste, Elizabeth remained a devotee of instant coffee all her life. 'I don't know what all the fuss is about the real stuff.'

Spices, lemons, blue cheese, dried salt fish such as anchovy, all stimulants to the palate and vital in small quantities to enliven a meal of otherwise nondescript ingredients, were almost impossible to find in England. Rice had disappeared fairly early on in the war, but rabbit was not rationed, nor were game and fish, and for those living in London there were the possibilities offered by Soho, then the only part of the city with shops selling 'foreign' produce in any amount. Vegetables were not rationed but restricted. Cooking fats were limited, even lard was rationed. The general consensus concurs with the reminiscence to the author of this period by Elizabeth's future friend the novelist Paul Bailey: 'You could only find olive oil in a chemist's – with a doctor's prescription. You weren't meant to eat it, to use it in *cooking*.'

Lord Gowrie, in the previous administration Minister for the Arts, recently Chairman of the Arts Council, first met Elizabeth as a young man in the 1950s. He described the post-war situation to the author: 'Farming was efficient. Woolton had sorted out diets, but one chafed against the controls after the war. After all, we had won, but we looked as if we had lost, with the persistence of powdered egg and synthetic custard, imported tinned Spam. Growing up in austerity was incredibly nasty from a culinary point of view. I mean, the food was really disgusting. You've no idea how nasty it was.'

The question arises: Why? Rationing was a necessary measure during wartime, but did it have to continue for so many years afterwards? Explanations deriving solely from national financial constraints are insufficient. There is one convincing conclusion: the food was 'really disgusting' because most people did not sufficiently care that it was disgusting.

England was the pioneer industrial nation. Industrialism, which harmonized so well with Puritanism, completed the job of destruction of the peasantry and peasant culture, chronicled in the melancholy novels of Thomas Hardy, and reiterated later by Flora Thompson. Chapel replaced Church and the urban barns of the town-dwelling Baptists and Methodists frequently displaced the beautiful parish churches. A single statistic is a salutory reminder. By 1893 the English folklorists had collected 140 'fairy tales'; between 1870 and 1890 France and Italy had yielded over 1000 each. Puritanism and Industrial Capitalism had been replaced, by 1945, by Socialism and Scientism, but the underlying spirit was much the same. And these were the principal reasons why Sir Stafford Cripps was enabled to be quite as effective as Cromwell's Major Generals at stamping out premature rejoicing when the British thought they had won the war.

Celia and John Herbert were friends of Doreen Thornton and lived in a top-floor flat in John's mother's large house behind Barkers, in Kensington. They were going away and handed over the flat to Elizabeth in their absence (Tony was still in India). She at once installed herself in this Kensington eyrie, and in the conditions then prevailing in England, did her best to bridge the chasm between her previous and present life-styles and survive. With no job and nothing forthcoming, Elizabeth launched herself back into London life and took up her habitual entertaining again. Most of her friends, abroad during the war, had also returned.

After years in the Mediterranean and the Middle East there were almost no restaurants whose English atmosphere they found sympathetic, and whose food they were willing or could afford to eat. Even bread was rationed in restaurants. Those like The Ivy and L'Ecu de France, frequented by Elizabeth and her kind before the war, remained open and carried on a semblance of the style and sophistication which had made them famous. Their old clientèle continued to frequent them, as much for the social cachet, the atmosphere and predictability of interesting companions while you ate, as for the (reduced) quality of food. Gallati of The Ivy described in his autobiography (*Mario of the Caprice*, 1957) how 'I used to make a kind of mayonnaise with flour and water put into the mixing machine with vinegar, mustard and a bit of powdered egg. It made me shudder to serve it.'

Elizabeth's new flat was equipped with one of those ridiculous kitchens, not then uncommon in converted English houses, where a work table doubled up as the cover to the bath. This necessitated a tidiness to which Elizabeth was neither accustomed – servants had seen to that – nor naturally inclined. Nevertheless, with her gas cooker and her fridge she began to try out some of the dishes eaten in her years of wandering. Few other than her most intimate friends, literary or otherwise, realized the extent of her passionate interest in food, and neither then nor later did her sense of good taste permit her to indulge her passion with anyone unless they showed particular interest or were in some way professionally involved, but it had continued unabated for her seven years abroad.

Elizabeth's experience of cooking and eating places was by now enormously varied in both a geographic and a gastronomic sense. It included running a ship's galley, with primus stoves, managing a primitive kitchen on a Greek island, and in Egypt – and, to a lesser extent India – becoming familiar with the world of Eastern food, before the war unknown to her but for the beguiling Mrs Leyel and *The Gentle Art of Cookery*. Elizabeth's experience included eating in some of the best restaurants – both costly, and modest and unknown – in all these countries. Throughout her travels she had learnt the art, essential for both travellers and good cooks, of pragmatic adaptation and accommodation to circumstance. In spite of her youthful tendency towards extravagance, necessity had encouraged her to develop a sense of thrift and driven her to use her intelligence and ingenuity. She had written to Priscilla from Egypt: 'I feel that one of the main conditions of continued existence is that life should always be full of changes and surprises,' and we are reminded of her own determined and consistently creative response to these changes and surprises.

With parental example from early childhood at Wootton, Elizabeth had an imperative need for her surroundings to reflect her own aesthetic. She cared deeply about the look of things, always including her own appearance. This applied to whatever she was doing: writing during the war lengthy screeds on 'stuffs' and colours and designs for clothes sent or ordered from her sisters and mother; 'redoing' the digs in Oxford, the flats in London, the *Evelyn Hope*, the cottage on Syros, her apartments in Egypt, and most recently 'new covers and curtains' for her latest move; or now, using her knowledge and ingenuity to create edible meals for her friends. Without ever being effete, Elizabeth had an unerring sense of taste. It was never outrageous, it was instead taste at once fastidious, traditional, catholic and bohemian. She had an instinctive ability to apprehend and develop the potentialities in the tone of the present. Her detection of the pretentious, which became keener with time, was reflected in both her own appearance and the atmosphere she created in her surroundings.

Although Elizabeth's collection of recipes had been lost when the *Evelyn Hope* and most of her and Charles Gibson Cowan's belongings were confiscated by the Italian navy, she had not returned from her travels empty-handed. In the years abroad she had been alert to all aspects of food: watching, listening, eating and preparing dishes herself. She had kept notes of recipes wherever she was. Back in England she confidently set about re-creating the remembered dishes of her travels, saying, 'With whatever I could get I cooked like one possessed.' In London there was one undoubted luxury: bookshops, and Elizabeth began to replace what she had lost and buy unfamiliar books too.

Meanwhile, in 1944, André Simon and Louis Golding had brought out an anthology for the readers of the Wine and Food Society, aimed at giving hope to the down-hearted upper-middle-class reader, entitled *We Shall Eat and Drink Again*, the stress of course was on '*Shall*'. The differences between what one eats and how it is perceived, borne out by countless records of this in action during the war years, remind us that a nutritionally adequate diet can be close to torture, especially to those accustomed to a more than adequate one. The English did not starve during the war, but for the better off particularly, accustomed to more meat, cream, eggs and imported fruit, the war and its aftermath was a grey landscape indeed.

During the war years Elizabeth's diet, by comparison with those left at home, had been anything but monotonous. And despite the war's end her return to English rationing provoked in her a sense of deprivation of the spirit, as much in reaction to English attitudes as to the physical dearth.

It took her another fifteen or so years to write at length about the effect of the Levant upon English cooking and herself. In a piece originally for the *Spectator*, then reprinted more or less in full as the introduction to her book on *Spices, Salt and Aromatics in the English Kitchen*, she gives credit to Hilda Leyel, founder of Culpepper's, for probably first inspiring her to cook. As importantly, she describes how on re-reading *The Gentle Art* she came to the realization that here was 'Yet another manifestation of the English love affair with Eastern food and Arabian Nights ingredients'.

Knowing as we do the volume of personal history behind Elizabeth's lilting description of Levantine food in her *Spices, Salt and Aromatics in the English Kitchen* (with the customary dearth of personal reference), it now reads both as an evocative exposition and a masterly display of reticence.

> . . . circumstances had landed me in Alexandria and subsequently
> in Cairo. In my turn I fell under the spell of the beautiful food
> of the Levant – the warm flat bread, the freshly pressed tomato
> juice, the charcoal-grilled lamb, the oniony salads, the mint and
> yogurt sauces, the sesame seed paste, the pistachios and the
> pomegranates and the apricots, the rosewater and the scented

sweetmeats, and everywhere the warm spicy smell of cumin [we learn in the same book that this was an indispensable spice in her store-cupboard].

In another *Spectator* article of three years previously (9 December 1960) she had reminded us that while in the Middle East her menu consisted of the above, combined with 'rather rough, but highly flavoured colourful shining vegetable dishes, lentil or fresh tomato soups, delicious spiced pilaffs . . . The Egyptian *Fellahin* dish of black beans with olive oil and lemon and hard boiled eggs'.

What Elizabeth said she found on returning to England and 'the awful, dreary foods of rationing was that while my own standard of living . . . had perhaps not been very high, my food had always had some sort of life, colour, guts, stimulus; there had always been bite, flavour and inviting smells'. In 1947 she felt that 'These elements were totally absent from English food.'

In those first months of re-acclimatizing herself to England, with no job and nothing forthcoming, Elizabeth was depressed but launched herself back into London life. Many of her friends were, like her, intent not only on re-instating themselves in England but on maintaining the coterie they had formed in Cairo. 'Elizabeth rather liked to be part of a group of people, a clique, and didn't care much for those outside it,' says her friend Patrick Leigh Fermor. What he did not add was that Elizabeth always maintained a position in more than one clique at once. Included in the comings and goings were: Robin Fedden, now curator of Polesden Lacey for the National Trust, and his wife Renée; Xan Fielding; John Young, future Oxford zoologist and his painter companion Ray; Betsey and John Udall, phoneticists; Lesley O'Malley from the MOI (left by her unbalanced husband in Cairo but still suffering the frequent despair this caused her for several years to come); Cecil Gould the art historian; George Lassalle; J. M. Richards the architectural historian; Doreen Thornton; Mary and David Abercrombie, future professor of phonetics, whose description of Elizabeth as 'a myopic black swan' captures well her extreme short-sightedness, her reticence, her sinuous grace and that hint of the predatory about her.

Judith Lassalle recalls how for some time after the war 'They

all, these people, came and went at a furious pace. Again in England they were trying to get things back to the way they had been before the war – but they could never quite get it back to how it was . . . Elizabeth would have a few drinks and warm up and then she would always say, "I must tell you, I must tell you." You could always say something to Elizabeth to make her laugh. Even when she was miserable you only had to smile at her and she would smile back.'
'Yes,' says Patrick Woodcock, a future friend and later Elizabeth's doctor, 'she was a great sender up but she knew how to be so funny.'

Autumn that year soon turned to one of the nastiest winters in living memory; everything and everyone froze. Diana and her husband Christopher (working as a doctor in St George's hospital) were living not far from Elizabeth in Abingdon Road. Diana, expecting a baby, was not having an easy time and as she had previously miscarried everyone was concerned. Towards the end of winter Elizabeth wrote to Felicité in Vienna saying that London had been 'vile' for the past few weeks and that she had been 'chained' to the stove, making meals for friends or for Christopher and Diana, going out only to Abingdon Road to bring them nourishing soups and other dishes wrapped in napkins.

She made the most of rationed ingredients, ignoring the pow-dered and dehydrated foods to which the English had become conditioned. With a sense of passionate urgency she scoured Soho; found garlic, searched out lemons, olive oil, bootleg butter, in typical vein sending a young friend back to Harrods when she arrived with what was called butter (cream cheese), saying, 'Get me the real thing.' Visitors always came with contributions: 'Unexpected ones some-times. A wild goose. Snails from Paris . . . Mock liver pâté from Fortnum's . . . One of my sisters [Felicité, back for a visit] turned up from Vienna with a hare which she claimed had been caught by hand outside the State Opera House.' That autumn and winter of 1946–7 was a good one for game, which was not rationed and cheap.

In an article written for the *Spectator* in 1963 entitled 'John Wesley's Eye' Elizabeth praised her post-war landlady, Mrs Herbert down below, for her long-suffering patience at the 'cooking smells, the garlic, the onions, those eternal bacon bones simmering in the stock . . . about the heating she was, with the best will in the world, powerless. Literally. And gas-less.' Doreen Thornton says that in fact Mrs Herbert 'who should have been scandalized by Elizabeth and her friends, actually found her fascinating. She was intrigued.'

Tony was winding up his affairs and making final preparations to leave India for England but Elizabeth was already feeling tetchy at the prospect. In her dislike and rejection of freezing, ration-blighted England (vegetables that winter were sometimes only recoverable from the ground with pneumatic drills, animals froze and died, fuel was in short supply) she had attempted to organize a passage to 'the island', Syros. Here she had wanted to reinstate herself in the little house and stay there with Tony, his journey to England forestalled for a while. But she couldn't go, because Tony was being 'very tiresome' about returning straight to England. With acid pen she wrote that it was a pity, because she would have liked to get back 'before the Americans arrive in their hordes to preserve Greece for the Mid West'. As she is to be frustrated in her attempts to return to her beloved Greek island she adds, 'Feeling desperately in need of a change, respite from the telephone and some fresh air I have heaved myself up and am spending a few days in a place called Ross-on-Wye, don't ask me why and that's not meant to be funny.'

When Elizabeth later wrote about this episode it had been deftly transformed into the passage in 'John Wesley's Eye' mentioned above, justly famous for its description of her passionate response to the bleakness of post-war England. It is a heartfelt piece, moving in itself, but for anyone who knows Elizabeth's writing and has mused over, or made a more methodical search for an explanation as to why she began to write, it appears that here one has found some kind of an answer. She sets the scene with apparent nonchalance; in fact it is a careful crafting of a series of minor crescendos culminating with the final dénouement: the inception of her first book.

With the gas in her flat all but giving out, she wrote: 'At this moment somebody put into my head the idea of going to stay, at reduced all-in rates, in a hotel in Ross-on-Wye,' the little town on the Welsh border, perched above the wide, leafy valley of the river Wye. In walking up and down the town, encountering all the pubs on the way, Elizabeth came across one of those wildly unreconstructed places, with châtelaines as unorthodox as their contents, few of whom any longer exist.

'An interesting looking antique shop. A very large shop, with immense windows. These were filled from floor to ceiling with a fantastic jumble of every conceivable kind of antique. Lamps, china, glass, bedsteads, curtains, Sheffield candlesticks, desks, pictures, books, bookshelves, bronzes, Georgian silver, coffee pots, horse brasses, corner cupboards, whole services of dinner plates, soup tureens, sauce boats, statuary. The lady inside the shop was as unusual as her windows . . . If you asked to look at something she pulled it out from the morass regardless.' Elizabeth keeps the tension taut, building on our growing sense of the reckless disregard 'Miss D.' exhibits for her wonderfully various and insanely balanced merchandise. Several near misses and an avalanche or two of collapsing valuables later Elizabeth described how she would extract herself from the shop with a sense of triumphant relief that her purchases were intact. On this particular occasion she had just rescued a 'Leeds dish and put it in my basket before Miss D. had a chance to knock it flying. The friend I was with rescued from under the lady's foot, and gave to me, a frail white jug . . . As Miss D. took my cheque her elbow jogged the tap of a copper tea urn perched on top of a model four-masted barque in a heavy box frame. It knocked over a solid silver clock representing General Gordon sitting on a horse, which fell against a scrap screen, a japanned tray and a tortoiseshell and silver-inlaid musical box . . .'

To Felicité Elizabeth complained of the weather and that she was 'constantly reminded of my one disastrous expedition to The Hills in India. For all one can see through the blanket of snow Kanchenjunga might easily be in the background.' This refers to Elizabeth's unsuccessful holiday with Tony, escaping from the heat of Delhi by train to the cool clear air of Darjeeling, that exquisite hill-station high up on the Eastern edge of the Himalayas. The little town of labrynthine steps and terraces, of exotic village and hill people, of bazaars and markets, glowing, intense and fantastic, ringed around with pine forests and snowy mountain peaks, had been a favoured retreat of the British Raj since its nineteenth-century creation.

After her rest in the Welsh borders Elizabeth was planning a visit to Priscilla in 'Chippers' (Chipping Sodbury) in Gloucestershire *en route* back to the austerities of London, but she was caught and cut off in Ross-on-Wye by extensive flooding of the surrounding towns and villages. The terrible cold of the winter had turned to equally disastrous flooding. Root crops were destroyed, thousands of sheep and cattle died, the smell of burning corpses soon floated on the air. Elizabeth meanwhile told Felicité that the horrors of English hotel life had not lessened with the years. As she elaborated in her *Spectator* article: 'I stuck it out. It was an effort. By this time I was finding it very difficult indeed to swallow the food provided in the hotel. It was worse than unpardonable, even for those days of desperation; and oddly, considering the kindly efforts made in other respects, produced with a kind of bleak triumph which amounted almost to a hatred of humanity and humanity's needs.' We are treated to a sample of 'flour and water soup seasoned solely with pepper; bread and gristle rissoles; dehydrated onions and carrots; corned beef toad-in-the-hole. I need not go on.'

The aspect of this perfectly judged essay which has the greatest biographical import follows immediately on this little diatribe, when the reader believes he is witnessing Elizabeth's conversion of frustration and longing into her first piece of writing. The essence of what Elizabeth tells her reader is so often true and correct; her omissions are in the name of a respectable desire for privacy (she is writing about *food* after all, not herself), concision, clarity, and as importantly, her instinctive appreciation of what was artistically relevant and what superflous to a piece. Here, however, we are presented with one of those rare examples where an omission is outstanding, following to the letter the implication of her friend Norman Douglas's dictum 'One suppresses much' – because there is something to hide.

The passage evokes with exemplary accuracy Elizabeth's thoughts and feelings at that time; her discovery that England provoked as much animosity in her as when she had escaped it seven years earlier. Temporarily unable to leave the country, or even this small provincial town, the words she began to write were a perfect synthesis of her attitude: a wail of longing for what she had lost, and a description, penned in vitriol, of what she had found in its place.

> Hardly knowing what I was doing, I who had scarcely ever put pen to paper except to write memos to the heads of departments in the Ministry which employed me during the war, I sat down and started to work out an agonized craving for the sun and furious revolt against that terrible cheerless, heartless food by writing down descriptions of Mediterranean and Middle Eastern cooking. Even to write words like apricot, olives and butter, rice and lemons, oil and almonds, produced assuagement. Later I came to realize that in the England of 1947 those were dirty words I was putting down.

And here we come to the omissions; two important facts which she was disinclined to divulge to her reader, but which are fundamental to an appreciation of her development as a writer. First, she was not alone; second, the friend accompanying her was responsible both for the journey to Ross *and* for encouraging her at this moment to pick up her pen. The friend was George Lassalle.

Having married as his second wife the cousin of his first, George had been sent on a posting from Cairo to Istanbul where he carried on, with admirable subterfuge, his job for Intelligence. A double agent for a time, he was decorated by the Germans. He left the Army and returned to England in 1946. (His work for Intelligence in fact continued until the 1960s, partially explaining his succession of makeshift jobs over the next twenty years.) Struck down on his return to England by a rare form of paralysis, he was left with his legs wasted and unusable and was sent to hospital for several months.

Some time after Elizabeth's arrival from India, and probably just into the New Year of 1947, the two resumed their old liaison. They continued their affair for the next few years and maintained regular contact with one another for the rest of their lives. In this context George had suggested that before Tony's arrival in England they should escape to a place where they were unknown. George was a keen fly fisherman and knowledgeable consumer of all things from fresh and salt water. As a boy, at a London Benedictine Priory school, he had been initiated into the rites of fly fishing on a holiday in Ross-on-Wye with the benevolent Father supervising his French and choir studies. George subsequently described his stay as a semi-visonary experience; both Ross and fish were special elements in his past, hence his recommendation of the town to Elizabeth. Ironically, we see in the autobiographical *Spectator* article that Elizabeth too later claimed her stay in Ross as something of a road-to-Damascus conversion.

The weather turned the occasion into more than a brief episode, but George was his habitual entertaining, ebullient, unscrupulous self. Hardly to be trusted further than he could be seen, for him the occasion would have been a great joke. He and Elizabeth knew one another well, but each continued to hold a fascination for the other, recognizing something which went some way towards consolation. Amongst George's many and varied interests was not only a concern for fish but food generally, beginning with his first trip to Greece three years before the war when he had taught himself to cook. His experience of the war was, like Elizabeth's, predominantly a Middle Eastern one, and he also was dismissive of the food to which they were subjected in England. In spite of his disreputableness Elizabeth remained fond of George and spoke of him often. At different times they both said that if they 'hadn't each had a touch of the tarbrush they would have married'. However, in 1947 they were each already married to someone else.

With time to fill in, waiting for the floodwaters to subside, the conversation again turned to Elizabeth's shortage of money and means of procuring some. George was the ideal adviser, he was always short of money, yet, a natural hustler, he somehow always managed to extract himself from tight corners. One is reminded here of the comment made about Charles Gibson Cowan – 'He would have sold his grandmother for a truffle' – and Elizabeth's unerring ability to associate herself with men who could be relied upon for unreliability. (An old friend recently said with sadness, 'Oh, she was attracted to people in the most indiscriminate way.') Having dabbled with outsiders, Elizabeth was always interested in similar types. Generally the point at which she identified with someone was the point central to their own exclusion.

Meanwhile, she had long since rejected the possibility of acting, but was unwilling to see herself in the other role in which she had gained valuable experience – librarianship. It was too unglamorous and besides, as Patrick Leigh Fermor recently said of her, 'Oh, Liz chafed so under discipline, she was a terrible handful.' So it was that here in Ross-on-Wye, in this comfortable, friendly hotel serving up its appalling food, George encouraged her to write. He may have been a scoundrel but he was an intelligent, literate and multilingual one who was also endowed with generosity and enthusiasm, and could always talk to Elizabeth. In the retrospective *Spectator* passages in which Elizabeth outlined the origins of her writing career, she said of herself that she 'had hardly put pen to paper' but this was patently incorrect – the traditional disclaimer to patron and public at the beginning of so many good books.

In the very letter from the Oxford Playhouse, in 1934, in which she had maintained she couldn't write, while sub-editing the theatre magazine, we saw evidence of her nascent abilities. She had in fact been writing in a small way for years. There was the juvenile recipe manuscript written for her friend Marian Butterworth, more importantly the mysterious book with Charles Gibson Cowan. Then the building of her collection of recipes which she had hoped to publish, lost with the *Evelyn Hope*. Most recently, her work as reference librarian for the MOI in Cairo had provided ideal practice for concentrating the mind and discarding extraneous material. We recall the description of her activities, which entailed her reading newspapers, books and magazines, writing summaries, distributing material where it could best be used.

The essence of Elizabeth's statement that she had hardly put pen to paper was that not until now had she addressed the problem with any purposefulness; *how* would she go about writing? Perhaps her association with the very literary (mainly male) authors of fiction and criticism in Cairo, as well as stimulating her, may have smothered her own literary beginnings. She did perhaps for a time harbour the idea of fiction, but the manifest confidence and élan of friends like

Lawrence Durrell and Robin Fedden possibly intimidated her. Ultimately, however, the reason she did not finally take it up was because she did not want to. Perhaps, like the novelist Olivia Manning, in Cairo at the same time as Elizabeth, she realized her inspiration did not come from the imagination – although Manning managed quite well nevertheless. But as Elizabeth's future friend the novelist Sybille Bedford astutely observed of her in conversation with the author: 'She cared too much about truth. A novelist must be prepared to make things up.'

With George's encouragement then, in that ration-blighted hotel in Ross-on-Wye, Elizabeth sat down and made a beginning; a record of her Mediterranean experiences and memories of dishes eaten along the way. Together they had decided what it was she must write about, and the obvious subject was food.

With Tony's arrival imminent, Elizabeth eventually returned to London with those first notes, while George went off to pick up labouring jobs around the country. One of these, working for Elizabeth's Uncle Top at the Blackmoor estate in Hampshire, was organized for George by her. This was in spite of the fact that their stay together in Ross had ended in argument, and it took Elizabeth some time to forgive him – but then she always indulged George.

Tony David's return to England appears to have been a relatively insignificant event in the larger scheme of Elizabeth's life. For the moment, however, she essayed the role of married woman, introducing her husband to the family and taking him to stay with several of them. They were above all enormously relieved that Elizabeth had had the good sense to 'rid herself of that terrible actor and marry a man who could at least ride a horse'. Stella, still at Dedham near Cedric and Lett, thought him a decent young man and felt the two seemed well suited. One can hardly imagine the two artists Cedric Morris and Lett Haines being so enthusiastic about Tony, whose abilities as a good-looking, pleasant socialite and 'butler' would no doubt have been enlisted for their entertainment. Priscilla thought him 'absolutely charming'. So too did some of Elizabeth's female friends, but they could all see the possibility that this might be a mismatch.

However distasteful Elizabeth may have found her Uncle Roland, she visited him several times at Wootton with Tony. Having squandered old James (Stick) Gwynne's money on years of lavish entertaining, he had found it impossible to remain at Folkington and, after ousting the tenant (a Miss Hudson, who had entertained Virginia Woolf to tea there and been credited as 'frightfully chi-chi'), he had moved into Wootton. He was sufficiently impressed by Tony's horsemanship to allow him to ride his favourite black horse out on the Downs nearby; reputedly Tony was the only person who achieved this honour.

In the flat in London entertainment was constant and drinking carried on, as ever, at a furious pace, but Elizabeth managed to weather the hangovers. 'She never admitted to having one,' recalls George Lassalle's future wife, Judith. 'She would always say: "Oh, I feel terrible, so ill – I feel absolutely as if I'm going to die." And she would mix up some sort of hangover special. She smoked a lot. Always.'

Elizabeth's cooking was beginning to reflect something of her own travelled sophistication. Soho was then really the only place in London where some of the ingredients for the Mediterranean dishes she was trying out were obtainable, but under the stringencies of rationing these were still in severely short supply. Tony, apparently not a bad cook, was interested and sometimes useful in the experiments to which she was now devoting considerable energies, but Elizabeth's patience was always limited, particularly with those who were not as quick-witted as herself. Concurrent with her growing expertise at the stove was an expanding collection of books on cookery, although Elizabeth's literary interests were by now far too well developed for her to marginalize them in favour of an exclusive interest in cookery writing.

In the summer of 1947 Elizabeth, Tony and Doreen Thornton, now separated from her husband, set off in an old Rolls for a holiday in the South of France. 'Tony always did things in a grand way, so he took a day cabin – they were up on the deck – just for going from Dover to Calais. We sat and drank champagne for the crossing . . . Tony and I shared the driving, because Elizabeth never could. The Rolls was lent by Chris Grey, a terrible old thing. It was like driving a tank. Lizza and Tony were getting on very well most of the time –

perhaps the only time – which made it a bit difficult for me. I do remember one day, though, going round the ramparts at Avignon and we were all not speaking to one another.

'We went right on down to Italy, but it was hard going because we had this awful fifty-pound limit on expenditure abroad. We met up with Veronica [Nicholson, now working for *Harpers Bazaar*, and in France to review the fashion shows] in Paris on the way down. We had to go there so Tony could do some shady deal to get money. Veronica took us out to a fabulous meal at Plaza Athénée on her expense account.' Dior's cinched-waisted, swirling-skirted New Look was launched that year, and whilst many marvelled at the seductively feminine image its use of yardage created, others railed at the unseemly abandonment of sense this necessitated, when clothes were still rationed. Fashion, as always, overcame political stricture and the style was a wild success.

Paris after the war was almost without petrol and painfully short of food, yet, in spite of Occupation, or because of collaboration, many French women had maintained a high level of interest in clothes throughout the war. Audrey Withers, then editor of *Vogue*, had made a post-war trip to report on the designer shows and, like others from Britain, marvelled at the remarkable clothes. In the streets as much as on the catwalk, she saw outrageous hats and high platform shoes, made of wood in the absence of rubber, and worn for walking and bicycling in the almost carless streets.

The occasion of Elizabeth's visit is vivid in Veronica's memory because on one evening when they all met up for drinks Ernestine Carter, then editor of *Harpers*, was part of the group. Ernestine was a formidably ambitious American journalist (small and not particularly attractive), who reached the heights of English journalism and would later feature in Elizabeth's professional life. Elizabeth proceeded to ridicule her size and appearance to Veronica and Tony almost within Ernestine's earshot, and Veronica afterwards regretted not having chastised her. 'But the awful thing was that Elizabeth could be so funny, never mind that it might be at someone else's expense ... Yes, somewhere there was that feeling with Elizabeth that she had a chip, was defensive, and so would always rise to the attack before it might happen to her . . . which of course it rarely did.'

Another woman who remembers being slighted by Elizabeth at this time was the young wife of Elizabeth's ex-lover, the glamour boy P.L. who had been so badly wounded in Egypt at the time of the battle of El Alamein. It seems he was unaware of, or insensitive to, the depth of Elizabeth's attachment to him, for there is no doubt she had hoped he would marry her. And, despite her statements at the end of her life that she had been relieved at his return to North America, her subsequent comments to a select few stressed that he remained the most important man in her life. He brought his new bride to meet Elizabeth – and Tony. The young woman felt distinctly uncomfortable. She herself came from a family of considerable wealth, but was relatively inexperienced and unaffected in manner. 'Elizabeth was very smartly dressed and with a friend did an awful lot of giggling. I felt it was at me.' No doubt it was. Elizabeth was uninhibited about bearing grudges and quite capable of setting someone up as the butt of her ridicule if she thought it was deserved; never mind that in this case the party may have been unaware of her crime. Elizabeth's strong sense of justice was often selective and consequently not always aimed in the right direction. 'She was very unforgiving, very temperamental. Very severe in her standards,' says her friend Sybille Bedford.

For some time Elizabeth's mother had been feeling the strain of running a house as large as the Old Grammar School at Dedham, and in 1948 decided that she would move. Priscilla and Richard had separated and Priscilla moved with the little girls to a house in South Kensington. In the following year Stella bought an elegant Georgian town house in Brighton, which she then proceeded (with the dealer Hugh Schooling's help) to fill with another remarkable and eclectic collection of strange and handsome things.

By the time the Old Grammar School was sold it had become apparent to Elizabeth that Tony did not have anything like the money she had hoped for. Knowing almost nothing about him at the time of her marriage, she had not been particularly curious to discover more. But there were few of his family left and those remaining were unable to give him handouts. Since his and Elizabeth's first meeting he had probably been living above his means in order to impress her and, after returning to England without a job, the performance was impossible to maintain for long.

Elizabeth was disappointed in her husband, but she was realistic enough to see, as early as her return alone in the summer of 1946, that she would have to do something about their finances. She asked for Stella's assistance and it was agreed that Elizabeth would be bought a house with the proviso that, because Stella regarded her as financially untrustworthy, it was to remain in her [Stella's] name and Tony was gradually to repay her. By 1949 Elizabeth and Tony were installed in their pretty four-storeyed Georgian house in Halsey Street, a quiet Chelsea street lying almost equidistant from four of London's most fashionable and elegant shopping thoroughfares: Brompton Road to the west, Beauchamp Place north, Sloane Street east and the King's road to the south, with property in the vicinity correspondingly valuable. In the triangle nearby, where Brompton Road and Sloane Street converge, lies the vast acreage taken up by Harrods, at that period probably the most fashionable Mecca in the Kingdom; in 1948 it had celebrated its centenary with great panache.

Elizabeth set to and furnished her house in a style now confirmed as her own, English with touches of the Mediterranean. Most of the furniture (and the fridge from Uncle Jasper) which she had left behind in England before the war was lost, destroyed by a bomb, so everything, other than a few pieces from Paris, had to be replaced. Notwithstanding her ambivalent feelings for Stella, she always respected her taste and had a number of things from her with which to furnish Halsey Street. In this context she went round one day to visit Maudie O'Malley, now living close by. Maudie had been a student of Cedric Morris and Lett Haines at Dedham Art School and like many students had bought things from Stella at the Old Grammar School. Elizabeth looked at some chairs Maudie had from Stella with a view to buying them herself. With their mutual friendship with Cedric and Lett and an almost equal fear of Stella in common, they began 'a fair amount of to-ing and fro-ing' to each other's houses, Maudie told the author in interview.

Maudie, so named by Cedric Morris, was living and painting in

London with her husband Peter and later did some drawings for Elizabeth. 'Oh, Elizabeth knew several of the painters from Dedham, she would go and visit Cedric and Lett. Robert Buhler, who had been a student at Dedham, did a portrait of her. Her mother was such an autocratic old thing. Very grand. She was always shaking her head and had large dangling earrings, and they went up and down – everything tinkled.' Elizabeth now exhibited the same kind of confident mixing of objects at which Stella had always excelled. Amongst other oddities which Elizabeth had acquired, perhaps through a theatrical contact, was an enormous bath. Alix Coleman remembers going to the bathroom on her first visit to Halsey Street a few years later and asking Elizabeth why she had such a vast bath.

'"Oh, that belonged to Dame Marie Lohr," said Elizabeth with a smile. And we both laughed. Marie Lohr was one of those great old stage actresses. Played alongside people like Leslie Howard in the film version of *Pygmalion*. She had those sweet small features in a face now large, and a voice like cut crystal. She was *huge*, and hence the bath.'

A high four-poster bed was acquired for upstairs (for which many years later a friend, Andrew Patrick of the Fine Art Society, had steps made so that Elizabeth's ascent was facilitated) and she began her usual ordering of stuffs for curtains and covers. No. 24 Halsey Street followed the standard pattern for small Georgian town houses; a long hall off which led a sitting room to the front, a dining room to the back and behind that a kitchen-scullery. Downstairs was a basement with rooms similar to the ground floor. The stairs led up to two more floors of bedrooms.

Visitors from the early years, and later, remember the chill in Halsey Street in winter. 'Oh, Elizabeth and Tony kept it cold. She would turn on the oven in the kitchen to warm it up. Downstairs was the perfect larder temperature.' Veronica Nicholson then described Elizabeth's New World cooker bought at the purchase of Halsey Street, as 'one of those great machines'. In 1949 its rounded edges, ubiquitous by the early Fifties, were in reaction to the starker geometry of Thirties and Forties Art Deco. As time passed and cookers changed in efficiency and design, Elizabeth hung on to the style – in fact a version of it remained in her kitchen until her death forty-three years later. Long ago grown accustomed to cooking stoves of the most primitive order she was unperturbed by the inconveniences involved. But, for the moment, her cooker was the height of modernity.

The prevailing atmosphere of Elizabeth's kitchen was at some variance to the design of her cooker, however. Hers was not the austere, deathly modernity increasingly promoted by most women's magazines throughout the Fifties and Sixties and reflecting the postwar advance of the streamlined 'kitchen as laboratory, food as efficiency and technology' ideal. (The same ethos gave the appalling title 'domestic science' to the apparently benevolent, in practice usually sterile, school and college cookery lessons for girls.) In the new 'ideal' kitchens without servants, a practical linoleum floor, stainless-steel sink and rash of post-war labour-saving domestic appliances would become necessities for a fulfilling life. A 'dream' kitchen, shining clinically from the pages of magazines, sported ever-larger refrigerators in which to keep the rapidly multiplying range of processed and frozen foods, whilst the desirable fitted look was soon given even greater unity by smothering every available surface under acres of the new Formica in a rainbow choice of colours and patterns. A heatproof, wipe-clean material, Formica was in perfect harmony with an age now largely addicted to hygiene and thrilled by the wonders of technology.

Although more women now worked than before the war the domestic ideal was still a wife at home with one or two young children, mindful of her role as 'home-maker'. In 1949 most young women were aware of their shortcomings in home management and cooking; the better off because they found themselves without servants, the less well off because they had been deprived of practice by the dislocations of war and rationing, and the consequent loss of the last of an oral culinary tradition passed down from mother to daughter. At all levels cookery classes became popular, as did women's magazines and cookery books, and their popularity as organs of domestic instruction, inspiration and advice had soared by the early Fifties. Just as the rapid expansion of the middle classes during the nineteenth century had left them unsure and greedy for instruction in everything from recipes to etiquette from the likes of

Mrs Beeton, so now another age of expansion needed more of the same assurance.

Elizabeth's kitchen was a different sort from those pictured in magazines, including those she wrote for. In 1949 and 1950 her taste was eclectic, essentially an amalgam of English and Mediterranean *country* living. Floors were of oak woodblock, her walls painted pale colours, in part to counteract the lack of light in a long lowish room – it had been extended in the 1920s, not too well, and was always a bit damp. She had found a farmhouse dresser on which she displayed much of her (unmatching) collection of pottery and china: old, English (much blue and white) and some brought back from her travels abroad. She had a large old pine table set in the middle of the room and around it farmhouse chairs. An old china sink, like those still in place in many English sculleries, was left *in situ*, its cupboard not to be updated for another thirty years or so. This was flanked by the New World cooker and beside that another painted, early nineteenth-century dresser with more china and containers. On the end wall, beside the pretty porthole window leading on to her tiny yard, was a dark and voluptuous French *armoire* in which were kept glasses, cups, preserves, cake tins, pans. At the other end of the room was a Georgian cupboard with sliding doors in which were spices and more pots.

For the majority in England and the rest of Europe at this time the kitchen, often small, was for cooking. It was not a room in which the family relaxed or entertained their guests, who were kept beyond it in dining and drawing room. The designers of houses and arbiters of social etiquette had not yet faced up to the actualities of contemporary life. The situation which prevailed post-war, certainly when entertaining guests, entailed the housewife preparing the meal, then bringing it into the dining room with kitchen shut off from view. That way, by implication, there just might be someone helping out of sight.

Only in rural farmhouse kitchens had a more ancient tradition been sporadically maintained where master, servants and farm-workers had never become separated by 'the green baize door' and sometimes still sat at table together. Most farmhouse kitchens were large enough to accommodate numbers of people who could still benefit from the old range or Aga, painted or scrubbed pine cupboards, dresser for display of china, and a large pine table at which much of the meal was prepared and then sat up to by the family.

In keeping with this tradition and the largely Mediterranean and unpretentious food which she prepared, Elizabeth asked her visitors into the kitchen, where they almost invariably stayed. 'Elizabeth had made it such a pleasurable room, and so conducive to the consuming of good food and the making of good talk, that we rarely got round to moving,' says Veronica Nicholson. Elizabeth wrote from experience and heartfelt belief in the introduction to her second book, *French Country Cooking* (John Lehmann, 1951), that: 'Some sensible person once remarked that you spend the whole of your life either in your bed or your shoes. Having done the best you can by shoes and bed, devote all the time and resources at your disposal to the building up of a fine kitchen. It will be, as it should be, the most comforting and comfortable room in the house.'

Elizabeth and Tony gave good parties. Veronica recalls an early occasion in Halsey Street when Elizabeth gave a cocktail party (the word was unfortunately again in vogue after its demise during the war) and the drawing room was still occasionally in use for its designated purpose. Quite a collection of people was there: Stella, the Feddens, Walter Baxter, Stewart Perown (briefly married to Freya Stark), and a number of Elizabeth's homosexual friends and acquaintances, such as Brian Howard, for a few years the narcissistic exquisite *par excellence*, whose elegance with language gradually succumbed to drink and drugs.

In describing the occasion Veronica remembers being struck by the incongruous way in which Elizabeth and her mother behaved at this sparkling social gathering. 'Everyone was in evening dress and there Stella was seated on the sofa. She had soon to catch a train back to Brighton and Elizabeth brought her a tray, almost as you might when ill in bed, but not in quite such a gathering. She had made a boiled egg and cut the toast up as you would for a child – into soldiers – and Stella sat and ate. Quite oblivious.' Meanwhile Brian Howard was getting into his stride by loudly insulting the gentle Walter Baxter: 'Why aren't you in evening dress, everyone else is?'

Afterwards Elizabeth said to Veronica, 'I'm *never* going to give a drinks party again.'

Tony's presence was becoming irksome to Elizabeth and he would sometimes absent himself: 'She was getting so bored by him.' George Lassalle was often at Halsey Street. Since 1948 he had been living with Judith Richardson at her mother's Onslow Square flat while she was away in Monte Carlo. Judith's father had run the Army and Navy Stores before his death. 'Oh, everything came from the Army and Navy when we were young, including my mother, she worked at the chocolate counter.' During the war and just afterwards Onslow Square was almost empty of its eccentric inhabitants except for a few such as Daphne Du Maurier, the Venns, Viva and Willie King. It was still a fairly quiet neighbourhood when George brought Elizabeth to be introduced to Judith. She had a cooked meal, and Elizabeth's tart response was, 'Well, George, at least she can cook.' When the two were married in 1950 Elizabeth said to Judith, 'There's one thing you've got to remember about George, he can't face up to anything, he'll always run away from things. He's a terrible coward.' It so happened that the date of their wedding, 10 May, coincided with the marriage of Elizabeth's cousin Robert Palmer to Anne, Baroness Lucas, so she couldn't be present at the Lassalles' celebration. Judith remembers that in characteristically generous style Elizabeth nonetheless came round in the morning 'with a huge salmon for our party, all beautifully cooked. She couldn't come, but made up for it by getting away from her family as soon as she could. She arrived when we'd all drunk a lot – so had she – and the party was breaking up. She didn't want to leave. George said, "Someone has to take you home," and we had to get Mark Culme-Seymour, an old boyfriend of mine, to take her.'

Contemporary descriptions of the monotony, leadenness and lack of skill demonstrated in English cookery during and immediately after the war are too frequent for their testimony to be doubted. But it is worth remembering that the same was also true during the 1920s and 1930s, when there was little feeling for the sensuousness of food, either in cookery books or in practice. The novelist and gourmet Ford Madox Ford could write, sententiously but accurately, that: 'Nowhere is our English inattention to a proper appreciation of the intrinsic values of life more conspicuous than on matters appertaining to the domain of the table.' In 1926 in *A Mirror to France* (Duckworth) his disquisition on the merits of modern French cooking concludes that 'Food in Anglo Saxon countries is no more talked of than love or Heaven.'

One is left with two overriding impressions from books and personal accounts of the first half of this century: an obsessive concern with economy and efficiency, and the assumption that cookery is a burden to be dealt with as quickly as possible. This prevails whether it is the working woman of small means who has no time and little money (or skill) with which to feed her family, or her better-off counterpart who, not working, has time at her disposal, but no inclination to spend it in the kitchen. These richer women, until recently protected by a bevy of servants from the unseemly and distasteful business of preparing food, were left relatively helpless after the First World War and utterly so after the Second, when servants had almost disappeared.

With few exceptions, there were two kinds of food. For those who could afford it there was what amounted to bastardized versions of *haute cuisine*, where more often than not the appearance of a dish was more esteemed than the subtlety of its taste. On the other hand there was 'plain wholesome food', based on the use of suet and dripping rather than butter and oil. 'Wholesome' meant heavy main courses, accompanied by vegetables stewed until soft; this was then reinforced with the ubiquitous boiled, baked or steamed puddings. (An undoubted English skill did still endure in the domestic tradition of sweet baking: cakes, pastries, biscuits.) English cooking practice was in strong contrast to the French one where cookery books and women's magazine articles took as their premise that not only did the French housewife *enjoy* cooking, being prepared to devote lengthy periods of time to its perfecting, but she had also inherited from her forebears a certain degree of basic culinary skill.

Of course some enthusiasts in England had been labouring for years before, during and after the war to inculcate an appreciation of good food and a consequent demand for it. Knowledgeable essays were produced by cultivated and cosmopolitan writers like P. Morton

Shand who, in *A Book of Food* (Jonathan Cape, 1927), as well as appreciating the best of our food, produced the well-rehearsed argument that 'for the last hundred years our national cuisine has provoked the world's grimace', or Romilly Fedden (Robin's father), who reiterated these sentiments in *Food and Other Frailties*. The cookery book writers continued the struggle. Amongst their offerings were Hilda Leyel's *Gentle Art*, her little books on salads, Elizabeth Lucas's *Pretty Kettle of Fish* (Chatto and Windus, 1925) and another on vegetables, André Simon's numerous publications with the Wine and Food Society, Constance Spry and Ambrose Heath's endless flow of material to inspire, not forgetting the Countess Morphy and Marcel Boulestin.

Ambrose Heath's *Good Food* of 1932 (Faber) was already using an extract from Norman Douglas's *South Wind* as his epigraph reflecting the spread of Douglas's influence amongst a travelled and literate minority. 'The ideal cuisine should display an individual character . . . a menu reflecting the master's alert and fastidious taste.' Heath then launched into his introduction with the argument: 'First, to show how easy good cooking can be; and second that it need not be expensive . . . it is often cheaper in the long run, for many of the famous dishes are derived from peasant and bourgeois kitchens, where it is essential that everything should do its full duty, and a little always went a long way . . . There are two essentials, however; the giving of a little time and a little trouble. Food that is worth eating cannot usually be flung together . . .'

He adds that those appreciating his book will be 'ready to give up some time and thought and care to the preparation of their meals'. Alert to the now servantless wife from Elizabeth's background, 'Those whom our present distress has forced to take, shall we say, a more active interest in the affairs of the kitchen', Heath's principles are commendable (even if the dated combination of ornament and tasteful restraint occasionally make his language verge on the comical). And the intention of introducing the reader – via a calendar layout – to the best and freshest foods available at all times of the year is a useful one. 'Good things out of season are but a ghost of their true selves.' Mr Heath recommends his book also to those who 'possibly from sentiment . . . would like to taste again . . . some of the dishes which they remember having eaten with delight in a restaurant, on a holiday abroad'. Finally, his little volume came jacketed and decorated throughout by one of the most astute, humorous and stylish artist-illustrators of the day, Edward Bawden, whose other illustrations included the famous Shell advertisements, fabric designs, posters for the cinema and decoration of the prestigious Fortnum and Mason catalogues.

The man whose work most influenced the eating habits of the younger artistic and literary circles of the Twenties and Thirties, and whose message is clearly disseminated in Ambrose Heath's writing, was Boulestin. A vital culinary influence upon Elizabeth, Marcel Boulestin was the latest in that tradition of colourful French chefs and gastronomes who first adopted the English and then encouraged them to care more about their table.

The culinary dialogue between England and France was an ancient one, set in motion as long ago as the Norman Conquest of Britain in the eleventh century. It seems that the links between European courtly food at this period and on into the later Middle Ages were much closer than hitherto recognized, meaning that what appeared as the culinary conquest of Britain was not such a simple matter: England was not as barbaric as some have thought and competition between French and English court cooks was an openly waged battle. With skirmishes flaring up over the ensuing centuries, references to the French victory are occasionally observed by the late Middle Ages. There were many cooks and writers in England, nevertheless, who staunchly maintained their English ground until the restoration of Charles II in 1662. The returning royalist court, bringing with it the sophistication and refinement of Versailles, for a time made everything French the vogue. Henceforward all self-respecting aristocrats kept a French cook, who would often be a religious (Protestant) refugee – although pastry-makers were preferably Italian. French recipes became ubiquitous in cookery books and this vogue extended to bills of fare, frequently done out in French.

Even one of the new eighteenth-century breed of acclaimed English domestic cookery writers, Hannah Glasse, catering for a less exalted and more middle-class audience, and whose fame derived in part from staunch English rejection of 'fancy' French food and the overblown notions of male cooks, was less 'patriotic' than she would have us believe when she wrote that much-quoted passage from *The Art of Cooking Made Plain and Easy* (London, 1747):

> If gentlemen will have French cooks they must pay for French tricks . . . I have heard of a cook that used six pounds of butter to fry twelve eggs; when everybody knows (that understands cooking) that half a pound is full enough or more than need be used. But then it would not be French. So much is the blind Folly of this Age that would rather be impos'd on by a *French Booby*, than give Encouragement to a good *English* Cook.

It transpires that Hannah in fact lifted a number of (inadequately understood) French recipes directly, and indirectly, from at least two monoliths of French cookery literature: La Chapelle and Massialot.

This reaction against what was perceived as French extravagance (a misconception of French cooking based on courtly books and courtly emigré cooks) took hold in England. But France was again to be in the culinary ascendant, this time partially instigated by an influx of French refugees during the aftermath of the French Revolution early in the nineteenth century. By the end of that century this French influence was properly understood by few. The omnipresent nineteenth-century tenets of thrift and economy gradually coupled with the misconceived idea that only *complicated* food was good food, drew the exasperated complaint from the great nineteenth-century chef Escoffier that the English cared more for show.

With his grace, good humour and sound French principles Boulestin set out in his restaurant and his writing to purge the English of the parsimony and misjudged attempts at 'What they think is "French" cooking. Which results in strange concoctions and alarming sauces, either simplified or elaborated with names equally vaguely French.' To readers like Elizabeth he became something of an icon.

Opened in 1925, Boulestin's restaurant had not only served beautifully prepared, unpretentious and authentic dishes from the French bourgeois cooking repertoire, but also provided delightful regional ones passed on by word of mouth from generation to generation and as yet uncommitted to paper. The spirit of the times was in reaction to what many felt was their parents' empty Victorian formality. Boulestin's message was perfectly in tune with the growing desire for (sophisticated) simplicity, reflected in the rapid success of his restaurant, more truly French than anywhere else in London, with the discerning élite of the Twenties and Thirties; the rich, the literary and artistic and travelled.

CHAPTER THIRTEEN

A Cooking Book
(1949–1950)

SHORTLY AFTER ELIZABETH and Tony's move into No. 24 Halsey Street Veronica married John Nicholson, a solicitor. Tony and Elizabeth went round to their mews flat off Kensington Church Street and made up the marriage bed. (During the commotion they met Walter Baxter, their next-door neighbour and future proprietor of the influential Old Brompton Road restaurant, the Chanterelle, a place Elizabeth would often visit in the Fifties.) Universally liked, John Nicholson was a gracious man of principle and humour and he and Veronica were to remain good companions throughout a long and harmonious marriage. His relationship with Elizabeth was maintained, however, increasingly for the sake of his wife. He was mystified at Veronica's attachment to her, his own reservations remaining intact.

Veronica was working on the staff of *Harpers Bazaar*, the quality magazine which competed on fairly equal terms with Condé Nast's influential, international oracle of style, *Vogue*. And towards the end of 1948 Veronica had persuaded Elizabeth that she should be introduced to *Harpers'* editor, Anne Scott-James, with a view to writing for her. A tall and elegant young woman, Anne Scott-James's cool and refined English beauty complemented her incisive intelligence. Her editorship of *Harpers* had established her as part of that brisk, well-educated, increasingly powerful, yet still rather embattled breed of women journalist-editors. Several of them came, like Anne Scott-James, from families noted for their literary and cultivated inclinations.

Anne Scott-James told the author she found Elizabeth 'reserved' but realized too that 'she obviously had a lot new to say' and, after discussing possible ideas for articles, asked her to write one for the magazine. Elizabeth's first attempt was accepted – she was asked for more – and in March 1949 her maiden article was published. It was entitled 'Rice Again' and the reception from editor and readers was such that she continued contributing to *Harpers* in her capacity as cookery columnist for the next six years. In this time she passed from the position of unknown journalist to sought-after writer of four successful books.

The article for *Harpers* was a modest single column, a standard 1000 words, whose introductory sentence led off with the information that rice was again available after years out of circulation, 'and with it come possibilities of pilaffs, risottos, curries – all those beautiful savoury dishes, snowy white, pale yellow with saffron or fried golden brown, spiked with scarlet of lobster, or black of *truffe*'.

Noticeable for the self-conscious stylishness of phrases like 'scarlet of lobster' and 'black of *truffe*', a flourish which seems to have little to do with her inexperience as a writer, and occurring as it does at intervals throughout all but her final writing, from the outset we see Elizabeth in characteristic mode – authoritative, practical, tart, evocative. And unlike so many cookery writers, now or then, she made the reader aware of the taste that the dish should have. She told them that as the rules for cooking rice, which are very simple, seemed to be 'insufficiently known', she made 'no apology' for stating them again. The notoriously difficult subject of rice cooking, in which each person claims the infallibility of their own method, was glossed over. Elizabeth's way was correct 'and that is that', as she would say.

Four recipes followed, each using rice: a pilaff, a *riz en salade*, a risotto and a rice stuffing. Elizabeth's Cairo cook Suleiman was immortalized, with his pilaff the first recipe of this debut article, although here she calls it Turkish. A year later the pilaff was honoured with Suleiman's name and had become 'one of the most comforting dishes imaginable'. Here one is presented with one of those slight elusive statements typical of Elizabeth and inducing in any reader alive to the hints in her prose the desire at once to lie back and muse *and* to sit up and think. 'Comforting' is a word more often applied to the hot, warming soups and slowly matured, relatively herb-free meat stews associated with cold northern climates, than to this dish so redolent of the spice-filled savour of the Far and Middle East. Did Elizabeth mean comforting to herself in the heat and sometimes despair of Cairo, or for herself and her readers here in these cold northern wastes to which she felt at present confined, as a reassuring reminder of lightness, brilliance and sun?

Her first article was not a dazzling piece of prose, nevertheless, she included so much that was herself that it can be read as an understated exemplification of what her writing would come to represent. The quality, presentation and style of recipes and writing exhibited those features which remained her trademark to the end. Admittedly, the qualities are easier to see with the hindsight of later writing, but the series which followed bears out Anne Scott-James's judgement of her work that 'It was as if her prose sprung fully formed from her pen.' The one feature, so characteristic, which Elizabeth did not yet quite have the confidence to display was her wit, but that she would remedy quite soon.

For her second article in April, she was again given 1000 words, and dealt with the possibilities of 'Easter Lamb'. Once more none of the recipes (except the last) was English: Anatolian Kebabs, *Tranches de Mouton Sauce Catalane, Gigot à l'Infante*, and for accompaniments she added Potato Kephtedes, *Concombres à la crème* and Mint Chutney. But neither were they tired French fare; rather, when not recipes from Greece or the Middle East, they were examples of a mellow southern earthiness like the *Gigot*, a leg of lamb marinated in olive oil for twelve hours, 'well seasoned with salt, pepper and herbs, including rosemary and marjoram. Put the *gigot* into a braising pan with half a pint of *malaga* or *marsala*, a quantity of small onions and 1lb of small sausages. Cook it in a very slow oven for several hours.' In conversation friends and relations remember the private version of this frequently voiced dictum: 'Cook it dead slow.'

In June Anne Scott-James was confident enough – her magazine staff were as impressed with the articles as the public – to unleash Elizabeth; she extended her to three columns for 'Gourmet Picnics'. The more expansive style this permitted meant that her entire first page was without a recipe and Elizabeth was now well into her stride. In urbane, informative prose, subtly her own, she described the rules pertaining to the complicated game of make-believe – sophisticated rusticity – called a gourmet picnic. Two menus followed, each with a page of recipes. The note of authority, tinged with that caustic humour familiar from her letters, made it clear that the writer had actually partaken of the picnics she described. The reader need have no qualms about the efficacy of the recipes, all that was now required was to get up and try them.

For all but the most wealthy or resourceful and enterprising cooks amongst the magazine's readership this, however, was impossible. Owing to a combined lack of demand and rationing, the ingredients – courgettes, green and red peppers, aubergines, garlic, olive oil, olives, anchovies, fresh pasta, pitta, almonds, raisins and garlic – were virtually unobtainable anywhere except in a very few shops, situated almost entirely in the capital, and even those largely in Soho. And in those bleak post-war days Elizabeth made little concession to the current dearth of Mediterranean ingredients. For hers are Mediterranean recipes, with only one or two (alternative) recommendations such as 'chopped chives, or the green top of an onion or leek' instead of basil, no reference to saffron, and 'grated cheese' in place of Parmesan. 'A lot of the food she was talking about was like fiction,' says Joyce Molyneaux, an early devotee and now a renowned chef, 'because it was food that you had never seen or thought you were ever likely to see.'

But this deterred neither *Harpers'* editor nor Elizabeth herself, who continued to provide this delightful 'fiction'. To the well-heeled young wives who read *Harpers Bazaar*, as yet unfamiliar with the attractions of the Mediterranean and its table, her writing provided a certain exotic stimulation. The rest, *au fait* with the Mediterranean's 'blessed shores' from Riviera holidays pre-war, were propelled into reminiscence; the anticipation of adventure while speeding southward on the luxurious Blue Train, hopefully soon to return.

Recently Anne Scott-James was surprised on being reminded that Elizabeth was born in the same year as herself, saying to the author, 'When we met she seemed older. I have no memory of her dress. She didn't strike me. But she was very grande-dame, very sure of herself; there was an egoism of quite an advanced kind. I thought she was pretty formidable, and didn't instantly warm to her.' But personal feelings were unimportant when the magazine's editor had discovered such a contributor and she let Elizabeth largely dictate her own material. 'She knew exactly what she wanted to do. The article would always be about a particular subject, for example vegetables. She was quite poetic about them.'

Elizabeth was soon demonstrating the breadth of her reading on her subject with confidence and flair. At a glance her writing made it abundantly clear that here was no culinary novice with a sentimental attachment to the 'shores of that great lake' as Forster had called the Mediterranean Sea. Though many may not have recognized it, the readers were being presented not simply with good recipes, but with a synthesis, a distillation of Elizabeth's varied experience, and her knowledge and literate understanding of the development of European (but particularly French and English) cooking. In *The Presentation of Food* she briefly outlined a history of what, in her belief, had been the misguided fashion for display. She launched in with a lengthy quote from the absurd and facile marathon which describes how to make *Lobster à la Newmarket* 'in a book called *A la Mode Cookery* published in 1902. It is typical of the inanity of fashionable cooking at that period. Mrs Brook . . . even went so far as to suggest that flowers, food and yes, wine should be chosen to match the hostess's gown.'

We are then treated to a passage of historical information, smoothly incorporating wit as a device to inform us effortlessly of her opinion. She describes how the First World War had called a halt to most of these 'preoccupations . . . and I suspect that most women who have the time and talent for this form of self-expression prefer to exercise it on the devising of lampshades. The inspiration for this upholstered food had come of course from France. Mid and late nineteenth century French cookery books abound with engravings of elaborate dishes carried out in the grandest possible manner.' This custom, initially so favoured by the great French chefs, was questioned by Prosper Montagne who according to André Simon 'originated the movement to put an end to the extravagance and waste of time and materials which all this fancy work entailed'. (And this movement was continued by Boulestin.)

Elizabeth's style of delivery – accurate information, opinion couched in wit, with enough conjuring and mystery calculated to intrigue and inspire – already evident in the very earliest pieces of her writing, was much in the spirit of her beloved mentor Norman Douglas. In the South of France at the outbreak of war, with his erudite talk of the Classical past and the Mediterranean present, Douglas had both concentrated her mind and expanded its vision. She had imbibed the essence of his message, as too the ethos of elegant simplicity and authenticity shared by some of her favoured cookery writers, Leyel, Boulestin, Pomiane. But she was never a copyist. Elizabeth had already arrived at a voice, uniquely her own.

Anne Scott-James's confidence in Elizabeth's writing sprang from two sources. 'She struck the exact right moment. With freedom again and the expectation of holidays once more, without ghastly restrictions or bombs.' She also recognized that Elizabeth 'wrote beautifully. Right from the start. You could smell the shrimps, hear the fishwives talking on the quay. She was old enough to write well, and it was quite clearly not run of the mill. There was this feeling that she wasn't thinking how to do it, but was always associating it with places, always with places – with mountains, with ports, with beautiful villages. There was a Proustian quality about it.'

By December of that year Elizabeth was writing another long piece, entitled 'Style in the Kitchen', in which she hinted at principles and intent. She described types of cook and cooking to be fostered and avoided in the amateur arena. Anathema: the flamboyant, ostentatious, or 'false chic style of cookery advocated by certain classes of cookery school. Sausages in jelly mould decorated with carrots, sponge cakes topped with tinned peaches and whipped cream . . .' Although they 'may be well executed with professional skill', just as with the 'pompous *Poulet à la Lucullus* of the International Palace Hotel, you may be able to disguise inferior ingredients, but not the wrong outlook on food'.

Esteemed was the style of cooking practised by those who often, like herself, had unconventional culinary backgrounds – writers such as Edouard de Pomiane, the son of Polish émigrés to France, who became, with radio broadcasts and books, one of France's most popular cooks. Sometimes scorned by the contemporary exponents of the Grand Tradition, his cheerful disregard for the sacrosanct and pompous aspects of French *haute cuisine*, combined with flair and a knowledgeable enthusiasm for food, enamoured him to many. Of his *Cooking in Ten Minutes* (Bruno Cassirer, 1948) Elizabeth told her readers that 'His recipe for skate in black butter is almost the perfect example of a delicate, rapidly prepared dish for these days.' And she sets down Pomiane's delightfully clear and inspiring instructions.

She writes that the experience necessary to make the perfect gratin or soufflé was 'hard to acquire nowadays, for it entails a certain recklessness in the matter of cream, eggs, and butter, plus a searching knowledge of your cooking stove, to achieve the perfect degree of creamy smoothness and the inimitable crusty golden coating of a successful gratin'. Who better to tell her reader how to achieve it than the great Prosper Montagne with his recipe for *Gratin Dauphinoise* (although Elizabeth's own far simpler version, given in *French Provincial Cooking* ten years later, is much better).

Only 'slavish attention to the rules' laid out by her dear Marcel Boulestin in *Finer Cooking* will save the amateur food-rationed cook from 'the ghastly anxiety endured by the hostess who has flung caution to the winds, entombing a month's butter and eggs and the last of the Grand Marnier into a soufflé'. In that dramatic image of eggs and butter 'entombed' this *Harpers* piece bears out Anne Scott-James's judgement on the fully fledged nature of Elizabeth's earliest writing. From the beginning she manifested a style of economy and elegance.

Elizabeth was not interested in analysis beyond a certain point, either then or in the future, and although highly intelligent, was not an intellectual. She could classify, but was not interested in the abstract. Her approach had already given her a firm (eventually profound) grasp of both the historical and aesthetic principles of her chosen subject; it was determined (at times stubbornly so) and passionate. Equally important, she had the imagination and peculiar discipline of an artist. Her synthesizing and refining intelligence and her formidable memory were often at their sharpest in her work. But this dedication and passion with which she approached her work could cloud her judgement when it came to others; a constant problem for her, in the years she spent as a journalist, was the length of her contributions.

'Oh, she was a very tetchy contributor, there would always be difficulties. One page, 1200 words, was what she had. But she never fitted in with you in any way.' Anne Scott-James would say to her: 'Elizabeth, I can't make the magazine bigger for you.'

'As a journalist you have *got* to give, there is no one too grand not to be able to accept changes and alterations. I'd say, "Elizabeth, there are too many words, you've got to cut them. Are you going to do it or shall I?" She wouldn't come in and I had to do it. She was unbending, couldn't see it, nothing mattered but her piece. In August I asked her to do me a Scottish article.

'"I don't know anything about Scottish food."

'She thought Scotland was barbarism.' With time Elizabeth would come to think differently about Scottish traditions, but for now 'Everything was Mediterranean. She sort of compromised with the Scottish number by putting a whole lot of other people's recipes in. She was very exciting, but very rude, you know. She was confident her work was good, and it was. I was rather frightened of her. It was hard, for women particularly, to like her, but with that knowledge, that imagination, you couldn't not respect her.'

Anne Scott-James had advised Elizabeth to hang on to her copyrights, then unusual for a cookery writer, and from the beginning Elizabeth utilized her literary labour to the full, making it bring in the best possible rewards. Practising this right (and insisting on it for all her subsequent journalism during and after the *Harpers* pieces), she was able to incorporate as much *Harpers* work as she chose into her other present endeavour. Before the end of 1949 she had put together a coherent collection of recipes in such a way as to feel she could call it a book. Veronica, George and Felicité were asked to read it through and had a number of comments to make. Apart from the benefit of George checking over the Greek pieces, they were all at pains to stress that there was too much reference to Norman Douglas. They believed much of him would have to go.

After persuasion Elizabeth grudgingly made the cuts and the manuscript was shown by a friend, Robin Chancellor, to several London publishers. It duly came back with the rejection notes. Food wasn't a good subject at the present time. But one, the entrepreneurial John Lehmann, publisher of the adventurous and prestigious Penguin

New Writing, was to become involved, almost in spite of himself. His own brief résumé of events is the best.

'One day there came into my office a disreputable piece of paper – several pieces of paper – typewritten, which said they were a cooking book.' Later, Lehmann and Elizabeth were to become friends and he told her that the manuscript was the untidiest he had ever received. She had been using it to cook from.

'I couldn't make very much of it myself, not being a cooking expert, but I had Julia Strachey with me and asked her to report on it. She came back and said, "I think this is a masterpiece."'

Now intrigued, Lehmann read it again but still needed persuasion. Julia Strachey later told Elizabeth that it was with the recipe for Turkish Stuffing for a Whole Roast Sheep that she had finally cajoled Lehmann into a realization of the book's strength and strangely alluring appeal: 'Imagine, a whole roast sheep, and the meat ration a few ounces a week.'

Lehmann continued: 'I was very thrilled at this and went through it. Though not an expert I (now) saw that it was a very remarkable piece of work. That was the typescript of *A Book of Mediterranean Food*.'

Without Julia Strachey, that small pink and brown linen book, encased in its enticingly vivid dust-jacket, may well never have become the icon it did for a generation of upper-middle-class readers. However, in Julia Strachey it could not have found a better ambassadress. As the niece of Lytton Strachey, the enemy of the Victorians with his *Eminent* ones, she had grown up at the centre of Bloomsbury life. For all Elizabeth and her family's dismissal of the inhabitants of Monk's House and Charleston Farmhouse and their charmed circle, what she propounded with such conviction was very much to their taste. Through her evocative descriptions of unpretentious peasant and bourgeois Mediterranean food and its places, Elizabeth championed with a singular literary grace the ethos of Marcel Boulestin: 'Faites Simples.' This had already, by 1927, been exemplified in Virginia Woolf's gloriously sensual description of the *Boeuf en Daube* dinner in her novel *To the Lighthouse*. And the Bloomsbury Group and others of the literary and social élite, such as Cedric Morris and Lett

Haines, had identified to such a degree with this ethos that their devotion had helped make Boulestin a success; several of them had been inspired to spend time in the South.

On the subject of *Mediterranean Food* John Lehmann continued: 'I always, perhaps not justifiably, believed that one of the causes of its success was a misprint in the first impression. In those days it was difficult to get eggs. Elizabeth had written take 2 to 3 eggs for a particular recipe and the printer had put "take 23 eggs".

'Well, I pretended to myself that that fascinated and excited people very much. And so I left it. I was struck by the imagination and knowledge of what she was writing about, and her style. Her command and subtle use of English, and only then did I begin to see her importance in a general sense.'

Without any particularly well-articulated understanding of its merits beyond its quirkiness and Mediterranean escapism after years of uniform war-time puritanism, Lehmann now sensed something of the book's potential appeal. Summoning Elizabeth to his office, he laid out his proposal for publishing her book. He would pay her an advance of £100: £50 on signature of contract and £50 on publication. But he did not like Elizabeth's title and asked her would not 'The Blue Train Cookery Book be better?' Elizabeth demurred, suggesting that the train had never reached Egypt. She was privately reluctant to have her book associated with a life-style which she felt had ceased with the war, and with which she didn't particularly wish her labours to be linked. She was correct that the life had gone for ever – and as Norman Douglas had predicted to her and Charles Gibson Cowan, Europe was irrevocably changed – but in fact this was the very core of the audience to whom her evocative nostalgia would appeal. Elizabeth was in a sense writing for herself, and her past self had some of its roots in that life. She was always ambivalent about this and never publicly professed it.

Elizabeth's persistence paid off. Having instructed her to think about the title, as would he, Lehman asked her to write an introduction. A few days later he wrote to her saying that, on reflection she was right, the title 'should stand'. Being right was something Elizabeth was rarely in doubt about, but she 'admired the good grace with which John, a man who – as I was to discover . . . was far from easy-going, conceded that I must have my own way over that *Mediterranean Food* title. Now of course it seems unthinkable that it could have been anything else.'

In spite of her confident prose, flowing as it does with such apparent facility, writing was never easy for Elizabeth, and for every finished page there were a number of false starts. An introduction called for a distillation of thought which she was later to make out hadn't been given much, when calling the result 'pretty perfunctory'. This is the comment of hindsight, of a more experienced writer. In essence, what she had arrived at was a synthesis of those first 'agonized cravings' put down in the Ross-on-Wye notes, and her more measured versions of them written out in the articles for *Harpers Bazaar*. It purports to be an introduction, and it is. It is also a challenge and a battle cry.

But first Elizabeth paid her friend Veronica the tribute of dedicating the book to her and years later, in her thanks for an honorary doctorate from Essex University, she described how Veronica: 'chivvied me, coaxed me, badgered me, in fact bullied me into writing about cookery at all'. As we now know, Elizabeth's motivation to write sprang from more powerful sources than a coaxing friend, but Veronica was, like George Lassalle, undoubtedly one of those significant few who recognized in Elizabeth something unique which needed airing. In musing over it Veronica has recently said that '*Mediterranean Food* was a very reserved book.' She felt that Elizabeth's passion and intensity and that shattering yet invigorating wit were too modified and 'her own voice didn't entirely come over'. Her friend was understandably disappointed in the loss of the 'person' Elizabeth. But Elizabeth had transcended the personal, had (like any artist) transformed real life, and herself. With her unusual combination of romance and utter practicality Elizabeth had reached out to her audience with the instinct of the born communicator.

Her introduction begins with these words: 'The cooking of the Mediterranean shores, endowed with all the natural resources, the colour and flavour of the South, is a blend of tradition and brilliant improvisation. The Latin genius flashes from the kitchen pans.

'It is honest cooking, too; none of the sham Grande Cuisine of the International Palace Hotel.'

'"It is not really an exaggeration," wrote Marcel Boulestin, "to say that peace and happiness begin, geographically, where garlic is used in cooking."'

The inclusion of Boulestin's outrageous hyperbole in her first page clearly demonstrates Elizabeth's viewpoint. The message she had purveyed for several months in her articles for *Harpers Bazaar* was here thrown down gauntlet-like at the feet of her unsuspecting English readers. But Elizabeth is concerned with evocation, she is not really interested in persuading: she is an artist, a myth-maker, not at heart a propagandist. Names flow one after another as an incantation, and within moments she has conjured images of those distant lands encircling the shores of the Mediterranean. In her mind's eye, and now ours, their significance resonates with her own journeys of discovery. These countries, to most readers mysterious and strange, were to her also vivid and real. And, as the book unfolds, one is reminded constantly of Charles's diary of their voyage on the *Evelyn Hope* and Elizabeth's letters to her family, where food was described almost incidentally but was actually at the heart of a celebration which was Elizabeth and Charles's life together: along the Rhône to the sea and the South of France, on the Riviera at the outset of war, and on into Greece and the harsh, isolated beauty of life on the 'Isles of Greece', and afterwards the more voluptuous, worldly years of Middle Eastern living in Alexandria and Cairo.

At a level only half understood by Elizabeth herself, this book rejoices in the romance of her life with Charles (inextricably bound to her experiences of the Mediterranean) and is a lament for all that she has lost. The essential core of the vision she is conjuring in *Mediterranean Food* is found in the poetry of her life on the lost 'Isles of Greece'. The dream is central to her vision, yet so intimate that she was never able to refer directly to it in her writing. Only much later does she make oblique reference to aspects of this period, and then only because with time she had buried and de-mythologized its significance for herself.

Elizabeth traces the routes: 'From Gibraltar to the Bosphorus, down the Rhone Valley, through the great sea ports of Marseilles, Barcelona, and Genoa, across to Tunis and Alexandria, embracing all the Mediterranean islands, Corsica, Sicily, Sardinia, Crete, the Cyclades, Cyprus . . . to the mainland of Greece and the much disputed territories of Syria, the Lebanon, Constantinople . . .'

The ever-recurring elements in the dishes of these countries of the Southern and Eastern Mediterranean were, as she later described them,

> the oil, the saffron, the garlic, the pungent local wines; the aromatic perfume of rosemary, wild marjoram and basil . . . the brilliance of the market stalls piled high with pimentos, aubergines, tomatoes, olives, melons, figs . . . the great heaps of shiny fish, silver, vermilion, or tiger-striped, and those long needle fish whose bones mysteriously turn green when they are cooked. There are, too, all manner of unfamiliar cheeses made from sheep or goat's milk; the butchers' stalls are festooned with every imaginable portion of the inside of every edible animal (anyone who has lived for long in Greece will be familiar with the sound of air gruesomely whistling through sheep's lungs frying in oil).

Of course, almost no one in England reading this in 1950 would have been familiar with that sound, or the dish which was its end, and the image is unexpected and powerful. During the war in England some had attempted, without too much success, to utilize those (unrationed) parts of animals for food which had before the war already fallen out of favour, but even these were hard to come by. If anyone – like the writer Theodora FitzGibbon, who asked her butcher if their scarcity meant that animals were no longer born with 'tongues, tails, hearts, kidneys, livers, or balls' – succeeded in obtaining the odd trophy it would have been unlikely to include the lungs of a sheep. Writing about such things Elizabeth added to the hint of the unattainable, the exotic, evident in her descriptions and recipes which followed. E. M. Forster said of Virginia Woolf: 'The passages in her books describing food were a sharp reminder that here was a woman alert sensuously.' Unquestionably this applied to Elizabeth too. The sensuousness in her writing was communicated to the reader on several levels: the form and content of her prose, evoking the shapes, colours, aromas and scents of food, was always set in context, in a place.

She takes her reader outside the kitchen and into the realm of the travel writer, one of whose attractions lies in the allure of the unknown, with descriptions of the strange and mysterious places of her experience. She tells her English reader, in the grey aftermath of war, that in the Mediterranean 'There are endless varieties of currants and raisins, figs from Smyrna on long strings, dates, almonds, pistachios and pine kernel nuts, dried melon seeds and sheets of apricot paste which are dissolved in water to make a cooling drink' [always a favourite of hers]. These and the ingredients she listed 'make rich and colourful dishes. Over-picturesque, perhaps, for every day; but then who wants to eat the same food every day?' And here Elizabeth is reiterating one of Norman Douglas's typical maxims on food: 'The longer one lives, the more one realizes that nothing is a dish for every day.' For Norman Douglas, unlike most, had no fear of life, only death.

The next section of the introduction is neither entirely clear nor always accurate, dealing as it does with the possibility or even desirability of reproducing Mediterranean meals, and for subsequent editions of the book it was cut. What Elizabeth stresses is that although 'the variety and quantity of ingredients called for in some of these dishes seem, at first sight, alarming, it is because I preferred to give the authentic recipes and leave it to the resourceful cook to improvise her own substitutes when necessary'. With these words and the following – 'I hope to give some idea of the lovely cookery of those regions to people who do not already know them, and to stir the memories of those who have eaten this food on its native shores, and who would like sometimes to bring a flavour of those blessed lands of sun and sea and olive trees into their English kitchens' – she has distinguished what will be the essential tone of her book. Whatever difficulties the reader might find in reproducing the recipes, the book's authentic voice was abundantly clear.

In part because at that time publishers did not employ specialist editors for cookery editing, and also because John Lehmann had recognized the quirkiness of the text, Elizabeth's manuscript was left intact with few alterations. The war had, by necessity, conferred on many English housewives a more French-Mediterranean resourceful-ness in matters of food and some of these were intrigued enough to try recipes for dishes such as: Soup Basque, and Iced Beetroot Soup made from baked beetroots whose 'resulting delicious flavour happily bears no resemblance to the bloodless things sold ready cooked by the greengrocers . . .' Avgolémono (*The* Greek Soup); Soupe au Pistou, vegetables and vermicelli, with the addition of *Aillade*, that fierce Southern paste made of pounded garlic and basil.

There is, inevitably, more than liberal use of garlic throughout *Mediterranean Food*, including, famously, the recipe for *Gigot à la Provençal*, left in French and whose author, 'rather severely remarks, this dish is supportable only to those who are accustomed to the cooking of the Midi'. Instructions are to lard the leg of lamb with a dozen cloves of garlic and serve with another litre of them blanched. How this must have shocked the English reader when the attitude of most towards garlic in 1950 differed little from Tobias Smollet's, that querulous eighteenth-century traveller who remarked that in France 'I am almost poisoned with garlic, which they mix in their ragouts and all their sauces; nay, the smell of it . . . perfumes . . . every person you approach.'

The insertion of the Provençal *Gigot* recipe is also a forceful reminder of the transformation of Elizabeth's attitudes. In her letter to Priscilla regarding preparations for the 1935 journey to Munich by train, she had said they were to travel third class, although it would be uncomfortable. She discovered they could stay the night in Cologne, which would prevent them sleeping on 'hard benches smelling of garlic and disgusting tobacco'. From the South of France after the outbreak of war, she wrote again to Pris that she had taken to garlic, which went into absolutely everything – they 'lashed' it into salads there, and she hated to think of having to cook without it.

When it came to the Savoury Omelette Elizabeth could see no better possible way of describing the method than to 'quote "Wyvern's" wholly admirable views on the subject' from his book *Fifty Luncheons*. 'Wyvern' was the pseudonym of a nineteenth-century Indian Army colonel, Kenney-Herbert, whose *Culinary Jottings for Madras* (first published in 1878) went into several editions and of whom Elizabeth was later to write: 'His recipes are so meticulous and clear, that the absolute beginner could follow them, yet at the same time he has much to teach the experienced cook.' There follow three pages of instructions on the cooking of an omelette.

Rognons Braisés au Porto . . . How many of her readers could lay their hands on a truffle? Never mind, they could at least salivate and imagine the day when it would be possible to try out 'the beauty of this dish', depending 'on the aroma of the truffle permeating the wine'. Or *Pissaladina*, that lusty onion, olive and anchovy Southern French pizza, 'one of the delights of Marseilles . . . where it is sold in the market places and the bakeries in the early morning and can be bought piping hot, by the slice off big iron trays.' *Anchoïade Croze, Grenouilles Provençales, Fish Plaki*: 'this is a typical Greek way of doing fish and appears over and over again in different forms.' Roast Lobster 'is a lordly dish', *Moules Marinière*, Spaghetti with Mussels, *Bouillabaisse* from Reboul's *La Cuisinière Provençal, Raito*, 'one of the traditional dishes of Christmas Eve in Provence . . . a ragout made of onions, tomatoes, garlic, pounded walnuts, thyme, rosemary, fennel, parsley, bay leaves, red wine, capers and black olives, all simmered in olive oil. In this sauce dried salt cod or eels are cooked.' *Arní Souvlákia*, 'eaten on the terrace of a primitive Cretan taverna, flavoured with wood smoke and the mountain herbs, accompanied by the strong red wine of Crete, these kebabs can be the most poetic of foods'.

'Octopus and Cuttlefish': in Robert Byron's Greek mountainside banquet, from *The Station*, 'We learnt what is meant by a Feast of the Church,' with his gothic descriptions of the gargantuan octopus feast presided over by a bishop, 'recently of Asia Minor, at a table set for seventy'. Each of Elizabeth's chapters was introduced and sometimes interspersed thus, with instantly evocative passages from writers who were, like herself, reminiscing on their love of France and the Mediterranean. None of them (except Douglas, and then it was for a joke) wrote cookery books. Rather these cameos, sometimes from novels, more often from travel books, were observations and memories by the literate and educated for others of their kind. Such was Elizabeth's book too, the food of her travels.

She gave us Henry James on the exquisite simplicity of fresh boiled eggs, bread and butter which was such 'poetry' that he 'ate a pound or two of it' in Bourg en Bresse; Tobias Smollett on the variety of fish on the Côte Niçoise in his eighteenth-century travels; an exotic, the vastly rich William Beckford, another eighteenth-century traveller, on an ecclesiastical feast in Spain; D. H. Lawrence on the abundance of vegetables – 'Piles of white and green fennel, like celery, and great sheaves of young, purplish, sea-dust-coloured artichokes, nodding their buds, piles of big radishes, scarlet and bluey-purple, carrots, long strings of dried figs, mountains of oranges . . .' from his *Sea and Sardinia*; Compton Mackenzie on his soul responding to the exquisite selection of ices in an Athenian café; Osbert Sitwell in *Great Morning* lunching on truffles, Pecorino cheese, grapes, pasta and red wine of the neighbourhood at his beautiful Tuscan castello, Montegufoni.

And finally to Elizabeth's beloved Norman Douglas in a passage from *South Wind*, which to the generation after the First War had been a liberating revelation in its challenge to modern morality and manners. 'All culinary tasks should be performed with reverential love, don't you think so? To say that a cook must possess the requisite outfit of culinary skill and temperament . . . The true cook must have not only these externals, but a large dose of general worldly experience. She is the perfect blend of artist and philosopher . . . If she drinks a little, why it is all to the good . . . It proves she possesses the prime requisite of the artist; sensitiveness and a capacity for enthusiasm.'

Elizabeth's identification with this was of course complete and like Douglas her 'artistry' was supported by sound knowledge and practice. Only very rarely, and then expressly stated, were recipes for dishes ever included in her writing which had not been tried out by herself. Simply making a dish, however, was not enough, it must *work*, be completely understood, before Elizabeth would include it. Many friends over the years had a dish given them once, twice, three times. 'I want to see if the soufflé needs 14, 15, or 16 minutes,' she might say. But this concern for accuracy came more from attempting to get the 'feel' for a dish so that she could then communicate it; she watched the clock and weighed and measured, but only to understand the principles, not for their own sake. A propos Elizabeth's concern for the 'rightness' of food she said to Judith Lassalle, 'I'd rather cut myself in half than a potato. You find the right-sized potatoes and cook all the same size together. You don't cut them, you just find the right size.'

Mistakes and failures were carefully noted; friends were not resented if they didn't like the dishes. Judith Lassalle remembers 'an awful cold Greek soup she would insist on doing. And a thing made of dried apricots, it was a complete flop. Sometimes we would laugh. Oh yes, she could, she could be so relaxed and jolly. George and she always had so much to talk about. He was very well read, he spent all his time reading, they both liked the French. And his languages were always a help to her. But it was often food. She loved finding out about it. When other people had a portrait on the wall Elizabeth would have a picture of a fish.'

Amongst the literary and artistic coterie of homosexuals whom John Lehmann patronized and befriended was the young John Minton. Minton was a painter, one of whose outlets, like many of the best of his generation, was book illustration. Lehmann had sent Minton with a friend, Ian Ross, to write up and illustrate a holiday in Corsica. Published by Lehmann as *Time Was Away, A Notebook in Corsica* (1948), it subsequently became a post-war classic of travel literature and book illustration, capturing the feeling of sultriness, the heat, the elemental timelessness and brooding history of the island. Elizabeth did not know the book, had not heard of John Minton when Lehmann showed it to her and said he proposed having him do the illustrations for *Mediterranean Food*.

Minton, with typical flair, captured perhaps the most important aspect of this book for the post-war audience: escapism. On a brilliantly eye-catching dust-jacket he used his by now well-established repertoire of images and the free-script lettering in vogue at the time to create an intense Mediterranean image of food laid out on crisp white cloths, wine, boats on a blue, blue sea and, somewhere up above, a blazing sun. Throughout the book his stylized pictures of a cornucopia of Mediterranean largesse by the sea, on rustic tables, in simple kitchens, with their setting often seen through a window, are skilfully integrated with the text.

On the Sunday following publication Elizabeth Nicholas, respected *Sunday Times* travel writer, wrote her unqualified praise of *A Book of Mediterranean Food*. To Elizabeth's delight she had appreciated the author's unwillingness 'to make any ignoble compromises with expediency' and was entirely in favour of a serious book which made no concessions to suit 'present, we hope transitory, weaknesses in our own victualling service'. She praised Minton's illustrations and Elizabeth's choice of quotation, and almost as importantly to Elizabeth, she noticed the absence of Brillat-Savarin's rather tedious strictures on the 'culinary art', then almost ubiquitous in any work on food.

With the completion and publication of *Mediterranean Food*, Elizabeth had reached the end of a lengthy period of gestation. Paris is claimed by others – and for simplicity's sake by Elizabeth herself – as the locale of its conception; the Paris of months of girlish academic exercise and good bourgeois food twenty years before. But in effect, her whole life had been a preparation for this synthesis of her beliefs and ideals. Elizabeth's writings *were* her beliefs and ideals, those lost and those still cherished. What she later wrote of herself in reference to prying eyes and pens is quite true: 'All there is to know about me is in my books.' What she did not add, though, was that so much of it was so cryptic as to be indecipherable unless one had the key. Her statement should be rewritten: 'All I understand of myself or *want* you to know about me . . .'

Her 'life's love' and a vital aspect of her biography about which she was quite open, even proud, was her relationship with Norman Douglas. In *Mediterranean Food* her tribute to him was simple: 'Above all I owe a debt of gratitude to Mr Norman Douglas, whose great knowledge and enchanting talk taught me so much about the Mediterranean.' Douglas had, from the time of their earliest meetings, given Elizabeth greater confidence to be herself. Hence her oft-quoted maxim of Norman's in her essay on him 'Have it Your Way', after his death: 'Always do as you please, and send everybody to hell, and take the consequences.' Like him, albeit sometimes with less gusto, she had done just that and, like him, she had reaped the benefits and the sorrows which this had so far entailed.

As often with Elizabeth the qualities of some of those she admired, perhaps above all Douglas, were frequently attributable to herself. This in no way implies emulation, rather an admiration for superior knowledge and a confirmation of what was already her own approach to life. Mark Holloway, in *Norman Douglas: A Biography* (Secker and Warburg, 1977), quotes him writing of the South: 'I am only dreaming through the summer months to the music of the cicadas.' Holloway adds: 'Dreaming perhaps, but sharply aware, and weaving scholarship, impressions, fact, and fantasy into an intricate fabric ... enchantingly entertaining ... This atmosphere is created without fuss, with economy and elegance, with style and verve, with measure and serenity, eminently considerate to the reader, good-mannered, enticing, satisfying.' I leave it to the reader to decide how much fantasy or serenity Elizabeth's writing demonstrates, but most of the other qualities Holloway ascribes to Douglas are eminently hers in writing.

CHAPTER FOURTEEN

The Only Real Paradise is the One We Have Lost
(1950–1951)

FROM THE COMMENCEMENT of her daughter's writing career Stella took an intelligent and appreciative interest in her progress and, despite her history of defiance, Elizabeth did want Stella's approval. This feeling of mutual respect grew on both sides and gradually tended to balance resentful youthful judgements. It is reflected in Priscilla's recent comment: 'Mummy was better company, took more interest in us when we were grown up.' This mother whom many of her friends were given to believe Elizabeth disliked was in fact the dedicatee of her daughter's second book. Although there is consensus on Stella's fearsomeness, friends and family are not consistent in their estimation of Elizabeth's relationship with her mother. Dislike is too simplistic a word here. A certain fear which Elizabeth never entirely outgrew, a certain sense of inadequacy in relation to her; resentment combined with a grudging but real admiration, might be a more adequate description. (Ironically, of Stella's four daughters there is no question that Elizabeth became the most like her as she grew older.)

An anecdote from some years later reflects Elizabeth's attitude. Veronica and John Nicholson were living at that time at Glynde Place, a beautiful Sussex house not so far from Wootton, and Elizabeth had been driven down from London for a large party they were giving. The following day Veronica and Elizabeth were due to lunch with Stella in Brighton. As they drove over Veronica became hopelessly lost and by the time they finally arrived in Brighton, over an hour and a half late, Elizabeth was very agitated at the prospect of facing Stella. 'Oh, it was a rather awful lunch, and all my fault; Stella was not amused,' said Veronica. 'We arrived so late that there was nothing of the day recoverable really. Elizabeth did remain in awe of her mother.'

After her return to England, notwithstanding disagreements of sometimes volcanic proportion, Elizabeth maintained regular contact with her mother. One particular event, whilst highlighting the tensions of any parent–child relationship, also illustrates Elizabeth and Stella's inadequate methods of resolving them. The event occurred several years later, by which time Elizabeth was an established authority on food.

Stella would come up to London, go round the auctions, see one of her daughters for lunch and return to Brighton on the evening train. On this occasion she and Elizabeth were having a meal at Halsey Street. Elizabeth made her mother cauliflower cheese and Maudie O'Malley remembers: 'They had a frightful row about it. Liz said that there was "no goodness in it whatsoever," and her mother said, "I totally disagree with you."

'Stella wasn't much of a cook, she could cook an omelette and cauliflower cheese and that was about it. Well, they started knocking back the whiskies and having this terrible row at the same time. And then Stella finally left in an awful huff. She stomped off down the road to Sloane Square underground going to get a train back to Brighton and fell down the steps and broke her leg and ended up in hospital. They had such arguments, quite tremendous.'

Tony David was now concerned to make something of his money before it ran out; he still had no job. Apparently he and Christopher Grey's brother came up with the idea of an up-market club and accordingly bought a property in Herbert Crescent. Doreen and her small daughter stayed there for a time in a top-floor flat. Simultaneously with these negotiations Elizabeth was spending money having Halsey Street altered to divide it into three more or less self-contained apartments to accommodate tenants as it already had done on an informal basis. It was arranged that Felicité would take one of the apartments. She agreed to Elizabeth's terms, paid her a lump sum for the tenancy and contracted to move into the top flat by late October 1950.

In the letter thanking Felicité for her cheque Elizabeth said that it did seem quite a lot of money. She hoped Felicité would consider the flat as apart from the family in every way – she should do as she pleased and live as she chose, and Elizabeth would continue to do exactly the same. (Echoes here of the Norman Douglas maxim on how to live.) Elizabeth wrote with conviction when she said she would be delighted when Felicité moved in. She also told Felicité that her cheque had enabled her to send off dozens of her own and added with that hint of the expiring actress which she never really lost: 'The relief of paying the bills has been so great that I feel dreadfully light-headed and I have retired to bed to recover.' Already a favourite place of respite for Elizabeth, in future it would become more so. Finally she complained to Felicité about a recent appreciation of their Aunt Violet (she had died in 1948). She didn't think very much of what Sir Osbert Sitwell had written on Violet, as it gave 'no real idea of her at all, except the colours she wore and the 'mulish' expression of obstinacy that they all knew only too well.

The tenant moving out before Felicité's imminent arrival was 'Denis' with his then companion. Elizabeth related to her sister the 'drama' of the ex-tenants' departure: some of Stella's furniture was being removed, but was immediately returned when Elizabeth telephoned to say she was observing the proceedings 'through her periscope'. With both her wit and territorial antennae here finely tuned, and impressively displaying her determination not be pushed around, one is reminded of Elizabeth's resoluteness in negotiation with the broker, Jewell, when recovering the insurance money after the pre-war robbery at her flat in London.

Another tenant at Halsey Street was the art historian Cecil Gould (known by Elizabeth and her friends as Goldilocks) whom Elizabeth met in Cairo while he was in cypher with the other Cecil, Robson. Patrick Woodcock says of Gould: 'Oh, Cecil's cooking was appalling. He gave a dinner to which Ivy Compton Burnett was invited. Champagne and cherries, it was absolutely awful. He was terribly pretentious and it was agreed that Elizabeth would give him cooking lessons, and she got her wires crossed with him as she often did with men. She really rather fell for him but it was useless. He was not that way inclined.'

It was Gould who had recruited Lesley O'Malley to Bletchley Park, the seat of British Intelligence, early in the war. Lesley, Elizabeth's close friend from the MOI in Cairo, was also back in England looking for a job. After a long and worrying search she eventually found work with Royd's advertising agency, where she remained for the rest of her working career. Some time in the early Fifties Elizabeth offered her the basement flat in Halsey Street and she accepted. The flat shared its stairs with Elizabeth's central part of the house and also, with a typical touch of eccentricity, a fridge at the top of these stairs. With Lesley's arrival the occupancy of No. 24 Halsey Street was established as it would remain for another thirty years.

Felicité and Lesley's presence and relative 'positions' in her house were significant factors in a subtle shift of Elizabeth's allegiances emerging during this period. Allowing for her periodic absences abroad – for several weeks, sometimes months, almost every year until her death forty-two years later – she was to develop a particular dependence on her sister Felicité. And, just as her reliance on and identification with Felicité grew, so her dependence upon her elder sister Priscilla diminished. Elizabeth had become aware, not unsympathetically, of Priscilla's position over the last year or so. Priscilla's life (and Diana's) had become more absorbed with the time-consuming responsibilities of motherhood. Sisterly loyalties were unchanged, but Priscilla simply had less time to devote to the role of surrogate mother. After her sister's separation from Richard in 1948 Elizabeth did not take to her present man perhaps exacerbated by her impatience with Priscilla's position before the separation. Family loyalties were divided here. In England again, Elizabeth was once more faced with her mother and sisters and the rest of her family after the years of emotionally less fraught communication by letter. Before and during the war, when Pris could always be relied upon to get them out of a fix, either financially or sometimes as go-between, she had represented a figure of permanence for her sisters. Their own pressures during the war had left Elizabeth's sisters remarkably uncritical of her. Despite their own consistent contribution to the war effort they would always judge Elizabeth by different standards. For all their own individual force of personality Elizabeth's sisters never quite overcame the slight awe in which they held her. And as she grew older and became more of a 'personage', as the family would have said, she herself did little to modify this response.

With two small daughters to care for, it was not easy for Priscilla to reshape her life. Here, Elizabeth's relative lack of interest in children would soon become more apparent, extending to a greater or lesser degree to Diana's family too. Although feeling few qualms about favouring one above another, as her nieces and nephews grew and developed Elizabeth was a fond aunt – but she was never a motherly one.

Elizabeth's position regarding children was not a simple one and the complexities of her character were revealed in her attitude towards them. She had stated from youth that she did not like them or want any of her own – taking steps accordingly to prevent it on more than one occasion. But, as she grew older she became more 'crustacean' and more ambivalent regarding both her earlier boast to Priscilla that she couldn't bear any one man hanging around her after the first six months, and her determination never to have children. Already by 1952 when she came to see George and Judith Lassalle on the arrival of their first child, her response at seeing the baby was to burst into tears, saying to Judith, 'Oh, I don't want to see your children.'

When her love affairs were failing Elizabeth was quite capable of inflicting wounds, but she did not always escape unscathed either. With her feline sensuality and magnetism, she instinctively knew how to treat a man, but the sheer force of her intelligence, sometimes thrusting and impatient, and her flights of temperament and wilfulness were not ultimately calculated to support the fragilities of a male ego. Her forte lay more in the arena of courtesanship than in the sometimes duller but more enduring one of conjugality. Nevertheless, with each renewed search for a lover, she was also reasserting her belief in the possibility of companionship and fulfilment.

After her years abroad, during which time all four Gwynne girls had developed more defined and adult personae, with her resumed proximity to her sisters Elizabeth found Felicité's unmarried and childless state one with which she could identify most closely. To an extent this was because Felicité was never subject to the emotional and time-consuming strains of child-rearing, but it was also because she remained, like Elizabeth, someone for whom literature was an utter necessity. Her library grew on a par with Elizabeth's, until Halsey Street became a house weighted down with books.

The publication of *Mediterranean Food* extended Elizabeth's audience, its enthusiastic reception alerting John Lehmann to a greater realization of her earning potential as an author. His immediate approach to her for another book on 'escapist' food was, then, only natural. But 'This time I was ready for him,' Elizabeth later wrote. 'I had a small collection of French recipes which hadn't been suitable for the Mediterranean book.' This would be published a year later, in 1951, as *French Country Cooking*. With her monthly articles for *Harpers* and other pieces of journalistic writing now being commissioned, Elizabeth was in demand. Amongst the first of the professionals to recognize her value was André Simon, the grand old man of the Wine and Food Society; and it was he who had the foresight to commission her first non-recipe-based article for the Society's journal, her brilliant essay, 'Two Cooks'.

While working in the bookshop Allan's, and before moving into Halsey Street, Felicité had already been helping Elizabeth with her new book. Elizabeth's boast to her sisters from Cairo of her newly learnt typing skills was premature. After *Mediterranean Food* (much of which was typed on a machine borrowed from Richard Longland) almost all Elizabeth's writing, both articles and books, was done in long-hand and subsequently expertly typed by Felicité.

As Elizabeth wrote in her introduction to this most usable of little books, *French Country Cooking* was not another work seconding the 'nonsense . . . talked about the richness of the food to be found in all French homes'. Not wishing to appear ungracious, nor debating the higher standard of French middle-class cooking compared to its English counterpart, she described 'the proportion of rather tough *entrecôtes*, rolled and stuffed roast veal, and *sauté* chicken' in French homes as 'exasperatingly high . . . Those who care to look for it, however, will find the justification of France's culinary reputation in the provinces, at the riverside inns, in unknown cafés along the banks of the Burgundy canal, patronized by the men who sail the great petrol and timber barges to and from Marseilles, great eaters and drinkers most of them . . .'

As always Elizabeth was writing from experience. She knew at first hand about those barges along the grand North–South French artery from Burgundy to its culmination in the salty Carmargue marshlands and the Rhône delta beyond Aix-en-Provence. The cooking she described was that encountered in 'hospitable farmhouses of the Loire and the Dordogne', the Auvergne, and the Normandy known since her youth, 'in sea-port bistros frequented by fishermen, sailors, ship-chandlers and port-officials'. This was the cooking experienced and enjoyed with such savour along the route she and Charles had followed in the French part of the voyage of the *Evelyn Hope*. When, however, she wrote: 'In such places the most interesting food in France is to be found,' she was not only recording her own opinion but also aligning herself (however unconsciously) with a well-established tradition. This was represented by that small group of travelled English men and women – most recently by writers such as Ford Madox Ford, Morton Shand and Romilly Fedden – for whom wayside France, its table and wine, was a place of infinite discovery.

A few passages from Romilly Fedden's *Food and Other Frailties*, well known to Elizabeth, illustrate the theme. Elizabeth had known Robin Fedden and probably his family since before the war, possibly staying as a guest in their Brittany house, Chantemeusle. When, years later, Elizabeth told her god-daughter Frances, Robin and Renée's daughter, that she had been engaged to Robin, Frances surmises that 'This must have meant an affair.'

Referring to the inter-war period Romilly wrote: 'On another occasion we were touring, in a car . . . and we had lunched and dined and slept at many international caravanserais. Be it known, you cannot eat superbly at any of these tourist-ridden hotels. There is a sameness about them, something standardized. You eat passably . . . but not with bliss . . . Perfect food is to be found rather in the out-of-the-way corners of Europe. Both in the country and in small market towns where you shall eat exquisitely.' He continued with the reminiscence of a fine small village inn 'renowned to a few initiates for its cooking', and described the lunch given by 'Madame' to himself and his party of friends in the garden, 'where a rough lawn led down to apple trees and a bubbling stream'. They ate 'perfect' melon from the garden, 'delicious' *quenelles de brochet*; ('why is it that in England pike is such an insipid nasty fish?') a 'perfect' foie gras, chicken *à la broche* with a consummate salad, and the whole complemented by an Auberdière Vouvray and 'a Bourgeuil of 1902'.

Romilly described another superlative yet not lavish meal of sole, pheasant, a chicory salad, a fondue 'the succulence of which still steams in memory', taken at the invitation of an elderly commercial traveller in an insignificant country town, at a resturant down a side street through an arch and a courtyard 'painted a sickly green'. Thence they passed through the enormous kitchen 'backed by a vast range and endless pots and pans in brass and copper. The chef, a huge person all in white, was bustling with his three subordinates ... We passed into the *salle à manger*', where, after they had finished with a fine house brandy, the waiter bawled out the *addition* across the room to 'Madame, fat and placid at the desk'.

In the same idiom Elizabeth wrote in *French Country Cooking*: 'the shopkeepers, the lawyer, the doctor, the curé, the gendarme and even those stony-faced post-office officials are exceedingly addicted to the pleasures of the table; and, being thrifty as well, you may be sure they know where the cheapest and the best of everything is to be obtained.' She maintained that as the peasant farmers were prosperous and thrifty too, 'Every scrap of food produced is made use of in some way or another, in fact in the best way possible ...' She told us that it was in the depths of the country that one learned about the variety of foodstuffs and ways of preserving them; meat products, charcuterie, sausages, smoked ham and pâtés. (A friend later commented that Elizabeth loved all pork products so much that she could have written a book about them, and indeed the section on charcuterie in *French Provincial Cooking* is inspiringly written.)

> The cheeses and creams, the fruits preserved in potent local liqueurs, the fresh garden vegetables, pulled up before they are faded and grown old, and served shining with farmhouse butter, the *galettes* ... the mushrooms ... gathered in the forest, the mountain hares, pigeons, partridges and roebuck ... the fried trout straight from the river, the sustaining vegetable soups enriched with wine, garlic, bacon and sausages, the thousand and one shell-fish soups and stews, the *fritures du golfe* ... of France's lovely prodigal coast ...

Elizabeth's proclamation of the virtues of the food of France was not, therefore, original, but her own experience and particular voice had a singular relevance and enormous appeal to those of her class and generation who had recently survived the war and were presently surviving the dreariness and boredom of its aftermath. Her introduction to *French Country Cooking* continued: 'Rationing, the disappearance of servants, and the bad and expensive meals served in restaurants, have led Englishwomen to take a far greater interest in food than was formerly considered polite ...' She identified her readers as those who in the country had grown and produced much of their own food, and those in the city who 'take trouble over their marketing, choose their meat and fish carefully. . . . keep a good store cupboard' and are 'equally interested ... in good and interesting meals ... [as often with Elizabeth there is more than a hint of the prescriptive] which derive from French regional and peasant cookery, which, at its best, is the most delicious in the world ...'

In the same year as the publication of *French Country Cooking* and in sharp contrast to it, *100 Meat-saving Recipes* by Anne Robbins (Nicholas Kay, 1951) appeared. In spite of its genuine efforts to provide an interesting post-war cookery book, it still revealed that underlying mentality of compromise Elizabeth was reacting against and attempting to counteract in her writing. *Meat-saving Recipes* (in its very title) makes the concessions and short-cuts Elizabeth was unwilling to make in her own book. And, although Anne Robbins tried her best to give 'tasty and flavoursome' dishes (unappetizing words), one is left remembering comments like: 'The recipes ... do not require endless time and pains' and are for 'the housewife who wants to prepare really good meals with a minimum of fuss and trouble'. Of course she does, who doesn't often feel the same? But with a little culinary experience one is reminded of Elizabeth's introductory words (not for the first time) both as exhortation and inspiration:

> Good cooking is honest, sincere and simple, and by this I do not mean to imply that you will find in this, or indeed any other book, the secret of turning out first-class food in a few minutes with no trouble. Good food is always a trouble and its preparation should be regarded as a labour of love, and this book is intended for those who actually and positively enjoy the labour

involved in entertaining their friends and providing families with first-class food.

Elizabeth's introduction ended with the reminder that it is not so much the merits of cuisines which are most important, but 'the spirit in which cooking is approached; a devoted, a determined spirit, but not, it is to be hoped, one of martyrdom'. Commendable ideals, but her readers might have argued that Elizabeth David, with no husband or children interfering with her 'labours of love', could easily talk. However, although those who became her devotees may not always have achieved such a high standard, it was that *spirit* which they were inspired to emulate.

Martin Lam, now chef-patron of Ransome's Dock in London, became friends with Elizabeth more than twenty years later. In describing one of her great strengths as a writer on food he says, 'As a teacher she was able to impart ideas very clearly, without always going into great detail.' Others have criticized this aspect of her writing but those like Lam see it as a virtue.

'She won't always give specific quantities, but she was the most precise person where precision was important. She will presume a certain amount of knowledge and understanding about a style of cooking and then describe a particular recipe that will fall into that style or method. Other times she will be quite specific. Being of that frame of mind she was able to talk about food generally and convey an awful lot – without going into pounds and ounces, without going into specific measurements.' And here Martin Lam makes an observation central to Elizabeth's ethos: 'Cooking is more than responding to ingredients.'

Referring to what was an essential part of Elizabeth's credo, implied in her introduction to *French Country Cooking*, Lam points out that 'She knew what the best was and wasn't going to accept second best, not in any sense of being élitist or wanting the most expensive, but just knowing.' In reference to this theme Sybille Bedford says, 'Liking what is best is different from what is snobbish.' Elizabeth herself had written in a *Harpers* article entitled 'Windfalls':

Sometimes the simplest luxury proves the most delectable. Last October a friend brought me fresh Normandy butter and new-laid eggs. Anxious that those eggs should lose nothing of their fresh bloom, and wanting to share the feast with a favourite guest, I decided it should consist simply of perfectly boiled eggs, and fresh brown bread spread with that lovely butter, to be followed by a pound of English field mushrooms, grilled, buttery and black, their flavour unmatched during the brief autumn week of their season. After the mushrooms we had Comice pears, which were at their wonderful best that particular day. A meal which heaven knows was nothing an Englishman would not have taken for granted a few years ago, but it was the startling simplicity of the fare and the quality of the ingredients which made the occasion a memorable one.

Martin Lam continues: 'She liked a particular restaurant because they had fresh crab salad. It was nothing but boiled crab, but they did it well and she would go there for that thing only, which in many ways would typify her approach to food. It didn't need to be five processes of cooking to achieve some very fine dish. She would be as happy with the best raw ingredients treated interestingly and sympathetically. Something which comes over time and time again with her – the ability to arrive at simplicity. But you have to go through several processes to get to the simple result.'

This attitude, sometimes explicit, always implicit, was evident throughout the whole of Elizabeth's work. This was what she meant when she wrote that 'Good food is always a trouble,' later expanding on this with the comment: 'Even more than long hours in the kitchen, fine meals require ingenious organization and experience *which is a pleasure to acquire* [author's italics].' She added several other points, by now fundamental to her approach to food and appreciated by few English cooks at this time. 'A highly developed shopping sense is important, so is some knowledge of the construction of a menu with a view to the food in season, the manner of cooking, the texture and colour of the dishes to be served in relation to each other.' These strictures were those understood by any ordinary Mediterranean housewife. They had little to do with fancy ingredients and were something for which the French of course were renowned. But although still as alien to most English cooks in 1951 as in her youth, Elizabeth's own familiarity with these principles had begun with Mrs Leyel's *Gentle Art* even before her adult sojourns in France.

She had written in *Harpers Bazaar* in 1949:

> How pitiful that a generation is now growing up which has scarcely known what good cooking is; which has never made a sauce with real eggs, never eaten parmesan cheese on pasta, never heard of *Cèpes à la bordelaise* or seen ham and Cumberland sauce on a breakfast table ... Unless young people learn now about the art of cooking, and eating and drinking wine, one of the great pleasures of life will be lost to them, and how can they learn to cook if they don't know how food should look and taste and smell?'

(Cumberland sauce was a favourite of Elizabeth's and she later described its genesis and virtues in *Spices, Salt and Aromatics in the English Kitchen*, calling it: 'This best of all sauces for cold meat.')

French Country Cooking again followed Mrs Leyel by concluding with useful lists (actually nuggets of comparative social history) of foods, 'preparations' and proprietors to be relied upon, some in France, most in London. Again it is interesting to note that where those shops recommended by Mrs Leyel still existed, Elizabeth recommends the same, and we are reminded that her familiarity with these exotic oases of 'foreignness' extended as far back as her reading of Hilda Leyel in the Thirties. We are recommended by both Mrs Leyel and Elizabeth to that Mecca of food, Hediard's, in the Place Madeleine in Paris – the shop about which Elizabeth wrote, 'Every exotic product in the world can be obtained [there], with particular emphasis on the French Colonies.' We are then given a hint of the passionate interest she already had, not simply in the recipes and their ingredients, but also in their social history. 'The firm was inherited from Hediard by his son-in-law, an Englishman, members of whose family are still in the shop, and who take great pleasure in explaining the origin and uses of the wonderful foodstuffs they sell.'

Elizabeth next sent her reader on to the Marché St-Honoré for 'cheaper foods unobtainable in England' and where 'It is a fine sight to see, and the Parisian housewives doing their shopping provide a notable lesson in the art of marketing.' And through the dearth of so much of such produce in England a vividly contrasting picture of it (and Elizabeth's attitude) emerges: 'Soissons, the good white beans for making cassoulet, fresh Norman butter and cheeses, baby courgettes . . . aubergines which will *not* cost 2s. 6d. each or whatever ludicrous price one pays in England, dandelions for salad, sorrel and all manner of simple and forgotten delights.' (Here and elsewhere, she already reveals her acute awareness of an English heritage so buried in this period as to have been almost lost.)

Continuing with her recommendations of where best to find the basic ingredients about which she writes, it is noticeable that almost all are foods which now sit on any supermarket shelf: lentils, split peas, haricot beans, rice, macaroni, spaghetti, etc., dried mushrooms, salami sausages, olives and their oil, good-quality dry biscuits, lemons, garlic, shallots, almonds, figs, other dried fruits, good jams and preserves (including quince and damson cheese, then more appreciated than now). Noticeable too are the recommendations for buying and growing herbs in pots in the garden, at a time when their absence was then so conspicuous from most shops. The purchase of spices was apparently most reliably to be done at Harrods and Selfridges food halls, Whiteleys, and an Italian family shop which occurred repeatedly in Elizabeth's (and Mrs Leyel's) references to all sorts of foods – Parmigiani of 74 Old Compton Street – and several more of their shops along the same street. Other recurring names were Roche, Delmonico and King Bomba.

Yet these shops (in London situated largely around Soho), which were frequently Italian, had not previously been so unusual in larger cities as Elizabeth's text might here imply, arising as they had from the tradition of the Italian warehousemen. Established in England since the early eighteenth-century, Italian warehousemen or oilmen had sold a variety of Italian foods: olive oils, anchovies, salami, pasta, parmesan, as well as those other foods which we now associate with high-quality grocers and delicatessens. Their stock later included some of the earliest tinned goods and many bottled sauces, pickles, chutneys, jams, dried fruits, almonds, pistachios, chocolate, coffees, teas and spices without which no sophisticated household could function.

The introduction to *French Country Cooking* preceded sections on *batterie de cuisine*, wine in the kitchen and the construction of a menu, each eminently readable for its own sake and again exemplifying Elizabeth at her confident best; terse, acerbic, opinionated, useful and accurate. But more, where this vital material could be made dry and dusty as it was in many contemporary cookery books, here it was replete with perspicacious observation of physical and human detail infused with touches of wit, the whole elevated to a cameo on the fine art of living. This, the art of living, was the whole of which food was a fundamental part. The *batterie* section proclaimed her passionate and visual sensibilities as much as registering her practical turn of mind: the appearance, the shape, colour, design as well as function of everything in the kitchen was always of the utmost interest and concern to her, ultimately as important as the food itself.

Elizabeth's practical and very English soul responded to the deeper significance of objects. And here it is worth remembering that her forebears were experienced engineers; both the Ridleys with their coal-mining successes and the Gwynnes with their pump. Elizabeth's nephew Johnny Grey (son of Diana and Chris), now a noted kitchen designer, remembers her fascination with, for instance, ironmongers' shops. 'Aunt Liza loved all those things: knobs, gadgets, hinges, hooks, handles. Walking along the street we *couldn't* pass an iron-monger's by, would always have to go in and look. Even a metal grating on the pavement fascinated her.'

Elizabeth maintained: 'One thing is quite certain, and that is that if Englishwomen paid more attention to having the right equipment in their kitchens, we should hear a great deal less about the terrible labour of good cooking. How many times have I been told: "Oh, I haven't time to fiddle about with that kind of thing," just because a recipe called for putting something through a sieve or chopping up a few vegetables.' On the subject of knives she said: 'Take the greatest care . . . keep your kitchen knives in a special box or compartment of the knife drawer [she was eventually to keep her own on one of those magnetic blades on the wall]. Let it be understood by all members of the household that there will be serious trouble if your knives are borrowed for screwdriving, prising open packing cases, cutting fuse-wire or any other purpose for which they were not intended.' One trembles at the thought of the reprisals for such crimes in Elizabeth's own kitchen.

Her friend Sybille Bedford describes this 'largish, longish room' in Halsey Street with its 'very long table, on which you could make and eat food. Everything was open, all the shelves. The stove, the sink, everything was in order, but a working order.' Reinforcing this subtle comment on Elizabeth's superficially disordered house, many friends have said that with the passage of time it became more likely that in order to sit down at her table you sometimes had to move a pile of books off a chair or papers to one side. But the overriding impression was of the most 'artistic' clutter: a bowl of purple plums, a plate of salted almonds, a bottle of white wine in a stoneware cooler, jars of gleaming fruits and preserves on the dressers, olives black and shiny against a terracotta dish, placed with apparent nonchalance but always with a painter's eye.

Elizabeth never had a study, working mostly from that large kitchen table and always in longhand. Latterly she almost always wrote in green ink and, with her knowledge of army hierarchy, probably with wry awareness that this usage was permitted only to those of the very highest rank. The kitchen functioned as the hub of her house: as her workroom . . . here she cooked and experimented; as her study . . . here she wrote; and finally as her room for socializing . . . here visitors were made welcome, dined and were entertained. In this kitchen she increasingly kept her utensils outside of cupboards, in earthenware pots, on the dressers, many others eventually hanging (like arcane pieces of metallic sculpture) on the walls – as was in fact the tradition with old ironmonger's shops – and noteworthy in this period when it was thought unsightly by the majority to display anything which indicated that a kitchen, even more a dining room, was actually a room in which to prepare or to eat food. She wrote in *French Country Cooking*:

As time goes on you accumulate your personal gadgets, things which graft themselves on to your life; an ancient thin-pronged fork for the testing of meat, a broken knife for scraping mussels, a battered little copper saucepan in which your sauces have always turned out well, an oyster knife which you can no longer afford to use for its intended purpose but which turns out to be just the thing for breaking off hunks of Parmesan cheese . . . an earthenware bean-pot of such charm that nothing cooked in it could possibly go wrong.

And later: 'Earthenware casseroles and terrines for oven cooking should be in every household.' The early nineteenth-century expansion of the china clay potteries in the Midlands and the subsequent development of enamelled tinware had put an end to the extensive use of earthenware (certainly of semi-glazed) in most metropolitan English kitchens. 'For some of the French farmhouse and peasant dishes described in this book they are essential; with time these rustic clay pots acquire not only a patina but an aroma all of their own, which in the course of long, patient simmering communicates itself to the *cassoulets, choux farcis, daubes* and *civets*, onion soups, and terrine of game which would lose something of their flavour and a good deal of their charm if cooked in an ordinary saucepan.' Elizabeth was here saying something novel for post-war England. Her plea for those cooking pots was a heart-felt cry for the agrarian-based, pre-industrial Europe of the South, a state long since lost to England. She was mourning this (and paid homage to it in her own pot collection) when she later wrote: 'Look at the friendly browns, and warm terracottas, the ivories and greys and the pebbles-on-the-beach colours of old English earthenware and stoneware.'

Significantly for future events, she recommended purchase and retinning of copper pans at Cadec's of Greek Street and Jaeggi's in Dean Street – both in Soho and then frequented largely by the catering trade. There were at this time no 'kitchen' shops as we now know them, only ironmongers, hardware shops and specialists like the above or the larger company, Ferrari of Wardour Street, for the trade. 'A very heavy copper sauté pan . . . is the most convenient pan in the world for braising a whole chicken or duck on top of the stove, for it can be left unattended without fear of disaster . . . They [copper pans] are fairly expensive and their upkeep takes time, but they look lovely.'

Again regarding appearance, 'A long platter for serving fish is important; the appearance of a fine salmon is ruined by being brought to table on too small a dish . . .' And elsewhere she would write: 'You see that utterly plain unadorned long white fish dish? On that dish a whole pink and silver salmon trout [a favourite fish] is unimaginably elegant.' These qualities, a 'painterly' eye and a passion for the products and seasons of agriculture, were central to Elizabeth's writing.

Following the section on *batterie de cuisine* was an exemplary short essay on wine in the kitchen, that most intimidating of subjects to the English housewife. The piece was a contracted version of a very useful little booklet done on the subject for Saccone and Speed, the vintner company, in the same year as *Mediterranean Food*.

On the composition of the menu she wrote: 'I should be surprised to hear that anybody had ever followed any cookery book menu in every detail; all that is needed to design a perfectly good meal is a little common sense and the fundamental understanding of the composition of a meal.' (This last was of course precisely what a good proportion of several generations of English women no longer did properly understand.) Referring to the present dearth of knowledge Elizabeth wrote: 'The restrictions of years of rationing have been the cause of some remarkably unattractive developments in the serving of food in restaurants, but if some ignorant or careless restaurant managers still serve chips with spaghetti or boiled potatoes and cauliflowers heaped up in the same dish with curry and rice, there is no need for us to do likewise at home . . .'

The precedent had long ago been set for good (and indifferent) cookery books with advisory sections like those Elizabeth incorporated into *French Country Cooking*. But hers were successful because they encapsulated several of those elements which made her writing so appealing: at once intimate in its detail, it enabled the reader to feel party to the experiences she described, be inspired by her enthusiasm and intrigued by the sense of mystery she purveyed. She had both the common touch necessary for communication and an aloofness calculated to provide allure. And although no one element of this writing was outstandingly original, each had its vital function in what became a powerfully fused whole. It was the manner in which Elizabeth put together these elements which singled out and made original their totality. As with any artist of merit this elusive touch lay both in reflecting something of the spirit of the time, and being just sufficiently ahead of it (in Elizabeth's case always just half a step) to stimulate question and change. In an interview with the novelist Paul Bailey he made an astute observation regarding Elizabeth's writing: 'And the tone of voice I liked. It was accessible to the reader, but not bending over backwards to them. It wasn't treating the reader like an imbecile . . . Hiding herself behind her prose . . . There is another message there to do with Art and the whole seriousness about life. She was so reticent, she would never talk to me about her private life . . . she uses style as a way of hiding something, which is a time-honoured tradition. It really was a case of *le style c'est l'homme.*'

There were contemporary and near-contemporary cookery book writers who had offered advice on marketing, the store-cupboard, the hazards of composing the 'right' menu (this had been one of the prime functions of Mrs Isabella Beeton's writing for an aspiring nineteenth-century middle-class), the *batterie de cuisine.* Others had held forth authoritatively on many of the same French dishes as Elizabeth (few on the Middle Eastern, Greek or Italian ones). Authors in more literary genres had written inspired and erudite travel books on France, the Mediterranean and beyond; many writers had colonized and created their art from the territory of the wistful, sometimes obsessive, semi-melancholic Proust's *A la recherche du temps perdu* (1915–27). (Elizabeth would no doubt have concurred with Lesley Blanche's statement in one of her books: 'Yes, Proust was right . . . the only real Paradise is the one we have lost'). None of them, however, had organized such a finely wrought and, potent mix of all these elements in cookery books which spoke to a generation of English men and women in search of relief from a lack-lustre drabness, loss of purpose, and the insecurities of a society still reeling from the aftermath of war.

Grey Gowrie remembers the effect of Elizabeth's writing 'on one's parents, who had gone to war. [Elizabeth had known Gowrie's parents in Cairo and in fact later told a friend that she had come across his father much earlier, dancing with him at her coming out.] They looked upon her work as part of the Liberation that had gone on afterwards, an indication that civilization was going to restore itself. There was an element of pornography about it, when you were living in Austerity and you were reading about sun-kissed peppers ... it had an immediate dynamic ... I think there was this tremendous feeling of joy when one read her books, of hope.' Growing up in Ireland, Gowrie subsequently met Elizabeth at the house of a mutual friend, also from Ireland, the painter Derek Hill, and was 'very amused by her, which I did not expect. She was salty, witty, sometimes shocking. She had what would now be called politically incorrect habits.' He remembers a later occasion when 'I was watching her cook a paella whilst chain-smoking, and some of the ash dropped in. She didn't care and just shoved it on. She drank reasonably, and she wasn't a precise cook. To follow her work well you need some basic knowledge of cooking.'

Elizabeth wrote in a subsequent preface to *French Country Cooking* that she was 'anxious to stress the fact that this little collection gives no more than an indication of the immense diversity and range of French regional cookery. It is a subject of such scope that half a dozen large volumes of recipes would scarcely exhaust it.' She added that as French regional cooking was so 'very much alive', and therefore perpetually evolving, it would be 'almost impossible ever to compile a complete collection'. Nevertheless, she was to make her own significant mark in this field nine years later with the publication of *French Provincial Cooking*. Not only a major contribution to the subject, *French Provincial Cooking* was a masterly work of cookery and literature. In one sense *French Country Cooking* reads like a sparkling trial run.

Among those seeking Elizabeth out after the success of *Mediterranean Food* were the editors of two magazines then in their infancy. One, *Contact*, described itself as a 'Magazine of Pleasure' (a title now assured to raise eyebrows); it had commissioned an article on Spanish food. Another, *Go*, 'The International Travel Magazine', was edited by Elizabeth Nicholas, who had reviewed *Mediterranean Food* with such enthusiasm and who had recently commissioned Elizabeth to contribute a long section to *The Sunday Times Travel Guide to the Continent* (1951). This book, for the educated tourist, included distinguished writers such as Georgina Masson, Lina Waterfield, Denys Sutton and Tamara Talbot Rice, noted for their interest in cultivated travel.

Elizabeth's contribution of over fifty pages had included potted histories of the more interesting towns, information on hotels, shops, wine and restaurants of note throughout the whole Riviera and Provence region. A feat of concision, as she once again visits some of her pre-war haunts, her piece offers up glimpses of her past. At St Tropez, 'In spite of trippers who crowd in at weekends, noisy film stars ... in great yachts, millionaires in Packards, and Existentialists from Saint Germain des Prés ... there is nothing to stop one bathing by moonlight, a most exquisite Mediterranean pleasure.' At Marseilles, 'to the right of the Vieux Port ... are a number of small cafés and restaurants where one can eat Italian and Provençal food in noisy but characteristic surroundings'. At Antibes she refers the traveller to 'The Ship Bar in the Place de Gaulle' and says 'it is a pleasant drinking place; Rudolf, who has presided there for years, knows everything that goes on and ... serves ... the best steaks on the Côte d'Azur.'

This is the same Rudolf she referred to in a war-time letter to Charles Gibson Cowan when he was collecting material for *The Voyage of the Evelyn Hope*. In spite of previously breathless comments to Priscilla that she had seen 'Mistinguett doing the marketing ... and this morning Lillian Harvey was in the bar, and once I saw the Windsors' car but I don't think they were in it', she had written to Charles that Antibes was, for her, 'Norman Douglas, and champagne cocktails'. The Riviera people, she said, made almost no impression on her. They may have made one on Charles, because that was the first time he had encountered the type. She advised him against including them, they were too well known. Rudolph the international barman had been, perhaps, the most interesting. She had said to Pris shortly before leaving Antibes in 1940 that she would rather listen to Norman's conversation or spend the day with him, aged as he was, than fifty of the 'warped and sodden sea kales who have made the Côte d'Azur a sort of *White Man's Burden*'. She thought the men there mostly resembled the 'Man who Stayed' in the play *White Cargo* (in which Elizabeth had given a 'celebrated' performance, in her words). 'The character in the play who, quinine soaked and gin-sodden, warns all the young men against going native and finally sends them home when they start babbling in delirium of green fields ...'

In Elizabeth's *Sunday Times* piece, another of the frequent covert references to her war-time stay in the South of France occurs a couple of lines after the Rudolph comment: '*Chez Felix au Port*, on the harbour in a lovely setting, has been famous for years for bouillabaisse, langouste and soufflés; it has become very expensive.' It was here, in 1940, that Elizabeth had written the letter to Felicité in which she said the gales of the past month had made the boat 'rock like a shell', so she had been obliged to write in a restaurant.

Aix, Arles, Avignon, Biot, Nice: 'The great food market is a spectacle calculated to drive the English visitor into a frenzy of envy . . .' And 'the flower market in the Rue St François de Paul in winter . . . and in summer is another sight to dazzle English eyes.' Elizabeth had first marvelled at this demonstration of Southern fertility (just as had Van Gogh half a century earlier) on one of those treasured days spent with Norman Douglas in the early part of the war. She had written enthusiastically of it to Felicité from Antibes. The country, she said, was very beautiful, the flowers glorious: wild hyacinths and tulips, daffodils and anemones, in profusion; when the sun came out it was marvellous. The flower market at Nice seemed to stretch for a quarter of a mile, and was stocked with the most glorious flowers: marigolds, narcissus, fruit blossom, mimosa, daffodils, violets, hyacinths – pink, purple, blue and white – all for practically nothing. One day she went in and bought thirty-five francs' worth of flowers; she couldn't carry them all and had to bring them home in a huge basket, then had no idea what to do with them all.

Many more towns and villages are mentioned in the *Sunday Times* piece, from Toulouse to Toulon and Perpignan to Palavas, concluding with a section on food and wine. Dealing with such a large area it was, inevitably, condensed, but Elizabeth still managed to evoke a good part of its style and atmosphere. The lengthy piece sometimes has an untypically commercial ring; Elizabeth had obviously been instructed to keep the family in mind, and mention as many entertainments – casinos and dancing – as she could. With few words she also conveys her dismal feelings at the encroaching modern style of tourism – she must have been aware of the irony that this very guide would encourage more of it. 'The islands of Porquerolles . . . are just across the bay from Hyères; they are wild and beautiful and were once the cherished refuge of artists and writers; as usual the crowds have followed them there, but there are still quiet and deserted beaches to be found and wonderful bathing from the rocks . . .' Le Lavandou had her conclude: 'There is a casino and the usual distractions.' At St Aygulf she said that the Relais, 'across the road from the beach, has the lovely background of the Alpes-Maritimes, but unfortunately, and nearer, there is also a camping ground'.

When the restaurants were to be dealt with she was clearly more enthusiastic. Of one in Le Lavandou she said: 'the entrance is through the kitchen where Madame Loulou Rossi is to be seen bent over her cooking pots, stirring a great pan of Langouste a la Provençal, all the perfumed aromas of the Mediterranean cooking issuing from the scarlet orange stew . . . The couple next to us were devouring soup, followed by two helpings each of roast pork perfumed with garlic and all the herbs of the hills, followed by two great platters of macaroni, and melon to finish. The grilled sardines, the aubergines and the haricots verts we ate were perfectly cooked, and the fried potatoes exceptional.' At St Raphael, 'After the host of "little" restaurants, furnished with gingham curtains, decorated with hideous pottery, and serving pretty indifferent food that have become a positive plague along the coast, it is with a sigh of relief that one enters a serious restaurant, where one knows at once by the smell of the place that the food is good.'

Writing to Felicité from France in the following year, 1951, Elizabeth said that she had been offered the job of going to Rome to write a 'sort of guide' for *Go*. She said that she had told Elizabeth Nicholas that she would accept it if the pay were large enough, but, as she neither knew Rome nor spoke Italian, it was unlikely to be an easy job. This publication appears not to have materialized, possibly because Elizabeth's 'pay' demand was too large but also, and more significantly, because the magazine folded during that year.

The above letter to Felicité was written soon after Elizabeth had given the manuscript of *French Country Cooking* to Lehmann, for which he commissioned another Minton cover, again striking and flamboyant. This time, knowing Minton better and with more experience, with her sure visual sense, Elizabeth knew what she wanted the illustrations to do for her book. She later said that she had encouraged 'a theme which recurred in all, or nearly all, of my subsequent books. I wanted the illustrations to convey information not just atmosphere.' Hence we see that the food in the pictures is better integrated into its surroundings than in *Mediterranean Food*. For instance the cover shows the interior of a provincial kitchen ready for work and the frontispiece portrays a woman inside her kitchen surrounded by the food she is about to cook.

After the exertions of finishing her book Elizabeth was, as so often, short of cash, wanted to get away from England, and was implementing plans for future publishing ventures. She had packed up her favourite valuables and thrust these and a number of her books and other belongings into Felicité's custody upstairs – 'I trust the books are not falling out of the wardrobe on to your head' – and decamped to a huge draughty house in the South of France. By this manoeuvre she was establishing early what would remain standard practice in Halsey Street whilst also continuing her long-established peripatetic habits. For some months of almost every year she would let Halsey Street (at a good price owing to its desirable location) and rent somewhere abroad, thus enabling her to have a holiday, with money left over for living. Always maintaining her journalistic obligations, and keeping notes with historical references, recipes and practical observations – all of which were subsequently used in future books – these periods away from England were usually successful in getting her bank balance out of the red.

'How you would laugh your head off if you could see me in this tumbledown old Castle of Otranto, with Romney [Summers] stacking logs on a great open fireplace as large as the town hall, and carrying his little khaki bag down to the village every day for the shopping. The weather has been a disgrace, the place as cold and wet as Charity. A fog comes up from the valley (or down from the hills) every night and in the morning you can't see out of the windows.'

This had been Elizabeth's introduction to several months in the rambling Provençal house, its grandeur by no means château-like, more that of a semi-fortified *manoir*. As she wrote, first in a *Harpers* article of 1955, later in a powerful passage in *French Provincial Cooking*, the house at Menerbes was set in a 'crumbling hill village opposite the Lubéron mountain', where the 'relentless screaming' of the Mistral brought herself and her friends 'perilously near to losing our reason'. In her letter to Felicité she provided more detail. The gas worked only spasmodically, and on the first day there was a tremendous explosion that blew off Romney's eyelashes; 'since when it has been difficult to whack him into lighting it'. Her bedroom housed bath and toilet, and Romney's the gas geyser. The whole arrangement, she wrote, might well have been 'invented by Emmett' (a contemporary cartoonist).

Romney Summers had been a friend of Elizabeth, George and Robin Fedden and other more exotic social luminaries, such as Edward Gathorne-Hardy, in Cairo during the war. Harold Acton said of this languid friend in his *More Memoirs of an Aesthete* that he was 'perhaps the only undergraduate who had a private house instead of lodgings when we were at Oxford . . . and received . . . in princely style . . . He maintained the same hospitable tradition at Gezira . . .'

Elizabeth's complaints to Felicité about bad weather were modified: when the sun came out it was warm enough to eat outside and even to lie on the terrace. 'The wine is 1/9 a bottle, new laid eggs 3d each, butter alas is 6/- a pound, and meat pretty expensive too.' The charlady was not too expensive, the cooking arrangements, surprisingly, fairly adequate, and the people in the village charming. Although the rent 'Mrs Bootface is extracting from me is sheer banditry', Elizabeth felt confident it would be 'delicious' there in two or three weeks' time.

The village of Menerbes in the *department* of the Vaucluse is in the heart of Provence. Set back inland from the towns of Aix, Cavaillon and Manosque, the beautiful, high, wooded Lubéron range with its string of fortified villages was in an area then frequented only by more adventurous tourists. Elizabeth took the house with two or three other friends. Apart from the other woman, Georgina (who paid rent to Elizabeth), being replaced for a time by Lesley O'Malley, this group remained fairly constant throughout the months Elizabeth was there, although there were also the friends who passed through at a hectic pace for much of the period.

Far away in her Provençal retreat, Elizabeth taxed Felicité back home with her financial arrangements. Always paying lip-service to the social niceties of gratitude Elizabeth was nevertheless demanding, and now worried about the lack of rent from the Boultings, tenants she already knew socially (Mrs Boulting's twin sons were to become film directors of some note). 'I have written to beat the agent about it . . . I hope all is well in that quarter and that they are not flinging my favourite lamps on the floor and grinding them underfoot.' For all her ability to appear disorganized Elizabeth was in fact very much the disciplined artist; periods of hectic activity and concentration were followed by periods of intense relaxation, usually lunches and evenings of entertaining and drinking. She was also most particular, almost neurotic, about the care of her possessions, giving rise to the occasional scene in the future which, if she had not taken it so seriously, would have been comical.

By May the weather 'continues perfectly appalling' and Elizabeth was writing under some strain, her letter prefaced by an apposite quote from the nineteenth-century poet Flecker: 'They knelt on the rotting Poop to Pray.' She told Felicité it stopped raining about 'once or twice' a week, at which time the Mistral started to blow with deafening force. The sun, when it did come out, was hot, but that was a rare occurrence. She was tired and disaffected with her Provençal retreat, saying that she never seemed to have a moment. Cooking two meals a day for four people on two gas rings without much in the way of resources, while at the same time trying to do her writing, took up all her days. These commitments had included 'plodding through' a 1500-word article on cheese for the *Children's Encyclopedia*, her monthly articles for *Harpers*, '& odd bits for French C. C. [*Country Cooking*] . . . I shall be grateful for a small amount of typing now and again.'

The 'daily' seemed 'continually in poor health and finds herself quite unable to walk up the hill', so wasn't much use to Elizabeth who had to do 'a good deal of washing up and general organizing . . . Romney bosses around and does a lot of shopping, Hamish doesn't get up till lunch time and most of his working hours are occupied fetching wood for the fire and doing the flowers. [Hamish was Hamish Erskine, son of the Earl of Rosslyn, whom Nancy Mitford had made the hero in her novel *Highland Fling* and had hoped to marry. He was, according to Doreen Thornton, 'very sympathetic'.] Georgina is a dear, and very good about helping but the poor wretch is supposed to be on holiday and paying heavily for the privilege of sitting in extreme discomfort on this dripping hilltop . . .' In reference to passing friends who couldn't 'resist coming to see my Provençal Paradise', she said, 'such arrivals are invariably the signal for a tremendous blind, the guests are then incapable of driving their cars away and have to spend the night. Bedlam then breaks loose, with Romney giving up his room to everybody in turn, a general shambles, and the whole company waking up still tipsy. However as 7 or 8 people can drink themselves into a stupor for 36 hours for the sum of about £2 one can hardly complain.' [She had previously apologized to Felicité for cleaning her out of gin before leaving Halsey Street.]

Doreen was one of the 'passing friends' who remained for a time and remembers that the house was full of people, so she was 'given the *dependence* to stay in. Hamish walked me down the garden each night in the dark. One day I found a scorpion in my shoe and that was it. I refused to stay there any longer and moved into the main house. The dining room was very large with an *enormous* table, rickety like the rest of the house. The weather was terrible and we sat about all day at that table, with a barrel of awful wine. What you could get then wasn't always very good.' (Writing later of wine in Avignon in an essay first published in T. B. Lanyon's *Besides* (1959), Elizabeth said that 'The wine of our own village *was* notable though: the worst I have ever consistently had to drink.')

Doreen continued: 'The house was dreadful, in the most gorgeous position. Hamish loved flowers. He knew a lot about them, and we would go out looking for things like wild orchids.' Elizabeth had 'tried going for a walk one day, and bore up very well, but upon our return collapsed in tortures of backache' and again later she was 'bent double with appalling backache . . . so shan't try again'.

In the *French Provincial Cooking* piece Elizabeth said: 'It does not do to regard Provence simply as Keats's tranquil land of song and mirth. The melancholy and the savagery are part of its spell.' This response to the elemental, sometimes threatening aspect of a land as ancient as Provence goes well beyond the comforting tourist's vision. The grumbling house, the appalling weather, in combination with too much bad wine – and 'it was the kind of wine it was wisest to drink out of a tumbler so that there was room for a large proportion of water' – succeeded in rousing Elizabeth's demons, so carefully kept at bay. She wrote a witty postcard to Doreen illustrating the *Castellet* in which they were staying, describing local events whose harsh discord reflected and confirmed her own sense of gloom:

'The butcher took to drink, kept 4 mistresses & was murdered by his brother-in-law in self-defence. The café proprietor's wife died 4 years ago, the proprietor of the little hotel committed suicide, the curé & his mother both dead, Madame Fernende had a stroke – How did we all escape? Love E.' She described herself to Felicité as experiencing 'such a bout of depression I was convinced death was imminent and have in fact made a new will, which I had better tell you about'.

She regretted not being able to leave Felicité her flat as long as the house was not in her name and had made ample provision for her both for the lump sum Felicité had paid her and for having to move should the house be sold. She made out a letter giving personal items to friends and said to her sister, 'If I fall off the precipice I'm afraid all this will be a bore for you, but you are the only person competent to cope.' Her previous reliance upon Priscilla in all these matters had now been largely diverted to Felicité. She continued: 'My collection of cookery books is to go to Veronica, but you will of course get all the rest' (Felicité's interest in food and its literature was of a limited nature). She ended, typically, with no further explanation, 'Enough of gloomy goings on'.

When the landscape was visible through heavy mists and Welsh rain it was becoming more beautiful every day. Three weeks previously all the gardens had been full of the most exquisite lilac she had ever seen. Elizabeth told Felicité that the household was getting hard up for reading matter, particularly 'tecckes' [detective stories, which Dorothy Sayers called 'the sport of noble minds']. She requested any new Penguins or Pans that were about, or anything else Felicité thought she might enjoy. She 'adored Scott Fitzgerald', especially 'The Diamond as Big as the Ritz', described the latest Ada Leverson [reprint] as having been 'locked up with Georgina and Hamish and I can't wait to get my hands on her', and wanted Evelyn Waugh's novels, soon coming out in paperback.

A friend arrived in a sports car and 'We were all very envious of him,' Doreen remembers. 'We had to go everywhere on buses, it was awfully hard to get about.' Elizabeth wrote to Felicité that there were some lovely villages there, and that in one of them they found an excellent restaurant, very cheap; there were probably more but communication was 'fearfully complicated'. Almost twice weekly Elizabeth, with one or two others, would take the bus the twenty or so winding miles into Avignon to shop for provisions on market days. Here they found one of those 'totally unpretentious' little French restuarants which Elizabeth loved and subsequently mourned the loss of in a more 'modern' France.

This little restaurant and its omelettes were to be enshrined in the title essay, originally printed in T. B. Lanyon's *Besides*, of Elizabeth's most popular later book, *An Omelette and a Glass of Wine*. This late collection of her journalism contains not only some consummate pieces of essay writing but also some vital clues to her personality and her thinking about food. *An Omelette and a Glass of Wine* is an insight into both how she perceived her own work and how she wished to control this perception for posterity. The book was published in 1984 when Elizabeth was seventy-one and in the pieces which she chose to reprint, as well as her editorial comments which preface them, she came as close as she ever did to extended autobiographical writing. In the title piece she wrote:

'Physically and emotionally worn to tatters by the pandemonium and splendour of the Avignon market, tottering under the weight of the provisions we had bought . . . we would make at last for the restaurant Molière to be rested and restored.

. . . the proprietors had always been angelically kind [how Elizabeth hung on to a few of those vapid words so beloved of Thirties socialites], welcoming and generous' and often plied Elizabeth and her companions with a fine after-lunch *marc de Champagne* before return to 'the rigours of our Mistral-torn village'.

Having outlined the story of Madame Poulard's rise to fame on account of her omelettes of 'exquisite lightness and beauty', Elizabeth admits that 'cookery after all does contain an element of the ritualistic . . .' She concedes that each must observe their own rituals – citing her own favoured pan in which she cooks her omelettes – but says that 'As to the omelette itself, it seems to me to be a confection which demands the most straightforward approach.' She wants the taste of fresh eggs and butter and 'visually, a soft bright golden roll plump and spilling out a little at the edges. It should not be a busy, important urban dish but something gentle and pastoral ... And although there are those who maintain that wine and egg dishes don't go together I must say that I do regard a glass or two of wine ... as an enormous enhancement of the enjoyment of a well-cooked omelette.' And she tells us that this, the accompaniment of a fine cheese omelette with a glass of wine, was to be had at that little Avignon restaurant.

Provence was the part of France with which Elizabeth was most intimate and about which she gives us the most detail and insight. Even here, though, she continues her habitual practice of only partially revealing herself. Her 'art' lay properly in the arena of the impersonal, and she herself remained only partially knowable until the last.

She had no plans after the end of June when the lease was up on the Menerbes house and by which time she would have finished the proofs of *French Country Cooking*. If the Rome venture for *Go* was to materialize she would travel there and then on to Capri to see Norman Douglas and, finally in August, return to England. Always needful of money, Elizabeth didn't plan on reinstating herself in Halsey Street if Mrs Boulting and her brood still wanted it. Elizabeth's plans, as so often in the past, were very fluid, including the possibility of returning to stay with 'Sib, Veronica, some rich American Friends in Cleveland Row or if I find some other house in these parts, less broken down and less expensive, I might stay here until September'. She in fact did spend June 'in frenzied despair correcting proofs' for her book, but by July was in Capri to visit Norman Douglas.

After leaving the Vaucluse Elizabeth was held up in Naples, as she told Felicité, 'in a state of utter collapse and had to stay in bed two days before I could totter on to the Capri boat'. Her youthful heavy drinking and late nights had not significantly diminished and despite a constitution robust enough to withstand the punishment she had meted out to it, now close to forty years old, her hard usage of herself began to tell. She already tended towards a preoccupation with her health, combined with a good dose of English stoicism. Barbara Doxatt, someone Elizabeth had known from schooldays, says: 'she was a bit neurotic, hypochondriac,' but the 'utter collapse' is an early indication of ill-health, eventually to become a chronicle of physical mishap. In Naples and now Capri she succumbed to 'something called water on the ankle', and it had become chronic. Capri is composed entirely of steep hills, so she could hardly have gone to a more unsuitable place. As long as she spent the day boiling up compresses and staying in bed, all was well; but as soon as she put her foot on the ground it swelled up 'like a bolster'. Apart from the inconvenience of being unable to walk and the exasperating pain, she was distressed by having her ankles look worse than they normally did – her legs were, by common admission, not her best asset. She contemplated asking Diana's husband, Chris, a trusted doctor and friend to Elizabeth and several members of her extended family, to engage a room for her at St George's hospital for the second half of August.

On Capri Elizabeth had taken a room in a private villa, large and cool, where she could work a little and put compresses on her foot. She said she hadn't much to do there, but was catching up with her sleep, which she badly needed. Menerbes had been enjoyable the last few weeks, but exhausting. She had certain vague commitments which included some pieces for Elizabeth Nicholas at *Go*. She told Felicité that she agreed with her judgement of the magazine – which was soon to fold. She hadn't heard from them for a while, and had no idea whether they were going to publish her articles on food. She had been asked to write a piece for them on housekeeping in France, but she had no will to begin it. She then makes what is an accurate and damning judgement on the present attitude to food in England as reflected in its magazines. 'Mrs N [Elizabeth Nicholas] seems to be quite sold on that technicolour food, & if that's what the public cares for who can blame her.'

Elizabeth was on Capri above all to see Norman Douglas, but said to Felicité that she couldn't afford to stay very long on 'this preposterous island . . . full to bursting with Neapolitan grocers and Americans. The piazza in the evening is a perfect nightmare of noise and screaming.' In spite of these complaints, and contrasted with a

Britain still labouring under rationing, she described shops stuffed with all manner of agonizing temptations, particularly the shoes, which she reluctantly admitted were not really for such as them, particularly with water on the ankle.

'The stuffs are lovely too, and the food, as long as one sticks to fish and vegetables & pasta, is not at all bad.' In the light of John Lehmann's future suggestion and subsequent commission the following year that she should write a book on Italian food, these and similar comments elsewhere are a surprising revelation of her relative lack of enthusiasm for it. With her sharp eye for the truth and the Gwynne memory for slights, Elizabeth still harboured memories of Italy's fickleness during the war and her own mistreatment when 'imprisoned' with Charles at Naples in 1940. In writing her 1963 Penguin introduction to *Italian Food*, the ambivalence she felt towards the country in the 1950s was clarified as springing from a profound source. 'Italy was a country to which I had come long after Provence and Greece had put me under their lasting spells. Towards Italy I felt more critical, my emotions were less engaged.' This is one of those statements Elizabeth makes from time to time which are so condensed as to reveal little more than the tip of the truth. Consequently the full significance of this comment can only be understood when recalling how seminal her experiences had been in Provence and on her 'beloved' Greek island in those early years of the war.

Since 1947 Norman Douglas had been settled and surrounded by his library in the ground-floor flat of Kenneth Macpherson's large and comfortable Villa Tuoro, some distance above the main town of Capri. This small and mountainous island, inhabited by the Greeks, was already famed in Roman times, the magnificent and profligate emperor Tiberius retiring there. With a view of mainland Naples, the island rises up precipitously out of the sea, its perilous cliffs making the coast almost inaccessible; while caves and extraordinary rock formations make it both beautiful and forbidding. For at least the last century and a half the island has been home to a succession of expatriate artists, writers and eccentrics, some of quite exotic proportions. The endless sunshine and skies of exquisite blue, extraordinarily lucid air and luxurious vegetation – fruit and olives grow in abundance – have long attracted those in search of an earthly paradise.

Under the benevolent and watchful eyes of Macpherson and his companion Islay Lyons, Douglas was to spend his last years at the Villa Tuoro. Emerging daily to wander the town, often in the care of his young friend Ettore, talking to old friends, both local and those from abroad, he ate and drank in company at favourite trattorias such as Savoia and the Caffè Vittoria. Something of a cult figure for many short-term visitors, Douglas weathered this, at times revelling in it, but his general attitude to post-war Capri was critical. He wrote that 'At this moment Capri is in danger of developing into a second Hollywood, and that, it seems, is precisely what it aspires to become . . . roads blocked up by lorries and cars [until this period there had been almost none], steamers and motor-boats disgorging a rabble of flashy trippers at every hour of the day.' Amongst this heaving mass of humanity it was possible to slip into less frequented haunts and Elizabeth and Norman happily entertained themselves in each other's company.

During those first meetings in Antibes in early 1940 Douglas had been as much taken with Elizabeth as she with him and he had shown consistent concern for her welfare during the course of the war. After his escape from the South of France to Portugal and the safety of Neil Hogg's Lisbon apartment, by June of 1941 he was fretting to Felicité about Elizabeth's whereabouts. 'I write to ask whether you have any news of your sister Liz, of whom I was very fond. I used to know her in Antibes and the last letters I had from her were from the Island of Syra (Greece). Since then – nothing!' [Douglas means Syros; Syra was the name of the main town.] Felicité soon told him what she knew of Elizabeth's recent escape from Syros and her present location in Cairo. Douglas, by early July, having left Portugal for his 'exile' in London, responded quickly. 'I was so glad to get your letter . . . with the – relatively – good news of your sister. If you hear anything more from her, would you please drop me a line? Neil and myself are going to send her a wire, as letters are quite uncertain' (he had received one from his brother [Quintin] in Egypt two days ago; sent off in March!).

Ten years later, in 1951, on Capri to see him, Elizabeth said to Felicité that Norman was still very spendid but not at all well, not liking the heat and grumbling because he couldn't drink as he used to. Nevertheless he would emerge from his house at six o'clock in the evening, when she would go to meet him at one of the cafés. Afterwards they might eat together and, in an article for *Gourmet* written in 1969, Elizabeth lauded Douglas's approach to food, in and out of restaurants. Harold Acton, who had known Douglas for much longer than Elizabeth, recalled that his culinary habits were wayward well before this period. Elizabeth's respect and fondness for Norman were not so coloured that she could not see his foibles, however, it is an idealized Douglas that Elizabeth presents. His understanding of food was more idiosyncrasy than taste, often astonishingly, although eccentrically, knowledgeable, but sometimes so erratic as to be merely puzzling to those with a wider range of understanding. Her writing on Douglas is an example of both Elizabeth's generosity of spirit and her creative sureness in concentrating on the best that a remarkable man could give. Writing for her super-refined *Gourmet* readers, and quite aware of the toes she might be bruising, Elizabeth revealed that 'His way was most certainly not the way of the wine sipper or of the grave debater of recipes . . . Authenticity in these matters was of the first importance to him . . . Cause and effect were eminently his concerns, and in their application he taught me some unforgettable lessons.' In demonstration of these she continues:

> Once during that last summer of his life . . . I took him a basket of figs from the market in the piazza. He asked me from which stall I had bought them.
>
> 'That one down nearest the steps.'
>
> 'Not bad, my dear, not bad. Next time you could try Graziella. I fancy you'll find her figs are sweeter.'
>
> He knew, who better, from which garden those figs came; he was familiar with the history of the trees, he knew their age and in what type of soil they grew; he knew by which tempests, blights, invasions, and plagues that particular property had or had not been affected during the last three hundred years; how many times it had changed hands . . . that the son now grown up was a man less grasping than his neighbours and was consequently in less of a hurry to pick and sell his fruit before it ripened . . . I may add that it was not Norman's way to give

lectures. These pieces of information emerged gradually, in the course of walks, sessions at the tavern apropros a chance remark. It was up to you to put two and two together if you were sufficiently interested.

Elizabeth's imbibing of these Douglas lessons had already been integrated into her work with the completion of *Mediterranean Food*. One of the qualities which she singles out in her tribute to him (above) and often glossed over by the English reader, but so fundamental to an understanding of the Mediterranean, was an appreciation of the 'variations in climate and soil' as she succinctly put it in *Mediterranean Food*. With this, and his profound respect for the seasons in mind, Elizabeth describes the famous Douglas habit of rarely eating in a restaurant unless he had 'first, in the morning . . . looked in; or if he felt too poorly in those latter days sent a message. What was to be had that day? What fish had come in? Was the mozzarella cheese dripping, positively dripping fresh? . . . Giovanni's wine will slip down all right my dear. At least he doesn't pick his grapes green.'

These attitudes of mind were to prove invaluable to Elizabeth in the following year and helped to bring about her complete conversion to the food of Italy. In talking about her work recently Grey Gowrie said: 'The writing had a sense of optimism and hope and the old Mediterranean world was still there. One of the consolations of being in my fifties is that we can remember the Mediterranean world before the age of tourism.'

That summer on Capri Elizabeth and Norman might have been forgiven for believing in the irreplaceable loss of an older world, but as they ate and drank and talked and listened, they were in fact experiencing a culture which (like much of Italy) was in some ways still in touch with its Greco-Roman past. Elizabeth's friend Sybille Bedford also saw a good deal of Norman in these last years and he would regularly drag her off on the famous post-prandial walks. 'He liked to walk for two hours after lunch. He liked his food and drink, he would talk about food, but he was not a gourmet. The moment you walked for a few minutes out of the piazza there is a rock path and we would make our way along it out into the country. He knew a vast amount about nature, he knew something about everything.

He was very tough, very virile, he had beautiful manners. He always liked a woman with him. He was violently atheistic, was very much afraid of dying.'

Norman's penultimate book, a final autobiographical work of 1946 entitled *Late Harvest* (Lyndsey Drummond), was a disappointment to him for its 'austerity' production on 'authorised economy standard' paper. To some of his friends its content was similarly insubstantial; they had hoped for a more organized and coherent account of his life, hardly realistic though with one as difficult to categorize as Norman. On her departure in late August Douglas gave Elizabeth a copy inscribed: 'For Liz. Farewell to Capri.'

CHAPTER FIFTEEN

Italy

(1951–1954)

HALSEY STREET WAS still full of Boultings, and Elizabeth's need for money kept them there until the following year. Returning to London at the end of the summer of 1951 she needed somewhere to stay beyond a few days here or there with friends. George and Judith Lassalle had moved to a basement flat at No. 14 Eccleston Square a few months after their marriage in the previous spring and, quickly re-establishing contact with George, Elizabeth was soon set up next door to them. (The two basement flats in fact took up Nos. 14 and 16 and No. 16 was temporarily vacant.)

Judith Lassalle describes the accommodation: 'It was another of those flats with the cooker in the bathroom, or you might say the bathroom in the kitchen. Anyway, the bath doubled, with a lid on it, as the kitchen table. She would knock on the door [which divided the two flats] if she wanted to borrow something or say something. She was in a way very polite. In John's kitchen she had hardly any facilities to cook on. It was camping gear really. She cooked a lot of bacon bones and Continental lentils. After she'd come through the connecting door and been with us for a while, talking, she'd often say, "Well, I must go and eat my lentils." She'd eat them cold or hot. Other times she would bring a bottle of wine and say, "I can produce this, what have you got?" and that way we'd spend the evening together.'

That autumn and winter in Eccleston Square Judith noticed how 'Elizabeth already sounded knowledgeable. She could take a teaspoon of something and analyse it, tell you what *wasn't* in it and what should have been in it. She and George talked a lot about food. She was writing about what we were eating . . . Then, and later in Halsey Street, Elizabeth was always having people round. But she was someone you didn't just pop in on.'

Elizabeth's now ingrained habit of dividing up her life, and accordingly her friends, is something which most of them have commented upon. As Alix Coleman says: 'She didn't keep open house, but people came often as guests, frequently they came separately too.'

Judith Lassalle remembers that during the Fifties and early Sixties, when they saw much of each other, 'We were rarely there with anyone else. Friends would wait to see Elizabeth in The Australian, the pub round the corner from Halsey Street. As we arrived someone would often leave . . . George said that Elizabeth needed a drink to get confidence. And she smoked like mad, tipped Gauloises. She was very shy, often put out a tough front to cover this up. If she didn't want to hear something she would just turn around to the wall or take her glasses off or put them on and screw up her eyes so that she couldn't see them . . . She never got into an argument, she would simply shrug her shoulders and walk away.' Other friends not only commented on Elizabeth's extreme short sight but also noticed her habit of putting her glasses on and off. George once said that 'when Elizabeth answers the door to you [without her glasses] she smells who it is'. One is reminded of that description of her as 'a myopic black swan'. One of her most distinctive qualities was this habit of separation, so extreme as to amount to a disciplined schizoid behaviour. This is the 'compartmentalization' of her life so frequently referred to by colleagues and friends. There are many who thought they were intimate with Elizabeth, indeed were, and yet knew nothing about whole strands of her experience.

Audrey Withers, editor of *Vogue* for whom Elizabeth would eventually write, had great respect for her writing and worked with her over a number of years. Nevertheless she has said of Elizabeth: 'She was I think, the most private person I have ever known. I had the feeling she had drawn a line around herself and it would be unwise to cross it without invitation.' The markedly different aspects of Elizabeth's personality were managed by existing in the different regions of herself at successive times. These regions were skilfully kept apart, just as she kept separate many of her friends. This type of existence, not uncommon in anyone of any complexity, and particularly artists, was in Elizabeth's case extreme. The distinctness and sharpness of the separations she engineered necessitated a high degree of practical management and self-government.

In her earlier life Elizabeth's ceaseless movement, her unsettled nomadic life-style, usually made unnecessary any serious management of these different selves. The boredom and satiety which she so easily experienced were kept at bay, avoided by change ... whether of occupation, associates, her milieu or her physical environment. Back in England after the war the problem became more pressing but in the short term she did her best (unconsciously) to keep moving, frequently changing her place of abode, launching herself feverishly into cooking, entertaining and trips abroad whenever possible. When young Elizabeth's sheer vitality sustained the most bizarre juggling acts, but with age the resource of raw energy diminished. To her own future cost she avoided the difficult emotional work of integrating her disparate and often warring selves, work so necessary for long-term equilibrium. Increasingly these unintegrated parts of herself demanded some kind of attention. She managed them in two ways: through anaesthesia (alcohol – induced oblivion) and by a meticulous manipulation of scene.

Several events took place early in the New Year of 1952 which deeply affected Elizabeth. First came the untimely death of the King, George VI. This upset her considerably and she repeated to the Lassalles, 'Why did he die? He shouldn't have died, it's so sad.' Despite her rejection of aspects of England she was at heart deeply English and her high Tory background made her monarchism entirely predictable. She dabbled with being an outsider, but at heart Elizabeth was a traditionalist, not a radical.

Another event shook her. 'On a dark drizzling February day ... news came from Capri of Norman's death.' With his going Elizabeth lost her revered mentor and friend and she was deeply moved. His paternalistic friendship had been one of the most significant features of her adult life and unquestionably one of the chief spurs to her writing. His life and writing remained a model for the rest of her days, and she truly mourned him. Before Norman's death Elizabeth had taken up John Lehmann's suggestion and agreed to write a book on the food of Italy. The book could almost be seen as a kind of tribute to Norman and the Classical land in which he had spent over forty years of his life. Elizabeth now began to research her new subject with thoroughness. Judith Lassalle remembers Doreen (who had come to know Italy while in Rome before the outbreak of war) and Elizabeth 'poring over maps and planning routes for Elizabeth and what presents to take for the journey. They decided she should stock up on tea and coffee, France still being very short of them. They were even short of gas.'

Tony was not now always in evidence although there was nothing formal about their degree of non-cohabitation, and he and Elizabeth continued to see each other for some time yet. Judith says that 'in this period Liz was broke and unsure of herself. Ian Erskine [the future Lord Rosslyn, brother to Hamish who'd stayed in the house in Menerbes], amongst others, used to take her out.' A lover from around this period (1951–2) was to become more prominent in her life, eventually having one of her books dedicated to him, as P.H.

By March Elizabeth was writing to Felicité from her apartment in Rome and the tone is reminiscent of those earlier letters to Pris, who for a great part of her youth and early adulthood had 'managed' so many of the mundane details of Elizabeth's life. 'A million thanks for all your coping. The newspapers have started to arrive, for which blessings to you.'

Though not always consciously, in transferring this role to Felicité Elizabeth was allocating her younger sister to a subordinate role in their relationship. Although they had literary and aesthetic interests in common, and her knowledge of these matters was as impressive as that of Elizabeth, Felicité did not have her sister's drive . . . the demon was not there. Felicité was not weak, but in comparison with her sister she was more malleable, a sweeter personality who ultimately complied with Elizabeth's assignment of her role. Elizabeth's appreciation of her was genuine – as it had been with Pris – but she also had an instinctive understanding of how to use the willingness of others. Judith Lassalle recalls a scene in Halsey Street which illustrates this trait. 'Elizabeth must have been without a cleaning lady at the time because she said to George, "I've got no one to wash my floor."

"I'll do it for you in return for a meal." And he did! Oh, Elizabeth could get people who didn't do things for others, to do things for her.'

One recalls Elizabeth's knowing comments from Egypt during the Flap of 1942 when, with a bandaged foot, she had people assisting her with her baggage, and noted that: 'the system has its advantages'.

Her Roman apartment was in the Palazzo Doria and she wrote that she was very comfortable in her little attic. She was on good terms with her landlady, but only too aware of how briefly that might last. Her rooms were small but pretty, with a good view over the rooftops of Rome. The kitchen was small and primitive, but she had, philosophically, long ago given up supposing that she would discover a decent kitchen anywhere but in her own house. And, as Elizabeth had spent so much time out of Halsey Street and was planning more months away in Italy, the use of this 'decent kitchen' was not possible in the foreseeable future.

Elizabeth had moved to the palazzo from a 'gloomy' *pensione* and had concluded like so many before her, and since, that Rome was a very noisy city. She spoke little Italian and although some of her friends were extremely knowledgeable about the country, most of her contacts were in fact English people; exiles of one kind or another. Friends like Archibald Lyall from the Ministry of Information in Cairo during the war, Archibald Colquhoun, recently acclaimed for his beautiful new translation of the most notable Italian novel, Alessandro Manzoni's *I Promessi Sposi* (The Betrothed). In writing about Italy, as compared with France, Elizabeth began with a disadvantage in that she just did not possess the same ease and familiarity with place and language.

This knowledge, that she was less *au fait* than usual, made her uneasy and was reflected in her general feeling of malaise. She was not at all happy about her book, or about her finances. Money was always a problem for Elizabeth because of her incurable tendency to overspend, even when she was being careful. Unfortunately her 'Irish Signora [landlady]' was fairly grasping, and Elizabeth had to pay her almost twenty pounds a month for the two rooms. I am paying her nearly £20 a month for her two rooms . . .' Elizabeth worried too about her prospects of reaching most of the places she needed to visit. Several of those to whom she had introductions had taken her out, but this would not be sufficient. Her next comment is consistent with her general opinion of Italy: 'So far I have found the food only fair and Italian wine disagrees with me.' In these negative comments Elizabeth is still careful. She knows that she doesn't yet have enough information with which to make an overall dismissal of the cooking as she almost does with the wine. Despite profound concerns about her work, concerns which never left her, however 'magical' her final prose might have been found by her readers, she responded to Rome itself with an understandable enthusiasm, saying it was lovely, and that she would have enjoyed it enormously if she had friends there. But she then reveals that fear which constantly beset her, 'the fearful agonies of writing and finance hanging over my head'.

Elizabeth's need to surround herself with a group of friends, at whose centre was a well-known clutch of intimates, was more insistent than with most normally sociable people. Her carefully constructed mechanisms to avoid more than a minimum of self-reflection would inevitably be less effective in a strange environment, especially where she didn't have the language to locate herself. She ends her letter by asking after the health of Felicité, soon due to have an operation and was also regularly indisposed with migraines. Ill-health disregarded, in Elizabeth's absence Felicité continued dealing with house bills, ensuring that all went as smoothly as possible with the Boultings downstairs, sent on Elizabeth's newspapers and mail, kept her up with the latest in interesting book catalogues and dealt with the resultant orders from Elizabeth who said she couldn't thank her enough 'for all your help and good works on my behalf'.

In a few weeks she was writing more happily about Rome while on a visit to Capri: many people had been kind and hospitable, and if she went on eating at her present rate she would have to go and take the waters at Montechatini, the famous Italian spa town. She now apologized for having left London in 'rather a shambling kind of way, but I really felt dispirited (and also too poor) for any sort of festivity'. Norman's death only days before her departure had added a great burden of gloom to her sadness over the demise of the king. 'Nobody wanted, quite rightly, to give a ball. The time for that will be when & if my book is finished, & when that will be it is hard to say.'

Having read more and moved about Rome and its environs she felt she had partially organized her task, saying that although she had collected enough material, she would not be able to cook it while in Italy. This illustrates that thoroughness which was one of Elizabeth's trademarks as a cookery writer, and for which she was at times feared by those who knew her. She assumes that the recipes cannot go into any book to which her name is attached until she has tried them out, sometimes several times. Taking the recipes down, watching them being made was, to her mind, insufficient evidence upon which to base a book of cookery. Confusion and inconsistency, common enough in her personal dealings, were rigorously excluded in the description of recipes. These descriptions included on the one hand the daily round, and that within it which is universal. In her writing she could bring all her knowledge, intellect, honesty, clarity, sense of poetry, history and the romantic to bear simultaneously. One of the important reasons Elizabeth stood above her contemporaries, still does above most who write about food, was that without in any way relinquishing her personality she transcended the personal. As a result they are authentic, authoritative cameos of Truth.

Elizabeth said to Felicité that she would have to do her experimenting on her return to England when, with Halsey Street still rented out, she would 'go and stay alternately with Doreen and Sib, & make free with their kitchens'. She wrote retrospectively that she 'had been naggingly aware ... that a tremendous task still awaited me when I should return to England'. In a letter to Felicité she said the book was, according to the contract, due for delivery at the end of November, but she would soon have to break it to John Lehmann that there was no hope of having it ready by then. Most of the rest of 1952 was spent in Italy and in 1953 she was back in England, reading, cooking and writing. It was a long and arduous task but one whose outcome she seemed ultimately to prefer to her other literary achievements. She commented on this in the Penguin (1963) issue of *Italian Food*, but on careful reading one is left unsure of what she actually thought about the *merits* of the book as apart

Elizabeth at twenty-two in a publicity photograph. She wrote her credentials on the back: 'Work. 5ft 6ins. Fluent French and German.' She was more than 5ft 6ins.

Lawrence Durrell, writer
and *enfant terrible*.

The celebrated travel writer
Patrick Leigh Fermor in 1945.

Elizabeth at her desk at the Ministry of Information in Cairo in 1943.
Note the cigarette in hand and the glasses – always removed for photographs.

Veronica Nicholson, the dedicatee
of Elizabeth's first book, in Italy
at the end of the war.

Anne Scott-James, editor of
Harper's Bazaar, in about 1949 when
she published Elizabeth's first article.

Viola Johnson. She and her husband
Arthur looked after Elizabeth in Italy.

The painter Derek Hill,
photographed by his friend
Cecil Beaton in the 1970s.

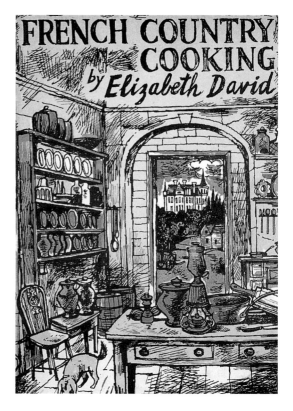

The Eggs by Cedric Morris
was donated by Elizabeth to
the Tate Gallery.

Right: The first edition
of *French Country Cooking*,
designed and illustrated
by John Minton.

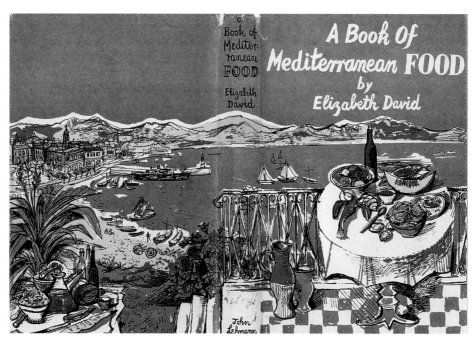

The first edition of *A Book of Mediterranean Food*, published in *1950*.
The jacket was again designed and illustrated by John Minton.

The Provençal 'Castle of Otranto' where Elizabeth stayed in 1950.

George and Judith Lassalle on their
wedding day, June 1950.

The photographer
and interior designer
Anthony Denney in 1960.
He collaborated with
Elizabeth for many years.

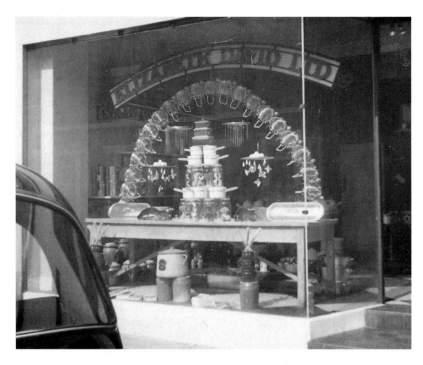

The window of Elizabeth's shop with a display designed by the artist
Gilli Gretton. Elizabeth called her 'a genius' for it.

Elizabeth in her drawing-room,
photographed by Cecil Beaton.

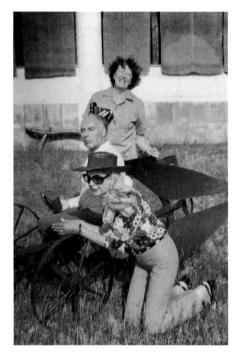

Doreen Thornton, Anthony Denney
and Elizabeth in the mid-1970s.

Elizabeth in her kitchen, drawn by John Ward RA in 1958.

Judy and Hugh Johnson.

Elizabeth photographed by
Derek Hill in the mid-1960s

Above: Elizabeth with Squeaker, her beloved cat, photographed by Cecil Beaton.

Elizabeth's grave in Folkington churchyard.

from her *feelings* about it. Elizabeth's lack of clarity here reflects her own ambiguity on the whole Italian venture. It is only with recourse to later comments that one concludes she did think it her best book.

'Writing of the feelings of authors towards their own work, Mr Raymond Mortimer . . . observed that they usually prefer, perhaps wrongly, the book which has given them the most trouble. That this book was uncommonly troublesome cannot be denied.' She said she 'felt . . . less detached from it than any I have done before or since'.

Writing from Capri, Elizabeth told Felicité that George Menasce – the wealthy Egyptian banker who had befriended and been kind to her in the war – turned up in Rome the day before she left for Capri, and that it was 'nice to see a familiar face'. A familiar face which she mourned in Capri was Norman's and she wrote that she had so far not been down to the Piazza, and didn't much want to, knowing she would not find him sitting there. She knew that V. S. Pritchett had written something about him in the *New Statesman and Nation* – 'any good?' – and that Brian Howard had written an angry letter about Harold Nicolson's article in the *Spectator*. Harold Acton had last seen his old friend Norman only days after Elizabeth left Capri the previous autumn. He wrote that 'The meal was punctuated by bursts of laughter and arteriosclerosis was sent to blazes. By the time we reached the funicular [by which Acton would descend to the steamer bound for Naples] Norman was almost buoyant.' And Acton sums up his last impressions thus: 'Standing there in his loose overcoat and shabby beret, he had the elegance of a Scottish Jacobite in exile. He was the most sanguine of the octogenarians I knew [Acton knew many]: his physique, like his intellect, belonged to the eighteenth rather than to the twentieth century.'

Over the years Elizabeth was to write several tributes to Norman herself. One, for *Wine and Food* in 1964, was built around a denunciation of a posthumous publication of Douglas's. A spoof on aphrodisiac cooking, *Venus in the Kitchen*, had an introduction by his friend and summer resident of Capri, Graham Greene, and was 'decorated' by Bruce Roberts. 'Defacements would have been a more accurate description,' spits Elizabeth. And in her anger and disappointment she went on to berate the emasculation of her friend's 'instructive and

entertaining little collection of recipes, mainly . . . of ancient Mediterranean origin . . .' She said, 'What makes this . . . anthology notable
is not the recipes. It is the characteristically irreverent Douglas spirit
which imbues them . . .' On the banal illustrations which so trivialized the tone of the book she was at her attacking best: 'Anything
more anaphrodisiac than [Roberts's] simpering cupids (in Bathing
trunks), his bows and arrows and hearts, his chefs in Christmas
cracker hats, his amorphous fishes and bottles and birds, his waiters
in jocular poses, sexless couples seated at tables for two, it would be
hard to imagine.' Elizabeth's criticisms are just but, for all her wit
and waspishness, the adulatory tone of her comments about Douglas
does sometimes begin to verge on the schoolgirlish. Other examples
are found in the tributes to him which she chose to print in her fine,
late collection of journalistic essays, *An Omelette and a Glass of Wine*.

Obviously she could not have been party to his friendships with
other homosexuals, and those with men such as Pino Orioli and
Harold Acton sometimes give glimpses of a life so much more
sexually forthright than the one his good manners allowed Douglas
to reveal to Elizabeth. When Elizabeth wrote, for instance, that John
Davenport's portrait of Douglas was 'beautiful, lucid and truthful'
some might not entirely agree; Acton was obviously one of them. She
wrote, 'We made friends easily. He reinforced my own growing love
for the Mediterranean shore. Our shared enjoyment of wine and food
had a certain reckless quality.' With admirable succinctness she then
described her own position vis-à-vis the whole subject upon which
she was now acclaimed as a distinguished authority. (Here Elizabeth
is capitalizing, as often, on having kept her copyrights by reworking
and expanding on something she had previously written. The passage
usually improved each time she reworked it.) 'We had in common a
dislike of meanness, and an aversion to fuss, interference and pretension. Solemn sippings and grave debatings were not for Norman, nor
were or are they for me.'

'What Norman taught me above all else was to distinguish
between the second-rate and the authentic in matters of food and
wine, and in the course of our friendship . . . he gave me many lessons
in the art of seeking out the sources of the best fruit, the olive oil
with the right smell, the freshest white cheese, the choicest Parmesan.'

This was a generous credit to Douglas but Elizabeth could not have imbibed the message with such certainty if he had not touched something which was already there in her. This search for the 'authentic', becoming something of an obsession, was one of the qualities which early singled Elizabeth out from other cookery writers of her day.

Some time after the publication of *Mediterranean Food* she had been at a dinner where the publisher André Deutsch was also present. Elizabeth was already sufficiently well known for him to ask if she would act in an informal way for the firm, as a kind of roving editor. If she came across something she thought worth publishing it would be a recommendation to them, and similarly if they were sent something upon which they needed advice it would go out to her. In this way a number of early Fifties André Deutsch cookery books were described by them as being under the general editorship of Elizabeth David.

Diana Athill shared editorial directorship with Deutsch. She was only four years younger than Elizabeth but says: 'She was a very formidable person. I was a little bit frightened of her. She made you feel inadequate . . . but she was invaluable in teaching me how to get the really authentic in a work of cookery, and avoiding the sham . . . My position in charge of commissioning and editing the cookery books was a joke really because when I started out I could hardly boil an egg. But food was always given to women. Elizabeth would never have done as an editor herself, her hair-sieve was much too fine for the more everyday books which we also did. But she was extraordinarily scrupulous and one could always trust her judgement, which came with admirable speed.'

Elizabeth talked to her about how difficult it was to be regarded as a cookery expert, saying that: ' "It wasn't taken seriously." We would laugh over what she called "the tinkling mandolin syndrome".

'What I got from Elizabeth was how one should approach food. Her sensuous and aesthetic appreciation of it. She always remained a touchstone for me long after she had become too big for us . . .'

The Deutsch cookery series consisted of genuine little books with unpretentious workable recipes and a few quite unusual ones.

Some of those Elizabeth recommended to Deutsch included: two books by Gertrude Mann, on berry cooking and apples, one on mushrooms by Garibaldi Lapolla, one on Indian food which Elizabeth [ironically] particularly liked, *German Cooking* by Robin Howe and another by her on *Italian Cooking* published in 1953, a year before Elizabeth's own *Italian Food* came out.

In discouraging her from taking on Lehmann's commission Elizabeth's friends were reflecting the general English attitude: 'All that *pasta* . . . We've got enough stodge here already; you won't find much else in Italy. You'll have to invent.' More than forty years on, when the English love affair with all things Italian shows little sign of abating, it is hard to realize that in this period when rationing still hung over England, Robin Howe's *Italian Cooking* would have been quite unusual. Indeed under the auspices of Diana Athill it was not a bad little book. Howe recommends the use of Italian ingredients, then hard to come by but all of which are now so familiar we often taken them for granted: olive oil, garlic, 'zucchini and aubergine . . . dried beans of all descriptions, a dozen or more different kinds of pasta and the Roman and Parmesan cheeses without which you can hardly begin Italian cooking'. She doesn't encourage substitutes and, if rather short on explanation for the uninitiated, the book is certainly not 'sham'.

Why was this then not received with the acclamation of Elizabeth's book one year later, in 1954? The answer is that Robin Howe's book simply lacks Elizabeth's weight, inspiration and sheer dazzling prose. She does not summon up readers' imagination, transporting them to another world. Describing her 'voyage of discovery' in Italy as 'far from easy', Elizabeth wrote that gradually 'the sense of discovery that Italian food brought me was . . . potent. As recipe after recipe came out and I realized how much I was learning, and how enormously these dishes were enlarging my own scope and enjoyment, the fever to communicate them grew every day more urgent.' That was Elizabeth. On returning to England after the war she had 'cooked like one possessed', eventually producing *Mediterranean Food*, and now she was 'feverish' to let her readers know what she had discovered: that Italy was, after all, extraordinary.

Of all the spectacular food markets in Italy, the one near the Rialto in Venice must be the most remarkable. The light of a Venetian dawn in early summer – you must be up at about four o'clock in the morning to see the market coming to life – is so limpid and so still that it makes every separate vegetable and fruit and fish luminous with a life of its own, with unnaturally heightened colours and clear stencilled outlines. Here the cabbages are cobalt blue, the beetroots deep rose, the lettuces clear pure green, sharp as glass. Bunches of gaudy gold marrow-flowers show off the elegance of pink and white marbled bean pods, primrose potatoes, green plums, green peas. The colours of the peaches, cherries, and apricots, packed in boxes lined with sugar-bag blue paper matching the blue canvas trousers worn by the men unloading the gondolas, are reflected in the rose-red mullet and the orange *vongole* and *cannestrelle* which have been prised out of their shells and heaped into baskets. In other markets, on other shores, the unfamiliar fishes may be vivid, mysterious, repellent, fascinating, and bright with splendid colour; only in Venice do they look good enough to eat. In Venice even ordinary sole and ugly great skate are striped with delicate lilac lights, the sardines shine like newly-minted coins, pink Venetian *scampi* are fat and fresh, infinitely enticing in the early dawn.

The gentle swaying of the laden gondolas, the movements of the market men as they unload, swinging the boxes and baskets ashore, the robust life and rattling noise contrasted with the fragile taffeta colours and the opal sky of Venice – the whole scene is out of some marvellous unheard-of ballet.

Such a lilting and evocative description of the sheer wonder of an Italian market has rarely been accomplished. And that shimmering, watery marvel of a city, with its 'blissful . . . respite from trains and traffic . . . the most gorgeous city in the world' had so captivated Elizabeth that she leaves her reader too, longing for '. . . the light of a Venetian dawn in early summer . . . so limpid and so still'.

It was in Venice that Elizabeth met Renato Guttuso, who was to do the drawings for *Italian Food*. Archibald Colquhoun, like

Guttuso a Communist (Lehmann, who had met Guttuso in about 1950, was also a one-time party member), was the intermediary. In his second volume of autobiography *More Memoirs of an Aesthete* (Methuen, 1970) Harold Acton remembers him: 'Archie Colquhoun . . . had been a liaison officer with the Italian partisans, who had converted him to Communism. His conversion had been more emotional than intellectual, for he told me they were more handsome than the bourgeoisie and entirely free from middle-class prejudice. "The salt of the earth and the honey." So far so good: I was glad he had enjoyed his war experiences but my temper rose when he remarked: "How lovely it will be when your villa and garden are handed over to the proletariat!" [Harold lived in a very large and beautiful fifteenth-century villa on the hills above Florence.] I could picture them stoning the statues, wrecking the flower beds, killing the goldfish and running bicycle races through the box hedges in the public garden . . . at the foot of the hill. "But you would be employed as a caretaker," he said to soothe me, "if you behaved yourself." '

Elizabeth wrote to Félicité from Venice: 'I found all kinds of fascinating characters assembled here for the Biennale . . . John Lehmann in most cordial mood . . . I had a great talk with him about the illustrations, for I really do feel very strongly the necessity for a change . . . He is doubtful about dropping John Minton, but has at least conceded that if I find someone suitable he will consider the matter.'

Elizabeth told Alix Coleman that she and Archie Colquhoun in Venice had been sitting together after a party when Guttuso walked by; Elizabeth had already admired his paintings in the Biennale exhibition. Colquhoun said, 'There's Guttuso – we'll ask him to do the pictures for your book.'

Moving on from Venice, having become 'oblivious' to the cacophony of Genoese traffic because in the market she was 'spellbound by the spectacle of the odd fish which come up from these waters', Elizabeth moves us 'Along the coast at Santa Margherita' where 'the fish market is famous; here the fish are less forbidding and savage of aspect, but their brilliance of colour is phenomenal'. And finally in this superb scene-setting for the chapter on fish, we are at 'Cagliari, in the island of Sardinia'. Elizabeth wrote later that 'when planning my Italian venture I had for some reason become interested in Sardinia – perhaps D. H. Lawrence's *Sea and Sardinia* was partly responsible'. Lawrence's book, with some typically fine prose, Elizabeth had already quoted in *Mediterranean Food* and one sees in *Italian Food* the influence of his luminous descriptions.

In a letter to Felicité referring to her curiosity about Sardinia she said that people had been mystified: 'What on earth can take you there?' She was determined to see it – the island being unknown to tourists and D. H. Lawrence so 'grumpy' about it, she thought there must be something attractive to be found.

In *Italian Food* she wrote of Cagliari market:

> Spread out in flat baskets large as cartwheels are all the varieties of fish which go into *ziminù*, the Sardinian version of fish soup: fat scaly little silver fish streaked with lime green; enormous octopus, blue sepia, mauve and turquoise, curled and coiled and petalled like some heavily embroidered marine flower . . . silvery slippery sardines; rose-red mullets in every possible size, some small as sprats, like doll's-house fish; the fine lobsters for which Sardinia is famous.

Before this joyous display of sensual delight might topple over into an orgy of purple, with consummate timing Elizabeth draws the passage deftly to a close. She makes one of those agile transitions at which she excelled, from the *genius loci* to the cooking stove and sound, practical advice.

> The mullet, the slices of fresh tunny, the little clams, seem [in Sardinia] to have been washed straight from the sea to the frying pan, so fresh and tender is their flesh. In such conditions there is no necessity to create complicated sauces and garnishes; and, indeed, for the cooking of fish Italian cooks are mainly content to concentrate their skill on the arts of frying, grilling, and roasting.

She fell for the island, calling her two-week stay there 'bliss . . . And I have decided to go back there, often . . .' She enjoyed her time on Sardinia as much as she did because she imbued it (however unconsciously) with a dimension beyond its obvious attraction as a wild and beautiful island off the mainland. She clearly experienced there something of that sense of remote simplicity found only on her now mythic 'Isles of Greece'; and which remained for her a kind of shining inner light. As time passed this light grew dimmer, but anything which rekindled memories of the purest happiness she ever experienced – on Syros with Charles – was inevitably close to her heart. She described 'a wonderful beach, miles of soft white sand, and clear, clear sea ... How unlike the refuse strewn and stuffy little playgrounds of Capri, Positano, Sorrento, & all the International Southern Blackpools of Italy and the Riviera.'

As she watched and ate and read Elizabeth recognized one of the fundamental differences between Italian and French cooking. 'What the Italian kitchen misses in the form of concentrated meat glazes, *fumets* of fish and game, the *fonds de cuisine* of the French, it makes up for in the extreme freshness and lavishness of its raw materials.' Should her English reader have mistaken these words for a call to outrageous luxury (the book was published in 1954, rationing ended only in that year), she was at pains to establish the fact that Italy too had fared badly in that last few years, 'and since the war Italian cooks have had to learn to make a little go a long way'. The purpose of her comments was to show how the Italian reaction to dearth is so unlike our own and that we could learn from it. We 'attempt to produce an imitation', whereas in such circumstances when an Italian wants 'to cook one of the traditional extravagant dishes ... her method would be to produce some attractive and nourishing little dish out of two ounces of cheese and a slice of ham, or a pound of spinach and a couple of eggs. A hefty *pizza* made of bread dough and baked in the oven with tomatoes, cheese and herbs costs very little and is comforting, savoury food. *Gnocchi* ... are cheap and easy to make, so are little envelopes of paste containing slices of cheese and *mortadella* sausage.'

Here one remembers some of those simple, inventive Italian variations on the theme of eggs, cheese, ham and spinach. The recipes Elizabeth gave included: *Uova al Tegame al Formaggio* (Fried Eggs with Cheese), *Uova Stracciate al Formaggio* (Scrambled Eggs with Cheese), *Fonduta* (Piedmontese Cheese Fondue), *Crostini di Provatura* (Cheese Croûtons), *Spinaci con Uvetta* (Spinach with Sultanas), *Piselli*

al Prosciutto (Green Peas and Ham), *Maccheroni alla Carbonara* (Macaroni with Ham and Eggs), *Crochetti di Spinaci* (Spinach Cro-
quettes) . . . all delicious and none hard to make. A mixture of
spinach, ricotta, eggs, Parmesan and nutmeg to taste, favoured in
Tuscany and called there ravioli, but perhaps better understood as
gnocchi, is fiddly but infinitely worth the trouble. As Elizabeth
rightly said, 'The most delicious of all the tribe.' The above is hardly
a hint of the good Italian food the book contains, but in answer to
those who believed that Italy's repertoire was a limited one, Elizabeth
later said: 'Invent indeed. I had so much material that a vast amount
had to be rejected.' And it is true, her book covers a fraction of what
there is.

Back in Rome after her visit to Capri, her plans were coming to
fruition. She had told Felicité that the Italian Tourist Board had
promised free tickets on a number of trains which, if they materialized, would be quite a help to her. Despite understandable wariness
at the *sprezzatura* of such an Italian undertaking, they kept their
promises and Elizabeth was treated 'royally'.

With the details of living wearing away at her, she resents the
time taken to organize them. Whereas in Halsey Street much was
undertaken for her by Felicité, here in Italy where such matters can
become quite tortuous she had no such factotum. Nevertheless the
recounting of it is tinged with a weary wit. 'I can't say my path here
is very smooth, my landlady although quite an endearing old trout,
is so dotty that no servants will stay, so my fine arrangements about
laundry and so on have broken down, & life is a long struggle to keep
a clean white blouse.' (As long ago as her years in Cairo Elizabeth was
noted for her slightly mannish white shirts.)

At this point she had already searched out enough to be saying
that eating and drinking were exhausting her to collapsing point. To
make matters worse, the Italian Tourist Board had fulfilled their
promise and the following week she was 'leaving to eat her way
through a gruelling marathon': Perugia, Bologna, Florence, Venice,
Milan and Genoa, at the expense of the Italian state. The Tourist
Board had organized an itinerary with some thought and care and
Elizabeth learned much from the trips they funded for her in the next
three months or so. She wrote to Felicité that they had fallen for her

'hook, line and sinker, but their enthusiasm will I fear be the death of me, for they are laying on 36 meals in 15 days, travelling in between so that as someone very rightly said I shall come back like a stuffed turkey. If I come back.'

Friends then in Rome included Archibald Lyall, and Elizabeth asked Felicité to continue in her role as book scout by finding for him 'the Augustus Hares about Rome'. (Augustus Hare was one of those remarkable literate and travelled Victorians whose books on Italy remain some of the best in an illustrious genre.) In requesting Felicité to search out these two volumes for her friend she demonstrates both her own memory for a book and the pains she expected her sister to take over the task.

'I am almost certain I saw them, and a lot more besides, in that good bookshop near South Ken ... not the Beauchamp – the one with the books outside. Or perhaps you have them in Allens [the bookshop where Felicité worked]. If so, or if you can lay hands on them do send them to him ... He might prove a nice customer to you. He is doing something about selling books for English publishers in Rome. (He wrote that book called 25 languages, without which I never move) ... The Augustus Hares to go on my bill – a way of returning hospitality ... Do tell Mrs Boulting that her friend took me out to dinner & was perfectly charming. And tell Tony, Diana and so on that I will write soon. Joyce Murchie has been ... in Rome. So it has been cheerful to see her & a good deal of drinking.' (Joyce Murchie was a lively friend who lived near Elizabeth in Halsey Street.)

Elizabeth returned to Rome and her little attic rooms overlooking the endless variety of terracotta roofs, common to all Italian towns but in Rome almost an undulating sea. Before her return she had visited many of the major cities, 'pilgrim routes' as she called them, of Italy. In July she wrote to Felicité from Verona, saying that Aunt Violet's gondola would have been just the thing there. She was being royally entertained and had worn out six pairs of gloves shaking hands with officials. She also made the revealing comment that: 'In Verona had to exercise considerable tact to avoid the toils of a haggard, dissolute but still handsome character, just my cup of tea but it would scarcely have done.' Elizabeth had not changed much; she still hankered after the echoes of a Charles Gibson Cowan.

To Priscilla she wrote a summary of her experiences: 'Rich living in Bologna and Venice, Milan, Como, Genoa and the Italian Riviera to follow in rapid succession. Oh for a boiled egg on a tray!'

In Florence Elizabeth visited Derek Hill, in Italy since 1948. He was the painter friend of Lesley O'Malley (soon to join the Halsey Street *ménage*). In 1952 Hill had been invited to stay in the Villino, the exquisite *dépendance* in the garden of the art historian Bernard Berenson's villa I Tatti, while he painted the grand old man. Set amongst the cypress slopes of Settignano, above Florence, I Tatti was Berenson's masterpiece: a dignified Cinquecento house, Italian art and a library, where he entertained and was entertained by some of the most artistic and articulate of America and Europe for almost half a century. Derek Hill also painted Harold Acton, who lived nearby and was a close friend of Berenson. When asked if he liked the painting Acton said: 'Like it no, but it is exactly like me.' Amongst other things he disliked his premature baldness.

Derek Hill's cook Giulia, who had been maid to Berenson, impressed Elizabeth with her elegance and delicacy. Years later she wrote of her: 'In bearing she was more the fastidious aristocrat than the sturdy peasant.' Elizabeth felt that her cooking followed the same principles. 'Subtly seasoned, but with unexpected contrasts, as in the cold, uncooked tomato sauce which she served with hot dry rice. Conversely, *riso ricco*, or rich rice, consists of plain white rice left to cool until barely more than lukewarm, when a hot cheese sauce resembling a fonduta is poured over it. Not an easy dish to get right.' In the 1963 revised Penguin edition of *Italian Food* Elizabeth calls this 'a very tricky dish . . . but when it comes off, glorious'.

Elizabeth's comments on the cook Giulia were put together with two others as an essay entitled 'Mafalda, Giovanna, Giulia' in *Petits Propos Culinaires*, 1980. The Mafalda piece is one of those glimpses of personal recollection which make her writing so intriguing at times. It demonstrates too the dedication and persistence Elizabeth needed and was prepared to give in order finally, and triumphantly, to secure a recipe. 'Come back in the summer and I will show you,' Mafalda had said when Elizabeth asked about her delicious bottled pimentos. Mafalda and her husband ran a small restaurant in Anacapri where Elizabeth stayed briefly on that visit down from Rome. In the summer she returned, also to Mafalda. A good part of the research for the book now completed, she removed herself, as do all Italians who can possibly afford it, from the summer heat of the city, and withdrew to Capri.

That summer Elizabeth paid her only visit to Norman's grave and wrote in an article on him for *Wine and Food* in 1965, entitled 'South Wind through the Kitchen'; 'I had never shared Norman's rather melancholy taste for visiting churchyards. A more fitting place to remember him was in the lemon grove to be reached only by descending some three hundred steps from the piazza. It was so thick, that lemon grove, that it concealed from all but those who knew their Capri well the old Archbishop's palace in which was housed yet another of those private taverns which appeared to materialize for Norman alone. There, at a table outside the half ruined house, a branch of piercingly aromatic lemons hanging within arm's reach, a piece of bread and a bottle of the proprietor's olive oil in front of me, a glass of wine in my hand, Norman was speaking.

'In the shade of the lemon grove I break off a hunch of bread, sprinkle it with the delicious fruity olive oil, empty my glass of sour white Capri wine; and remember that Norman Douglas once wrote that whoever has helped us to a larger understanding is entitled to our gratitude for all time.'

For the second time Elizabeth was the guest of Arthur and Viola Johnson, who normally lived in Rome and kept a summer villa on the island. She had been introduced to Arthur and Viola by Norman Douglas and they soon became close friends. The Johnsons were refined, cosmopolitan – Arthur was an international lawyer and authority on modern art; both he and his wife were knowledgeable about wine – and appreciated Elizabeth (though interestingly, Viola later commented to her son John that in a way she found Felicité a more interesting person than Elizabeth). John recollected in conversation with the author: 'Mother and Father avoided at almost all costs having their friends staying *in* the villa. The form was to stay close by, as Elizabeth did, and take all meals with them at their Casa Molino a Vento.' Elizabeth's 'cool room' was five minutes' walk from the bottom of the Johnsons' garden.

Viola and Elizabeth would make early-morning assignations together: 'Oh, I remember they would go out very early. At five a.m. they'd be off to the market and come back conspiratorially with mountains of aubergines and other things. I used to think they were completely dotty. That first summer they met [1951], on leaving Capri my mother had asked Elizabeth to look after Norman for her while she was away.' The Johnsons were close to Douglas and young John too found him 'delightful', in spite of being 'a very naughty old man . . . He once got me drunk at a café, I was about twelve, and my parents forbade more visits, but of course I went all the same. I pretended I was going swimming. He was a great charmer. He said that if he married again he would marry my mother. I would go round there often. He had a huge bronze pot filled with all the visiting cards collected during his life and we would play this game of "Looking Back" over his life. His stories about people were so interesting. It was great fun.'

Elizabeth was to spend six weeks on the island this time and, knowing that 'these pimientos were rather a speciality of Mafalda's and . . . were by far the best I had ever tasted' she made repeated visits to the restaurant in the hope of securing the privilege of watching her bottle them.

John Johnson describes Mafalda as a 'tiny little lady, she was wonderful'. Wonderful maybe, but not to be hurried in her bottling of pimentos. So Elizabeth went off with the Johnsons for a week or so, travelling around the Gulf of Salerno to some of the ancient towns of the Italian South. They went to Sorrento, Salerno, and down to the coastal village of Agropoli. 'An awful flea-bitten little town,' says John, who accompanied his parents and Elizabeth. He recalls an episode revealing the grip of superstition under which most of Southern Italy still functioned, about which Douglas had written so descriptively in *Old Calabria* and of which Elizabeth was uncomprehending. 'Liz and I were going for an early morning swim there and some little boys clamoured at us that if we didn't cross ourselves before we entered the water we would turn into devils. Of course we didn't and so when we emerged from the water they were terrified because they thought we *must* be devils.'

They visited ancient Paestum on its wild and lonely plain of whispering sun-bleached grasses. The city was famous in Greek antiquity for roses and violets even before its domination by the Romans, but the population gradually dwindled owing to the ravages of malaria, and was finally sacked by the Saracens in the ninth century. Not until the classically minded eighteenth century were its majestic golden Doric temples marvelled at and fully revealed, making it a place of pilgrimage almost as moving as Athens. 'At Paestum we clambered about,' says John. 'My father had read classics at Oxford and was intrigued, wanted to look at everything there. We spent ages going round it. We had a picnic. It was a beautiful, strange place and we went back again a few days later whilst staying in a converted Carthusian monastery in Positano. I remember Liz met in Positano by chance a friend of hers. He was boiled lobster red. He was very suave, a well-known homosexual photographer of the fifties.

'Another suave man friend I remember. One day an enormous luxury yacht came into the harbour whilst we were at the Marina Grande, at Capri, and Liz knew this chap in the party on board. We went to lunch on board the yacht and the Yugoslav captain was very taken with her and kept asking her to take off her sun-glasses so that he could see her eyes. But she wouldn't of course because she wouldn't have been able to see without them. Liz insisted that I must go for a trip on a yacht and so it was arranged that I should go off for a few days on this great luxury ship.'

At Ravello in the hills above the coast the Johnsons and Elizabeth ate and drank better than for days. As Elizabeth wrote, 'In the south, it is true, careful cooking is not common.' Her caveat that apparently food in Calabria – she didn't travel that far south – had improved a good deal since Douglas's First World War denunciations of it is still only partly true. She had hoped also to go to Sicily, but had had to give up the idea as her finances were in poor shape. Elizabeth had recently written to Félicité that her finances were 'worse than they have ever been (*not* to be passed on to *anybody*)' and, owing to her practice of rarely putting recipes into her books unless she had seen them *in situ*, there are few from the island. This was a pity because it made some of her judgements about Italian food less balanced than they would otherwise have been. Sicily has a fascinating culinary history, if sometimes lacking in finesse: its location, and consequent invasions, made it for a time one of the most cosmopolitan and cultivated places in the Mediterranean.

One of the recipes, *caponata*, which Elizabeth did include from that beleaguered and beautiful island, she described as only 'interesting'. She is mistaken. Why she also gave a Frenchman's version of it is obscure. When done well, and well in advance, it is a powerful and memorable hors d'oeuvre with true echoes of the Greco-Roman civilization of which Sicily was a part. When she wrote that 'Considering that aubergines have been cultivated in Italy since the fifteenth century, it is odd that the Italians should never have evolved a dish of aubergines half as good as the Balkan *moussaka* or the Greek purée of aubergine with oil and garlic . . . or the Provencal *ratatouille*,' I would take issue with her. *Caponata* is more odd, but at least as good as *ratatouille*.

A dish from the South, *crespolini*, which she appreciated and took down from the chef at that 'comfortable' hotel at Ravello was one which she said became 'a lasting favourite of my own as well as being much taken up by later cookery writers'. One detects here that wail of 'plagiarism', to which cookery writers have always been so ruthlessly subjected, and about which crime Elizabeth was to become so sensitive that it sometimes verged on zealotry. If sometimes mistaken and misplaced, her sensitivity was understandable. The recipe which Elizabeth took from the chef at Ravello is for 'delicate little pancakes filled with a mixture of spinach, ricotta and chicken livers'. After being cut into triangular pieces the *crespolini* are put into the oven 'until the cheese on top is melting, golden brown and crusty at the edges'.

Another unexpected pleasure of the hotel at Ravello, 'far above Amalfi and the coast', was their own 'unusual' *Gran Caruso* red wine. Elizabeth enjoyed two other wines with the Johnsons in Rome. They owned a vineyard at their fine eighteenth-century villa outside the city at Grottaferrata and here was produced for them a wine 'red and heady and one of the treats of the months I spent in Rome,' she wrote much later in the 1987 extended version of *Italian Food*; '. . . another was a white wine, fresh and frizzante, from the Veneto estate of Franco Marinotti, a . . . friend of the Johnsons'.

On return to Capri Elizabeth writes to Felicité with more book orders. As gifts for hospitality: '*The Romantic Exiles* [E. H. Carr, with notes on the English who had lived in Sicily] is for Arthur Johnson, the Beerbohm is for *Mrs* Arthur Johnson. For that matter they can both go in the same parcel if you have them at the same time.' She next asks Felicité to organize supplying *another* Mrs Johnson with Tony's tea coupons: he never used his, and she wouldn't be in England for long.

'At last Mafalda relented: the weather was fine, the moon no doubt was in the right quarter, the peppers were fat and fleshy, the price was as low as was compatible with the goods being in their prime. As it turned out it was well worth waiting for, because year after year I have used Mafalda's method of bottling peppers with great success. A number of people have questioned whether it is possible to do this preserve without oil. . . . yes it is, I think it is because of this that they are so good, for the addition of oil tends to make the peppers soggy. [The roasted peppers Elizabeth loved so much, and reproduced several times, appear in a little booklet she wrote for the Le Creuset cast-iron ware company in 1969, one of the rare occasions when she wrote for a commercial enterprise.] The acrid-sweet smell from the roasting peppers fills the kitchen with what is, to me, a most potent evocation of a warm October day in the Abruzzi and the unforgettable scent, all pervading, of charcoal-charred *peperoni* in an inn on the mountain road down from Aquila to Ascoli Piceno and Ancona on the Adriatic Sea.'

Before the middle of October Elizabeth was back in Rome for the last time. Just returned from Sardinia and the final two-week phase of her Italian journey, she called it 'bliss' and eventually included many recipes from that large and culturally remote island which Italians still don't really regard as Italian. The Sards would agree. Elizabeth tells Felicité on 11 October: 'Books arrived – many thanks. Leave Rome 16th to Turin, Paris; London 25th. See you soon. Love E.'

In England, with Halsey Street still let to the Boultings,

Elizabeth did indeed 'make free' with Doreen's kitchen as she had planned from Italy. She was with Doreen and her husband Colin Thornton for over three months, experimenting, cooking, writing. 'This was fine,' says Doreen, 'but what wasn't was that when we had people to dinner Liz would invariably say "I'll cook" and she wouldn't produce dinner until eleven o'clock at night. Once my step-father was staying and it was awful. He needed to eat and Liz had hardly started by nine o'clock. She'd have spaghetti hanging all over the kitchen chairs to dry and everything in general disarray. Every-thing in *Italian Food* was practised on us. She'd make the most lovely food. There was a chocolate cake she made, the most divine thing imaginable, uncooked and made with layers of chocolate and biscuits.' [This is *Torrone Molle*, which came from Lina, the Johnsons' fine Tuscan cook.]

Elizabeth was using all her practical and synthesizing abilities to make coherent the food of Italy. It would be a difficult task for anyone familiar with its great variety and differences but, even for someone of Elizabeth's gifts, beginning in relative ignorance, the task was formidable. Whatever the book's shortcomings it undoubtedly accom-plished most of Elizabeth's professed objectives. One of these had been to describe her joyful discovery of the regionalism still very much intact after Italy's relatively recent unity. At the end of the nineteenth century, in symbolically attempting to encourage this new unity many towns had ripped down their still near-perfect medieval walls, and Elizabeth wrote in the introduction to *Italian Food*:

> Whereas only the very credulous would suppose that Italians live entirely upon *pasta asciutta* and veal escalopes, the enormous variety of their local dishes is quite unappreciated outside Italy, and the highly regional aspect of the food is not grasped at all . . . The term 'Italian' used in relation to food would in fact mean very little to most Italians. To them there is Florentine cooking, Venetian cooking, there are the dishes of Genoa, Piedmont, Romagna; of Rome, Naples and the Abruzzi; of Sardinia and Sicily . . .

Elizabeth continued:

It is not yet a hundred years since the creation of United Italy. Not only have the provinces retained their own traditions of cookery, but many of their products remain localized.

In London or Paris can be found . . . the best of everything which England and France produces. In Italy the best fish is actually to be eaten on the coast, the finest Parmesan cheese in Parma, the tenderest beef in Tuscany . . . How many transatlantic travellers landing in Genoa have dined in some Grand Hotel . . . and gone on their way without ever suspecting that Genoa possesses a cookery of a most highly individual nature, unique in Europe? Everyone has heard of the *mortadella* sausage of Bologna, but how many hurrying motorists drive past the rose and ochre coloured arcades of Bologna quite unaware that behind modest doorways are some of the best restaurants in Italy?

Forty-five years later many Italians will still tell you first the province from which they originate before informing you that they are Italian. This regionalism has long been recognized in Italy as a problem as much as a virtue. Its days may be numbered.

Jane Grigson, a friend of Elizabeth and one of the few cookery writers of a younger generation who was as literate and as fierce against fuss as she, said of *Italian Food*: 'Elizabeth was the first person to tell us why Italian food works in certain ways. She points out that . . . Italy is dominated by regionalism in a way that France isn't . . . When you begin to see Italian food like that the whole picture clears and you begin to understand how it works and why you put certain things together. She did the same for French food; she taught us about the background to eating.'

In her introduction to *Italian Food* Elizabeth continues: 'In Italy, therefore, it is always worth finding out what is to be had in the locality in the way of wines, cheeses, hams, sausages, fruit, and vegetables. They should be asked for . . .' In appreciating this she cannot help but notice something which in Italy one never tires of; that

The beautiful colours of their food is one most characteristic point. The vivid scarlet dishes of the south, the tomato sauce and the pimientos, the oranges and pinks of fish soups, the red and white of a Neapolitan *pizza*, contrast strikingly with the unique green food of central and northern Italy; the spinach *gnocchi* of Tuscany . . . the green *pesto* sauce of Genoa, the green peas and rice of the Veneto, green artichokes in pies, in omelettes, in salads; the green and yellow marbled stuffings of rolled beef and veal dishes – such food can scarcely fail to charm.

A vignette, written as Elizabeth's sensuous response to the unerringly successful Italian combinations of colour, shape and taste, was put into one of her articles for *Vogue* a few years later.

A handsome round white dish, quite flat, entirely covered with slices of pale rose Parma ham, cut so thin as to be almost transparent, with edgings of opaque silky white fat; in the centre a little pyramid of purple figs fresh from the tree, their honey-sweet flesh bursting here and there through their skins; a glass of fresh, cool white wine.

She called this the 'most perfect of all hors d'oeuvres'. And in the introduction of the chapter on Hors d'Oeuvre and Salads she wrote that 'Among Italian *antipasti* (hors d'oeuvre) are to be found some of the most successful culinary achievements in European cooking.' Of Parma and San Daniele ham she said they were 'at their best perhaps the most delicious hams in the world . . .'

An anecdote incorporated into the *Vogue* piece attests to Elizabeth's stubbornness and insistence on what was 'right' in food. Little did the 'magisterial assistant' of the 'celebrated store' realize with whom he was contending when he told her that to cut the Parma ham 'in doorsteps', as she said he was doing, was correct. 'I left him in undisputed possession of his massacred ham and his individual notions, wondering what would have been the reaction of the Italian friend who was so frequently my host in Rome and whom I had known to send her cook back to the shop with the *prosciutto di Parma* because it was only as thin as writing paper, whereas, she maintained, it should be perfectly transparent.' Viola Johnson was capable of being almost as formidable as Elizabeth.

In direct relation to the regional nature of Italian food Elizabeth mentions something which is a vital aspect of her book. 'But at the same time it should be borne in mind that as in any country which relies largely on its own agricultural produce, the seasonal character of the food remains intact.' On revising the book in 1963, in spite of her sorrow at the advent, since 1954, of the deep-freeze, she believed that this was still largely the case. Awareness of and respect for the seasons in cooking was already one of Elizabeth's tenets, and its discovery at the heart of Italian cooking was a happy one and something she tried to convey throughout *Italian Food*.

> There are dishes which are made in certain seasons or for certain festivals and at no other time of the year. Heavy winter dishes such as the *polenta pasticciata* of Lombardy, the *lasagne verdi al forno* of Bologna and the brown bean soup of the Veneto give way after Easter to lighter dishes of *pasta in brodo*, or *antipasti* . . . of raw vegetables, or little *crostini*, fried bread with cheese and anchovies.

Together with her descriptions of 'how to get the best out of Italian food in whichever province one happens to find oneself', these were messages taken to heart by many readers on visits to Italy. And Elizabeth wrote: 'This is reward enough for the work I put into the book.'

For the first time she was permitted to give a [brief] bibliography and demonstrated how she had made herself conversant with the Italian literature on the subject, both ancient and modern: *Cuoco Secreto di Papa Quinto* (1579) by the famed Bartolomeo Scappi, cook to Pope Pius V; *La scienza in Cucina e L'Arte di Mangiar Bene* (1890) by Pellegrino Artusi; *Il Talismano della Felicita* (c. 1932) by Ada Boni, as Elizabeth truly describes it 'one of the great modern classics of Italian household and regional cookery'. Amongst the several other books was the Touring Club Italiano, one of the several guides to food and wine which she cited. An enlightened Italian attempt at recording and thereby preserving regional Italian food, Elizabeth found it invaluable in her researches and itinerary planning. She combined her reading of all these to give, in two succinct, useful and elegant pages, the history of Italian food. At the beginning of the book, in 'The Italian Store Cupboard', she tells the reader with her usual practical and {increasingly} historical thoroughness what is essential to Italian cooking. For the 1963 revised edition, at the end of the chapter she attached the whereabouts of purveyors of Italian produce, there now being a sufficiently large number to give 'a cross-section'.

In 1963 she wrote that 'On the whole I think it is easier to find the best Italian cooking in Italy than to come by its English equivalent in our own country.' The tide in favour of all things Italian which Elizabeth described as turning between the publication of *Italian Food* in 1954 and its first revision in 1963 did not abate. In the last thirty years it could be described as having become a tidal wave. The best of the myriad eating houses which now serve menus based on Italian can be excellent; the majority, however, still produce Italian food which runs from the mediocre to travesty.

After months of labour the book was nearing completion and Elizabeth made a trip to Scotland for a couple of weeks to write up the index with Lesley O'Malley's help. She and Lesley set off for a working holiday in a friend's borrowed bungalow on the West Coast of Scotland. 'On their way up to Plocton they stayed with us,' Mary Abercrombie told the author. Her husband David (then running the newly-formed phonetics department at Edinburgh University) was an old friend from Cairo. 'David had once left a party with Elizabeth when she had said: "If you're not doing anything come and have pot luck." Pot luck turned out to be roast suckling pig!'

It rained solidly for two weeks and when they got back to Edinburgh they greeted the pavements with joy, put on their 'walking shoes' and spent the day doing the antique shops of Edinburgh. During that same visit 'We ran out of mayonnaise at lunch, my son and I fled to the kitchen and made some on the spot, winding the egg beater. We felt very daring giving Elizabeth mayonnaise made with a metal spoon. She said it "wasn't bad", and we breathed again.'

In the Penguin introduction to the book there are some hints which on careful reading reveal their barbs. Elizabeth felt she had suffered from most shabby treatment at the hands of her publishers during the making of the book. And, justified though she was, one notices the litigious Gwynne in her asserting itself again. Once

Elizabeth felt that she had been wronged her sense of outrage could rarely allow the matter to rest. During 1953 and the writing of *Italian Food* John Lehmann's ailing publishing firm ground to a halt. In spite of being one of the most entrepreneurial and prestigious contemporary publishing names Lehmann was making a loss, and the printers Purnell told him they couldn't subsidize him any longer. The final insult came in a meeting of directors when Lehmann was told, 'What we need, Mr Lehmann, is a few rattling good yarns', at which he left in frustration and fury.

Another more aggressively market-orientated and hence financially successful firm under the Purnell aegis was Macdonald. They had been offered Lehmann's list of authors by Purnell but had agreed to take on only two. One of these was the American Paul Bowles, already synonymous with Morocco, and acclaimed for his novel *The Sheltering Sky*. The second was Elizabeth. She was furious, but could do nothing to extract herself from what she felt were Macdonald's clutches. (Bowles, much cannier, quickly escaped from his contractual obligations to Macdonald.)

As a result *Italian Food* was not published under the John Lehmann imprint but instead that of Macdonald. Elizabeth's ire was still sufficient for her to vent some of it in her Penguin introduction ten years later. She was good enough to call Macdonald 'endlessly patient and generous in the matter of production' but she let it be known that they had 'looked at it coldly. I had been a long time about it – it was twice as long as they had been led to expect ... paper shortage ... printing costs ... they hoped the expenditure would be justified.'

Macdonald's chief director, Eric Harvey, was a ruthless operator whose foremost interest was sales, and on delivery of her manuscript he said, 'Do you mean to say that Mr Lehmann contracted to pay you £300 for this book? For a *cookery* book? No wonder his firm wasn't paying. Ah well, let's hope we get our money back.' As it turned out they did, many times over. Harvey's treatment of Elizabeth still rankled more than thirty years on and so she recorded some of the details in the final edition of *Mediterranean Food* published in 1987, saying that Macdonald had 'certainly proved a sorry exchange for John'. Elizabeth knew how to use her pen in reprisal and never hesitated to do so. And, like any Gwynne, she was a formidable opponent.

While she was writing *Summer Cooking* Macdonald approached her to ask if she was interested in an offer Penguin had made them to publish *Mediterranean Food* in paperback. Rather to Macdonald's surprise and in spite of indignation at the meagre 50 per cent of the royalty she would be given, Elizabeth jumped at the chance of extra circulation. She wanted to spread her message, and also needed the money. She was always most keen to see her books in as many venues as possible and complained about her publisher's unwillingness, or inability, to do this better. As well as the 'vastly increased readership' she knew Penguin would bring her, Elizabeth always wanted 'a younger one which would include students, young married couples and many professional women sharing flats or living on their own but still needing to cook for themselves and to give the occasional dinner party ... the paperback was to be 2/6, a price within the reach of nearly everybody'.

Perhaps most important of all was the fact that apart from Bee Nilson's perfectly respectable but uninspiring wartime book the *ABC of Cookery*, *Mediterranean Food* would be one of the few paperback cookery books on the English market. This was thanks to the enlightened efforts of Eunice Frost at Penguin. The only woman director, with the support of Allen Lane, the firm's founder, she had stubbornly pushed through the offer to Macdonald.

Interestingly, the biographical details of the author on the back cover of the Penguin book take careful account of the contemporary anti-German climate of opinion: Elizabeth went to school 'in Switzerland' rather than her actual stint with the aristocratic German family in Munich in the Thirties.

The reviews for *Italian Food* could not have been more gratifying, with praise from culinary luminaries such as Margaret Lane. More impressively, the grand old man of wine and food, André Simon himself, wrote: 'It is the pattern of what a cook book ought to be which introduces the fare and wines of a land foreign to its readers; it is informative and reliable without any traces of pedantry; it is valuable because of the first hand knowledge and original appraisal passed on to the reader with ease and grace.'

But *Italian Food* was more than an exemplary cookbook, and consequently the praise from writers of more literary genres than the one with which cookery books were then usually associated was of still greater importance. These were people who were seeing in Elizabeth's books the writer as much as the cook, and this refers to more than her style alone, consummate though it could be. Those of her audience who were not primarily cooks recognized that here was no mere collector of recipes. The distinguished traveller and writer Freya Stark was amongst this group, but most pleasing of all for Elizabeth was the accolade from Evelyn Waugh. In the Penguin revised edition she wrote that 'When Mr Evelyn Waugh, a writer whose books have given me more pleasure than I have powers to acknowledge, actually named this book in the *Sunday Times* as one of the two which in the year 1954 had given *him* the most pleasure I was, and still am, stunned by the compliment and by Mr Waugh's tolerance of my amateur's efforts.'

Ingratiating herself didn't sit well with Elizabeth, and knowing her personal style the reference to herself as amateur is irritating, however much it falls into a respectable rhetorical tradition. She was no amateur, and no one who knew her or her work would have thought her one; certainly Waugh recognized that that was precisely what she was not. However, as he was for many of her generation arguably the greatest living English writer – she had recently crowed with delight at having wheedled a proof copy of his latest novel out of her friend Archie Lyall in Rome – the praise could not have been more gratifying.

CHAPTER SIXTEEN

Summer Cooking *and Consolidation*
(1955–1960)

DURING THE COURSE of 1954, while waiting for *Italian Food* to go through the first stages of production and printing, Elizabeth had been at work on a new book, one which she later described as 'less taxing'. So incensed had she been by Macdonald's treatment of her that this time she would publish with another firm, the Museum Press. Called *Summer Cooking*, this little book was another attempt to encourage the English to look at the principle which Elizabeth had seen at work in the Mediterranean and France and again repeatedly in Italy during the previous year: that the preparation of the right food at the right time and in the right place was the most desirable way to live. She described the object of this new collection of recipes as providing dishes 'with emphasis on two aspects of cookery which are increasingly disregarded: the suitability of certain foods to certain times of the year, and the pleasure of eating vegetables, fruit, poultry, meat or fish which is in season, therefore at its best, most plentiful, and cheapest'.

In her introduction to the revised Penguin edition ten years after the book's first publication in 1955, Elizabeth's argument is substantially the same but, with an enormous increase in the English consumption of frozen and convenience foods, she makes her point more forcefully this time:

> As I understand it, summer cooking means the extraction of maximum enjoyment out of the produce which grows in the summer season and is appropriate to it. It means catching at the opportunity of eating fresh food freshly cooked. It means

appreciation of treats such as new peas, fresh little carrots, the delicate courgettes now home produced and to me as delicious as the finest asparagus. There are ... omelettes flavoured with fresh green chives, chervil, tarragon, parsley ... a few heads of purple-sprouting broccoli or a pound of tender little string beans cooked for just seven minutes, to be eaten cold – as a separate course, with an olive oil and lemon dressing – but quickly, almost before they have cooled.

She explains that because many think summer is for cold food, this does not mean that it should be 'over-refrigerated lifeless food'.

After the months of financial worry and what had often seemed like gorging herself in Italy – 'Italians are on the whole abstemious drinkers but big eaters' – Elizabeth could enjoy writing a little book which had no obligation to tourist boards or magazines. *Summer Cooking* is a lovely varied collection of pieces from around her travels. A good number of course are from France and, with her recent discoveries very much in mind, several here could have gone into *Italian Food* ... Some are from her years in the Middle East, others still from the English tradition.

Accompanying the usual sections on soups, fish, meat, etc., there are also chapters on 'Jams ... and Other Preserves', 'Buffet Food', 'Improvised Cooking for Holidays' and 'Picnics'. There is also a chapter on eggs and an instructive and well-judged little essay devoted to fresh herbs, then sorely needed in England. There are mentions of angelica for salads, savory for broad beans, lovage for haricot beans: 'marjoram is almost essential to strew in small quantities on mutton, pork and lamb chops . . .' The next comment reveals in its necessary description how uncommon pizza then was in England.

> ... wild marjoram ... is an essential ingredient of the Neapolitan pizza, that colourful, filling, peasant dish of bread dough baked with tomatoes, anchovies and cheese ...
>
> Fennel ... has many uses besides the sauce for mackerel found in all old English cookery books ... there is a Tuscan

chicken dish in which the bird is stuffed with thick strips of
ham and pieces of fennel bulb and pot-roasted . . .

. . . the leaf of the sweet-scented geranium gives a lovely
scent to a lemon water ice and an incomparable flavour when
cooked with blackberries for jelly.

With reference to those dishes whose use of herbs reflect 'an
essential rather than an incidental flavouring', Elizabeth says that this
is something to which she wishes to

call attention, for it is this aspect of cookery which is passed over
by those writers who enjoin so much caution in the use of herbs.
Sometimes it is a good thing to forget that basil, parsley, mint,
tarragon, fennel, are all bunched together under the collective
word 'herbs' and to remember that the difference between leaf
vegetables . . . and herbs is very small, and indeed at one time
all these plants were known collectively as 'salad herbs'. Nobody
tells you to 'use spinach with caution', and neither can you be
'discreet with the basil' when you are making *pesto* sauce, because
the basil is the essential flavouring . . .

She uses again the recipe from *Italian Food*, but here without the
comment that the Genoese 'claim that their basil has a far superior
flavour to that grown in any other part of Italy, and assert that a good
pesto can only be made with Genoese basil'.

'How one learns to dread the season for salads in England.'
Perhaps at last, close to half a century after Elizabeth wrote this, we
can say that there are many in England who now know how to make
a good salad. There are still many who do not, but in 1955 Elizabeth's
dread was even better founded, for these latter made up the majority.
The following diatribe has a grim ring of truth to it: 'What becomes
of the hearts of lettuces?' (One is reminded of Theodora FitzGibbon's
search for animals' 'tongues, tails, hearts, kidneys, livers, or balls'.)
Elizabeth continued: 'What makes an English cook think that beetroot spreading its hideous purple dye over a sardine and a spoonful of
tinned baked beans constitutes an hors d'oeuvre?' She acidly questions

why we make the cold salmon, already beyond its best by the summer season, 'look even less appetizing than it is by serving it on a bed of lettuce leaves apparently rescued from the dustbin?' Anyway, Elizabeth preferred salmon trout, finding it 'one of the most delicate of all fishes'.

Dispensing with the endless instructions for lettuce salads in cookbooks she says that: 'it seems to me that there are only three absolutely essential rules to be observed: the lettuce must be very fresh; the vinegar in the dressing must be reduced to the absolute minimum; the dressing must be mixed with the lettuce only at the moment of serving'. An admirably precise and succinct description of a much mangled task. Her friend Sybille Bedford noticed that 'she always mixed salad with her hands, saying that this was the only way that every leaf was properly covered in dressing'. As for dressings, 'however mild the vinegar, I prefer lemon juice, and very little of it'. She next makes a swingeing attack, concluding with a typically tart finale: 'The grotesque prudishness and archness with which garlic is treated in this country has led to the superstition that rubbing the bowl with it before putting the salad in gives sufficient flavour. It rather depends whether you are going to eat the bowl or the salad.'

On the same theme she gives an invaluable list of instructions for the care of lettuces. Amongst these she advises that: 'Porothone food bags, which are now sold in most large stores and in stationers are excellent for keeping greenstuff fresh.' Elizabeth was always fascinated by any kind of simple new gadget or container and, knowing that her readership was now considerable, she enthusiastically mentioned them in her journalistic pieces. Judith Lassalle recalls her excitement at the advent of tin foil. 'She loved all those new things as they came out. I remember her holding up a Pyrex dish and saying, "You can actually hold something up and see when it's done." '

Regarding the preparation of summer food Elizabeth gave that same advice which had become her hallmark: keep the dishes simple, don't mix things when they can be left separate. Accordingly: 'The simplest hors d'oeuvres are the best, looking clean and fresh . . . When devising a mixed salad be careful not to overdo the number of ingredients . . . one of the nicest of country hors d'oeuvre is the

Genoese one of raw broad beans, rough salame sausage, and salty sheep's milk Sardo cheese; each of these things is served on a separate dish . . .'

She gives A Summer Hors d'Oeuvre:

A dish of long red radishes, cleaned, but with a little of the green leaves left on, a dish of mixed green and black olives, a plate of raw, round, small tomatoes, a dish of hard (not too hard) boiled eggs cut lengthways and garnished with a bunch of parsley, a pepper mill and a salt mill, lemons and olive oil on the table; butter, and fresh bread. Not very original perhaps, but how often does one meet with a really fresh and unmessed hors d'oeuvre?

Paupiettes of Sole in Lettuce is an elegantly simple and delicious recipe using cooked prawns and sole fillets rolled up in lettuce leaves; it is followed by several more for that same fish. From the chef of one of the most understatedly elegant establishments in Italy, the Gritti Palace Hotel in Venice, fillets of *John Dory Marechiaro* shows Elizabeth's ease with unpretentious grandness. Her next recipe for the earthy *Routes à la Provençal*, or the utterly simple herring – 'A plain grilled herring really fresh is one of the most delicious of fish' – shows the skill with which she could migrate from complex sophistication to total simplicity.

Her Spiced Grilled Chicken, a variation on the Indian 'kubab' chicken, is a refreshing and interesting change from the simpler European ways of grilling the bird. She had adapted the recipe from a recondite nineteenth-century gem entitled *Indian Domestic Economy and Receipt Book* (1850) which she had recently discovered. In 1955 when recommending this recipe chicken was a sought-after meat which had not yet been transformed into the tasteless, drug-packed batteried thing turned over to millions of supermarket customers in suffocating polystyrene packaging. Elizabeth could then write what now only pertains for free-range varieties: 'A grilled chicken is perhaps one of the nicest foods at any time . . . and although expensive . . . it could be much less rare than it is.' As well as a large number of French chicken dishes, there is an Italian fricassee, an English Parsley Pie and a Grouse Pudding, the last two from the *Cookery Book* of the estimable Lady Clark of Tillypronie whose posthumously published recipes Elizabeth later described as valuable for their ideas, historical aspect and 'the feeling of authenticity, the certainty that these recipes were actually used and the dishes successful.'

A stock made from old grouse can be used in several delicious ways, 'notably for stewing mushrooms', and in the vegetable chapter we find Mushrooms Cooked in Grouse Stock; but for Mushrooms Cooked in Cream we must turn to 'Improvised Cooking for Holidays', as much because of Elizabeth's association of this dish with the idyllic aspects of her childhood at Wootton as because any holidaying reader might really find them out in the fields: 'To make a really good dish of mushrooms in cream very fresh little button mushrooms from the field are needed.'

'Sweets' is replete with light, simple, enticing little dishes redolent of English summer days and evenings at their best. Fresh fruit purées, mousses, creams, fools and ices, made of strawberries, gooseberries, blackcurrants, redcurrants, raspberries, apricots and cherries. The traditional open French fruit pies are there, as are melons stuffed with raspberries, Sugared Nectarines, and Crémets d'Angers to be presented in those little heart-shaped moulds. Lemon Ice Cream. Chocolate Chinchilla with its earliest of chocolate's accompaniments, cinnamon, and that quintessential English dish Summer Pudding: 'Although nearly everybody knows of this wonderful pudding, authentic recipes for it are rare . . . Thick cream is sometimes served with summer pudding but it is usually served without.'

'Cold Spiced Beef, Shooter's Sandwich, Bacon and Lettuce Sandwiches, Figs and Cream cheese'. From one of her earliest articles written years before for *Harpers Bazaar* Elizabeth extracted and expanded a little essay wittily and authoritatively instructing the reader on how to make the perfect picnic. These instructions, followed by the few recipes, are a dialogue with her own past and are there to inspire, to stimulate the reader's imagination as much as any precise rules which can be followed: 'As for the food, preparing it always seems to me half the fun. The possibilities are almost without limit, and fantasies can be indulged.' She tells us that on the whole elegant food is to be eschewed in favour of the rustic. 'The simpler charms of salame sausage, fresh cheese, black olives and crusty French bread are enhanced when they are eaten on the hillside or the seashore.'

Summer Cooking concludes with six pages of extracts from those who have written on the art of the picnic, a pastime the English have always approached with particular thoroughness. The practice of using other authors sometimes assists the writer only in revealing the inadequacy of his or her own means of expression. Needless to say, Elizabeth excelled at it. Being well read, she was able to select with an informed mind, knew who to turn to, where and when, and one only wishes for more. She would have made a fine anthologist. From the start, in both her *Harpers* articles and *Mediterranean Food*, she appreciated how to surround the atmospheric prose she was creating with passages which added to the texture and weight of her own writing. Here one is reminded of that presumption pervading her work and inherent to the reader's understanding of her art, that we will share a knowledge of at least some of her material. The passages of quotation, sometimes only tenuously related to the topic, will nevertheless find a sympathetic and eager audience in many of her readers. Henry James tells us that a perfect picnic must be 'not so good as to fail of an amusing disorder, nor yet so bad as to defeat the proper function of repasts'. We have Ford Madox Ford picnicking in pre-war Provence, William Hickey [*père*] with the Archbishop of Canterbury and Mrs Beeton's 'Bill of Fare for Forty Persons'.

Indian picnics are recorded for us by one of Elizabeth's favourites, the redoubtable nineteenth-century Colonel A. R. Kenney-Herbert ['Wyvern']. From his *Culinary Jottings from Madras* (Higginbotham and Co., 1948) come: 'A nice piece of the brisket of beef salted and spiced . . . is a very handy thing for a tiffin basket; and a much respected patron of mine recommends . . . a really good cold plum pudding in which a glass of brandy has been included.' This naturally leads into Elizabeth's own experience of Indian picnics and she regales us with the disastrous evening beside the Qutb Minar outside New Delhi.

Next she tells us about the *fellucah* party:

An agreeable form of picnic taken in Cairo . . . on board a hired
Nile sailing boat Arab servants would carry the food; there were

copper trays of pimentos, small marrows [courgettes, such favourites of Elizabeth's] and vine leaves stuffed with rice, large, round shallow metal dishes filled with meat and spiced pilaff, bowls of grapes and peaches and figs and melons cooled with lumps of ice . . . there would be music and the wailing of Arab songs as the boat swung rather wildly about, the crew made Turkish coffee and we drank the odd . . . red Egyptian wine . . .

Elizabeth is calling up her past for us, one *fellucah* party in particular spent out on the Nile reclining on cushions with George Lassalle, Romney Summers, and Robin Fedden 'prancing up and down [according to Lassalle] like an elegant monkey in the rigging'.

The release from the quotidian, the sophisticated game of make-believe necessary for picnics to succeed, was a fantasy in which Elizabeth loved to indulge. Her sense of irony, her wit – not infrequently a masquerade, the protective shield of the sophisticate – she held always at the ready. The conclusion to *Summer Cooking* is made by Bernard Berenson's brother-in-law Logan Pearsall Smith. Elizabeth selects the piece on 'The Ideal Picnic' from his *All Trivia* in which he expresses both his exasperation with England (he was settled here, an Anglophile American) and his projection of a vision, only partially ironic. He has returned, disillusioned, from a day's wet picnicking and says: 'If I had dreamed a dream incompatible with the climate and social conditions of these islands, had I not, out of that very dream and disenchantment, created, like the Platonic Lover, a Platonic and imperishable vision – the Ideal Picnic . . . the wonderful windless weather, a Watteauish landscape, where a group of mortals talk and feast as they talked and feasted in the Golden Age.'

Elizabeth creates a unity out of a huge range of social and cultural elements. She presumes that the elements of food which she singles out . . . the bottled pimentos on Capri, the octopus of the Greek islands, the wild mushrooms of her childhood . . . these and their like will resonate for others; as also the people whose characters come briefly and vividly alive for us as individuals or types: Norman Douglas, Kyriakou the deep-sea diver cook in Alexandria, Mafalda of the red peppers on Capri. And finally there is the context in which the food and people are set, the places, the countries themselves.

These are the building blocks she uses in creating that single extended work of art which is – far more than with most writers – her whole body of writing.

During 1954, while *Italian Food* was going through the press and Elizabeth was writing *Summer Cooking*, a young man, Terence Conran, was launching himself into a related venture, a King's Road coffee bar-restaurant which he called The Orrery. An orrery is a clockwork model of the solar system whose name derives from the seventeenth-century Earl of Orrery; one of them hung from the ceiling of the restaurant. Conran said subsequently that he was much influenced by Elizabeth's books. The coffee bar in 1950s England – with modern furniture, an Italian espresso machine and its appeal to the now more solvent young – was sufficiently novel and prevalent for the *Architectural Review* to run a feature on the phenomenon. The Orrery, with its young proprietor, was included in the article. His aim was to serve not only espresso coffee, but also a small menu of good simple food, including a few soups, omelettes, perhaps a fruit flan, good French bread, and all at reasonable prices.

Conran had trained at the Central School of Art as a textile designer, but under the democratizing influence of the Bauhaus he rapidly extended his vision beyond simply designing materials to the concept of complete interiors. His métier was the marketing of simple, effective and affordable designs for the high street rather than élite artistic salons. His creative genius lay in the area of public communication: he was selling a vision, a way of life, not a collection of items. So was Elizabeth, but Conran, as befitted the next generation, was more clear-headed about what he was doing. From the outset he was aware that he was appealing to the rapidly growing mass-middle class . . . middle-class in taste, whatever their professed opinions and however modest their incomes. *Mediterranean Food* was originally addressed to an élite, but by the time of the first Penguin paperback (1955), Terence Conran and Elizabeth were speaking to the same loosely constituted but large social group.

The orrery was the kind of learned gadget which appealed to the austere natural philosopher sages of seventeenth-century England. By the mid-twentieth century Terence Conran had the wit to realize that an element of antiquarian science could be presented as fun. In 1953 he had travelled for the first time to France with several friends, staying in a cottage in the Dordogne owned by Nancy Cunard, Thirties socialite and eternal rebel. Talking and drinking 'the roughest red wine' Conran told the author he had ever tasted, 'She was finishing her book on her old friend Norman Douglas and talked about him a good deal.' Conran was struck by 'the plenitude of France compared to grey England. For someone who had grown up in England during the war, going across the Channel, and the further south you went, where there were piles of aubergines, lemons, peppers, garlic – nobody had *heard* of it in England. The ordered disorder of masses of cooking equipment muddled up with hammers and saws, nails, everyday things you could see all around you in the markets and iron mongers. Simple, wonderful, practical, durable designs in the little shops and markets as well. Piles of porcelain and flowers and plants.' The more robust life-style of rural France, with an easier sensuality than could be found in England, was something Conran was trying to suggest in his coffee shop. This holiday and his subsequent visits to the cafés, little shops and markets of Paris made a lasting impression upon him.

Since those first ventures Conran had prospered, and when Veronica Nicholson's friend and neighbour Walter Baxter needed a designer for his new restaurant, the Chanterelle, Conran was the young man he chose. The restaurant was credited by the *Architectural Review* with having an instant air of 'sophistication and solid comfort . . . by the use of natural woods and finishes combined with a warm but subdued colour theme'. Throughout the Fifties the Chanterelle remained one of the best and most favoured restaurants in London. Patrick Woodcock remembers that it was at the Chanterelle in the later 1950s that he met Elizabeth one day with friends.

'She was wearing a beautiful black dress and was very pulled together. We were all sipping away and we got on well, so I asked her to dinner with the councillor to the French Embassy, Gerard André. It was because of him that she got the French order of the onion.' (Patrick Woodcock refers here to Elizabeth's being honoured as a Chevalier du Mérite Agricole some years later.) Patrick and

Elizabeth became close friends and she later stayed in his house in the South of France. Patrick is generous and perceptive, with a talent for friendship, and his observations on Elizabeth are some of the more enlightening of those made by her friends. Patrick was friendly with a number of the better English artists of the time, including Keith Vaughan, John Craxton, Robert MacBride and John Minton, who had illustrated Elizabeth's first two books. 'She was this curious academic figure, too. In her way she knew herself to be a great comic figure. She was a great sender-up, had such a sense of humour. She was awfully funny.'

Summer Cooking was published with illustrations and dust-jacket by Adrian Daintrey. Daintrey, never more than a moderate artist, turned out some truly mediocre work for *Summer Cooking*, and the portrait drawing he did of Elizabeth, used on the inside of the dust-jacket, is similarly uninspired. Nevertheless, the book's content was acclaimed as another fine Elizabeth David achievement, confirming her position not only as one of the foremost cookery writers of the day, but also as someone to be read on the Mediterranean – as useful abroad as a good travel writer.

In the summer of 1955 Elizabeth was asked by Leonard Russell, long-standing Literary Editor of the *Sunday Times*, if she would join the paper as a cookery columnist. She agreed, but despite her liking and respect for Leonard Russell her column in the *Sunday Times* also brought her up against someone who proved to be one of her most unpleasant adversaries and whom she grew to hate unreservedly.

Ernestine Carter was that formidable journalist, by now editor of the *Sunday Times* women's pages, with whom Elizabeth had already crossed in the Parisian hotel just after the war. One might guess that Mrs Carter's attempts to decapitate Elizabeth's work were a sustained effort of reprisal. It seems, however, that she applied the same tyrannical methods to all her contributors. More than one talented female journalist has observed, like Alix Coleman, that 'as soon as you began to do well Ernestine began to cut your work'. Suicide for the paper, one would have thought, but there were always those prepared to step in when others, defeated, had left.

Elizabeth had herself been a 'tetchy' contributor when Anne Scott-James was editor at *Harpers Bazaar* (by 1951 Eileen Dickson had taken over and Anne had gone on to the *Sunday Express*). As she had observed, not only Elizabeth's prose seemed to have sprung from her fully formed but her sense of 'being someone too'. Clearly from the beginning Elizabeth commanded respect – albeit sometimes qualified by irritation or fear – but her insistence that her work should remain unaltered made more than one hard-working editor's hackles rise over the years. Her inability to function comfortably in a team came about because to an extent she lacked the imagination and the ability to stand outside herself. Protecting The Word, her art no less, inevitably made writing journalism problematic both for herself and any editor who employed her. She enjoyed the power journalism gave her to disseminate her message, but was not happy for this message to be constrained by the relentless demands of a page layout.

After six years under Ernestine Carter, however, although never in the least servile or manipulable Elizabeth had become a little more willing to accommodate herself to the needs of an editor. For the thirty years that she wrote journalism, some of it very good and much of it influential, she was never truly comfortable in the role. She was too much the innovator, the maker, whereas the good journalist remains a purveyor of messages, not (in his journalism at least) the creator of them. Elizabeth was too much of an artist to be satisfied by simply purveying her own message, she also needed time to create it.

Through her journalism and the popularity of her books Elizabeth spoke to more and more people. Her initial audience was that fairly small number of people, an élite, with whom her writing had in a sense been a group collaboration of responses to shared interests and social background. As time passed, as The Word which was the Mediterranean was spread by Elizabeth's books, the circle of her élite devotees began to extend until gradually her converts came from a broader audience, the same audience which Terence Conran had quickly identified. The lively middle-class young of post-war England may not have experienced that passionate pre-war contact with the Mediterranean which Elizabeth expressed for her generation, but others like Conran shared enough – travel abroad to France and beyond – to find her books a practical means to an expansion of themselves.

By 1956 Elizabeth had agreed to two other journalistic commitments. Audrey Withers had been up at Somerville and after Oxford had made the rapid transition from 25 shillings-a-week girl at Bumpus, bookshop to the rich and aristocratic, to editorship of the oracle of style, *Vogue*. A discerning and hard-working editor of the magazine since 1940, Audrey Withers had long been an admirer of Elizabeth's writing. She told the author: 'In 1956 we got in touch with her. She was immediately recognizable as a person you couldn't push, so we wooed her.' Audrey succeeded, and Elizabeth left *Harpers* to write a monthly article not only for *Vogue* but also for another of Condé Nast's sister publications recently brought to England, *House and Garden*. For the next several years Elizabeth's energies went into journalism: with the *Sunday Times*, *Vogue*, *House and Garden* and other pieces here and there she became a skilled professional with a flourishing and mounting following. Her trips abroad, even when not directly on behalf of a journal, usually ended by finding their way into her writing. In that sense she was deeply autobiographical, she never wrote about what she hadn't experienced.

Remembering a trip to France in 1955 with her husband, Audrey reminds one how Elizabeth's articles for *Vogue* about the largesse of France and the Mediterranean were as uplifting to her readers as her first articles for *Harpers* had been in 1949. 'We went to a food fair whilst in the South of France and it was so extraordinary seeing all that agricultural produce. And butter, still so rare in England. We could have bought mountains of it. We had so little spending money compared to the rest of Europe that on that holiday we could hardly afford to buy a cup of coffee.'

When Audrey Withers had asked Elizabeth to write for *Vogue*, they agreed she would begin with a series of twelve articles, one each month, on 'the finest foods in season'. The first one, 'Food at its Best in May', set the precedent. 'It was', said Audrey Withers, 'a straightforward account of what she considered met the title description and how it should be cooked. It occupied a full page in the centre of the magazine . . . continued on two turns, and was faced by a full-page colour photograph by Anthony Denney . . . illustrating one of the dishes she described.' Elizabeth had initially said to Audrey, 'You can't do colour pictures of food. I think they're bloody awful.' (And so they were at that time.) Elizabeth was emphatic that the photographs wouldn't work in studio conditions and at her insistence they were all done at Halsey Street. 'Audrey gave it such a lot of room . . . Audrey was the first to put my articles in the middle of the magazine with a picture.' Elizabeth felt she was being treated as her work deserved. There was of course, as Audrey Withers knew, something less than straightforward going on in Elizabeth's articles. They were not simply well-written recipes got up in pretty prose; Elizabeth's writing was throughout a crusade, a cry to the English to make more of life. And here her considerable skill as a writer was revealed. Bearing in mind her temperament, it is notable how she refrains from the temptation of easy victories by deploying her acerbic wit: instead it is a sustained crusade of seduction, not one of assault.

> According to tradition it is in the month of May that all the spring vegetables come in; duckling and green peas, followed by green gooseberry tart, should be the Sunday treat, and the scents of mint and buttery potatoes fill the kitchen. The opportunity to enjoy these first fruits of summer is to be seized with both hands . . . Tiny broad beans, baby peas, miniature carrots and early asparagus are best prepared in the plainest and most obvious way, cooked in the minimum of water and served with butter melting over them as they come to the table.

Elizabeth tells us that the obvious choice for the main course is lamb or spring chicken 'split in half, coated with oil, and grilled'. And as she has written before, she says that 'few dishes are more delicious'. The basic ingredients she has described are English; they have to be because the point she is making is one about 'catching the moment as it flies', something she once told her sister Priscilla from her Greek island that she was so good at. Freshness from each season and in spring and early summer . . . 'the tenderness of very early youth' . . . is the basis of her food. In her *Vogue* articles the elements she uses to make a more complex picture are more often than not from abroad, especially France or Italy. The salami for the Genoese hors d'oeuvre she loved, with its requirement of the pungent sheep's cheese, Sardo, were imported, but so long as they came from a reputable shop could be almost as good as in their homeland. The third and simpler element, broad beans, came fresh from the reader's local English greengrocer; Elizabeth's respect for freshness and how to harness it is at the heart of her message.

The recipes themselves throughout the first *Vogue* articles are for dishes mostly French, sometimes Italian and English, occasionally other. For June there is Cucumber and Prawn Salad, French Beans and Tunny Fish; July offers Iced Sorrel Soup [Russian], *Langouste en Brochettes*, Herb Gumbo [Creole]; for August: 'Holiday Cookery in hired houses, the picnic season, huge breakfasts for hungry children, are upon us . . . Cold ham, or bacon and spiced beef in the larder is invaluable because it is acceptable to children and grown-ups, whether for breakfast, luncheon, tea, supper or picnics . . .'

Times have changed and Elizabeth's words here read almost like something from a previous age, but her justified fascination with things like spiced beef remained. It was she who inspired the Harrods master butcher Mr Ducat to make it again from the recipe she gave him and printed in the Christmas number of *Vogue*, in 1958. Its popularity was instant and the beef sold in vast quantities. Elizabeth described it as 'one of the very best in the whole repertory of our national cookery'.

September has *Ratatouille Niçoise, Poulet Sauté aux Olives de Provence*, English Field Mushrooms, Blackberry Water Ice and the extraordinary Buttered Grouse, for which she says: 'Have the courage to serve . . . quite alone in its beauty, for any salad, sauce, watercress or other accompaniment would simply get in the way.' For years to come Elizabeth continued to berate the English for their suspicion of the admirable French habit of eating dishes unadorned, in splendid isolation. Related to this was Escoffier's guiding principle, 'Faites Simples', which in turn produced Elizabeth's article for the *Spectator* in 1961 entitled, 'Letting Well Alone'. As an inspired young cookery writer, Jane Grigson, said of the English: 'They always love to gussy things up.'

In October's *Vogue* Elizabeth is talking of late harvests and partridge, grouse, hare and the first pheasants of the season. 'English autumn vegetables and . . . imported aubergines are still abundant, the first chestnuts, onions bought from the Breton onion boys' (in the days when they sailed across the Channel and rode around the English countryside selling them from their bicycles). She sings of 'home-grown Comice pears' and celebrates the quince, 'that curiously scented and beautiful fruit, hanging golden and ripe in English orchards, ready to be made into jellies and marmalades, creams, pies and preserves'. Elizabeth always loved the quince, associating it as other Europeans do with some of the best-loved traditions of each of their countries, and she wrote often about this singular fruit.

In December she says: 'As to the more substantial part of the Christmas cooking, the turkeys and goose must go to their inevitable fates in the oven. Every year . . . the thousands upon thousands of English women cooking, for one week of the year, as if for their very lives, patiently chopping and pounding . . .' Elizabeth tells us that these women, skinning, mixing and stuffing, with their 'mountains of brussels sprouts, cannot but command respectful admiration'. Lukewarm praise for those gargantuan efforts. Elizabeth cannot hide her distaste for English Christmas fare and in confirmation gives recipes entirely untypical: pâtés and terrines. The fact was that she hated Christmas turkey, loathed Brussels sprouts, and had said before and was saying again, by implication, that English women would do better to look to the quality of their simpler daily fare rather than this unique impressive annual burst of effort. Many years later in her beautiful book *Spices, Salt and Aromatics in the English Kitchen*, she used some of this article to vent her real feelings on the subject in a delightful piece describing the dinner she prepared for her Greek neighbours on Syros with Charles for that Christmas of 1941.

In May 1957 Elizabeth began another series for Audrey Withers. This came about because 'during the course of the previous year Elizabeth and I had often discussed her contributions. Early on she had only wanted to give us recipes. It was only when we began talking that I realised how interesting, how witty she was and how varied was her experience of France. I felt that if her recipes incorporated the story of how she came by them her articles would be even more popular. I was wary but began to suggest that she could think of writing them in that way.'

Revolutionary for cookery articles though Elizabeth's *Vogue* articles were in having much more discursive material than recipes, she was still obliged to follow what she called 'the strait-jacket of convention' – although with considerably more freedom under Audrey

Withers than was permitted to other cookery writers at that time. Elizabeth described the convention thus in *An Omelette and a Glass of Wine*: 'The old routine had been to open with a short introductory piece relevant to the products of the season, or to one particular type of dish ... or it might deal with the cookery of a specific region of France or of Italy, or perhaps it might be a little moan ... about the poor quality of something or their rarity in the shops. Whatever it was, once the opening piece was dutifully concluded, you filled the rest of your space with appropriate recipes and that was that.'

In a posthumous tribute to Elizabeth, Audrey Withers wrote in *Convivium*, a quarterly dedicated to 'good eating', that she found her the most private person she had ever encountered. 'She had drawn a line around herself and it would be unwise to cross it without invitation. The question was, where exactly was that line.' But Audrey told the author she 'just knew that I mustn't intrude. I have never felt it so much with anyone else, but understood I had to tread so carefully, had to be very, very cautious. One had to respect her or it seemed she might bolt. I felt that there was such a protective fence around her. I can't therefore call her a friend.' These perceptive observations made by Audrey Withers were put into practice, she was a sensitive and facilitating editor; they paid off because Elizabeth agreed to write the French Regional Cookery Series on the 'more intimate personal lines' *Vogue*'s editor had suggested. She says: 'I felt the thrill of success.' These articles, combined with some from the *Sunday Times* written during the next four years, were eventually to form the heart of Elizabeth's next book, *French Provincial Cooking*.

The articles for the *Sunday Times* and for *Vogue* were the result of specific trips to France taken in these years. Elizabeth never drove, and in enlisting the help of someone who did, it was often her old friend Doreen Thornton whom she asked to accompany her. From the first the *Vogue* articles and those Elizabeth wrote for *House and Garden* were accompanied by photographs. Her earlier writing had been complemented by the illustrations of artists, such as John Minton. When she had some say over the matter, however, as with the illustrations for *Italian Food*, it was Elizabeth who had chosen to drop Minton, not the publisher Lehmann. Her liking for Minton was immaterial in her judgement that he picked up too much on the escapist theme present in her work. And although in 'decorating' *French Country Cooking*, Minton had put a little more emphasis on the informative aspects of the book rather than simply conveying an atmosphere, this was still not sufficient for what Elizabeth believed to be her purposes. She did not want the fantasy decoration of the Mediterranean but instead more of the reality. Guttuso's unromantic 'drawings' with their almost monumental quality were much more to Elizabeth's present taste. (Note the change of nomenclature under Elizabeth's influence. Minton's illustrations, like so many illustrations in books at this time, were described as 'decorations'.)

Notwithstanding that a certain level of fantasy was precisely what Elizabeth was purveying, she was doing more than that. Part of her early achievement lay in the fact that she was also translating that fantasy, that illusion, into a working reality; her recipes were, increasingly, to be used. Accordingly she wanted the illustrations to her work to be as much about information as atmosphere.

Anthony Denney and Elizabeth had already been friends for a number of years when he began taking the photographs to accompany her magazine articles. Denney started out as a painter, but after Audrey Withers had 'acquired' him to work for *Vogue* he became one of Condé Nast's major photographers. *Vogue* and *House and Garden* were full of his work. 'He was absolutely top of the tree, he was the best,' said a former *House and Garden* editor.

Denney was married and had three children before he divorced in 1950, after which his flamboyant homosexuality became common knowledge. During this period he graduated to interior designing; he knew 'everyone who was anyone in London society'. Denney's photographic assistant was the young Anthony Armstrong-Jones, later Lord Snowdon; clients included Jacqueline Kennedy and Aristotle Onassis – Denney decorated his yacht. His position as one of the arbiters of taste was sufficiently established for his houses to be photographed in some of the earlier books on 'style' to emanate from this period. He began to amass a large and valuable collection of modern art.

His photographs for Elizabeth's articles are amongst Denney's quietest and finest work, some of the best food photographs of the time. The problems of food photography had long been appreciated by magazines and book publishers but few had yet sufficiently understood how to solve them; Denney instinctively did. Their friendship was an important factor in the success of his and Elizabeth's partnership, and their shared visual sensitivity made for a considerable bond, a partnership then unique. Photography is not a substitute for still-life painting, but Denney's ability to capture and enhance aspects of Elizabeth's message is without doubt. It is also noticeable that as photographers like Denney gradually became more 'artistic', the worth of their images decreased. Too much soft focus, too much reliance on faux still-life compositions, corporate designer-led book imagery; all have trivialized much recent photography of food. Denney's photographs for Elizabeth in the Fifties and Sixties avoided these pitfalls and were often unlike anything seen before.

When Doreen drove Elizabeth on her French trips for *Vogue* and the *Sunday Times* Anthony usually came too, accompanied by his boyfriend; like Elizabeth, Anthony didn't drive. 'Anthony and Alex went in another car, neither did we drive in convoy. We'd arrange to meet up at some place for lunch or the hotel where we were going to stay for that night . . . Elizabeth and Anthony would spend ages talking about what to photograph, and then Anthony would take hours and hours doing it or get something in a flash that had happened by . . . A market stall piled up with things, waiting at some odd angle for the light to be just right, a sudden flock of geese walking past, a table after lunch.' The discussion of photographs for Elizabeth's articles was equally thorough when Denney was to take shots of made-up food; Elizabeth would cook the dishes, for example the pâtés and terrines, in Halsey Street, and they would then set about displaying them. Denney's photographs of food for Elizabeth were almost invariably taken *in situ*, a fact whose importance future photographers and designers underestimated.

In France: 'Oh, there were ructions,' says Doreen. 'They would sometimes forget to photograph something and have to go back and do it. It could be chaos . . . And Anthony would take those wonderful photographs. Once, after a morning's wait for the right shots, we'd driven to the next place and Anthony wailed, "Oh no! There was no film in the camera." Liz and I'd share a room. One day in the South of France we arrived at the hotel and she was hurling suitcases about. There was no calming her like that. And I said to Anthony, "*I* can't deal with her, you do it." *Something* was wrong. So Alex and I left them to it. We went in the car to the beach for a swim, it was lovely, and they were stranded.' There were few like Doreen who could withstand Elizabeth's real furies. But over the years Doreen remained consistent in her down-to-earth devotion to her friend; she remained equally determined not be to dominated by her. As a result not many knew Elizabeth so intimately and there were few whom she respected so much.

'Like her mother Stella, Elizabeth never minded in the least showing if she didn't like someone . . . her behaviour could be appalling . . .' One remembers the episodes like Elizabeth's near-vendetta with Ernestine Carter, who was obviously an unpleasant and difficult taskmaster on the *Sunday Times*, but Elizabeth's nature was not a forgiving one. Her need for revenge continued beyond the grave, in her posthumous page of diatribe against Mrs Carter's 'cutting shears'. However, it was more than simply anger; it was that same driving spirit which made her, in spite of her reticence, believe so absolutely in her work and defend it with messianic vigour. 'Elizabeth was different from *all* the other people,' says Doreen.

CHAPTER SEVENTEEN

French Provincial Cooking

(1960–1965)

WITH THE BIRTH of their first child in 1952 George and Judith Lassalle had moved out of London to a large house in Sandwich, but George retained a stall in Bermondsey Market selling antiques and books. Judith, who had bought and sold since she was very young, came up to London to run the stall two or three days a week. 'Sometimes we would go to Elizabeth in Halsey Street; she came down to Sandwich too. She and George often talked about her work. "Can you describe what I'm trying to say better than me?" she'd sometimes say to George. He found her books. Once he had a Wycliffe bible, had it for nothing and sold it for £500. He knew a lot about books and with his languages he did well. But he was so unscrupulous. Once he borrowed some cookery books from Kitty Gaunt, wife of William Gaunt, the editor of the *Studio* magazine and gave them to Elizabeth. She was very pleased. Kitty Gaunt kept asking George: "When am I getting my books back?"'

'And he'd keep telling her some story. She was furious, but he never told Elizabeth, and Kitty never got her books back ... Elizabeth once said to him: "You'll either be in prison or dead in twenty years' time, George."'

'George always had an effect on Elizabeth, and she was the only person who could keep *him* in hand.'

Elizabeth's circle grew as she became well known, but she always remained close to a number of friends made before and during the war in Egypt. If it turned out that she didn't quarrel beyond reconciliation Elizabeth could be a devoted friend. Amongst the closest of this group were Robin and Renée Fedden. Of their two children the younger, Frances, was Elizabeth's god-daughter. Robin had continued his advancement within the National Trust since returning from Egypt after the war; his associations and friendships were legion, his affairs frequent. As Veronica Nicholson said: 'Yes, Robin *loved* women, often had an attachment, usually pretty. Renée took it in good part and had her own friends.' Staying the night once after a drunken party, Robin said most graciously to Veronica in the morning, 'I'm *so* sorry, Veronica, I forgot to seduce you.'

To his wide interests – he wrote books on suicide, Egypt, ski-ing, the National Trust – and gift for friendship he also added great knowledge and a passion for buildings: he was Secretary of the Historic Buildings Commission for many years and an honorary RIBA. James Lees-Milne wrote in his obituary of Fedden that 'He was very hard to define. He had numerous interests, and many accomplishments . . . everything he did seemed effortless . . . He moved in many worlds and shone conspicuously in them all. He was alert, witty and informative . . .' There was a steeliness there in Fedden too. And this, combined with his 'elegance' and 'vitality', had attracted Elizabeth from the first. Lees-Milne said: 'He was no ordinary man.'

Neither was Renée any ordinary woman, but she was a more private figure than her husband, and only those who knew her well realized quite the force of her personality. Veronica Nicholson says of her, 'She seemed somehow wooden, perhaps even dull at times.' Elizabeth would insist that this was not Renée. Renée was intelligent, vital and to some beautiful. But like Elizabeth she could be very reserved. Their intimate and long-standing friendship was to have significance for them both in this latter part of their lives.

In the late Fifties Priscilla had moved to Catherine Street, Stella's London house where she entertained and cooked her way through many of Elizabeth's recipes. Although Elizabeth now usually turned to Felicité as her closest adviser and advocate, Priscilla appears once again the lynchpin of the family. So, although they might eat at favourite places like the Chanterelle, it was here that Stella, on her weekly visits to London, would be most likely to see Felicité and Elizabeth for lunch. On a typical occasion Priscilla invited their old family friend, the painter Lett Haines, with the young, as yet unknown, Robert Carrier, Stella and Elizabeth.

As well as looking at an auction Stella usually visited the dealers' stalls at Bermondsey Market. Judith Lassalle looked forward to her visits. 'She was so eccentric and didn't care a bit. She wore sand-shoes and a long white Fair Isle knitted coat and a blue veil. She'd always pick out the *one* thing on your stall that was unusual, tell you something interesting about it, never haggle and get out her Coutts cheque-book. The other stallholders loved her for it. I loved her telling me things. Elizabeth was quite sniffy about me dealing with her. "Oh, you see her, do you?"

'As if it wasn't quite the thing to do.'

Judith 'met Stella in the V&A once with a young man in his twenties. She said, "Oh, how nice to see you," and introduced me to the young man, her nephew. "This is Nicholas Ridley, your next prime minister!"

'She told me once that she'd been round the Queen's Gallery with the director [the distinguished art historian Oliver Millar]. "That man Millar, he'd got the captions on the paintings wrong, so I put him right" [knowing Stella she may well have had one or two significant contributions to make].

'I thought Stella was great fun,' Judith concludes.

Elizabeth liked Judith Lassalle and 'was always so generous. Whenever you arrived she'd immediately open a bottle of wine. She was tall and slim and would sometimes give me her clothes; they were always beautiful, made by fabulous people like Worth, Maggie Rouff, Hardy Amies. She wore superb clothes . . .'

From the beginning of George and Judith's marriage he and Elizabeth sometimes went out together. 'And Elizabeth would always ask: "Is it gracious living, George?" '[Her way of gauging the formality of the invitation.]

'On Saturday nights when George came down from London he'd often bring some food sent down by Elizabeth after he'd been working at Bermondsey. Elizabeth would ask me now and again: "Has he given you any money recently?"

' "No."

'And she would say, "Well, you'd better have some then."' At that point Judith was bringing up three small children and George sometimes left her with no money.

Elizabeth's sister Diana, still in London with her doctor husband Chris Grey, had by now four more children: Johnny born in 1951, Christabel born in 1952, Stephen born in 1954 and Christopher in 1957. Sometimes one or other of them would be brought to visit 'Aunt Liza'. For Johnny, and later Stephen, these visits were to prove especially significant.

Meanwhile despite Elizabeth's finances frequently causing her concern, her reputation as a writer was growing apace and friends like Patrick Woodcock remember that in the late Fifties 'She was an icon for many of us.' With her steady journalistic output this status amongst that first élite group was spreading out so that by the end of the decade Elizabeth was something of a middle-class cult. And, although she complained about the pains journalism caused her – 'the dreaded deadline' – she had now become a true professional. In so doing she had completed a vital shift of orientation. She had made the transition from writing for an élite to writing for a mass audience, from writing for a few people whom she knew or could imagine, to writing successfully for a wide range of distant, anonymous individuals.

The ability to make this shift – not an easy transition – sprang from the same source which had enabled her to appreciate and live with Charles Gibson Cowan. This was the reason Elizabeth was a greater artist than her Aunt Violet, whom in several ways she resembled. Violet could not transcend the gap between a refined and privileged élite and a less exalted but still discerning mass. Violet had no desire in fact to make herself available to a wide audience, hence her great artistry is now remembered by few.

Elizabeth's management of her increasing status reveals much that was typical of her; at heart it was a use of public power deriving from a private style: a distaste for publicity inherent in her social background. From the start Elizabeth treated her celebrity with an almost Garbo-like reserve, somewhat easier then than now. She was aware of her growing power to sway opinion. Her response to the comparative success of her campaign to teach the English how to live – and it really was no less than that – was mixed. She did not always approve of those who were, in however remote a fashion, her followers. Perhaps they themselves were not always aware of the degree to which Elizabeth David was the bearer of the *zeitgeist* which they themselves reflected.

Others were writing good cookery books and articles at the time: Elizabeth Craig, Ambrose Heath, Constance Spry, Sheila Hutchins in the *Daily Express* and Philip Harben in *Woman's Own* and on television (Marcel Boulestin, the first television chef, had died during the war and was followed by Harben). They were all influential and popular, partly because they were willing to make concessions to the Englishness of their audience. Elizabeth rarely did, but this did nothing to limit the growth of her readership. In a different category was André Simon, the spirited advocate of a fine Gallic palate, through his Wine and Food Society and its Journal, whose members and readers remained predominantly upper-class throughout all the major contemporary social changes in perception and behaviour.

Alan Davidson, one of the most distinguished and stylish writers on both cookery and its historical significance, stressed to the author that: 'Nothing can detract from Elizabeth's position as the leading public figure in all this. Her books became the standard-bearers of these changes . . . they were emblems for people who were taking a fresh look at food and cookery . . .' But Alan believes that 'It must be remembered that to an extent this would have happened anyway. She was not the only force. There were all sorts of invisible ones at work. These shifts were going on in post-war Britain and even if Elizabeth hadn't taken up writing on food they would have continued anyway. Books like Patience Gray's [Patience Gray and Primrose Boyd, *Plats du Jour*] were influential, but it's hard to overemphasize Elizabeth's importance. The main thing she did was not to influence people to "Keep it simple" but to "Lift up your eyes to the Continent and take an interest in exotic ingredients."

'I can still remember olive oil being a tiny bottle you only bought in the chemist (for medicinal purposes such as unblocking ears) and people would have been astonished if you had suggested it had another use. That was the kind of world Elizabeth was operating in in the 1950s. She often referred to shops in Soho and I remember it because working in the Foreign Office then, I used to go up there in the lunch hour and bring things back for the evening. Soho was a showcase for good European ingredients: Italian, Spanish, French . . . They had all you would want and you could explore the whole subject by shopping there weekly. There was an Italian shop which had a dazzling array of types of pasta. Up and down the streets of Soho you would have salamis and charcuterie which you wouldn't have any-where else at that time. The ripples spread out from there.'

I would differ with Alan over the 'keep it simple' issue; it seems inextricably bound up with the philosophy Elizabeth is propounding. She writes over and over with only minor variations, sometimes almost *ad nauseam*, to the effect that we are a nation which has 'a curious distrust of the primitive and simple in food, and so carefree a way with the specialities of other countries that while retaining names, we have no inhibitions about complicating, altering, travesty-ing and degrading the dish itself'.

A new development in Elizabeth's writing occurred with a request from Leonard Russell of the *Sunday Times* soon after she began working for the paper. In the introduction to *An Omelette and a Glass of Wine* she recalled Russell asking, 'Would she review a book?' 'Appalling me with a task I had never before tackled,' Russell 'proceeded to cajole, coax, persuade' until Elizabeth agreed. 'I don't think he found me very good at reviewing, and given that among his regular reviewers were Cyril Connolly and Raymond Mortimer, it took some courage to even accept the few books he entrusted to me.' Elizabeth reprinted all but one of these pieces in her *An Omelette and a Glass of Wine* collection. These few reviews and one or two later ones from the *Spectator* which she put in the book are good, concise pieces of criticism. Interestingly, almost every one of them is in some way related to interests which were to preoccupy Elizabeth in years to come: the restaurant in France, Middle Eastern food, English food.

A related interest was highlighted by the first book she was sent. This was a slim volume called *Home Baked* (Faber, 1954) by Celia and George Scurfield and Elizabeth found that 'The book is a sympathetic one.' So it is, right down to the pleasing simple exuberance of the yellow and black dust-jacket; the kind of book design Faber excelled at. Elizabeth wrote an enthusiastic review and 'a little research into the history of English bread-making proved instructive'. She said: 'For at least 250 years the bad quality of English bread has been notorious' and cited a nineteenth-century writer, Eliza Acton – who was beginning to take on heroic status for her – saying that our bread was noted 'both at home and abroad, for want of its genuineness and the faulty mode of preparation'.

Elizabeth agreed with the Scurfields that 'the only remedy for those who rail against the travesties of '"genuine wholesome bread" sold by bakers is the same as it has always been. It must be made at home.' As it turned out, her review helped to sell many copies of the little book on bread. Writing about it again in 1984 she said, 'It has gone into many editions since, is still in print . . . and must have helped thousands of readers to learn how to make their own bread.' She added the generous comment: 'For me the book eventually opened up a whole new field of study and of cookery.' Although this little volume triggered off in Elizabeth a serious interest in bread-making, it was to be several years before it became an obsession, and finally a book.

Long before these events were to take place, in 1960 Elizabeth brought out another book, by far her longest so far; the culmination of much travel, research and thought. Published by Michael Joseph, it was called *French Provincial Cooking* and in the opinion of many is Elizabeth's masterpiece. The book is undoubtedly a very fine achievement for its great knowledge of French culinary developments and provincial traditions, accurately, thoughtfully and beautifully written down. Indeed, probably no other English person had ever managed to convey these matters with such authority and enthusiasm. This was the considered development of what Elizabeth had begun in *French Country Cooking* nine years earlier. The French too regard the book with respect. And in England France's self-appointed gastronomic respresentative, André Simon, hosted a lunch in Elizabeth's honour at the book's publication.

French Provincial Cooking was based on years of familiarity with French food – eating in France, living and cooking in France – and a deep knowledge of the cookery literature; the bibliography is exhaustive and demonstrates Elizabeth's impressive range. She describes the success of the French between the world wars at rescuing their regional cooking, initiated by such men as Curnonsky, Marcel Rouff and Austin de Croze. But she also makes the salient point (of which these dedicated men were aware) that this would have turned into an exercise in nostalgia if there had not existed in the provinces of France the wherewithal to effect their task of preservation. Elizabeth writes here with coherence and understanding about something which was an essential, part of her motivation and had been an essential, albeit unarticulated, spur to her writing from the very beginning. What she says about France applies, more or less, to all the Mediterranean countries about which she had written in reaction against the depredations which the industrial revolution had wrought upon the traditions of her own land.

> France is still largely an agricultural country and the right conditions for the preservation of their traditions still prevail. These traditions are constantly being renewed from within; the professional cooks and the housewives adapt the old methods to changing tastes and altered conditions without thereby standardizing all the food ... the tourist organizations work hard to foster their own local products and cookery magazines publicize them in a sane and sober way, so it is not so surprising that the regional cookery of France is a profitable and flourishing industry as well as a beneficent one.

Although she says that good food is not always as good as it was, for those prepared to look, 'One of the great points about the cookery of France is that it is so extraordinarily varied.'

With this in mind she continues: 'To compile a comprehensive volume of French regional recipes would take a lifetime of work and research', and she concludes that it would still be impossible 'because ... cookery is continually evolving'. Elizabeth tells her readers that she has selected recipes 'which have pleased me and which can be reproduced in English kitchens without too much difficulty'. Although 'difficult' is a relative term her judgement is a true one for those with care and time to give. She creates possibilities where before there were none; she describes, draws pictures, instructs, until the regions of France become a manageable and comprehensive map across which her reader is drawn with that enticing sensual prose, and the desire to make these dishes becomes an urgent and pressing need.

'We ate all the way through *French Provincial Cooking* over the late Fifties', says Judith Lassalle. 'Elizabeth would invite us all around for endless meals. She would come herself or send things down to us at Sandwich too. We were guinea pigs – "It's for four or six" she would say. "Let me know how far it goes round . . ."' Pies, prunes, plums, apricot things. A woman came down to do drawings of the things Elizabeth made. (These are some of the drawings of unpretentious clarity by Juliette Renny which head each section of the book. Kitchen equipment: pots, tians, marmites, mandolins, knives, ramekins, fish kettles and much more are illustrated.)

It is in this book that Elizabeth describes her first and subsequently revelatory experiences of French food as a teenager, in that claustrophobic Parisian household practising such exquisitely refined greed. It is here that she gathers together her *Vogue* articles and gives us a beautifully clear résumé of the food of each region of France. Amongst those she discusses: Paris, the Ile de France, Normandy . . . its beautiful northern fish . . . Breton artichokes, 'shining leeks; and fluffy green-white cauliflower . . . Carefully bunched salad herbs' and with them all the memories of the France of her youth: Brittany where there is fine salt-marsh lamb, 'Nantais ducklings served with the tiny green peas or the baby turnips of the district . . . the delicious fresh cream cheeses called *crémets* which are eaten with sugar and fresh cream. . . . At restaurants in Nantes, Tours, Angers . . . Amboise and many other places along the banks of the Loire,' she describes 'the unique speciality of this country, the famous *beurre blanc* . . . Anjou's great contribution to the regional cookery of France.'

Amongst the regions it is clear that Provence holds a special place in her heart. She is sufficiently aware of this to write: 'If I seem to be biased in favour of the food of the South, it is because the country itself has for me such a very powerful appeal.' It could not be otherwise when so much of her own development was bound up with this plenteous, beautiful, at times parched, sometimes 'bleak and savage' region. A single card to Felicité from Alsace in May 1957 sums up her feelings: 'Terribly cold, country rather like Switzerland. Otherwise all going well, plenty of good food, but would rather be in

Provence.' Her piece on Provence in the book is close to a creed, the nearest she gets to monotheism:

> Provence . . . to which I am always returning, next week, next year, any day now, as soon as I can get on a train . . . now and again the vision of golden tiles on a round southern roof, or of some warm, stony, herb-scented hill-side will rise out of my kitchen pots with the smell of a piece of orange peel scenting a beef stew . . .
>
> But to regard the food of Provence as just a release from routine, a fierce, wild riot of flavour and colour, is to oversimplify it and grossly to mistake its nature. For it is not primitive food; it is civilized without being over-civilized. That is to say, it has natural taste, smell, texture, and much character. Often it looks beautiful, too. What it amounts to is that it is the rational, right and proper food for human beings to eat.

Lorraine, its capital the beautiful Nancy, launches Elizabeth into a superb example of her Proustian-style rêveries, beginning with the bakeries and pastry shops whose enticing smells beckon her inside to buy early-morning *croissants*. Here she is beguiled by the counters piled with 'flat round orange and gilt tins, glinting and shining like little lamps in the pallid sunshine'. Filled with the *Bergamottes de Nancy*, 'little boiled sweets, scented with essence of Bergamot . . . one of the oldest specialities of Nancy . . . and as I walked away carrying my pretty little tin of childish sweets I thought how often some trivial little discovery colours and alters in one's mind the whole aspect of a city or a countryside.'

With Proust already in our minds she next tells us that: 'At the little town of Commercy originated the small, fragile, shell-shaped cakes called *madeleines* so beloved of French children, and which have become celebrated in French literature because it was the taste of a *madeleine* dipped in a cup of [lime] tea which Proust used as the starting point of his long journey back into the past.' A signpost to Epinal triggers another of her own childhood memories 'of primitive coloured pictures and sheets of brightly uniformed soldiers, the *images d'Épinal* which have the same primitive charm as our penny-plain twopence-coloured prints'. And one travels with Elizabeth in her mind's eye to the decorations she made from the same little paper soldiers for the cabin of the *Evelyn Hope*; and further back still to the Wootton nursery of her childhood. .

This and many more such interludes, along with the evocations of markets and shops, are the passages which support the recipes, the essential core of the book. Elizabeth later called these fine pieces 'informative background material, local colour and general chatter'. There is a shift here, and also a degree of unawareness on Elizabeth's part. It was these passages as much as the recipes themselves which gained her devotees. For them she was not only creating a recipe which they could replicate in their kitchens, she was describing a world which could be imagined and summoned up amidst the cooking pots. This is several steps on from *Mediterranean Food*. She, like her first readers, has had to face the world and with it become more of a realist. The talk now is often of reliability: good reputable restaurants, as well as the apparently delightful little discovery down a back street, which may turn out a disaster. Elizabeth now describes these establishments, their dishes, their wines, their quietly remarkable fare, whether a local speciality or a house favourite, with poetry, confidence, authority.

Many of the trips to France for *Vogue*, *House and Garden* and the *Sunday Times*, during the late 1950s, were made with the purpose of discovering more about places with which she was not already familiar. These were the trips taken at the suggestion of 'the original and enlightened Audrey Withers . . . provided with £100 . . . to help cover restaurant meals, hotels, petrol and so on'. These were the journeys often in the company of Doreen and Anthony Denney and 'even though these trips were very much France on a shoestring, the knowledge I derived from them was valuable'. So also was the dedication with which Doreen supported Elizabeth during these years. In return Elizabeth concluded her acknowledgements by thanking 'my friend Doreen for driving me, with much patience and care, on many rather arduous journeys around and across France in search of good food . . .' She could not make the central dedication to Doreen because this had already been given: 'To P.H. with love.'

P.H. was a man whom Elizabeth had known for some time.

Indeed when he was given the dedication of *French Provincial Cooking* their liaison was already several years old. He was to be another of those doomed to disappoint her. Some friends have said that, even more than the lover who returned to North America, and to the arms of another, after being injured in Egypt during the war, this was the man whom Elizabeth most deeply cared for. He was a wealthy importer, of conventional good looks, whose pleasant personality nevertheless seems to have been sufficiently vague beside Elizabeth's for her friends to be unable to describe him with any particular verve. Some say he doted upon her, others say that he was 'undynamic, boring'. More than one friend thought the reason he did not eventually marry her was that his liking for money and the life-style a richer girlfriend brought him was greater than his love for Elizabeth.

In conversation with the author, Peter Trier recalled: 'I did think it a bit odd Elizabeth being attracted to a man like that. . . . Liz was far too intelligent for most men, she could run rings around most of them intellectually. She was frightening, because she was both intelligent and intellectual.' Perhaps, like the lover in America, it was not only a matter of money but also the comprehension that he was not strong enough to prevent Elizabeth consuming him that kept P.H. from marrying her.

The dedication of her book to this man is particularly poignant because in this same year, 1960, she was also finally divorced from Tony. Ironically, he was an old friend of Elizabeth's present lover; they had in fact been fellow-soldiers in India. In those days, in order for a divorce to be granted it was necessary to prove that there were 'sufficient grounds'; one of the parties must be deemed to be at fault. And as it was Elizabeth who took out the divorce petition she had to prove Tony to be at fault. This involved detailed descriptions of his errors, probable adulteries and other misdemeanours. But, however true these criticisms may have been, to a large extent this was an academic exercise necessitated by the requirements of divorce law.

Elizabeth and Tony's marriage had ceased to be a real one years earlier; Elizabeth certainly had maintained longer- and short-term affairs for the whole of this period, and the two had not effectively lived together for most of the last few years. Above all it should not be forgotten that Elizabeth was as quickly bored by poor Tony as her friends predicted she would be. And, however pleasant their short conjugal interludes may afterwards have been, their marriage did not really last beyond India. Elizabeth was irritated by Tony's inability to keep up with her and his failure to maintain her. But here she was playing a game of double standards. She wanted a marriage of convenience and couldn't support the consequences of it longer than she did whilst in India. She was quite conversant with what Tony was and was not and had married him with too much pragmatism. Her mistake had been to pretend to herself that she had sufficient self-discipline both to successfully manage Tony and herself into the bargain. It was too much to ask, and in her heart Elizabeth knew it wouldn't work, as more than one of her letters reveals in those weeks of indecision before her marriage.

There seems little doubt that with her divorce, and the dedication of her book to him, she was in a sense offering herself to P.H. They continued their liaison for some time after 1960. However, it was not Elizabeth to whom he made an offer of marriage; but instead the other woman who had been in the background for some time. Elizabeth and he continued seeing each other for several years, although less frequently following his marriage. When it finally came to an end Elizabeth believed herself heartbroken. 'She rang me in tears, she said P. is gone, she rang everybody,' says Alix Coleman.

'Oh, Elizabeth was so fond of him; she was devastated when he went,' says another friend.

Although Elizabeth was always responsive to men her drive to control and manipulate worked against her when their sense of self-preservation got the better of them. In the process Elizabeth was sometimes undoubtedly used. But her attitude to men, sometimes verging on dismissive, was noticed by some women as quite pronounced. Caroline Trier remarked to the author: 'She liked intelligent men but there was this feeling that women were really much more interesting and ultimately worthwhile. She was always very pro-woman which was unusual for then . . . she used to say: "I think that a woman's position is terrible." '

Women have repeatedly remarked on how extraordinarily supportive she was to them in times of stress. On reflection they are inclined to agree that the support was strongest when it involved conflict with a man. 'Oh, if you had a bit of a moan about your husband, she was *absolutely* behind you. One had the strong feeling that men were the inferior breed.'

In common with any number of other women Elizabeth appears to have believed that they were ultimately more respect-worthy than men. She may also at some point have had a romantic liaison with another woman. However, if this was so it can only be described as one element of her complex personality rather than an *essential* part of it. Elizabeth could never be described as having an aversion to men, her response to them was much too sincerely and consistently positive for that ascription to apply.

During the first five months of 1960 *Vogue* published a discursive series Elizabeth wrote for them on the markets of France in which she combines again more of the detailed practice, the whereabouts of the produce as well as the romance. Cavaillon, Yvetot, Montpellier, Martigues, Valence; under Elizabeth's mellow pen the names of these great centres for the buying and selling of local produce and foods ring out; as she said herself of 'the little towns round about Valence . . . like peals of bells compelling you to go and look at them'. And the reader was further intrigued and enticed by the accompanying pictures. The research for this series had been done on a two-week marathon with Doreen across France, with Anthony and Alex in tow to take photographs.

Doreen had been permitted 'to jump the queue for one of the first Triumph Heralds if I promised to write an article for their magazine'. And so it was that she featured Elizabeth's and her journey around the French markets in an article entitled 'Woman Driver's 2300 miles in a Herald'. One of the nattiest new little sports cars, the Herald created great interest as they sped through France. Doreen knew little about cars but satisfied her regular male interrogators with the statement that 'It was the first British car produced in any quantity to have independent suspension on all four wheels. Whilst the other members of the party were taking photographs of the market, the farmers and market police were gathered round the Triumph . . .'

Elizabeth's article in September *Vogue* on autumn fruits and preserves, a subject always dear to Elizabeth's heart, is accompanied by one of those sumptuous Denney photographs set in her Halsey Street kitchen. Anthony and Elizabeth always discussed beforehand how the photograph would be set up and, with their combined understanding of composition, colour, texture, craftsmanship and an instinct for the best image for the moment, they seemed almost unerringly to succeed. Denney's photographs accurately reflected Elizabeth's work in their contrast between the absolute simplicity of white plates and terracotta dishes of olives, radishes, fresh butter, new bread, golden and white halved boiled eggs, a green salad or a bowl of fruit; and in this instance the impression of autumnal largesse here, with an enormous *galette* of glistening jewel-like fruits on the table. As a backdrop, on the wall is a strange and Surreal image; a painted fish, cutlery and red plates stuck on to a canvas. Just as Surrealism's unsettling Alice-through-the-looking-glass displacement of reality would have a predictable appeal to someone of Elizabeth's personality, so this picture by the modern Surrealist Coetze (also collected by Anthony Denney) was one of her favoured possessions. Shortly after the publication of *French Provincial Cooking* Elizabeth very reluctantly agreed to be interviewed about it on Manchester radio by the novelist Elizabeth Jane Howard. Brian Redhead was involved too.

'The programme was about people who had just published books,' says Doreen. 'There was a young girl of about fifteen, Liz and some others. Liz came to stay with us because we were then living in Nottinghamshire. I'd persuaded her to do it and had to drive her over to the studios. She was *determined* not to go. It was spite. We stopped at a friend's on the way . . . had champagne, that helped. Elizabeth Jane Howard was very nice to us . . . met us, etc. Foolishly though she gave us lunch in the staff canteen . . . well . . . sandwiches like *that*. It was a bit silly of her, and Liz was terribly rude about it . . . She was awful on the programme . . . sounded like a bad-tempered school ma'am and said she never wanted to do it again. I said, "Liz, I'm terribly sorry."

' "That was awful, wasn't it?"

'I said, "Yes." '

Elizabeth's style of public performance did not improve with the increase of her reputation; with age it became worse. Nevertheless, the book was a great success. Charles Pick, then co-managing director at Michael Joseph, recalled to the author a dinner with Allen Lane, founder of Penguin, at which he said, 'You've published a wonderful book.'

At the end of 1960 Elizabeth gave up her column for *Vogue* and, with enormous relief, also left the *Sunday Times*. She had appreciated the intelligent and patient editing of Leonard Russell, but she could no longer support the bullying and tyranny of her immediate women's editor, Ernestine Carter. Elizabeth had some time previously become friends with a bright young journalist, Alix Coleman, who successfully persuaded her to move to a paper apparently inappropriate as a vehicle for Elizabeth David's melodious middle-class voice. This was the *Sunday Dispatch*, to which Alix Coleman herself had recently moved. Alix had worked on the *Sunday Times* and had also been subjected to persecution by Ernestine Carter. She told the author:

> Ernestine was terrible. The first time I was summoned to see her my speciality was interviewing. Anybody, from personalities to Barnardo's children. My pieces went down well so Ernestine called me in and told me I was doing too many interviews and that I'd have to cut them down. She would cut my copy mercilessly. If she thought someone was doing well she would stop them doing it. I left because of her. Margaret Costa took over from Elizabeth. Elizabeth told her that Ernestine was poisonous and she would be well advised to keep away, but Margaret thought she could manage. A couple of weeks later Liz told me that Margaret had telephoned her to say: 'You were wrong about Ernestine. She's much worse than you said.'
>
> Anyway, I left because of Ernestine. Anne Edwards was now the women's page editor on the *Sunday Dispatch* and I told her about Elizabeth; Walter Hayes the editor wanted Elizabeth and we managed to get her for the paper.

Later, in *An Omelette and a Glass of Wine*, Elizabeth herself wrote: 'In 1961, freed from the *Sunday Times* and the monthly stints for the Condé Nast magazines, I worked for a time for the moribund *Sunday Dispatch* and wrote my first contribution for the *Spectator* and, unexpectedly perhaps, thoroughly enjoyed writing for both publications.' Her articles for the *Sunday Dispatch* were as close as Elizabeth came in her writing to the opposite end of the social spectrum from the fashionably tasteful confines of *Vogue* and the intellectually prestigious *Spectator*.

The *Dispatch* was the Sunday paper of the *Daily Mail*. It was 'an earlier version of the *Sun*. With sleaze, girls, actresses and illustrated serialized versions of novels,' says Alix Coleman. 'Lord Rothermere had been told to write clean stories so they got us. Anne Edwards and I came from the *Daily Express*, and there was Kate Whitehorn too. With Elizabeth we were supposed to represent quality, style. Elizabeth had suffered so much under Ernestine that she was much more malleable now. She'd learnt a lot because of the *Sunday Times*.'

And again we see Elizabeth's ability to cross the social divide as few of her contemporaries or friends could. Her patrician voice is put aside and, alongside pictures of Marilyn Monroe in her shapeliest dresses and would-be Brigitte Bardot girls modelling corsets (as 'Page Three' precursors), Elizabeth steps out with a bright, unpatronizing style. She is still her authoritative and sometimes acerbic self but the language is jauntier, more down-to-earth. In short, says Alix Coleman, 'She understood what was required of her. She wrote these beautiful simple recipes' in a clear straightforward style, complemented by equally straightforward incitements to cook well.

Elizabeth's articles were sufficiently autobiographical to keep the gossip column devotees happy: in March 1961 we are told that she has had to refuse the services of her interior designer friend (Anthony Denney) to reorganize her kitchen. She describes it as 'a rather barn-like room with three outside walls and the fourth entirely taken up by french windows looking out on nothing but a blank wall'. In wishing to 'turn it into a lighter, warmer, more convenient room to work in – and to entertain in . . .' she wanted also 'to preserve its character . . . My kitchen's assets are its size . . . and its parquet floor . . . and old English pine dressers I've collected over the years and the massive table 5ft. 6ins x 3ft. 6ins. with a 2in. thick scrubbed wood top which I had made a few months ago to go on an old one I already owned – a magnificent table both to work on and to sit at.' She has modern spotlights set in, 'vital' heating and a new china sink and cupboard underneath. She buys 'a fine, old 19th century pine cupboard . . . to replace that battered old dresser . . . and a hard wood plate and dish-rack which I've had fixed on the wall above one of the draining boards.' (With the exception of the 'ravishing pink called Columbine' with which she warms up the walls – she later called it 'corset pink' – this was very much the way Elizabeth's kitchen remained for many years to come.)

In December Elizabeth was off to stay in Ireland with the intensely sociable painter Derek Hill in his expansive Donegal house, St Columb's. She told Felicité she was collected off the ferry at Belfast by another guest, John Bryson, who turned out to be great fun – he had organized the new Oxford Playhouse with Stanford Holme, was a friend of their Uncle Jasper, knew absolutely everyone and chattered away ceaselessly. Elizabeth found the swift, friendly service in the Irish shops much to her liking after London; her replacement of a forgotten petticoat 'would have taken me three hours in Harrods – and John Bryson went in to a confectioner's shop to buy sweets for the domestics while I was posting a letter and it was all over in half a minute.'

Elizabeth and Derek Hill had become friends through Lesley O'Malley, who was living in the basement of Halsey Street. In Donegal Derek was blessed for many years with his cook, the late Gracie McDermott, a warm and generous-spirited local woman devoted both to her cooking pots and her employer. He was a discerning and regular traveller and returned from around the world with recipes for her to try. The food at St Columb's was renowned, and Gracie loved the constant round of guests and meals Derek's hospitality entailed. After Christmas Elizabeth was writing to Felicité from her bed, one of her favourite places in which to work, with Derek's huge golden retriever lying in front of her fire. (For years Felicité kept a retriever upstairs at Halsey Street but Elizabeth's great love was always cats. Her own, Squeaker, had been a present from a litter produced by a cat of Doreen's. Elizabeth was utterly devoted to her and often mentioned details for her care whilst away. Squeaker appears in the Beaton photograph on the back cover of *French Provincial Cooking*. After many years Squeaker's death left Elizabeth distraught. 'Oh, she was inconsolable for a time,' says Doreen. 'I was glad I wasn't around when it happened. It would have been too much to bear.')

Elizabeth continues her letter: 'Terrific frost on the ground, and I don't suppose anything will stop Derek having a skating party on the lake if he can possibly organize it in between the lunch, tea, drinks and dinner parties which scarcely cease for an instant . . .' She made several visits to St Columb's; its combination of restfulness, stimulation and good food suited her. She tells Felicité, while fretting about Squeaker, to find 'a whole box full of white wine Veronica has given me, very nice and just the thing for visitors . . . that Muscat is not for every day.'

The quiet luxury of Derek Hill's hospitality was a pleasant relief for her: for now it suited her not having to put 'saucepan to stove', relinquishing the responsibility. She was later to use some of Gracie McDermott's recipes, saying that she was 'the greatest natural cook' she had ever met. Gracie herself – photographed each year by Derek's friend Cecil Beaton when he came to stay – found Elizabeth's books 'a great help to me because she explained things so nice and so beautiful that I was able to follow them'.

Back in London Elizabeth was again at work on pieces for the *Spectator*, a publication she truly enjoyed writing for. Looking back in *An Omelette and a Glass of Wine* in 1984, she wrote that 'they were stimulating years for me. Well, look at the company I found myself in. Katherine Whitehorn, Cyril Ray, Bernard Levin . . . Brian Inglis was my first editor . . . and at the end the lamented Ian McLeod.' In characteristic style, with her compulsion to settle old scores, Elizabeth remarks on the sharp contrast between the late Ernestine Carter's 'cutting shears' and what at the *Spectator* she found to be 'the co-operation, support and on occasions most beneficial editing by Cyril Ray and Katherine Whitehorn'.

The *Spectator* pieces were 'in the main topical . . . all over the place, from reviews of eccentric books . . . to harmless fun at the expense of restaurant guides and the baiting of public relations persons who made imbecile suggestions', to encounters with hitherto unknown foods and 'delicious wines'. Elizabeth's fine-tuned wit and English satire were particularly well suited to a magazine such as the *Spectator*. And she protests disingenuously when she writes that her fun and baiting were 'harmless'. They were no such thing, and the furious response which her badinage and satire sometimes provoked from those concerned was exactly their purpose: to draw attention to the 'disregard for the authenticity of other people's and indeed our own culinary specialities' and much else here of a second-rate nature to do with food. In a piece called '*Franglais*', written for the magazine in 1965, she gets right under the skin of the differences between the essential Englishness and Frenchness of dishes via a brilliant anatomy of a revered English (as it turns out, French) accompaniment: Cumberland sauce.

Elizabeth's friend Veronica Nicholson, like several others, believes 'Elizabeth wrote some of her best pieces for the *Spectator*. They were so funny. I've always thought Elizabeth a very good essayist. She couldn't handle a really long piece. In a way her books are bits and pieces. I told her that I had come to that conclusion. I don't know if she was pleased. I said I thought she played a beautiful minuet but not a concerto . . . that she was something like Lamb and Hazlitt and all those lovely writers whom she despised. She wasn't a story-teller.'

Amongst friends she was renowned and amongst enemies [by now she was collecting a fair few] feared for her hatred of anything or anyone with a whiff of pretension about them. Patrick Woodcock asked her to dinner with 'a fat old queen who was very knowledgeable. He came to dinner and Elizabeth said to me afterwards, "Thank you for asking me, Patrick . . . I was pleased to meet that phoney."'

Historical pieces, which were in a number of cases to prove of considerable significance in Elizabeth's life, and a rash of quirky reviews of eccentric books, were the other topics she dwelt on for the *Spectator* – books such as Sir Harry Luke's *The Tenth Muse*, first published by Putnam in 1954. She commends the *Muse* and says it has 'the collector's madness . . . Few authors are as modest as Sir Harry Luke . . . and fewer still provide the stimulus, the improbable information [it is replete with extraordinary asides], the travellers' tales, the new visions which to me make his book a true collector's piece.' In these post-colonial days Luke's book is a strange bird indeed. He had been a Governor of Malta and knew Elizabeth's sister Priscilla well. A photograph in the book has him sitting like an intrepid mouse beside the benevolent giant Queen of Tonga.

Viola Johnson's husband Arthur had died in 1958 and in 1962

Viola decided to come to England and try her hand at work. She bought a bookshop in Museum Street near the British Museum, whilst living in Sloane Avenue with her son John. Viola and Elizabeth had remained close friends since those days in Capri, and almost every Sunday Elizabeth went to eat lunch with them. John recalls: 'My mother and Elizabeth went on a number of trips around Piedmont and a visit to Venice together in the 1960s. They were an extraordinary pair. My mother became most eccentric, would tell people she was leaving town when she wasn't at all so that she wouldn't be disturbed.' In the autumn of 1963 a trip with Viola to Alba in Italy for the truffle festival there produced the article 'Truflesville Regis' for the *Spectator*, written hurriedly, Elizabeth said. Viola criticized the Italian spelling mistakes and corrected them for a later reprinting as she so conscientiously done for *Italian Food*. Elizabeth's journey to Italy with Viola ended with an inspirational visit to Turin where she unearthed a little confectioner's shop selling the candied walnuts of obscure and ancient Italian tradition. Triumphantly she carried some back home to England.

John Johnson describes how 'The trip to Venice produced risottos from Elizabeth when I'd go round there. Over time they became ever more minimalist, with eventually very little in them. Two peas and one prawn. You know, that sort of thing.'

John meanwhile had decided he wanted to be a bookseller and went to learn with Felicité, now working in another bookshop which she had helped to set up with the owner, John Sandoe, in the summer of 1957. Combined with her persistent habit of reading, Felicité's expertise in the buying and selling of books was considerable (she ran the paperback department at Sandoe's) and John recalls her warning him: 'If you work in a bookshop you'll never read a book again.' John ignored the warning and spent several months in the shop with Felicité. 'She wore her hair drawn back, and tweedy skirts and knitted tops. Much more a sensible country look than Elizabeth's. She rode about Chelsea on a bicycle and talked in very precise, clipped tones. She was very protective of her sister. She didn't cook, wasn't interested in it. Felicité was a lovely person. Her attitude to Elizabeth was rather a subservient one.

'A certain Mr Marks bought frequently from the shop, and he

often seemed to find things wrong with his purchases and would bring them back. Felicité was always very patient about this and would exchange them. One day something came up about his name and he said to Felicité, "Don't you know who I am?"

' "No."

' "Why, Marks of Marks and Spencer."

'He was so pleased that Felicité had been so civilized without knowing who he was that he immediately asked her to tea at his house. That way they became good friends.'

Elizabeth was also about to make a new friend. Having spent three years as a staff writer for Condé Nast publications, in 1963 the young Hugh Johnson (to become an expert on wine, and later horticulture) took over from André Simon, retiring editor of *Wine and Food*. The Spring issue was the first under Hugh Johnson's auspices with André Simon now Editor in Chief and Henry Yoxall Consultant. In his generous posthumous tribute to Elizabeth Hugh said: 'I first read her articles in the *Spectator*. . . . "Pale soups the colour of summer frocks," she writes, and the soups, and the mood, stick fast in your memory. I trusted her completely, and I believe that is the secret of her writing. It is transparent; never affected. Her readers cannot doubt for a moment that she is telling the truth. She is a writer who plunges straight in. Time and again I have picked up one of her articles and felt the strong grip that marks the start of a good story.

'And she could be as funny as Stella Gibbons [the author of *Cold Comfort Farm*]. The first piece in *An Omelette and a Glass of Wine* . . . tells the story of the dire conditions that provoked her to start writing . . . Ross on Wye in 1947, and Miss D's catastrophic antique shop where the proprietress laid waste her own toppling stock with every clumsy movement, still makes me shake with laughter.

'An ambitious editor could not *live* without such ravishing writing. I invaded Halsey Street . . . with little real idea of what I was asking for; just wanting my readers to feel the same exhilaration as I did.'

He told the author: 'Reading the introduction to *French Provincial Cooking* inspired me as a wine writer. I thought: That's how I want to write about wine.'

Hugh wonders why she made him welcome, sat him at her kitchen table and began 'to hypnotize me with the loaf she had just baked, the pale butter that asked for nothing else; the olives, the ungrand but totally vivid glass of wine I had scarcely heard of. Probably out of respect for André [Simon had insisted that Elizabeth be invited to his retirement party], and possibly because *Wine and Food* was a vehicle for longer pieces than the *Spectator*, and for more of the history and literature of cooking which was becoming more and more her passion . . . We got on like a house on fire and before long we were going out to meals together.'

Hugh Johnson was correct in saying that Elizabeth wanted a venue more amenable to the increasing length and more historical nature of her writing, but he was too modest in saying that she responded to him as she did simply out of respect for André Simon. Elizabeth saw and appreciated his enthusiasm, knowledge and willingness to learn. Her nephew Stephen Grey's assertion that 'Elizabeth didn't like people who didn't know what they were talking about' concurs with the opinion of everyone who knew her. 'She was intimidating to those who didn't.' 'Don't put up with nonsense merchants,' she would say to Stephen. As long as they were sincere and not 'phoney' and had something to offer which interested Elizabeth she was interested and interesting. There was now a growing band of younger devotees who, like Hugh Johnson, became her friends. One who later fell into this category, Alan Davidson, remembers an occasion when he and his wife Jan invited her to lunch with a Billingsgate fishmonger and his wife. 'Elizabeth got on famously with the fishmonger and his wife. They talked about fish, but also about family matters. Elizabeth could be a very sympathetic person; she was very curious about other people's lives.'

Hugh Johnson began his editorship of *Wine and Food* in the Spring of 1963 with a new cover design: huge bright lime-green script on a cream ground. In the very next issue, Summer, he had secured a long article by Elizabeth, entitled 'An Anthology of Ice Creams: these recipes cover briefly the history of ice-cream making, from 1720 to 1963', which immediately demonstrated Elizabeth's wide knowledge of sources, French and English: Menon, Emy, Hannah Glasse, Alexis Soyer, etc. As Hugh Johnson said, 'She was very accurate . . . the truth was very important.'

Nineteen sixty-three was a particularly hectic year for Elizabeth.

In the early spring she had made what turned out to be a disastrous commitment and one from which she fled early, with the help of Veronica Nicholson and her husband John. A rich homosexual, Rex Henry, recently married to a young and beautiful French model, was living in Marrakesh. He wished to entertain on a scale commensurate with his aspirations and employed Elizabeth to teach his cook to produce French cuisine. From the start Elizabeth and Rex Henry miscommunicated. With some apprehension she had agreed to stay in this ménage, lodged in her own apartment attached to the luxurious house. She saw the venture as a means of making a good sum of money and getting herself out of England to the sun. She was also curious to look again at the Mediterranean. In part this was out of nostalgia, but intertwined with that was also the urge to observe one of the kinds of place responsible for what she would eventually describe as 'the English love-affair with Eastern food and Arabian Nights ingredients'.

Morocco, only recently independent of France, was, like Alexandria, a hotch-potch of races: Phoenicians, Romans, Arabs, Jews, Muslims, black Africans, Spaniards, Portuguese, and finally the French; all of whom had left their mark in a country situated in the north-west corner of Africa yet only 8 miles from Europe. For centuries the cities of Morocco had been caught in the hustling economic and cultural Mediterranean cross-fire. Marrakesh . . . with an admixture of ancient custom and modern aspiration, a city of extraordinary beauty and wretched poverty; a city where can be found a dusty clearing at night hung with lamps lighting up the bustle of snake charmers, acrobats, beggars, competing with the call of water-sellers and food stalls, for the money of passers-by. This is called Djemma el Fna, the 'assembly place of nobodys'.

But Elizabeth saw little of life outside the kitchen, whether of the rich or the poor, and the allotted time which she had agreed to devote to this dubious task quickly became an onerous and frustrating burden from which she chafed to be free. She wrote to Félicité saying: 'Don't think I can make my escape until April 4th – from Tangier via Gibraltar – London. They are trying their best to be decent to me, but they are just perfectly awful people.' She knew she should never have gone, and vowed it would be the last time she went against her instincts and undertook any venture just for the sake of getting into the sun. The weather was the most perfect she could remember since Cairo, and she found the country fascinating, but, as she was in the kitchen or the back of a car the whole time, it hardly made any difference. She had not been allowed out to the souk or any shops except the market. The cook was charming, and good, but the task hopeless – her employers wanted elegant international food, composed of ingredients unavailable in Marakesh. (It is in any case unlikely she would have agreed to instruct in the preparation of one of the types of cooking against which she had spent so long reacting.) Rex Henry refused to listen to anything she told him about cooking and instead 'talked as if he were in the nineteenth century'.

At the same time Veronica and John had arrived for a holiday to explore Morocco. 'John didn't want to meet up with Elizabeth, but I told him it would be impossible not to. We were staying at this large hotel where one stayed and it was inevitable she would discover we were there. She couldn't bear it with these people any longer – got chippy about any possible kind of servant status . . . they had dinners to which she wasn't invited. They had certain social pretensions, which annoyed Elizabeth intensely. She begged us to save her, so we took her off on a journey through the Atlas Mountains for some days. It was very beautiful and Elizabeth was very obliging. But she did always have to have a butt. I put her in the front with John and I was reading out guide books from the back. She would keep making terrible fun of me . . . quite unfairly . . . I think it was part of her defences, she simply had to put something up . . .

'We stopped the night at such a beautiful town on the coast, called Mogador. It was whitewashed, very Arabic-influenced with those lovely arches and then that French Gauloise blue and then there was brown. We went round the market. She would have been up at four if necessary to do something like that. We all loved markets but John was into a passion to get it over with and Elizabeth was in a passion to stay. It was so *illuminating* to be there with Elizabeth. When I came home I made our ridiculous kitchen in St Anne's Terrace out in these colours. It was Elizabeth really, she had such an artistic view of things it influenced one.'

Back in England, after three weeks away and recovering from a complicated bout of flu, Elizabeth wrote in her regular *Spectator* article about a small and learned publication's attempts to classify and illustrate the edible fish of Tunisia and the central Mediterranean. She said that the author, a young diplomat, Alan Davidson, then on a posting to Tunisia, 'has a gift for conveying memorable information in a way so effortless that his book makes lively reading for its own sake.' A colleague of Alan Davidson's at the embassy in Tunis, Roger Eland, had worked with Elizabeth at the Ministry of Information in Cairo during the war and sent her the booklet. Elizabeth's involvement in Alan Davidson's fish interests continued and, as he subsequently wrote in his book of culinary essays, *A Kipper With My Tea* (Macmillan, 1988), 'years later when it had long been out of print she persuaded her editor, Jill Norman, that it should be turned into a proper book covering the whole Mediterranean.' This was *Mediterranean Seafood* (Penguin, 1972), acclaimed as the most authoritative book yet written on the subject.

Elizabeth later wrote of this period in *Spices, Salt and Aromatics in the English Kitchen* that she had 'enjoyed my compulsory leisure re-reading old favourites in my cookery library.' Some, like Mrs Leyel's *Gentle Art of Cookery*, 'had been my earliest kitchen companions', others such as Lord Bute's *Moorish Recipes* were more recent discoveries of which she had written in 1955 in a review, for the *Sunday Times*, 'a lovely little book of Moroccan cookery, beautifully written and illustrated . . . A cookery book concerned more with the authenticity of the dishes than with what the English housewife may make of them is a rarity. We are fortunate to get it. It is a collector's find . . . the fine free style in which the recipes are written and set out are most pleasing, and how elegant are the Moorish cooking pots and serving dishes shown in the illustrations.'

Another far more serious reason for Elizabeth's compulsory leisure was that shortly after her recovery from flu she was taken gravely ill. As Doreen says, 'She had been drinking too much spirits. A while previously Liz and I had had this crazy arrangement whereby I came up from Kent several times a week to help her with her papers and filing. Everything was in a terrible mess. She never threw anything out so there were piles of files and piles of papers and piles of books. It was simply ghastly, and we didn't get much done. But we had some lovely lunches. So many interesting people passed through. Afterwards I had a job working in the Harrods Food Hall and I'd come round for lunch most days.

'One day I went round routinely and there was Lesley [O'Malley] in a terrible state. Liz was lying there trying and unable to speak . . . she couldn't. It was awful. I got the ambulance and then Lesley and I followed it to the hospital [Edward VII]. It was all very dramatic. She'd had a stroke. Liz was in the same room as the actress Bebe Daniels. We would sit there making her [Liz] talk. Anyway she got better very quickly. After that Liz hardly drank spirits.'

Elizabeth only made this distressing event known to her closest friends; she didn't want it to jeopardize her reputation for working. Although it was fairly mild and she quickly recovered she was very young to have experienced an illness of such potential seriousness. At the time of the stroke she was forty-nine. Afterwards her fear, expressed to Veronica and Judith years before: 'I don't know what I'd do if I lost my sense of taste', was partially realized; she could no longer properly taste salt. One of her future colleagues, Peter Trier, remembers many occasions when Elizabeth would have him testing dishes for the salt when he called in. Veronica too remembers testing many times Elizabeth's favourite recipe (Suleiman's) for salted almonds. 'There'd be saucers out for you to try with the food salted to different degrees.'

During the same year she wrote a new introduction to *Italian Food* and revised the book for a first Penguin paperback edition. She says:

During the last decade provision shops and supermarkets selling a high proportion of Italian and imported produce have multiplied. In our big towns new Italian restaurants open almost monthly. The Espresso Coffee Bar, phenomenon of the early Fifties, has developed into the Roman or Neapolitan-type *trattoria*, and spreads far beyond the confines of Soho into the outer suburbs of London and our great industrial cities and seaports. Scarcely a week passes but somebody writes an article in a national newspaper or magazine extolling the glories and subtleties of Italian cooking.

She tells her reader that, added to this, relatively accurate Italian recipe books pour off the presses. But she is at pains to point out that many still do not understand two of the essential virtues of Italian food: a respect for the seasons around which the cooking revolves, and the regionalism which still dictates the type and quality of most of the produce and consequently dishes too.

Having said that reviewers had originally been 'unimaginably kind and welcoming' about the book, she adds that there had also been 'criticisms, queries, and corrections from readers'. Elizabeth's reputation was now sufficiently large for her to have a fairly voluminous postbag. She speaks to her following with these well-chosen words: 'I do not think there is one [letter] which has not been enlightening, constructive, and encouraging . . . It is in view of such criticisms and requests for more detailed explanations, and in the light of ten years further cooking experience, as well as in consideration of conditions much changed . . .' (A number of the criticisms she has in mind are from her friend Viola Johnson who again checked the recipes and corrected more of the Italian. Her son John says, 'Mother never could understand how it was that so many simple mistakes got into the text.') Towards the concluding section Elizabeth writes: 'What I in fact believe is that the English are now more creative and inquiring about cooking than they have ever been before.'

In the autumn Elizabeth appeared in *Wine and Food* again with 'Wardens an Unearthly Savour'. This fascinating piece traces the variety of delightful ways in which pears and quinces have been transformed into sweet dishes for the last 400 years. She once again demonstrates the breadth of her knowledge relating to the history of cookery literature, her discerning qualitative judgements clearly made from considerable familiarity. 'Among the most interesting fruit recipes to be found in the whole of English cookery are those in Robert May's *Accomplish't Cook* first published in 1660', the year of Charles II's restoration to the throne: tarts, pies, creams, all of quinces, that exquisitely scented golden fruit which so beguiled Elizabeth. More recipes follow for the quince confection so beloved of the Portuguese, Spanish and French, called by the French *cotignac* and by the Spanish *membrillo*.

With quotations from the great French traveller and essayist Michel de Montaigne's *Italian Travel Journal* (a copy was given her the year previously by Veronica) we are reminded of Elizabeth's appreciation of the literature of travel, used since her very first book. And with it she is now consistently reaching further back in time. Montaigne says: 'In the evening Signor Ludovica ... sent me a present of some boxes of very good quince jelly, scented, and some lemons and some oranges of extraordinary size.' The year is 1581. Elizabeth quotes too the great Massialot on pear compote: he was one of those ferociously determined cooks who, at the close of the seventeenth century, dragged French cuisine out of the Middle Ages and into a new, more simplified yet refined culinary aesthetic.

In *Wine and Food*'s Winter issue Elizabeth has 'A Nostrum of Neats Tongues'. She ranges from the seventeenth to the twentieth century in a résumé of recipes on how to get the best from a calf's tongue. 'Packed into shallow pots or white-lined terrines and sealed with a layer of clarified butter', this is, she later wrote, 'to my mind the best and most subtle of all English potted meat inventions'. Her recommendations include eating tongue hot with her favourite Cumberland sauce, or potting it in a variety of ways; whilst under the recipe for Lemon Mincemeat Eliza Acton, a more humble domestic writer than Massialot, is credited by Elizabeth with being 'unsurpassed for her taste, her meticulous instructions (her *Modern Cookery*, 1845, is to my mind unquestionably the finest cookery book every written in the English language)'. In these historical pieces Elizabeth is not just purveying nostalgia. What she consistently gives are usable recipes from the great cookery writers of the past.

Hugh Johnson had rapidly put his mark on the journal of the Wine and Food Society (of which he was Secretary), at first most noticeably in his stimulating layouts and designs. He illustrates the covers and inner pages of *Wine and Food* using reproductions of old still-life paintings, that hitherto almost ignored rich source for the history of food. Elizabeth and Hugh's friendship had quickly developed and he generously gives her credit for inspiring him on those regular visits to Halsey Street, and also while on their regular trips to try out new restaurants together. 'We would talk over the covers and illustrations throughout each issue and her great knowledge of art and her passionate interest in design was of immense inspiration and help to me.'

CHAPTER EIGHTEEN

Selling a Dream
(1965–1973)

IN 1958 ALIX Coleman had introduced Elizabeth to a young man who owned a company making copper pans. Among other enterprises Peter Trier also carried out the vital service of retinning these pans (an alloy of tin and nickel is used) both for the trade and for private customers; without the tin lining copper pans are dangerous to use. In conversation with the author he described himself thus: 'I was a tinker really.' Peter had sold to many of the reputable retail outlets – John Lewis, Selfridges, the Ferrari Brothers in Wardour Street and Madame Cadec. In 1960 he had also begun importing the French Le Creuset enamelware into England, with considerable success.

'Almost the entire first consignment was bought by Selfridges. The shops had said to us, "It will never go because the English housewife will think it too heavy amongst other things." They were wrong.'

'We had a lot of help from Liz over these things and other ideas. It was she who later got Le Creuset to make the blue and was the first shop to sell it. She was sick of the yellow and when she mooted the idea David Schmitt of Le Creuset asked what kind of blue she suggested, then: "That's the blue I want," and she pointed to a pack of Gauloises lying on the table – the cigarettes she always smoked. No one used that colour then except the Dutch in their black enamelware with the cobalt blue inside it . . .'

When the Le Creuset blue was finally launched in 1967 after two years of procrastination on the manufacturer's part, the French magazine *Marie-Claire* commented, 'C'est la couleur qui fera fureur.'

'She suggested we should make wooden chopping boards, bowls;

should make a mezza-luna chopper. She wanted people to have wooden draining racks, so we had them made and distributed all these things and more to other companies . . . [Peter's brother Stephen became involved here also.] By then Elizabeth knew her mind and was inclined to be dogmatic, but whatever she said there would be a public following for it. It became obvious that with this enormous clout that her name carried we would have been silly not to have gone with her ideas, the standards she had were so high . . . Liz had been thinking about the idea of setting up a shop for some time, and together I thought we had a lot to offer.'

Elizabeth, like Peter, knew Madame Cadec and her remarkable little shop in Soho, then one of the best and most interesting places in London to buy high-quality kitchenware: utensils, containers, pots and pans of all kinds from France. For those domestic buyers who knew of it Cadec's was invaluable; Madame Cadec was extremely knowledgeable. Among her eccentricities was a practice she commented on to Peter Trier: 'Purchase tax. Oh I don't deal wiz zat orreeble abit.'

Some time after Peter and Elizabeth's thoughts had started to take a more practical form, in May 1964, a large shop was opened on London's Fulham Road to great public acclaim. Called Habitat, almost overnight it became the place where mildly affluent young Londoners found design for their houses to reflect their belief that they were liberated, but without having to bankrupt themselves in the process. During the Fifties Terence Conran had developed his ideas about designing furniture and textiles and learned more about how to sell them. He was above all interested in reaching a wider public than most furniture and fabric companies then did. The Habitat look reflected Conran's interests and influences: a liking for pale Scandinavian woods, natural materials, an Arts and Crafts concentration on good craftsmanship to produce design which was both beautiful, functional and affordable. In the kitchenware Conran evinced his love of the Mediterranean.

Furniture, as one of the costlier types of object made for the home, was sold at that time in the rather hushed and precious atmosphere then considered appropriate for department stores and furniture showrooms. Disliking this, Conran decided that alongside his simple practical furniture and fabrics he would add kitchenware too. As these goods were cheaper their sale would give the shop a more busy, bustling feel, with more people going in and out, and helping to create a vibrant, instant and stimulating atmosphere. Conran himself had, since his first visits to France and subsequent reading of Elizabeth's books, always loved food and its objects, so this addition, like most of what he sold, derived from a personal interest. Habitat radiated an impression of being up to date, but was never so avant-garde as to be threateningly stylish; it was comfortable and durable too. Some of the things found there were obtainable in other shops, but Conran's instincts were masterly in giving his customers the things they wanted and the guidance and the reassurance that this was the way they could put them together. By showing how, he gave them confidence in surroundings which were both modern and not too difficult to emulate. He was a virtuoso at navigation within the English system, and at manipulating it to his advantage; at the same time he contributed to its reform, its mellowing.

Inspired by France itself, by Elizabeth's books and by what Conran had seen at Madame Cadec's in Soho, most of the kitchenware in Habitat came from France. One of the best retailers in Paris was Dehillerin in Les Halles. Here Conran found the tools for the kitchen: knives, mills for pepper and salt, sieves, earthenware bowls and containers, terrines, pots, copper pans. Crockery came from Scandinavia as well as England. A vital feature of the new shop, and one whose originality is difficult to remember because now ubiquitous, was the display of the kitchenware. Conran wanted to replicate something of the feeling of those French ironmongers which had so inspired him ten years earlier, more recently the warehouses too. Consequently he had all the merchandise displayed out front on deep shelves. Little was stored away in stockrooms behind. All the glasses were out, all the china, all the saucepans. This gave the combined impression of abundance and the functionality of a warehouse.

Central to the success of all this was that Conran was selling a life-style, but also, as he told the author, 'Habitat had a fashion connection. It was designed to be constantly changing, with new looks and new ideas. However, classic cookware and furniture was the permanent base of it all.'

Elizabeth was annoyed that the young Conran had pipped her at the post with his kitchen section in Habitat. He knew her socially by now and she felt that he had taken some of her ideas. 'She often referred to it as Shabbycat or Tattycat. I suppose she thought it was a bit vulgar really. But yes, she was quite fond of him as well in a way,' says Stephen Trier's wife Caroline, who worked in Elizabeth's shop for its first two years. Elizabeth need not have felt too concerned about the need to demean Conran's enterprise, however, or the threat of competition, because in him she had a magnificent disciple; he was part of that first, younger post-war generation which had been inspired by and was now proselytizing her ideas. But she was always ambivalent about her followers, and in any case was not consistent about what her writing and this new enterprise were about. Conran is generous towards her, though, and prepared to give credit when he says: 'Yes, I was incredibly influenced by Elizabeth.'

Meanwhile, plans had been going ahead in 1964 for Elizabeth to launch her own shop. Pam Pugh (then Llewelyn) remembers 'a meal at the Chanterelle where we all sat down and decided that we would go ahead with it'.

Before they opened Elizabeth had coaxed and persuaded her friend Renée Fedden to join in the venture. Whilst Renée's financial contribution came from her close friend Rosie Peto, Lady Hinchinbrook, Peter Trier's wife Jenny, using some money she had recently been given, bought the leasehold on a little shop in Bourne Street, off Sloane square and convenient for Elizabeth in Halsey Street just the other side of the King's Road. The tenants had wanted to buy it but Elizabeth's enthusiasm had inspired the others to go ahead. Pamela and Brian Llewelyn were asked if they would join as partners along with Renée and Jenny. 'Elizabeth provided little of the finance, but all the cachet in her name.' These four and Elizabeth were the directors (Peter, although intimately involved with the enterprise from the beginning, was never one of them).

Peter Trier and Elizabeth went 'in a beat-up old Bedford van on several buying trips to France. She wanted to have her own products in the shop and was prepared to scout the length and breadth of England and France to secure them.' Shops like Dehillerin in Paris were already known to her but she and Peter were in France to discover wholesalers. These they found by asking around and through the connections Elizabeth already had over in France.

'A little factory here, a small pottery there. I can see Liz twenty feet up in an old warehouse, picking out old dusty bowls and getting so excited about them. South from Paris and turn left and an old pottery there. Liz went bananas about it. "I've found the real thing," she kept saying.

'The shop was to be a serious kitchen shop. You could call it a grown-up Madam Cadec. We were gradually loading up a ton of big pots on the Jeep [someone else was driving this] and the old Bedford van and lumbered back home with it all. XYZ was her code name for the pottery; she was nervous about us being copied before we began. So we sent back a card saying: "We found XYZ."

'Anything to do with design for Elizabeth was completely handed over to Anthony [Denney, who designed the entire interior of the shop].'

The shop was not large, nor was it in a particularly well-placed position, with an unsympathetic meter merchant next door. Unlike Conran's Habitat on the corner of Walton Street and Fulham Road there was no view from a distance; but its proximity to Sloane Square and the area's potential for customers, a large proportion of whom already owned a number of her books, was not lost on Elizabeth. (At the time her shop opened all her books had been revised by her and published by Penguin in paperback.)

Denney's utterly simple design succeeded as the perfect backdrop for what Elizabeth and her partners were about to sell. His interior reflected the growing contemporary trend for public spaces to become more workmanlike. The spatial possibilities of old warehouses were being recognized; picture galleries, for instance, were now regularly sited in this type of building. Aspects of Modernism, its functionalism and clarity of line, had finally become acceptable to more than just the artistic élite.

But Elizabeth herself was not much concerned with trends and estimations. She was driven from within. She was not self-conscious like Terence Conran, did not have his sensitivity to the spirit of the age, seems not to have been much affected by the turmoil of the

Sixties — for it was in that decade that her shop and Conran's were opened. According to *Time* magazine this was the decade of Swinging London, the capital of Pop culture, the Place Where It Was All Happening. At the heart of Pop culture and design was a claim for the value of novelty, for the ephemeral, the temporary, the expendable, and for popularity as an ultimate criterion — all of this; on the other hand there was tradition, memory, permanence and the élite. Within this duality Elizabeth was on the side of tradition. The cult of the Mediterranean — Provence, Italy, and the Isles of Greece; and even further; the Spice Islands, the Mysterious East — is an old English passion. So Elizabeth's love of well-matched function and craft — craftmanship *is* tradition and memory — was one long established in England.

Pop culture was purveyed overwhelmingly by music, which entirely passed Elizabeth by, as did most other aspects of the movement. However, at the time she was seen as New, and therefore automatically a Good Thing. She did not flaunt her remarkable memory and knowledge of the past, her 'square' High Tory monarchism, or any other unfashionable mental habits.

Elizabeth Good, who had written a preview of Habitat in the recently instituted 'Design for Living' section of the *Sunday Times* the previous year, interviewed Elizabeth the day before Elizabeth David Ltd opened. She is described as 'shy . . . reserved . . . hates being photographed . . . is tall and slim' and her

style is muted, deceptively off-hand: she tucks her grey silky hair behind her ears and the large hornrimmed glasses she sometimes wears ride constantly halfway down her small schoolgirl nose. Her soft, almost expiring voice is often the vehicle for some pretty lethal comments on her profession. When words fail she resorts to long, effective silences.

Her voice quickens when she talks about cooking and the equipment she will sell . . . Handling each piece with familiar affection, an almost sensuous feeling for textures and shapes . . . she says, 'What I want to sell is traditional French and English cooking utensils and tableware. I want to make this clear. We are trying to get English things as well as French ones. I went to France to look for traditional regional pots, traditional shapes and materials. About 40% of our stock is French.'

Elizabeth Good wrote that the interior by Denney had interpreted Elizabeth's views 'simply and effectively: builders' finishes, black and white [tiled floor], the only colour is a soft blue-grey, the only decoration a leaf motif in cast iron which is used as brackets for cool marble shelves and as a rail to the stairs leading into the cellar.' (The cool shelves had come from Burketts, the recently closed-down high-class fishmonger opposite Harrods.) Denney said, 'I call it a no-decor shop. It's nostalgic, it evokes memories of bakeries, still rooms and larders. Elizabeth herself would not have used the word nostalgic. She called it "very professional looking, very solid. Not grand and not forbidding. I want anyone who passes to feel they can come in and buy a toothpick."' Alongside the toothpicks they would have found the warm browns of French earthenware diables, casseroles, jars, tians, terrines; the yellow and paler creams of glaze and salt-glaze, the steely glint of knives, one for every kitchen task; whisks of willow, spoons of china, wood and metal for cooking, serving; mortars, moulds, mandolins, hachoirs, white china Pillivuyt bowls, ramekins, cocotte dishes and much more, crammed in orderly display on shelves and on the floor; all the perfect little tools for those obscure kitchen tasks at which the French so excelled. Elizabeth Good wrote: 'Together they have brought off a difficult proposition: to make tangible an atmosphere and an attitude.'

Elizabeth David Ltd was quickly copied, and those involved in her shop became even more wary of disclosing vital sources of supply. An English supplier commented later: 'These cooking shops we sell to, they're all copies of hers.'

Peter Trier says: 'A lot of Elizabeth's friends came to the shop, it became a kind of club for her. Several of them worked there too. Those like Joyce Murchie whom Elizabeth had known since Cairo and spent time with in Italy.'

'Joyce was great fun, she was a very social being', says Caroline Trier. 'She had a small income and didn't really need to work but did it to help Elizabeth out. To the surprise of us all she turned out to be a brilliant saleswoman. She could sell anything to anybody.' Caroline

Trier recalls that this prompted one of Elizabeth's *bons mots*: 'Oh, Joyce could sell an egg-cup to cook a turkey in.'

Part of the reason for Elizabeth's success was that she had never been avant-garde, but instead had represented fashion in the traditional sense. At the heart of this was the now ageing idea of 'the prevailing customs of the upper classes', the ruling élite from which Elizabeth sprang. Elizabeth David Ltd was the first specialist kitchen shop in England to foster the ideas she had promulgated for over a decade in her books.

On the day of opening, 1 November 1965, 'You couldn't move in the shop,' says Pamela Pugh. 'Liz had let it slip to some other journalist or someone, anyway the word had got out and other papers had written something up about it as well as *The Times* who was supposed to have the scoop. We were absolutely inundated. We had started the whole thing off in such an amateurish way really that we were taken by surprise at the success of it. After a week our stock was gone. We had been driving over nearly every evening to the warehouse to restock. Our French suppliers were not exactly highpowered or speedy so we had to frantically get more stuff. It was lucky we were so young. It was very exciting and stimulating, you were learning on your feet ... I remember so well that distinctive and evocative smell in the shop ... Gauloises, and pâté, and there was always wine around.'

Peter Trier says: 'Liz would bring lunch in a string bag and even if it was just a boiled egg, it would be beautifully cut up with homemade mayonnaise and sprig of parsley and all beautifully arranged on a white plate.' His sister-in-law Caroline Trier remembers that 'Yes, every day Liz brought in a lunch for us. There was a crate of wine delivered at regular intervals and there was always wine there for lunch. It was Red Lisbon. The stockroom was small and very cramped but one squeezed in. There was one of those old Singer sewing machine bases with a marble top for a table and Liz would beautifully lay out whatever she'd brought for that day. One of us would remain in charge of the shop if someone should come in during the lunch period. We didn't really sit down for it though, just grazed in passing. It was always delicious.'

Elizabeth was in every day and Renée most days too. There were always one or two people there working in the shop helping Elizabeth. She wouldn't always be out front and spent a certain amount of her time in the back room. Two months after the shop opened Renée and Robin Fedden separated. 'Elizabeth was wholeheartedly behind Renée on this, she was immensely supportive of her,' says Caroline Trier.

Elizabeth David Ltd was to take up much of Elizabeth's time for the next seven years, and for the first part of that period she did little writing. In the months before the opening of the shop, however, she had a flurry of journalistic activity, including several pieces for the newly launched women's magazine *Nova*. The magazine was subtitled 'A new kind of magazine for the new kind of woman'. With articles on cooking and the home *Nova* set out to reflect a new attitude of self-fulfilment before duty. The *Nova* woman apparently cooked more because she enjoyed it than because she had to; a principle to which Elizabeth in her single state could subscribe.

Another pattern fixed by now was her division of the day. Since her months in India, and whenever possible before that, her periods of work and rest, reading and writing were not governed by any conventional norm though by now they were well known to her friends. Up at about five, she would often work from bed with her instant coffee beside her. In the evening if she wasn't seeing anyone she could work late. If there were guests, smoking, talking, listening, drinking, she usually prepared only one or two dishes. Guests would sometimes be asked to help wash up.

The novelist and wine connoisseur Sybille Bedford had met Elizabeth in 1963. She told the author: 'Then she wrote me a fan letter and I had written her one, our letters crossed . . . I was then living in the South of France. [Elizabeth had written in her tribute to Norman Douglas that Sybille Bedford, 'that magical writer', had assisted Norman on his cookery book *Venus in the Kitchen*: 'Sybille Bedford's succinct, quiet reveries on her friend are amongst the most perceptive and sensitive.'] When I was to be in England she invited me to dinner in Halsey Street. It was one of those Georgian houses . . . very narrow and when you came in it was made narrower by having bookcases on both sides of the passageway. It was like one of those First World War trenches and they felt as if they were going to fall in on you. The house was stuffed with books and ornaments.'

Hugh Johnson also had the same impression: 'Bookcases almost blocking the entrance hall, books silting up the sitting room, ziggurats of books on the dresser, the stairs, the bed . . .' Elizabeth kept her full *Oxford English Dictionary*, all fourteen volumes of it, doubling up as a table at the end of her bed.

Sybille Bedford continues: 'Felicité was there that first evening – we later became good friends. After drinks she didn't immediately absent herself and Elizabeth said, "Felicité, I had asked you for drinks not dinner," and she had to remove herself upstairs. That evening I had white Beaujolais for the first time. We went down into the kitchen . . . Everything was open . . . all the shelves . . . the china was white.' (The complete invasion of white was not to occur for another few years, when Elizabeth had grown more purist and got rid of much of her traditional blue and white.)

Sybille Bedford describes the meal as 'simple and delicious. We had kebabs, cheeses and apricots . . . From the beginning we had so much to talk about. Food; we always talked about that. It is very much part of my writing. But much else besides. We talked about painting, Shakespeare. Elizabeth was very erudite, on Shakespeare . . . and poetry. She was such a perfectionist. Elizabeth was someone who was very severe in her standards, she was so amusing, and very unforgiving. She didn't do a prima donna act, she enchanted people. I rose from the table to leave at 1.45 a.m.'

Elizabeth David Ltd was used by a number of friends, such as Sybille Bedford, to illustrate her generosity. 'She was immensely so, to the point of insanity . . . When she liked someone she would give them something, see to one's comforts. She gave me a bottle of La Tour, "Because," she said, "your standards of dinner are so high." I was later given a complement of white china from the shop.'

Doreen Thornton comments: 'Liz had not the slightest idea about money really. She was so generous. Right back when we were young, and she'd say about things, "Oh, put it on my account."

'I'd often come up to London and see her in the shop. There were always friends milling about as well as those officially there to help. I'd do something to lend a hand, one didn't just stand around, and she'd send me back with armfuls of lovely white things . . .'

'She was so generous materially but not about people,' says Sybille Bedford. 'She had fallen out with an editor [the débâcle with Macdonald over *Italian Food*] and fifteen years later she had not forgiven him. This trait became worse. Elizabeth was very, very temperamental. She had such an excess of fury.'

It is said that Elizabeth was essentially private, hated publicity and wouldn't give interviews. However, part of her always had an eye to some useful publicity: for a new book, or the shop. During the Sixties she gave interviews not only to most of the major newspapers, but also to a young journalist, Michael Bateman, for a book he was putting together on the best-known contemporary figures making food as their living.

Bateman began his record of the interview with the words: 'There's only room for one at the top and that place is occupied by Elizabeth David . . . For some years now books have been coming out from other writers in which they acknowledge a debt to her and her only. Katherine Whitehorn . . . says she is David inspired . . .' Bateman noticed, like everyone who entered Halsey Street, the tools of her trade surrounding Elizabeth in such profusion.

Despite several inaccuracies (Elizabeth wrote a sharp letter about him to a friend), Bateman captures something of the real Elizabeth. 'Her books . . . go to America and one by one get translated for the European markets.' He lets her, in her own words, give an idea of the international status she has by now acquired. '*French Provincial Cooking* was a notable flop in the US. I had fan-tas-tic notices in the US. Better than here, so it shows you that notices don't do anything for you. I just don't know the market.' [She never did understand her market well because she was often talking to herself.] By 1965 all Elizabeth's books had been brought out in paperback by Penguin, since 1963 under the auspices of a young editor, Jill Norman, on whose life Elizabeth's was to have a great impact.

The following year Elizabeth was interviewed by the new editor of *Wine and Food*, Pamela Vandyke Price, who belonged to the younger generation of people under Elizabeth's sway. She described her thus: 'Gioconda of the kitchen, she will smile and talk of other people. Elizabeth says, "Why should anyone want to know about me?"

'"Hundreds of thousands of people want to know about you," I tell her, "because you have made us think differently about food . . . You've sharpened up the standards of restaurants and become compulsive reading for men and women who don't cook at all. . . . It's your ideas, as well as your recipes, that dominate the entertaining of those of us who . . . grew up in the war, and ever since have had to cope singlehanded in the kitchen."

'Elizabeth counters that: "There was already so much wonderful work being done to encourage good cooking. André Simon, Ambrose Heath, Elizabeth Craig – where would any of us be without them?"'

In this same wilful vein, according to Pamela Vandyke Price, when she tries 'to trace her influence among food writers', Elizabeth says, 'For goodness sake, there's too much nonsense written about cookery – they'll be publishing books on Lowestoft cooking or Tunbridge Wells cuisine next.'

Between 1967 and 1969 while the shop took up most of her time Elizabeth wrote little journalism. Nevertheless she did have printed at her own cost four little booklets which she sold in the shop alongside the rest of her books, and a selection of paperback cookery books by other authors. The booklets are beautifully designed and printed. Elizabeth was obsessive about every detail as they went through the press. 'She had nightmares, there'd be hell to pay if anything was wrong with that kind of thing,' says John Johnson. The booklets were:

Dried Herbs, Aromatics and Condiments (1967). Elizabeth had 5000 of these printed, to go in a herb, spice and condiment pack sold by the shop. After two years the little booklets had sold out and she reprinted them.

English Potted Meats and Fish Pastes (1968), a version of the article she had first done for *Food and Wine* on 'Neat's Tongues', then expanded for *Nova* in April 1965.

The Baking of an English Loaf (1969) appeared in its first guise for *Queen* magazine in December 1968.

Syllabubs and Fruit Fools (1969), with some recipes cut, was published in the first issue of *Nova* in March 1965. Elizabeth republished the article in expanded form in *Queen* magazine in 1968, now under the editorship of her friend Hugh Johnson.

These were not Elizabeth's first ventures into the genre of pamphlets, and in 1972 she wrote one on *Green Pepper Berries: a New Taste*; she sold these berries, which fascinated her, in the shop. Despite their slightness these little books are interesting, giving eminently useful instruction and information at the same time. They were the seeds which grew into the works consuming the last years of Elizabeth's life.

In 1969 Anthony Denney married a young girl, Celia Royde-Smith, who had for some time been working in the shop, and whom Elizabeth had found sympathetic. She and Renée, amongst others, were very surprised at the event and for a time Elizabeth was deeply hurt. Apropos the marriage she made one of those criticisms most damning in her vocabulary: 'disloyalty'. (Elizabeth always had difficulty in accepting that those close to her might also wish to lead autonomous lives.) In time Elizabeth became fond of Celia and forgave Anthony, as much as she was able, going to stay with them in Spain on more than one occasion. As a result of his enormous earnings Anthony had effectively become a tax exile and moved much of his wealth to Spain, where he bought and restored a farmhouse near Alicante in the south-east of the country. Here in the mid-1960s, before his marriage to Celia, Elizabeth had stayed with him and his current boyfriend, an Australian, shortly afterwards writing about her stay for the *Spectator*.

In 1970 Elizabeth brought out a new publication. This was a synthesis of ideas which she said had come to her in a moment of comprehension while re-reading Mrs Leyel's *Gentle Art of Cookery* during her extended period of ill-health in 1963. She had realized that her old favourite was 'yet another manifestation of the English love-affair with Eastern food and Arabian Nights ingredients . . . The train of thought . . . is still incomplete, still no more than a glance into the English preoccupation with the spices and the scents, the fruit, the flavourings, the sauces and the condiments of the orient, near and far.' She called the book *Spices, Salt and Aromatics in the*

English Kitchen and said that it was the first volume in what was to be a series 'perhaps three volumes of five, it depends how much time I have, I write terribly slowly. . . . Later volumes will deal with bread, yeast, cakes, creams and cheeses and egg dishes, and meat and game.' Meanwhile, the first was an enlightening little treatise. Oddly, it is the only one of her books whose title is clumsy in its scansion; a rare occasion when one is reminded of Elizabeth's 'boredom' with music (in her later life she owned a television but no stereo system). And even those who know and admire the book often misquote the title, reversing the first two words to *Salts, Spices* . . .

A simple description – 'This book offers a sample . . . of the immense number of English spiced and aromatically flavoured dishes' – is inadequate. In the very first lines, with her accustomed elegance and mastery of her medium, Elizabeth captures the reader's imagination, evoking the past with one of her incantational lists.

> For some two thousand years, English cookery has been extremely spice-conscious, not surprisingly to anyone in the least familiar with the history of the spice trade in Europe and the part played in it, successively, by the Phoenicians, the Romans, the Arab conquerors of Spain, the Norman crusaders, the merchants of Venice and Genoa, the religious orders which fostered the arts of healing, medicine and distillery, the Portuguese explorers who opened the sea route to the Indies, the Dutch empire-builders who wrested the spice trade from Portugal, the British East India Company whose merchants in their turn made London for two centuries the greatest spice mart in the world.

Elizabeth continues with a fine résumé of the usage of spices and flavourings throughout the history of the English kitchen. She diverges from the [then] prevailing belief that the traditional English fascination with these things was largely a result of attempts to mask contaminated food, or to enhance 'a monotonous diet of salt meat or boiled fish', and argues that the reason they have such an honourable place in our cooking tradition was probably because 'the English have a natural taste for highly seasoned foods – as do most northern people – and since trade with the Near East and Southern Europe brought us early in the evolution of our cookery considerable opportunities for indulging the taste, we took to spiced food with an enthusiasm which seems to have been almost equal to that shown by the Romans at the height of their preoccupation with the luxuries of living.'

In 1968 a young woman, Claudia Roden, exiled through political upheaval from her Egyptian homeland and the city of her birth, Cairo, published a beautifully written book entitled *A Book of Middle Eastern Food* (Thomas Nelson). She said it was 'the fruit of nostalgic longing for . . . food that was the constant joy of life in a world so different from the Western one'. In evocative and judicious prose she presented 'humble peasant food, flamboyant Mediterranean dishes, the elaborate . . . as well as the everyday dishes of the middle classes throughout the Middle East'. She has generously given credit to Elizabeth as the person who 'with her brilliance and integrity' inspired her to write when she read her first book. In lifting 'the veil from the food which she [Elizabeth] had learned about when she lived in Cairo, Alexandria and Greece . . . her book of *Mediterranean Food* . . . slightly eased my nostalgic homesickness . . . In the early editions she intimated that there were many more dishes in the Near East which needed to be discovered; that was the spark that fired me.'

Claudia Roden's book was an instant success, and not only because the late 1960s was a period of fascination with anything 'ethnic'. The book is a delight to read and inspiring to use, but the degree of its success is a partial reflection of those very strands present in English history and the national psyche which Elizabeth sets out to draw together in her own *Spices, Salt and Aromatics in the English Kitchen*. Elements of Middle Eastern Food – as also other aspects of the cultures of the Middle East – had for centuries been brought back and made fashionable with the upper classes in Northern Europe. Certainly by the end of the eighteenth and the early nineteenth century the vogue for things Eastern was widespread among the educated classes: one thinks of Edward Fitzgerald's *Omar Khayyam*, Richard Burton's *Arabian Nights*, Persian miniatures, and the related vogue for Chinoiserie.

Elizabeth herself had personal experience of the east, of course: she had lived several years in Egypt, travelled in the Middle East, for a while in India, and had visited Morocco. Added to this she had an easy familiarity with many of the classic works on the East in her own library, including Doughty's craggy nineteenth-century masterpiece, *Arabia Deserta*, and Lord Bute's *Moorish Recipes* (Oliver and Boyd, 1956). To these she brought her now considerable understanding of the history of England's food and its dependence on the Middle East and the classical Mediterranean. In the most consistent celebration of English food she had so far undertaken, Elizabeth produces a book which is not a dry historical work but instead fulfils the claim she made for her beloved Mrs Leyel: 'Stimulus, that was the quality which Mrs Leyel provided and in plenty, for she had the gift of making her recipes sound enticing.'

Occasional comments throughout *Spices, Salt and Aromatics in the English Kitchen* point more clearly to Elizabeth's present inclinations. On the vexed question of the French influence upon English cooking she says, 'Towards appreciation of these points, increased familiarity with our own cookery history and its literature, so astonishingly rich, varied, and illuminating, would help.' And her own command of this heritage is now abundantly clear. At least by 1958, quite probably earlier (it was first published in 1939), she had become familiar with *The Englishman's Food: Five Centuries of English Diet* by that remarkable food-loving biochemist J. C. Drummond, in collaboration with his wife Ann Wilbraham. During the war Drummond had assisted Lord Woolton in masterminding wartime rationing – 'the best food for bad times' – along sound dietetic principles.

Drummond's book was the most comprehensive study so far undertaken on the history of the English diet and, although the subject is increasingly recognized as a branch of social history, with much primary literature published, *The Englishman's Food* has still not been superseded. Elizabeth rightly called it 'absolutely engrossing . . . an invaluable work of reference', written 'lucidly, with great learning and a nice dry wit'. Related to this is another group of books which Elizabeth cites in her bibliography and from which she quotes at length in the body of her book.

As long ago as the 1930s women had begun to collect and write down British regional or folk recipes; somewhat akin to the way in which Cecil Sharpe had made his great collection of the folk music of Great Britain. The aim of these English women was to record and make usable this traditional cooking before the industrialization of food had 'completely crushed [it] out of existence'. One of the chief of these, Florence White, started the English Folk Cookery Association to carry out the task. It died with her in 1940 but her book *Good Things in England* (Jonathan Cape, 1931) is a fine testament to her work. Historical collections of English recipes were not so new, one of the most recent being: *English Recipes and Others* (Methuen and Co., 1967) was by the well-known *Daily Express* food columnist Sheila Hutchins, who had a fine collection of old food books. But in 1932 Florence White had insisted that hers were those recipes still being used by living people. They were not 'museum pieces' but often recipes that had been in use in people's families 'for over a century. These are so many and so varied that the present volume is merely a small instalment of our kitchen and stillroom riches. England does not know her wealth.' Nor was this written by a zealot provincial. Florence White had trained and worked in France for several years, concluding that 'there is no reason why the famous French cuisine and our fine traditional English cookery should be bitter rivals. Both are absolutely distinctive.'

In 1954, as well as bringing out Elizabeth's *Italian Food* Macdonald had also published an extraordinary book by a woman called Dorothy Hartley. This was *Food in England*. After studying early manuscripts in the British Library, for many years Hartley had wandered around England (by bicycle) collecting and writing about the pre-industrial customs and crafts of Britain in a voluminous series of books and articles. Despite certain inaccuracies and an inadequate bibliography for tracing sources, *Food in England* is a remarkable, rambling compilation of traditions and practices connected with the making of English food, which the author illustrates with her witty and distinctive drawings.

Elizabeth's *Spices, Salt and Aromatics in the English Kitchen* is an extension of this genre, but also a reappraisal of her own knowledge, her sense of belonging, and the deeply deleterious long- and short-term effects of industrialization on our food. Her choice of English recipes is quirky and inspiring, with a stimulating selection from so many of the authors made familiar by her articles. Their inclusion springs from beliefs long held by Elizabeth, but only now finding expression in a more expansive form. (Even when generous and encouraging, as Audrey Withers or Hugh Johnson had been, they were still always bound by editorial constraints: a maximum of two or three thousand words.) With biting wit Elizabeth describes how, for example, a simple English butter sauce for fish was gradually transformed out of all recognition and 'we began to confuse good plain cooking with plain bad cooking ... What it did become was billsticker's paste, and on this basis egg sauce, parsley sauce, caper, anchovy, shrimp, mushroom, lobster and some half dozen other perfectly respectable sauces fell toppling to their ruin.' And from this sorry conclusion springs the crucial point of *Spices, Salt and Aromatics*: to restore them, and the whole body of English cookery, Elizabeth believes, 'We need to go back, far back, to the recipes of more than a century ago, to the early and mid nineteenth century, when an authentic and still strong English cooking tradition flourished amid the ravages of the Industrial Revolution.'

We are given two practical, learned and graceful chapters on 'Aromatic Herbs, Dried or Fresh' and 'Spices and Condiments': Allspice, Aniseed, Caraway Seeds, Cardamom, Cassia ... Cayenne Pepper ... Coriander, Cumin, Curry Powder ... Mustard Seeds, Nutmeg ... Peppercorns ... Poppy Seeds ... Saffron ... Salt'. And so on. None of these flavourings is particularly obscure, but amongst the remarkably varied collection of information on their origins and historical and present uses, there are many good tips on how to use and how not to use them. Elizabeth's own prejudices were always confidently displayed but her nephew Stephen Grey, for whom this book and her next were favourites, maintains: 'Most books have a feeling of what is right or wrong, but Aunt Lizza was liberal, in the sense that it is up to you how you want to have your bread. She only sets standards from an historical point of view ... she never rams things down your throat. The magic was in the stories ... and then to find out how easy it was was marvellous. But I wouldn't have bothered if I'd had to just read a recipe. You weren't left with much choice after reading it but to get up and make those things.'

Elizabeth was most certainly telling readers what they ought to do. But it was done with such subtle persuasion and absolute confidence in her opinions that the reader, by implication a follower, doesn't wish to be thought less tasteful than Elizabeth, so will most likely concur. She says:

> The use of herbs is very much a matter of association, taste, and prejudice, and cooks whose work I respect recommend a branch or two of rosemary in the dish with veal, chicken and lamb roasts (I prefer branches of wild Provence thyme); others suggest that the meat be spiked with the minutest pieces of dried rosemary and garlic. As for sage, Italian cooks, like ourselves, are fond of it, and use it for a number of veal dishes. To me, it deadens the food with its musty, dried-blood scent. [A lethal thrust. One has to steel oneself to reach for the jar of sage after that.] Instead of sage, it is worth trying dried mint or basil . . .
>
> To make a bouquet of herbs in leaf form . . . put a teaspoon of mixed basil, marjoram, thyme, savory, with a crumbled bay leaf, in a 4 inch square of muslin. Add three or four whole peppercorns and, if you like, a peeled clove of garlic crushed with a knife. Tie the little bundle with thread . . .
>
> Personally I find the little ritual of preparing herb bouquets one of the minor pleasures of cooking. Nothing would persuade me to relinquish it in favour of a bought bouquet made up in a factory . . . all as like as two — or rather twelve — teabags.

Another chapter is devoted to 'Sauces'. Commencing with one of those brilliant pieces of historical unravelling of culinary myths which she was so good at, Elizabeth wades through the quagmire of inaccuracies surrounding the true origins of her favourite, Cumberland sauce, 'the best of all sauces for cold meat . . .' This is the introduction to over twenty pages of 'emulsions sweet and savoury', taken largely from pre-industrial cookery books, written when she believed the English still understood the principle which Escoffier, then Prosper Montagne, had also maintained: 'that the basis of all good cooking must be good taste and common sense, and not mere fancy and make belief'. As André Simon says: 'Montagne believed, and never tired of repeating, that sauces and garnishes were not meant to camouflage, cover, or make acceptable . . . their function . . . was to help and not to hide, to add flavour, taste or consistency to the food which they adorned, and to do it discreetly.'

Elizabeth includes: Fruit Sauce for Game, from Florence Jack's instructive *Cookery for Every Household* of 1914; Sauce of Horse-radish from the inimitable seventeenth-century wit, man of letters, proto-scientist Sir Kenelm Digby and his *Closet Opened*; Gooseberry Sauce for Baked Mackerel from Eliza Acton's *Modern Cookery* of 1845; Drawn Butter from *A True Gentlewoman's Delight*, the posthumously published cookery book of the Countess of Kent, who died in 1651, a lady to whose book Elizabeth was particularly attached. She quoted from it often and made considerable researches into the life of the Countess, Elizabeth de Grey, sister to the Countess of Arundel; Granville Sauce for Salmon comes from Lady Llanover's *Good Cookery* of 1867. Elizabeth had some time ago fallen for the charms of the spirited Welshwoman Augusta Llanover's *Good Cookery* and had written an original biographical piece on her for *Wine and Food* in 1965. 'My aim', wrote Lady Llanover, 'has been to preserve or restore all the good old habits of my country, and utterly repudiate all immoral introductions which ruin the health as well as imperil the soul . . .' Wife of a local MP, Benjamin Hall, Augusta was 'formidably industrious, endowed with a high sense of duty towards her dependents and her husband's constituents'. She also

> devoted immense energy to the study of Welsh traditions and agriculture, to local folklore, music, literature, husbandry, cookery and housekeeping. After the death of her husband . . . [it is to Benjamin Hall that Big Ben owes it nickname] Lady Llanover evidently settled down to the writing of her cookery book. We can take it that everything she set down was first-hand, noted from direct observation and practical experience. When she gives recipes for rice bread, barley cakes, leek and plum broth, chicken and leek pie with cream, Welsh salt duck, Gwent short cakes . . . her authority is indisputable . . .

Elizabeth's verdict on Welsh duck in *Spices, Salt and Aromatics* is that it produces 'a deliciously flavoured and tender duck; and the melon goes to perfection with cold duck. . . . It is fortunate for us that Lady Llanover recorded such recipes . . . for they do not appear in other published works'. Elizabeth is not only here being something of a Welsh Nationalist (she had always loved visiting Wales but undoubtedly became more conscious of her Welsh origins on her father's side as she grew older), it is a book after her own heart. This is vividly illustrated when Elizabeth writes that Lady Llanover professed certain beliefs which were anathema to Victorian taste, saying that: 'In her repudiation of the marvels of Victorian progress and the products of what she called "mechanical talent" she was also reactionary. Or was she a visionary? To those of us who today yearn increasingly for authenticity and natural food, she appears sometimes to be writing of the 1960s rather than the 1860s.'

This was in 1965. Writing five years later in *Spices, Salt and Aromatics* Elizabeth reiterates: 'Now seeking means to combat the Chemical Age, we look to our forebears for help.' This is the repeated battle cry of the book. She says that she writes 'mainly out of a wish to preserve some memory of the seasonal aspect of fruit and vegetables, before everything green . . . disappears straight into the packet, the dehydrating machine, and the deep freeze.'

Elizabeth is trying to create a present world from the past, and herein lies the difficulty. At the outset, in *Mediterranean Food*, she used quotations from past writers to give depth and context to her representation of a world, but a world which still existed in the present. The Middle East, regional France, provincial Italy, were still growing and preparing food in ways often little changed for centuries, sometimes even millennia. The past, for Elizabeth, just as for the poet T. S. Eliot in his plea for the crucial place of tradition and history in the modern world, gave depth and added meaning to the present, as it had always done for every culture prior to the relentless West in the twentieth century. But in *Spices, Salt and Aromatics* Elizabeth has to overcome the problem that the English world she describes through her recipes can no longer be found in real time. Pre-industrial England had paid the price, had been swallowed up 'by the ravages of the Industrial Revolution'. It had lost, unlike the Mediterranean countries she had always written about, the traditions of a culture rooted to the soil and connected through continuity to its past; and in turn England had produced a kind of cooking no longer alive but recorded only in books.

In the section on 'Anglo-Indian Cookery' Elizabeth regrets having to record that since the time of her redoubtable and admired nineteenth-century Colonel Kenney-Herbert and his *Culinary Jottings*, little had changed in India. 'The kitchens which I myself had the opportunity of observing in New Delhi were still unbelievably primitive, and the food which came out of them an astonishing mixture of English nannies' puddings, cakes festooned in spectacular spun-sugar work . . .' and so on. She likes the Colonel because she can identify with his sentiments and sometimes his beautifully clear voice. It was he whom she had quoted verbatim in *Summer Cooking* on the making of an omelette. In her comments on the Colonel she is clearly identifying: 'Several good cookery books have been written by professional soldiers, and this is perhaps no coincidence. On the whole the most successful books of technical instruction, and this applies as much to cookery as to other subjects, are those . . . [where] . . . the author expresses his views with soldierly precision and is prepared to go to some lengths to defend them.' This applies to Elizabeth also, but at the same time she believed, as she said of Kenelm Digby's recipes for mead, metheglin, hydromel: 'all the best recipes . . . are runes, litanies, something even of magic spells'.

On 'Cured and Brined Meat' Elizabeth has this to say:

English food, so extravagantly overpraised by its advocates and so bitterly, and so often rightly, reviled by those who have suffered from British hotel and restaurant catering, is never seen to greater advantage than when it is presented in perfect simplicity, unadorned, and on a rather large scale. In other words, English party food tends to be very much more acceptable than English everyday cooking . . .

Let us consider some of our genuine English culinary assets. Among the best of them are our cured and salted meats. Hams, gammons, salt silversides and briskets of beef are not . . . so preposterously expensive that only about half of one per cent of the population can ever taste them . . . It is here especially that we get back to cooking in a certain quantity . . .

and the recipe for these dishes follows.

'Kebab Cookery' tells how to make perfect kebabs derived from 'the Levantine and oriental traditions to which English cookery already owes so much. To me, it is hard to improve on the flavouring of lemon and dried wild marjoram buds which give the lamb kebabs of Greece their sharply aromatic scent.'

Khichri is: 'The dish from which the English evolved kedgeree. The original contains no fish, and is simply a mixture of lentils and rice cooked with spices. It is very cheap and filling.'

Those potted meats about which Elizabeth has already written in articles and again in her little booklets are here repeated and augmented: Prawn Paste, Potted Tongue, Potted Spiced Beef, Pork ... Served chilled with hot thin toast, these simple and delicious little pots, for hors d'oeuvres and savouries, are quintessentially English and as such are perfect for wintry Sunday morning breakfasts in the country with a fire nearby, good strong coffee and fresh home-made toasted bread.

And as to 'Sweet Dishes and Cakes', here is a list of some of the most homely, delicate and luxurious dishes Elizabeth has yet recorded: Almond Rice and Hot Chestnuts and Prunes from Mrs Leyel; How to Make a Pippin Tart from *A True Gentlewoman's Delight*, by the seventeenth-century Countess of Kent, whose book was one of Elizabeth's favourite possessions; Thick Perkins, Dark Ginger Cake, 'this excellent recipe ... from my partner, Renée Fedden'; Chocolate Chinchilla, and here Elizabeth gives a little description of the fascinating origins of chocolate. She reminds us that the favoured flavouring for chocolate, newly arrived from the New World, was cinnamon: 'a dish which demonstrates how excellent is the combination of chocolate with cinnamon'. Cinnamon Ice Cream, from Cassell's vast compendium, c. 1880, and whose merits Elizabeth had long ago realized.

This ice cream has more recently been taken up by contemporary chefs, one of the many recipes which Elizabeth has not been credited with resurrecting. Good chefs and food writers have always looked at old dishes. Several of the best chefs and writers have had considerable collections of cookery books; but it is only in more recent years that grandiloquent versions, or what amounted to pastiches of old dishes, have sometimes been replaced in England with the original. The drive towards 'authentic' old dishes, which Elizabeth was partially responsible for launching with *Spices, Salt and Aromatics*, has been only partially understood by most chefs. The food they make is described as 'authentic', but for many it is really only 'quaint', and will be dropped at the next turn of fashion. Food has become part of the new leisure; the only time numbers of people turn from versions of fast food and really cook. One is reminded of Elizabeth's criticisms of the English for making an effort only for special occasions and not for every day.

The novelist A. S. Byatt gave *Spices, Salt and Aromatics in the English Kitchen* a perceptive review on its publication, saying:

> She has a sense of facts, of the history and geography of real food, quite divorced from the timeless fantasy and charade which we have whipped up in response to shining machinery and hygenic mass-production, our indiscriminate parade of Granny's old cambric nightdress, shawls and laced boots, cheap Indian bedspreads . . . her stone porringers were used in the seventeenth century and she suggests sensible modern equivalents. She treats the English language with the response she accords to food, and writes with a purely English combination of the flatly Anglo Saxon . . . and the lyrically Romantic . . . The new book combines practical and Romantic in its very subject, the history and illustration of the English addiction to spices and aromatics . . . the romance is English and earthy, solidly established in time and space.

Another reviewer said:

> Provincial France, Italy, the lands bordering the Mediterranean, those were the areas whose food she evoked so eloquently. And when I came to visit them years later . . . Yes it was all as she had said. But English cookery? It seems such an alien field, a vast gastronomic desert of pale blancmanges, stodgy suet puddings and boiled fish – could she do the same for that? The miraculous answer is yes, she can and has.

There were other writers now making claims about the importance of resurrecting old English dishes. Many of these books, however, were either exercises in nostalgia or ultimately too unwieldy and academic to be used as modern cookery manuals. Elizabeth's aversion to inaccuracy, verging on the obsessive, and her profound understanding of the history of her subject led her to avoid either of these pitfalls. For those who were prepared to read carefully, *Spices, Salt and Aromatics in the English Kitchen* was not only inspiring but also useful, with a degree of subtlety not always seen in her work.

But for the most part the book's reception was not as wholehearted as it had been for her previous ones. This latest message was a difficult one for many of her first followers to accept. For years Elizabeth's writing had inclined the Anglo-Saxons away from their own culinary traditions and taught them to savour instead the food of the sun. In this latest work she was telling them that at its best – found in recipes from the past – their own tradition had been as rich and rewarding as that of the Mediterranean.

As Elizabeth had so exactly characterized it herself, the 'runes, litanies and magic spells' had always been the unifying force in her writing; the evocation of place, the calling up of atmospheres and conjuring with the words, until her readers were in the place she recalled, ready to experience, however momentarily, a hint of paradise. These evocations were enhanced by passages from other writers, but the realist in her had always held the whole together with the recipes, the practical realization of those spells. Her descriptions may have been of the exotic, but there was usually the knowledge that if readers could only get there, get themselves to that obscure corner of Sardinia, Provence, Egypt, they would find the actual food Elizabeth was describing. In *Spices, Salt and Aromatics* Elizabeth was attempting something more difficult; she was conjuring with the past. And, for most of us, to travel in time, and then to bring back the past into the present, to re-create it, is not as easy as travelling in space; it demands a more imaginative commitment.

Spices, Salt and Aromatics in the English Kitchen was dedicated to Elizabeth's old friend and present collaborator in the shop, Renée Fedden. In early April of 1970, the year the book was published, Elizabeth had just returned from one of her buying trips abroad. Each year since Elizabeth David Ltd had opened, Elizabeth, usually with Renée, had made this journey once or twice. They would return to favoured sources of supply and were also searching for new ones. One of the results of these journeys was an essay written in 1980, entitled 'Eating out in Provincial France 1965–1977'. Elizabeth sadly but accurately recorded what she saw as a general decline:

> How is it that French restaurant cooking has so notably . . . deteriorated during the past two or three decades? Among [the reasons] I would say the main one has a good deal to do with the conservatism of the French themselves in matters of eating. In the vast majority of French restaurants . . . the order of menu has remained unchanged for fifty years . . . What has suffered from shrinkage is the quality of raw materials, of the cooking skills and also . . . the critical faculties of the customers . . . What has dismayed me as much as anything else has been the complacent attitude of customers and restaurateurs alike.

She says that on her buying trips for the shop she stayed 'an average of two or three weeks at a time travelling all over the country, staying in different hotels night after night, eating in every type of restaurant from village inns to the occasional . . . three star establishment'. She tells us that they kept largely away from the tourist haunts, motorways and the tourist season,

> staying often in hotels patronized by commercial travellers. During the subsequent three years my visits to France were less frequent and less extended and . . . I was free to pick and choose . . . restaurants . . . So it is with some experience that I record the melancholy fact that during those fifteen years I have eaten far worse meals in France, and more expensively . . . than I would have believed possible in any civilized country.

She remembers one of the exceptions: 'meals in a pretty and elegant country restaurant' owned by the mère Brazier whose other restaurant, in Lyon, Elizabeth had written about lovingly in *French Provincial Cooking*. This one was up out of the 'notorious fogs of the city . . . and for a time my favourite restaurant in all France . . . alas that it must be written about in the past tense . . . there was a gaiety and a grace about lunches at Col de la Luère which seemed to me to be most essentially French.' She sadly concluded that 'in France these days' culinary experiences of quality are 'more likely to be connected with a picnic than with a meal in a restaurant. Picnics in France combine so many joys . . .'

At about this time she hints at 'staff problems'. This included a manageress who was removing things from the shop, but more seriously Elizabeth was beginning to have fundamental disagreements with her partners. For some time the Triers and Llewellyns had been telling her that she must be more careful about how and what she sold, but she refused to bend.

'Liz wanted the shop to be a little museum, a place saying to people, "This is how you do it." But you couldn't do that without losing enormous amounts of money,' says Peter Trier. 'A big percentage of the stuff in the warehouse over at Vauxhall Bridge was stuff that we had bought and Liz had got fed up with. There'd be something selling well and she'd decide she didn't like it any more, so it would just stay sitting in the warehouse collecting dust. She was always fiddling about with stuff on the shelves. If someone wanted something from the window display they were told to come back in two months when the window display was changed.

'On many occasions I told her that we couldn't go on in the selective way in which we were without the shop folding. She just didn't want to see it . . . the shop was a social centre for Liz . . . It became a kind of club for her friends, that was part of the problem . . . It had such a smart clientèle; younger people like the Dimblebys, the Johnsons [Judy worked there for a time] and others like Peggy Guggenheim, Freya Stark, Princess Margaret and Lord Snowden. When John and Fanny Craddock came into the shop at the beginning to see what it was about, she hid in the loo; she couldn't stand them. Liz was in the shop so much of her time. For those years it was the centre of her life I think. But one of the overriding things about Liz was that she couldn't stand the average member of the public. She was intolerant of ordinary people. It was an entirely cerebral thing. It wasn't their social background, that didn't matter a bit.'

'Oh, but she could talk to anybody as well,' says Pamela Pugh. 'Yes, people of every type,' says Peter Trier. 'She didn't care as long as there was something they had in common. It could have been anyone. If they were talking about food or anything to do with it – pots, pans, recipes, she would be interested, would be open, would get so involved and stand there talking and listening – she could always listen – and offering advice. Whereas if it was more her contemporaries and she thought they weren't genuine, she wouldn't care who it was, she'd be utterly merciless right there in the shop. She could have been an academic and had the common touch too, that is the rarity. Her meticulous attention to detail overrode the crap. She would say: "That's absolutely crap." She was enormously kind too. When she went on her Paris trips she would always bring me back violet jam because my mother was called Violet. The letter that she wrote when my mother died was absolutely marvellous.'

'At the beginning it was all sweetness and light with everyone,' recalls Doreen Thornton. 'But the trouble was she expected everyone to work with her dedication and her hours. She had no family commitments like the others did. Renée worked so hard for Elizabeth.'

Renée was in the shop most days and her daughter Frances Fedden told the author of her own and her sister's annoyance at times 'because she wouldn't be able to get back home until quite late with the shop keeping her there ... At 5.30 one wanted to leave work. You wanted to go out, do other things, but Elizabeth found it difficult to understand. You were always being a bit disloyal if you insisted you had to go.'

Gilly Gretton, a young painter who worked in the shop, remembers that: 'One often had to leave late. Not only when the window was being done. Elizabeth was just so dedicated to the shop and her work there that she found it difficult to understand that anyone could want to do anything else ... It somehow wasn't really like a normal job. You felt part of this endeavour, sometimes kind of whether you liked it or not. But it did make you feel loyal to what the shop represented.'

By 1967 Elizabeth David Ltd had launched a catalogue service and it was clear to the other partners that this wholesale selling was going to be the only way of keeping the business afloat. 'The shop alone wasn't viable, we were unofficially becoming as much a wholesaler, with all the stuff having the Elizabeth David logo on it,' says Pamela Pugh. Renée and a young woman called Antonia Grahame now spent most of their time over at the warehouse looking after this side of the business.

In the summer of 1970, her Kensington house sold, Priscilla had moved back to the country and Wootton, which at Roland's death she would inherit. Roland, eventually a ward of court, had been in a home since 1965, while Wootton was managed by a pilfering cook and general handyman. They were seen off, and during 1969–70 Priscilla renovated the house to something of its former beauty.

In April 1971, after a debilitating illness, Diana had died – for years she had also suffered from that alienating condition, tinnitus. Elizabeth had sometimes spoken and written with impatience of Diana over the years; nevertheless she and Felicité deeply mourned their beautiful, scatty sister. Elizabeth was initially taken aback when Christopher, Diana's husband, for years Elizabeth's doctor, remarried some months after Diana's death. Elizabeth brought out the usual armoury of epithets used for those whom she regarded as 'disloyal'. Matters had not been helped by internecine family wranging over money and property (reminiscent of Elizabeth's grandfather's days) during the course of 1971, finally resolved largely as a result of Elizabeth's timely and decisive intervention. She had seldom returned to Wootton in the years since leaving it as a girl, but was pleased that her sisters had maintained closer ties with her childhood home. And now it belonged to Priscilla, the eldest of Rupert's daughters.

In 1971, almost thirty years after she had been forced by circumstance to leave, Stella also returned and was installed in a small flat. Since 1962 she had lived in Enfield, on the edge of London. The house was unremarkable except for the fact that it came with a double garden, and with the manual assistance of Judith Lassalle's son Patrick, Stella 'made a beautiful English herb garden when hardly anybody else was making one'. Her daughters tried to persuade Stella to move but she remained adamant in her refusal to do so until she grew too feeble to manage on her own.

By 1972 relations between Elizabeth and the other partners at Elizabeth David Ltd were becoming strained. It was evident that Renée had some sympathy with the others. Peter Trier remembers Renée as 'very quiet, she worked very hard, kept in the background at the shop. She was strong, but not dominatingly so. One or two have called her bossy, but she was a very kind person.' Sybille Bedford remembers her friend as 'highly intelligent, capable of being emotional; she was thin, severe, haughty, remote. She cooked beautiful Middle Eastern food.'

Negotiations were going ahead to open a branch of the shop in a large store. Elizabeth was reluctant. Peter Trier's analysis of what the shop represented for her – more a kind of permanent social gathering place, with herself as the centre – is correct. Also, notwithstanding her ambivalence about the public, at a level which Elizabeth herself probably did not understand, the shop was for her a way of giving, just as her cooking had always been; here she was the undoubted magnet for the clients and source of inspiration for the whole enterprise. The underlying message of the shop was Elizabeth's role as teacher: the pots, the tools, the simple gadgets, and finally she herself, were there as purveyors of her message.

For all her shrewdness and professed worldliness Elizabeth was not capable of making a business work enduringly. She had neither the managerial skills nor a good enough appreciation of how others were motivated to continue in any public or impersonal capacity for very long. Stephen Trier, Peter's musician brother, who saw a good deal of her at this period, says: 'Elizabeth had a streak of enormous kindness in her. She could manage while it [the shop] functioned as a club for her but once the others had made it finally clear that it had to work as a business, she couldn't do it.' The problem was insoluble. Elizabeth had been a brilliant communicator to large numbers of people with her mass-market publishing with Penguin, but here she had to face unique individuals whose ideas didn't coincide with her own. One is reminded of her frustration on the trip to Munich before the war to meet Priscilla, her new husband Richard and Felicité.

Their opinion of the city hadn't coincided with her own rosy-coloured vision and her anger had been extreme. She hadn't changed very much! Nonetheless the ideas about quality and design of cooking tools, how they were to be used and the style of the kitchens which housed them, had all been deeply influenced by Elizabeth's ethos, as seen in the myriad kitchen shops which soon opened in the wake of her lead.

Meanwhile at Wootton Stella had grown very frail and in early June 1973 Elizabeth was urgently recalled by Felicité from a visit to Italy. She returned and wrote that 'My mother was very ill and unlikely to recover. So I went down to the country where she lived . . . and spent several hours with her before she died – yesterday afternoon [9th June]. She was nearly 90.'

Soon afterwards Maudie O'Malley wrote to offer Elizabeth her condolences and received this letter in reply:

My mother really was a very remarkable person although she could be, as you say, alarming – and her personality was so strong that it is very hard to believe that she is no longer here.

I am thankful for her that it is over. She was not happy . . . could not have been, once she had lost her independence, and her garden. Indeed during the past year . . . I knew she felt that there was little point to her existence . . .

It would be futile to pretend that she was a good mother in the conventional sense but what extraordinary qualities she had in other ways – none of us, sadly, had inherited her genius for gardening, but . . . all our surroundings, came in some way or other from her. Her influence was very strong . . . and it was of course due to the somewhat erratic education and upbringing she gave us that I was able eventually to write my books and create my shop. Felicité asks me to thank you so very much for your letter . . .

With love to you and Peter
Elizabeth.

Stella was buried in the small churchyard at Folkington close by Wootton where she had attended services many times with her husband Rupert and small daughters half a century ago. Elizabeth wrote a card to Julia, Priscilla's daughter, thanking her for making the wake afterwards at Wootton such a remarkable occasion. On that one day, Wootton was once again Stella's 'domain. Even her vanished garden seemed to live again in the dazzling June sunshine.' And Elizabeth felt that Diana was in some way not left out.

By now Elizabeth was feeling that her enormously high standards in the shop were gradually being chipped away, compromised for the sake of profit. Her partners said, 'No, we are just trying to survive.'

Elizabeth David Ltd had never really been organized with formal directors' meetings. 'Everyone had basically just made decisions along with Liz. The choices about stuff in the shop had all ultimately been hers,' said Steven Trier. 'She'd have a turn in the shop. Oh, quite often. She'd say, "God, what are we carrying all this bloody rubbish for," referring to things on the shelves that she'd decided she no longer liked. And it would have to be cleared away into the stockroom and the other stuff would sit at Goading Street [the store under the arches near Vauxhall Bridge]. She would have a caprice in the shop like that. And that's how Elizabeth split from the shop. One day she had a turn and flounced out saying that was it. And it was. That was it. She didn't come back.'

As time passed and the event receded into the past it became fixed in Elizabeth's mind as unremittingly horrible; her principles being compromised by commerce, and to friends she was remorseless in her attacks on all but Renée. However, her fury and despair essentially arose from the fact that it was clear that she could not continue with the shop as she wanted it to be. Once her partners' repeated attempts to make her understand that they couldn't continue in the same way for much longer were clarified, Elizabeth's attitude to retaining a hold on the shop became more ambivalent, not admitted to anyone else and probably not to herself either. 'It came to the point where I thought, "We're just going to lose Jenny's money,"' said Peter Trier.

Elizabeth found it almost impossible to admit error, but turning her partners into vulgar 'monsters' relieved her from the pressure of taking any responsibility for the failure of the shop to make a profit;

a sad outcome of events. With her growing inclination towards the litigious aspects of her Gwynne nature she launched herself into the attack, vilifying her ex-partners for the rest of her life.

After she severed relations with the shop Elizabeth continued seeing Renée for a few months, but when Renée became more openly sympathetic to the other partners' ideas she could not accept this and would no longer see her. Indeed, after Renée's 'disloyalty', these friends of thirty years never saw one another again. On the 17 January 1974 Elizabeth wrote Renée a letter in which her gratitude does little to temper her damning criticisms. Overshadowed as it is by fury, Elizabeth's judgement is clouded, leaving her uncomprehending of Renée's, or the other partners' positions, and this remained the case until the end of her life.

> Dear Renée,
>
> Don't think, on account of anything I've said in the enclosed communication, that I underestimate your contribution to the business. It was enormous and very important, and I don't think we could have made Elizabeth David Ltd what it *was* without you.
>
> I just feel bitter and sad that my own part in it has been so belittled, and my requests for proper treatment so contemptuously rejected by the company.
>
> You invested your money in my name and its prestige, at least that's what you said at the time. I'm glad that its paid off for you, even if not in a very sensational way. [Renée in fact had little financial reward from ED, Ltd.] Again, it was sad that you grew to resent my name and felt it necessary to participate in the rejection of all that it implied so that the name has become a sham.
>
> E.D.

Only weeks after her sister Diana's death in April 1971 Elizabeth had travelled to France with Renée on a pre-planned buying trip for the shop. Following their return in May, Elizabeth wrote Renée a letter whose sentiments serve as an illustration of the depth of their now severed friendship.

Dear Renée

You will never know how much you have helped me . . . I didn't believe that I could manage the trip at all, and certainly with anyone else but you there could have been no question of my going away. As things turned out I think you were right, and anyway the job had to be done. You have done all the work, all the planning and coping, and at the same time you have comforted me and kept me going and provided many moments when grief was forgotten . . . and like every one of our journeys together this one produced what will prove to be happy memories . . . even sometimes a good meal.

You must be very tired. As I well know from my sessions with poor Diana during the last weeks of her life, sustaining somebody who is in misery is totally exhausting. Your patience and understanding are not gifts for which one can exactly say thank you I suppose. I can say thank you, my love, for using them so wonderfully.

Elizabeth.

Recalling this period of acrimony and turmoil, Sybille Bedford said, 'She felt that in Renée all her ideals had been let down . . . the break was definitive. For her it was like a mortal blow . . . Elizabeth's ability to see straight had narrowed over time.'

After another year or so Renée herself retired from working for Elizabeth David Ltd but the shop carried on with Elizabeth's name. She tried her utmost to withdraw from her partners the right to use the name, wrote long and emotional letters to friends and sought legal advice on the matter, including asking Veronica Nicholson's solicitor husband John to help. 'But,' said Peter Trier, 'if Liz had been more civilized about the whole thing we'd have let it go. High drama was Liz's thing and no doubt she dined out on it for years afterwards. She could be so destructive if she felt that way inclined . . . Liz made a lot of song and dance about it not being right after she left – "That terrible stuff being sold in my name" – but it wasn't really much changed.'

Peter did not fully understand Elizabeth's passionate relationship with her name. But as someone so preoccupied with controlling the various aspects of her life, her name was central. She felt that she had lost control of it and with it had lost part of herself. The loss of control in her carefully divided life was something which she feared and hated more than almost anything. 'Years later, when we met again,' Peter said, 'she chundered on about it . . . she had an obsession with her name.'

Twelve years on Elizabeth was at a book-signing for her collected journalism, *An Omelette and a Glass of Wine*, and someone there was speaking to Chuck Williams, an American devotee and friend of Elizabeth's who owns an enormously successful group of kitchen supply shops in the United States. Chuck Williams was told about the events which had led Elizabeth to leave her partners in the shop, and how she had not seen any more of them since that time. 'It wasn't that we had said we weren't seeing one another, we just didn't get in touch,' says Peter, who also 'wouldn't stand for crap'. He felt Elizabeth had behaved excessively. Chuck Williams subsequently rang Peter and said, 'What on earth are you doing being so stupid like this?' Peter gave it some thought, 'And I sat down and wrote Elizabeth a letter.' Afterwards he and Elizabeth saw one another regularly. 'When we took up together again I'd take her out. We'd go to places she then liked: Sally Clarke's, Simon Hopkinson at Bibendum . . . others. "You were such shits to me," she'd say more than once. But we weren't, you know. We had to make a living and Liz wasn't interested in that . . .'

At the end of 1973 Elizabeth was in hospital writing in low spirits to Marjorie Lloyd, a friend from the MOI in Cairo, and saying, 'Work progresses hardly at all. Disruptions continual, and swollen legs now joined to neuritic feet with inflamed joints. Temper often inflamed too, on account goings on of E.D. Ltd. Much love E.' Although during this year she was given the André Simon Memorial Award, the first public award made for her writing, her gratification was marred by exhaustion from anger. Time had not blessed Elizabeth with greater restraint, nor had her passion receded. The anger provoked by her partners in the shop was extreme, abating little with time; she had inherited to the full those relentlessly unforgiving aspects of her grandfather James Gwynne.

One example serves to illustrate the intensity and bitterness of her feelings and the remorselessness of her attacks. In one of her annotated first editions of *Spices, Salt and Aromatics in the English Kitchen*, inherited by her great-nephew William Harcourt-Smith, Elizabeth has scored through and made illegible every passage which refers to Elizabeth David Ltd. At the first reprinting and revising of the book in 1973, she was quick to benefit from the opportunity, and erased her public connections with the shop by omitting all reference to it in the biographical frontispiece and throughout the rest of the book. In all subsequent publications of this and other books she articulated her fury at the loss of her name with greater force still, by addition of the sentence: 'In 1973 Mrs David severed all connection with the business trading under her name.' A final and perhaps reconciliatory point worthy of note: Elizabeth never had the dedication to her estranged friend Renée removed from *Spices, Salt and Aromatics in the English Kitchen*.

CHAPTER NINETEEN

A Mediterranean Passion Cooled
(1973–1977)

ONE OF THE assistants working in the shop, April Tanner (later Boyes), had previously trained as a librarian and Elizabeth asked her to help catalogue her library at Halsey Street. Years of collecting had led to such an expansion of her library that it was now 'silted up' into the thousands. Described in some wonderment by friends, the books were everywhere: in piles on tables, chairs, the stairs, and badly needed organizing into some kind of system. April did her tidy and methodical best, and by early 1974 Elizabeth was writing to Alan Davidson that April was still working spasmodically on her books, the situation made more difficult by the presence in her library/sitting room of almost 'fifteen huge cartons of papers, utensils and oddments' retrieved from the shop. These required sorting, something Elizabeth felt unable to do at that moment. For years April arrived for part of the week to act as secretary-cum general factotum to Elizabeth, driving her to libraries and further afield outside London on many occasions.

In *Spices, Salt and Aromatics in the English Kitchen*, Elizabeth had said that the book was simply the first volume of a series which was to be nothing less than a thematic history of English food. Apart from Drummond's great work, *The Englishman's Food*, a notable recent addition to the field of serious histories of English food had recently been made with *Food and Drink in Britain* (Constable, 1973) by a Brotherton Librarian at Leeds University, C. Anne Wilson. A thoroughly researched book, which Elizabeth called 'admirable', it is nevertheless more history than cookery and not exactly the kind which Elizabeth believed she wanted to write. No one had yet undertaken such a literary and broadly cultural look at the whole subject by theme and there was plenty of room for her mammoth projected undertaking. Although one of these themes took over, Elizabeth was at present proceeding with the next two works in tandem. They were to be first, a book on bread in England, the germ of which had been the little booklet written for her shop entitled, 'The Baking of an English Loaf'; and next, the 'Creams, Ices, Sylla-bubs, Trifles' she had referred to in *Spices, Salt and Aromatics*.

Another writer who, like Elizabeth, combined in her work a felicitous mix of literature and history, was the then young (now late) Jane Grigson, who by 1974 had published three well-written books. Jane Grigson was Cambridge-educated and a prize-winning Italianist whose first book, *Charcuterie and French Pork Cookery* (1967), had been sent to Elizabeth as a typescript by Anthea Joseph of the publishers Michael Joseph. Elizabeth's response had been very positive, as she herself wrote of the book in her own posthumous tribute to Mrs Grigson in 1990:

> Here was a writer who could combine a delightful quote from Chaucer on the subject of a pike galantine with a careful recipe for a modern chicken and pork version of the same ancient dish, and who could do so without pedantry or a hint of preciousness.

The year following its publication Elizabeth had proposed Jane Grigson to the *Observer*. Jane's magazine articles gained her a huge following, notable, as Alan Davidson wrote of her in his *Times* obituary:

> Because she was above all a friendly author, equipped by both frame of mind and style of writing to communicate easily with [the public]. However much she knew about this or that . . . she never seemed to be talking down to anyone. On the contrary she is a most companionable presence in the kitchen; often catching the imagination with a deftly chosen fragment of history or poetry . . . [Jane was married to the poet Geoffrey Grigson.] How often have I heard people declare that her recipes are not just a pleasure to read – they always work!

Jane Grigson had from the first, in the introduction to her
Charcuterie, declared: 'Nobody can produce a cookery book these days
without a deep appreciation of Elizabeth David's work.' In an
interview with the author Paul Bailey defines the difference between
Elizabeth and Jane Grigson as:

> A very fine one . . . Jane was a scholar of a different mental
> discipline . . . it was Jane's tone of voice that Elizabeth liked . . .
> they were both on the same course. Elizabeth writes the more
> fine porcelain prose. But Jane is no mean writer. She is more
> robust, she is a more generous spirited creature than Elizabeth.
> She's not so aloof. But Elizabeth came from a different time, she
> was so reticent, and that squares with her hiding behind her
> prose . . . that there is another message there in her work to do
> with art, and a whole seriousness about life.
>
> Jane said she believed that the reason Elizabeth's writing
> was so good was because it came from some kind of compulsion.
> Most people who write about food write about it because there
> is a lot of money to be made from it . . . particularly nowadays
> . . . Jane sensed that Elizabeth had had something traumatic
> happen to her and that she therefore needed to write to express
> herself. But being an Englishwoman of a certain class and time
> and having a certain reticence . . . and being someone who
> appreciated food and had tasted all those flavours abroad . . .
> what better way to hide her real purpose, which was to express
> herself in the deepest possible way, than to do it in a scholarly
> way . . . As she grew older her books became more and more
> scholarly.

This is perceptive, but can be read as implying a self-knowledge
which I do not believe Elizabeth possessed.

In early 1974 she had not recovered from her self-imposed
severance from the shop and was at a low ebb. She wrote more than
one letter which shows clearly her difficulty in mustering her normal
enthusiasm. Her health too was suffering. To Alan Davidson she
wrote that she had been immobilized for a short while, because of an
ulcer on her right ankle, which refused to go away 'whatever I do or

don't do'. (The effectiveness of antibiotics in treating infection is of course severely limited when combined with alcohol, which Elizabeth refused to stop consuming.) She was attempting to get on with her two books, but without much conviction and didn't foresee either of them ever being finished.

In February she said to Maudie O'Malley, the painter who had attended Cedric Morris and Lett Haines's art school, that she was 'plodding away at my yeast book', but saw no end in sight. She had lost the will to write, and it was an effort to put pen to paper.

Elizabeth may have felt downhearted and without the will to apply herself, but disciplined mental exertion had long ago become compulsive, and we see the necessity to immerse herself in her books beginning to provoke stimulating thoughts and ideas.

During this year Jane Grigson brought out her *English Food* (Macmillan, 1974) with its lovely, usable recipes, never in the least misty-eyed or effete. Her lucid introduction is a well-judged balance between past and present, an overview which Elizabeth could not always manage so well. Elizabeth's daemon, which had driven her so relentlessly and to such creativeness, had not facilitated an integration of her spirit, already so clear in the young Jane Grigson. The subject, an appreciation of English food from the past, was becoming a popular one, but Jane Grigson's voice on this was amongst the very best in its integrity and unpretentiousness. Her sentiments were entirely understood by Elizabeth, whose creed they perfectly endorsed and who was vitriolic in her condemnation of those who jumped on the bandwagon of 'Ye Olde Englande'. For a description of the very task upon which Elizabeth had launched herself and whose essential nature she didn't always communicate too well, Jane Grigson's introduction to her own book seems entirely appropriate and is here quoted at length.

> The English are a very adaptive people. English cooking . . . is a great deal more varied and delectable than our masochistic temper in this matter allows . . . It is . . . true that a good many things in our marketing system now fight against simple and delicate food. Tomatoes have no taste. The finest flavoured potatoes are not available in the shops. Vegetables and fruit are

seldom fresh ... Cheeses are subdivided and imprisoned in plastic wrapping ... Words such as 'fresh' and 'home made' have been borrowed by commerce to tell lies.

In spite of this the English cook has a wonderful inheritance if she cares to make use of it ... My aim has been to put in dishes of quality ... I have also included a number of Welsh dishes because ... they are linked closely with much English food while retaining a rustic elegance which we have tended to lose ...

There's no avoiding the fact that the best cooking has come down from the top. Or if you don't like the word 'top', then from the skilled, employed by those who could pay and had the time to appreciate quality. In England on the whole the food descends less from a courtly tradition than from the manor houses and rectories and homes of the well to do merchants ... It hands down the impression of the social life of families in which wives and daughters weren't too grand to go into the kitchen and to keep a close eye on the vegetable garden and the dairy ...

One thing to note is that the great English cookery writers, from Hannah Glasse to Elizabeth David, have most often been women, in contrast to the French ... Our classical tradition has been domestic, with the domestic virtues of quiet enjoyment and generosity. Whatever happened when the great mass centres developed in the nineteenth century, English cookery books of the eighteenth century to early Victorian times had been written from an understanding of good food and good eating, a concern for quality.

This piece conveys with grace and apparent effortlessness some of the essential features of English social history. And, although later more pessimistic about the future of England's table, Jane Grigson wrote here that 'I finished *English Food* full of hope. In discovering at least something of our tradition for myself, I began to see that we did have a treasury to be exploited ...'

Elizabeth also was labouring: burrowing, searching, sifting, synthesizing, in order to illustrate for her readers just that 'treasury'.

She had long ago realized the importance of England's culinary past, represented in the present only by books. And, with the help of writers like Kenelm Digby, Elizabeth Countess of Kent, Robert May, Hannah Glasse, the Ladies Llanover and Clark of Tillypronie, her beloved Eliza Acton and many more besides, Elizabeth was continuing her task, begun with *Spices, Salt and Aromatics in the English Kitchen*, of creating a new world. Just as Jane Grigson did not deal in nostalgia, neither was Elizabeth's writing about the past ever quaint. She had too much integrity and knew too much of England's past either to prettify or trivialize it.

Jill Norman, her editor at Penguin, was one of those newer friends whom few of her older ones met socially with Elizabeth more than in passing. With Elizabeth's present book Jill Norman's position of support as editor and friend was at times to be crucial over the next few years, including a number of trips taken together, foraging for information and corroboration. With the successive reissue of Elizabeth's earlier books by Penguin in recent years, Jill's input had necessarily been a modest one; Elizabeth made revisions (always meticulously up to date) and revised or rewrote her introductions to the original hardbacks and Jill Norman simply checked the process. With *English Bread and Yeast Cookery* the situation was different. For some time Jill had been commissioning original books for Penguin and taking more editorial responsibility for them. One of these was Alan Davidson's first book, *Mediterranean Seafood*; at Elizabeth's suggestion commissioned by Jill. 'She worked with me for the entire book, she was a very good editor,' says Alan, now himself a publisher and an acclaimed author of several more books. Elizabeth felt the same about Jill's contribution to her present book, *English Bread and Yeast Cookery*, where her editorial influence was significant.

Meanwhile April Boyes continued with her cataloguing of Elizabeth's library – against Elizabeth's wishes she had pencilled shelf-marks on the books. She also drove Elizabeth on regular errands of research inside and outside London; the Guildhall Library, within the ancient City Square Mile, was an important source of material. If April dropped Elizabeth off in the morning rather than staying to help her she would be reminded to put the wine to keep cool in the pond in the little garden behind the library. At about two o'clock when Elizabeth had finished they would spread out a blanket on the grass, fish the cooled wine out of the water and take their picnic lunch in this incongruous little haven with the roar of traffic and the bustle of commerce just beyond the shielding walls.

'She was coming in and out then, often with Mrs Boyes,' says Irene Gilchrist, the Principal Reference Librarian at the Library. 'It was clear that she wasn't well. When the air became too much for her she would go and sit on the library steps, giving the City police quite a turn . . . Mrs David had already used the library before 1974 . . . In her writing it's clear she was only interested in history in as much as it could serve a purpose . . . She always respected the staff here, she looked up things herself. She did demand respect though, it was never put into words . . . I did feel she had a certain arrogance. We would see her several times in a few weeks and then not for months and months.'

Elizabeth's working practices were now settled into a pattern which did not vary much until her death. Writing to Marjorie Lloyd in 1975, she asks her: 'to come round for a glass or two of wine or a picnic-type lunch. (I've all but given up eating in the evenings and try not to drink more than a glass or two of wine, so that I can get to bed early and can then start work early – also I'm trying to make drastic cuts in smoking – it's not only the ridiculous waste of money, but I've been coughing so badly, all self-inflicted.) . . . My book plods on. It has become a burden and I am determined to get it over with very soon. But there's quite a bit still to do.'

There *was* still a great deal to do but Elizabeth's working regime rarely held to the one described above. She often laboured until very late into the night. Sybille Bedford lived nearby and, a late person herself, remembers passing on numerous occasions when Elizabeth's light was still burning at two or three o'clock in the morning. Elizabeth would then wake early, often work from bed, have lunch, at home or sometimes out – if with a friend probably long and bibulously – then sleep for the latter part of the afternoon. The cycle would then repeat itself with work late into the night. Nothing changed outwardly as Elizabeth worked her way through her book, except that over these years she became more difficult to please, more acerbic in her condemnation of those of whom she disapproved.

(Robert Carrier, for instance, whose ideas for his successful kitchen-shop Elizabeth believed had come entirely from her own, she called 'the thief'. It rankled that he even wrapped his kitchenware in black tissue paper as she had done in Elizabeth David Ltd.) As a consequence of voicing her disapproval Elizabeth was not without enemies.

Despite little outward change a final shift of emphasis was taking place in Elizabeth's writing. A change is manifest in *Spices, Salt and Aromatics in the English Kitchen*, a delightful little book whose sources are clearly and avowedly historical. With *English Bread and Yeast Cookery* the orientation is now unmistakable.

In Elizabeth's most intense journalistic phase, through the late Fifties and into the mid-Sixties, she had applied her formidable intelligence to aspects of the world which she had hitherto ignored. The small man, increasingly threatened by the large corporations, had been consistently championed in England by those such as Jane Grigson. It was so obvious as to be hardly worth saying that, in general, good food and cooking tended to go with a multitude of independent, small-scale centres of activity, and in *English Bread and Yeast Cookery* Elizabeth addresses these themes with unrelenting vigour:

> What is utterly dismaying is the mess our milling and baking concerns succeed in making with the dearly bought grain that goes into their grist. Quite simply it is wasted on a nation which cares so little about the quality of its bread that it has allowed itself to be mesmerised into buying the equivalent of eight and a quarter million large white factory-made loaves every day of the year.

Elsewhere Elizabeth notes from an *Assessment of the British Bread Industry*, carried out in 1974, that: 'British bread is the most chemically treated in Europe.'

Concurrently with these practical concerns which rightly infused the book Elizabeth was also launching herself on to themes of a grander nature. Nineteen seventy-three had been both her sixtieth year and the year of her mother's death. By nature an artist, like many such, Elizabeth 'builded better than she knew' with the writing of *English Bread and Yeast Cookery*. Throughout this exceptional book she is seeking to describe what enduringly exists by linking herself with something more real and permanent than that first wishful, nostalgic, Romantic-escapist vision in *Mediterranean Food*. After the solid and integrated craftsmanship and the restrained discipline of *Italian Food* and the beautiful, studied and mature gathering together of her years of thought on France in *French Provincial Cooking*, in *English Bread and Yeast Cookery* she at last brings to a halt her lifetime of escape.

In this magisterial work she is grappling with growing old, facing up to the terrors of mortality and the ineradicable human yearning for its opposite; the themes over which she ranges are often so deep and rich, so remarkably varied, that the book becomes impossible to paraphrase adequately. It is not a simple book whose themes are immediately available, and this proved a stumbling-block for many readers – as a consequence few have read it all the way through. Its many-layered historical approach does not facilitate appreciation by being dipped into, nor with its 547 pages is reading at one sitting very likely. Above all it is something to return to when there is an odd quiet hour to spare, in a spirit of dedication and with time for rumination. The advice Elizabeth had quoted long ago from that little book *Home Baked*, which had so inspired her, 'All that bread needs is time and warmth,' is eminently suitable for the reading of her own book. She need only have added: 'And a willingness to experiment.' For such readers the rewards will be manifold.

English Bread and Yeast Cookery is divided into two parts: Part I is a *History and Background*, while Part II gives the *Recipes*. Part I describes the varieties of grain past and present used for the milling of flour: Elizabeth tells us about the milling and the flour itself, the leaven, yeast, salt and flavourings, the remarkable variety of bread ovens, the bread factories, the commonplace and quaint names and shapes of buns, cakes, loaves, and much else besides. In Part II she states bluntly that the recipe for French bread from the eminent seventeenth-century English cook Robert May 'is extremely simple, a total refutation – there are many others in this book – of the belief too hastily assumed by home economists, cookery journalists and cookery-book reviewers, that any recipe earlier than Mrs Beeton is impracticable today.'

Setting down the anatomy of English recipes, she traces the development of the old ones over time, sometimes concluding (but only if she thinks it necessary) with her own modifications to the myriad baps and rolls, manchets and payndemayns, crumpets and muffins, French bread, pancakes and oatcakes, dumplings and dough-nuts, regional yeast cakes and spiced fruit breads, bakestone cakes, and much more.

As Elizabeth traces the histories of the materials and methods for making the innumerable varieties of bread, her book fairly resounds with quotation. In writing of bread, whose ancient craft and mysteries are interwoven with so many of the enduring myths and symbols of mankind, her thoughts turn again and again to tradition and its practices. She speaks of:

> The ancient rituals of ploughing and sowing and reaping, the gruelling work at harvest time, the thanksgivings and feasting when the corn was safely gathered in, the allusions . . . to the millstreams running dry so that no grain could be ground, the tales of dishonest millers, the portrayals of the poor humble gleaners bent double over their task of scratching the few last ears of wheat from the cornfields after the landlord's grain had been harvested – all these are more or less familiar to us through the works of our poets and writers. From William Langland to Shakespeare, from Chaucer to John Bunyan . . . from the Jacobean translators of the Bible to the eighteenth-century Parson Woodforde, all and scores more, travellers, diarists . . . have in some way recorded the years' cycle of growing and harvesting.

In a long letter to Veronica Nicholson Elizabeth writes at length about trying, through her readings of the Bible, to unravel the problem of the words leaven and yeast. She admits that her knowledge of the Bible was rather shaky, and hopes to be able to complete this book without having to quote it. She begins her letter in annoyance, but the subject soon claims her, provoking a disquisition; the germ of which became in her book, one of the most varied and interesting passages yet written on that elusive substance, yeast. It commences here in her letter to Veronica with a beautiful introductory passage: 'In Chaucer's England one of the names for yeast or barm was Goddis-Goode "bicause it cometh of the grete grace of God." These words imply a blessing. To me that is just what it is. It is also mysterious, magical . . . this substance which performs the ever-recurring leavening miracle . . .' And it is noticeable how often in the writing of *English Bread and Yeast Cookery* the words mysterious, magical, miracle, recur more than ever before as Elizabeth seeks to understand. 'First, leaven doesn't mean yeast as we understand it – and leaven not yeast is the word used in the Old Revised Version. It was like this. Before the days when yeast, or barm, was isolated as a fermenting agent taken in liquid form from the top of the cask of ale . . .' And the lucid explanation in her letter continues:

> The origin of the Passover was that the Israelites were getting ready to up sticks and get out of Egypt, so Moses told them to throw out their leaven, they couldn't take it with them – all those heavy jars and trekking across the desert – so when they didn't have any leaven they had to do without risen bread and bake just flour and water – biscuit – and ever after they kept the Passover with unleavened bread in memory of that time (I expect I've got all this garbled, it may be more Cecil B. de Mille than the Bible).
>
> I don't know whether St Paul was the first to use leaven as a symbol of corruption, and unleavened bread as one of a return to innocence, anyway that's what he was saying to the Corinthians. I don't know what they'd done to provoke the diatribe – that chapter is mostly about fornication . . . and in the Old Revised Version reads as if some lunatic sub. had been at work on it. But . . . I don't understand . . . all the references by St Paul to cleaning the leaven of evil, purging is the word used by the old translators who didn't use words for nothing . . . so perhaps there was . . . some way of cleaning a leaven, purging it, renewing it – a purification, a spring cleaning.

In my bible (given to me at my christening) there is a splendid Concordance ... According to this: 'Leaven is any substance that promotes fermentation. In the N.T. . . . a symbol of silent pervasive influence, usually of that which is corrupt.' Silent pervasive influence is marvellous. Pasteur must have thought something like that when he finally discovered that it was the bloom on the grape which makes the ferment in wine. But I'm sure he didn't think it was corrupt ... The Jews aren't the only people who are superstitious about it [leaven]. I think the Puritans were anti-leaven, they would be, and at different times I fancy there have been other outbursts against it.

In *English Bread and Yeast Cookery* Elizabeth is attempting to create a world. With the loss of so many traditional practices this is of necessity from the past and its records alone. In the latter years of her life, history becomes an abiding interest for its own sake, as well as a means to order her own inner chaos. History really is used as her handmaiden, and in her book she harnesses its battery with exemplary command, to evoke and capture our sympathy and imagination, with its recipes as the backbone of the very real work she *creates*. In her customary manner Elizabeth enlists others to add weight and lustre to her themes, and the cumulative effect of her quotes, from the far distant to the more recent past, is somehow more powerful than in any of her previous works.

One strand, quietly and consistently present throughout the book, is Elizabeth's easier acceptance of her own Englishness. The authors cited, like the themes, range far and wide over time and place. She quotes from *Centuries of Meditation* by the seventeenth-century cleric and poet Thomas Traherne in which he wrote that when he was a child it seemed as if 'the corn was orient and immortal wheat, which never should be reaped nor was ever sown. I thought it had stood from everlasting to everlasting.' And Elizabeth adds, 'magical and mysterious words'.

'"My bread is sweet and nourishing, made from my own wheat, ground in my own mill, and baked in my own oven,"' Tobias Smollett wrote in *Humphry Clinker*. For the twentieth century Elizabeth has York Ketteridge, quoted from *Five Miles to Bunkum*, as 'a most kind and understanding man who knew about wheats, their differences in height, colour and yield. He would snatch a couple of near-ripened ears, rub them in his horny hands to shed the husks, then blow into his cupped hands to winnow husks from grain. Husks clung to his whiskers as he tossed the grain into his mouth. "Wheat is life, boy. Don't let no silly bugger tell you different."'

George Eliot wrote on watermills in *The Mill on the Floss*: 'The rush of water, and the booming of the mill, bring a dreamy deafness which seems to heighten the peacefulness of the scene. They are like a great curtain of sound, shutting one out from the world beyond. And now there is the thunder of the huge covered wagon coming home with sacks of grain.' And later: 'then there was the smell of hot toast and ale from the kitchen, at the breakfast hour.'

From Henry Mayhew's revelatory study *London Labour and the London Poor* (1861): 'Perhaps no cry – though it is for only one morning – is more familiar to the ears of a Londoner than that of One-penny-two-a-penny, hot cross buns on Good Friday.'

Elizabeth illustrates an archetypal example of Englishness:

> one of our greatest naturalists, Gilbert White of Selborne, on a year's grain growing in Hampshire in the eighteenth century; with their echoes of Shakespeare's 'rich leas of wheat, rye, barley, vetches, oats and pease', these notes evoke a picture most essentially and intensely English. Gilbert White, author of the famous *Natural History of Selborne*, one of that wonderful breed of country parsons who have enriched our literature with their diaries and their meticulous records – William Harrison of Essex, from whom we learn so much of Tudor England, was another – kept his journals for nearly a quarter of a century, from 1768 to 1793. He noticed and noted everything going on around him. Such details as the exact 'delicate soft tinge of green rye', 'the millers complain for want of water' ... 'Farmer Knight's wheat of a beautiful colour ... Wheat, being secured by the snow, looks finely ... Great rain ... Rock-like clouds. Oats and pease are cutting ... Sweet harvest weather ... Much wheat bound up in the afternoon ... Goldfinch sings. Oats are cutting. ... White dew. Peaches ripen. Barley begins to be cut.'

Elizabeth knew Gilbert White's home ground from her youthful visits to Uncle Top and Aunt Grace, the Earl and Countess of Selborne, at their home Blackmoor House, whose estate almost borders on Gilbert White's beautiful pocket of the Sussex–Hampshire borderlands. In her tribute to the great naturalist, as more than once in this book, Elizabeth leads us to a place rich in memories of her childhood: 'The little water mill at Michelham Priory in East Sussex, founded in the thirteenth century, was restored to working order in the mid-seventies. Visitors to the priory can buy the freshly ground flour and see the workings of a small mill much as it was five or six centuries ago.' This was the same Michelham Priory which Elizabeth's grandfather James had restored, and of which her mother Stella was given the choice upon her marriage to James's son, Rupert Gwynne, seventy years before.

Another place of youthful memories and prominent in *English Bread and Yeast Cookery* is Wales, where Elizabeth made numerous journeys while writing her book. There she could still find a few small millers for whom one could buy best-quality flour. White Mill was near Carmarthen: 'Mrs Lickley, the miller's wife . . . makes her own blend . . . and, should there be none ready when you call at the mill, she will blend and pack it for you while you wait. Many a time I have brought White Mill flour back to London with me, and have also used it for bread to be baked in the old brick oven at Ty Isaf' [this was the old farmhouse near Llandeilo belonging to her friend Jean Bolland].

As ever, Elizabeth experimented, and for the five years it took her to write the book, often with the collaboration of Jill Norman, she baked constantly until she understood the recipes. She found the experience of using the oven in Jean Bolland's home – trying out recipes older than the old dome-shaped brick oven, itself identical in design to those used for centuries – a moving and instructive one.

Lady Llanover, to whose *Good Cookery* practices Elizabeth had become particularly attached, and whose delicate drawing of bound wheat sheaves she used as endpapers for her book, appears frequently in the numerous recipes from Wales. But perhaps Elizabeth's greatest favourite, the sensible yet 'poetic' Eliza Acton, finally has her day with regular references and quotes from her eminently usable books, *Modern Cookery for Private Families* (1845) and *The English Bread Book* (1857) about which Elizabeth says: 'It is not under 1845 that we find decisive instructions and definite directions for the making of bread and the management of yeast. What a blessing this book must have been to the baffled housekeepers and cooks of the time.'

Elizabeth was always adept at collecting 'loyal subjects,' some more 'slave-like than others', as Doreen Thornton put it. While her sister was writing *English Bread and Yeast Cookery* Felicité's role was, as it had been for many years, 'in a category unique to herself . . . the imaginative finder- and provider-in-chief of books for study,' as Elizabeth said in her acknowledgement. 'Without her remarkable eye for the relevant book I might perhaps have finished writing my own sooner, but I certainly wouldn't have learned or enjoyed so much while I was doing it.' The most effective book-scouting carried out by Felicité on Elizabeth's behalf took place not only through John Sandoe's bookshop where Felicité still worked, but also through the pages of secondhand book catalogues of which she and Elizabeth received a large number. Regarding Felicité's assisting her to learn and enjoy so much Elizabeth adds that she could say the same of her editor Jill Norman, to whom she dedicated the book. Jill had 'nursed it along chapter by chapter and stage by stage . . . and certainly worked on it as hard as I myself'.

In London and 'further afield' Elizabeth had April Boyes, and for trips to France Elizabeth Savage, both of whom acted as semi-official assistants. Elizabeth's warm thanks in her acknowledgements touchingly reflects these supportive female relationships upon which she was so dependent. 'In Wales Jean Bolland has done the same, driving me to mills, museums, libraries, bakeries, local markets – and as a bonus provided the cleaned-out old brick oven in her own house for me to try my hand at the ancient way of making bread. Nothing could have been more instructive or more enjoyable or indeed more fruitful for this book than my visits – rather prolonged some of them – to South West Wales.'

One of the loyal band of followers, the late Jean Bolland was happy to act as second fiddle, drive Elizabeth about in the car and have her to stay in her house. Mrs Priscilla Bain described Jean

Bolland in a letter to the author: 'As well as being great fun she was a very tolerant and unconcerned person and very restful to be with. In fact – and I say this with affection – she was basically lazy and happiest with the *Times* crossword, a cigarette and coffee or a glass of wine . . . She had a great sense of style and her house . . . always managed to look pretty.' Mrs Bain continued: 'She was pretty chaotic too – untidy, no sense of time – but one forgave her all because she was such fun . . . perhaps the perfect companion for E.D.'

Certainly Elizabeth delighted in her visits to Ty Isaf – another pleasure to be indulged in there was the drive across country for lunch at The Walnut Tree restaurant – and in *English Bread and Yeast Cookery* her enthusiasm for its old farmhouse oven is infectious: 'They are of extraordinarily skilled construction . . . once cleared out one of these old ovens will be ready for firing and for baking just as it was for centuries, before the commercial bakery took over the job of supplying our daily bread.' With this new experience Elizabeth was now particularly alert to the varieties of baking methods described by Eliza Acton in her *English Bread Book* of 1857:

> It is most of all in many of our villages that better accommo-
> dation is required than now exists for baking generally, and for
> baking bread especially; for great discouragement to the makers
> often attends the sending it to a common baker's oven, should
> there chance to be one at hand, which in many instances there is
> not.

In *A London Family* 1870–1900 (Oxford, 1946) Mrs M. Vivian Hughes recounts how the products of those initially unpopular iron ranges, which had often displaced the old brick ovens, were still, as Elizabeth writes, 'So much better than the London baker's bread that neither she, nor her children as they grew up, ever willingly ate bought bread. A familiar story.' Elizabeth may at times become incensed but her observations on, for instance, the inadequacy of the ovens in modern gas and electric cookers, 'which are too small and getting smaller', are made from experience surely so familiar to her readers that they cannot have helped but join in her protest.

In a sense Elizabeth wrote *English Bread and Yeast Cookery* for the ultimate, ideal English reader. She has all the English sensitivity to the passage of time, to history, to nostalgia. But in this she is neither quaint nor simply writing an antiquarian lament. Her book is more robust than that. As literature, as a work of art, it has none of the inconsistencies or erratic messages of some of her earlier writing. Her command of subject and her powers of exposition have matured and grown, making the book the work of a writer who can do all she once could but more besides and with greater sureness. Above all the writing here is not literary. It doesn't seek directly to please the reader but yet will please some readers more than any other of her books. Throughout her life Elizabeth took up the cudgels against the impoverishment and ugliness of life under Puritanism and the industrial system. And in *English Bread and Yeast Cookery* she creates a practical handbook of ways and means to tackle an alternative. This is the most reflective of her books, showing Elizabeth's interest in knowledge as a part from pure information. It is not really possible to read it unless one becomes absorbed, and then it compels thought in a way which her other books do not.

In *Bread and Yeast Cookery* Elizabeth makes her most concerted attempt at coming to grips with the actual world, at suggesting how to bypass the sterilities of modern society. She passionately fights her female corner in the name of effective individual skill and craftsmanship against the proliferating crudities of a desiccating technology. She does not overtly relinquish Norman Douglas and the world he represents, but here there is none of his disdainful paganism. In this, the last book published in her lifetime, Elizabeth has left something of her Mediterranean self behind. Norman Douglas is displaced by the likes of Kenelm Digby, the Countess of Kent, Eliza Acton and Lady Llanover, who augment the overall intensity and coherence of vision which the book gradually discloses. Along with her scholarship, knowledge and craftsmanship, Elizabeth has lost nothing of her passion, her driving daemon; never quite surfacing, it is nonetheless there, implicit throughout.

In addition, *English Bread and Yeast Cookery* often reveals an unmistakably affectionate tone, unusual in Elizabeth's writing. It encompasses the virtues of homeliness and friendliness, as well as the more spectacular and striking aspects of human nature. To a greater or lesser degree Elizabeth's Mediterranean books are well-judged mediations between fantasy and reality. Her lyrical passages wring every last drop of colour, texture and atmosphere out of those Mediterranean cameos, yet before the purple has a chance to cloy she moves over to the down-to-earth practicalities of food preparation and cooking. Similarly, in *English Bread and Yeast Cookery* the evocation of a past milieu, with all its rituals and traditions, is beautifully done. But before it can become an exercise in antiquarian nostalgia, with quaint spelling and suchlike embellishments, Elizabeth transfers us to the precise methods required to achieve some particular effect in breadmaking, showing how this can be adapted to modern conditions. When writing on the Mediterranean she so often had the actual practice before her, whereas in her writing on England she almost always had to commence with sources from the past.

Her first book, *Mediterranean Food*, in a way half denies the domestic aspect of cooking, or at least vacillates about it, but in *English Bread and Yeast Cookery* there is no such ambivalence. It is a friendly, comfortable book, as in the older sense of the word used in *The Book of Common Prayer*: 'comfortable words . . . those that give strength in time of need'. Perhaps the most moving and significant message at the heart of this singular book is that Elizabeth achieves that rare thing: a celebration of the domestic without denying romance.

English Bread and Yeast Cookery was published in the autumn of 1977 to considerable acclaim and won the prestigious Glenfiddich Trophy for 1998. It was evident, however, that most reviewers, intimidated by the book's size and its author's reputation, gave little more than a cursory glance at some of its obvious themes. Many did not take enough trouble to describe what Elizabeth had achieved. But perhaps this was because they had not fully comprehended its magnitude. One of the most perceptive exceptions was Claire Tomalin for the *Sunday Times*. She drew attention to much of the essential matter of the book, saying that Elizabeth had:

> made us nostalgic . . . for worlds most of us could not possibly
> know. For two and a half decades she has turned our faces away
> from England. We were a very willing generation to grow

greedy and reject our Anglo-Saxon culinary conditions . . . the war and rationing encouraged whole worlds of fantasy about food and travel to flourish in our heads. In the fifties standard English cookery books were still recommending the use of dried eggs and margarine, with a pinch of sage as the most dashing herb on the shelf. Against such a landscape Elizabeth David appeared as liberating and delightful as Homer Lane did to the young Auden. Our eclectic kitchens became the hearts of our houses. Now we are being led to consider our native traditions again.

Tomalin says Elizabeth's motivation was frustration at the standard of 'manufactured' bread and the sense that people might again be 'prepared to spend time baking their own bread'. Her interpretation here is essentially accurate, although with the benefit of greater knowledge we can see that Elizabeth's motivation was also more complex and varied than this. Tomalin continues, observing that 'We have lost our traditions here.' But *English Bread and Yeast Cookery* 'has much more than the touch of history and topography that one finds in all good cookbooks. It is a work of devoted scholarship, using all manner of records of the past to re-establish its practice.' She goes on: 'there is a formidable amount of detail involved, and some readers will be impatient to reach Part II . . . where the practical instructions begin. But even if you decide to start the book there, you will find yourself turning back for references and practical advice.'

In interview with Caroline, Terence Conran's then wife, Elizabeth said: 'This started out as a small book and I got more and more deeply enmeshed. My interest in the subject germinated in 1956' – she refers to the *Spectator* review she had written on the Scurfields' *Home Baked* – '. . . the research was done in libraries here and there . . . I most specifically didn't start out to crusade or to preach . . . but the more I found out, the more impossible I found it to forgive the cynical debauching of our bread. . . . if people want to eat factory bread they can, but they should be told, they should know more. . . . I've enjoyed doing this book so much. I've really behaved like a lunatic, eating yeast pancakes galore – and cakes like Sally Lunns – I love cooking with yeast, it's so easy.'

Elizabeth's originality lay in her ability to synthesize, and in parallel her fine-tuned reflection of the zeitgeist was unerring; consequently she was always just that one step ahead of her time. In the 1970s many were already disenchanted with the results of mechanization and would have agreed with Eliza Acton's comment in her *Bread Book* of over 100 years earlier that English bread was 'noted both at home and abroad for its want of genuineness, and the faulty mode of its preparation'. In 1977 they went out and bought Elizabeth's book. It sold 15,000 hardback copies in a short time.

Several other studies on the making of bread, from late last century and on into this one quoted by Elizabeth – William Jago's exhaustive researches on the principles and technology of breadmaking, John Kirkland's 6-volume *The Modern Baker and Confectioner* (1897), Frederick Vine's *Practical Breadmaking* (1907) and Walter Banfield's beautifully titled *Manna* (1907) – Elizabeth describes in her acknowledgements as 'splendid works'. Nevertheless, *English Bread and Yeast Cookery*, with its searching scholarship and meticulous attention to detail, its comprehensive, magisterial tone and passionate vision, is unquestionably the greatest book written on the history and practice of breadmaking this century.

In the year of the book's publication, Elizabeth was made a *Chevalier de l'Ordre du Mérite Agricole* by the French. The previous year, 1976, she had been awarded an OBE. On presenting it to her the Queen asked what it was for, to which Elizabeth replied that she wrote cookery books. 'That must be very useful.' And indeed *English Bread and Yeast Cookery* was exactly that.

CHAPTER TWENTY

Ice and Beyond
(1977–1995)

THE ENGLISH PEDIGREE for some of the recipes in *English Bread and Yeast Cookery* is, on first reading, dubious. But their presence is usually merited as imports which Elizabeth judged popular enough to have installed themselves in the English national repertoire. Often badly made on their home territory they here benefit from new instruction (Claire Tomalin's review refers to: 'A mournful chapter on the present . . . decline of traditional French bread'). In an interview Elizabeth made scathing reference to that relentless English practice of the 1970s: (bad) quiche with everything: 'Quiches, quiches everywhere. But they bear no relation to those lovely creamy tarts from Alsace and Lorraine. The pastry is unspeakable in what is laughably called a quiche in this country.'

Included, along with some mordant wit at the expense of the monstrosities offered in its name, is a recipe for the making of a good pizza and its relative, Elizabeth's favourite, the *pissaladière*. She wrote to Priscilla's daughter, Julia, on the eve of her marriage in 1976 with some advice: one of the things she needed to know in order to feed people fairly cheaply was how to make a pizza; all sorts of other good dishes could be made from pizza dough. Elizabeth had taught Julia's cousin Johnny Grey how to do this a year or so earlier: he had become the wonder and admiration of his brother's friends and made huge quantities and froze them successfully. Elizabeth offered to teach Julia, it was so easy and satisfactory. The pizzas Elizabeth made were light, unlike the 'repulsive brick things' served in pizza houses or bought frozen. And they cost a fraction of what people paid for those other 'con jobs'.

Johnny Grey was, like his aunt, compelled by an interest in design (trained as an architect, he has subsequently become a noted kitchen designer) and spent time during these years talking and listening to Elizabeth. In 1977, when her bread book came out, Terence Conran also published a large photograph-filled compendium, *The Kitchen Book*. Incorporating some of the most influential contemporary ideas, Conran's book was very popular, subsequently a valuable fragment of social history. One of the kitchens photographed in the Conran book is Johnny Grey's first attempt, an outrageously impractical neo-gothic reaction against the current vogue for streamlining and uniformity. Another kitchen in the book is an illustration of what was described, with a touch of satire, as Elizabeth David's 'Dream Kitchen'.

In mid-July Elizabeth wrote again to Julia saying that *Bread* was in its final stage. And then she was off again to Wales. In the years of research and work on *English Bread and Yeast Cookery* her attachment to Wales had grown sufficiently for her to think seriously of buying a house there. Developments in France had disaffected her and she said, 'Too many sad things have happened there. I want a house in Wales with water.' Elizabeth remained captivated by water all her life, and its presence is spur to some of her most memorable descriptions of place. In April of the following year she thanked Hugh Johnson for presents of his own honey on a card depicting a seventeenth-century English hunting scene, in the foreground of which is perched an elegant water mill in delightfully vernacular style. Elizabeth finished her card: 'As for the water mill . . . it's the one I'm looking for . . . Much love E.'

One of the quotes in *English Bread and Yeast Cookery* from M. Vivian Hughes's quietly celebratory autobiography *A London Family* refers to a tea with relations at the little town of Machynlleth in 1888. Elizabeth's reason for including this quote is undoubtedly as much autobiographical as for its reference to Welsh 'light cakes'. Her own particular memories of Machynlleth and its river valley extended as far back as the Gwynne girls' first idyllic Welsh holiday in the mid-1930s. And during the war Elizabeth had nostalgically asked Priscilla if she did not remember the little house they had seen on that holiday together. She recalled its position along a path by a river, which ran through the garden, and nearby was an odd-looking sugar loaf hill. 'I have absolutely got to have that house. I don't say I want to live there permanently but I have never ceased regretting that I didn't take it.' This was one of the regions of Wales in which Elizabeth still believed, over forty years later, that she wanted to live. Her dream was never to be realized. She was always concerned about money, but perhaps most importantly the energy, patience and determination required to buy, organize and probably renovate a house so far away from London was soon to be in doubt.

Driving back with Johnny Grey from another trip to Wales in the autumn, their car was involved in a major accident. 'It was terrible,' says Hugh Johnson. 'Liz was devastated by it. I don't think she ever really recovered properly.' Apart from broken limbs Elizabeth's right hand was left unusable and her jaw broken, resulting in permanent problems with her teeth. The broken limbs meant that she had to spend three months in London's Lister Hospital and in her own words remain 'effectively out of action for several more'. Friends concur with Hugh Johnson's view that 'Liz never fully recovered physically, but more, I think, it affected her whole psyche. She couldn't have written another popular book after this. She was simply more frail, had less zest for living.' Alan Davidson remarks that 'After *Bread* there *was* a diminuendo.' Elizabeth was only sixty-four, but she seemed unable to overcome this premature frailty brought about by the car accident. In subsequent years other aspects of her deteriorating health, combined with the increasing tendency to fall and – with osteoporosis – break bones, put her frequently in hospital, sometimes for many weeks at a time. In the London hospitals she frequented, her room with its little fridge was always filled with delicacies and wine, offerings brought by the stream of visitors.

Research on the next volume in Elizabeth's grand projected history series was already under way; material had been collected intermittently during the writing of *English Bread and Yeast Cookery*. As the years passed, and she became more fascinated by the byways of scholarship, the book's subject grew, taking on different perspectives and emphases until its focus became most concentrated on the use of ice and the creation of ices. The disentanglement of the history of ice was to fill the rest of her life.

Aided in her book-collecting by the indefatigable Felicité, Elizabeth had early decided against the habit of collecting fine first editions in favour of less precious later editions of books. This was for two main reasons. First, it meant that she could afford to buy more, and second, as she wrote in the first issue of Alan and Jane Davidson's journal, *Petits Propos Culinaires* (*PPC*): 'When it comes to cookery books . . . it is a fearful mistake to pay large sums for first editions and neglect later ones, and this applies particularly to works which have had a long life.'

She continued by making several points about old cookery books, central to her own book-collecting. She wrote that first editions of famous cookery books 'wouldn't be nearly as interesting to serious students of cookery as later ones, in which authors themselves have made revisions, corrected errors, added new recipes, brought cooking methods up to date, and incorporated recently introduced ingredients'. Elizabeth's comments here are interesting and entirely valid, but also miss the point about a first edition existing as an intact, fixed piece of history to which readers often feel considerable allegiance for personal associations as much as for literary value. (This point arose again when Elizabeth later republished, revised and augmented editions of her first four books, and was surprised at the adverse reaction this provoked from some readers.)

For all her capability to communicate in her writing Elizabeth was often unable to comprehend fully what it was she represented for her audience. With *Mediterranean Food* she had communicated, above all, a passionate dream of escape. With *Italian Food* and *French Provincial Cooking* a more sober *modus vivendi* for this dream and its relationship to reality was evolved. But in this last phase of her life it was the realities of history and tradition and their rightful place and value in the present which she was most concerned to promulgate. Elizabeth had written originally out of a need to express herself and in response to the vicissitudes of her own class and generation, and they had responded. Over the years her readership had not only grown it had become more heterogeneous. But for most the things which Elizabeth represented above all were still a vigorous and sophisticated commendation of simple things: uncomplicated authentic food, and escape.

Believing that the 'soul' had gone out of her writing in the later work, some of Elizabeth's readers wanted more of the familiarly evocative recipes and less history. As devotees they did not expect her to change and were unwilling to follow her along these more thoughtful paths, which was quite reasonable. But Elizabeth's own course was now ordained. In her pursuit of truth she never ceased to recommend the authentic – her recipes are always about this. But in these later years well-structured escape no longer fulfilled her and, if only subconsciously, she was confronting a more austere reality.

During 1978 Elizabeth was revising *English Bread and Yeast Cookery* for the American publisher, trying to answer some of the volume of letters received from her English readers, and staying again in Wales. Felicité had been suffering for some time from various ailments – but in August the following year her symptoms intensified and she was taken into hospital. John Johnson drove Elizabeth to visit her there and remembers being annoyed with her. 'She had some bizarre ideas about what was good food for Felicité, would make these extraordinary rich little dishes all beautifully got up in cloths and things and we'd take them in daily.' Elizabeth's life came to a virtual standstill for Felicité during the most intense period of her illness. Yet despite this concern friends and family were familiar with Felicité's timidity towards Elizabeth, and Elizabeth's neglect and insensitivity regarding her sister's physical and emotional needs. (The sisters now rarely entered each other's areas of the house, preferring to communicate by telephone or notes left on the stairs. An anecdote from this period is illuminating. Felicité increasingly felt the cold in her upstairs rooms. Elizabeth had always kept Halsey Street under-heated, but the deterioration of Felicité's health made her more susceptible than previously to the cold. Sabrina (Priscilla's elder daughter) bought a heater for Felicité, but everyone's fear of Elizabeth was such that Priscilla had to stand guard while Sabrina hauled the heavy and offending object to a quaking Felicité up above. Then the guilty trio fell on the sofa in relieved laughter as Felicité offered a drink to celebrate their success.)

The dynamic of the Gwynne sisters' relationship was, however, too complex to lend itself to judgement on the basis of such neglect alone. These two had shared a house for thirty years – 'leading', as

Elizabeth later wrote to Maudie O'Malley, 'our quite separate lives, but of course dependent upon each other for so much.' And, despite Felicité's presence upstairs, Elizabeth also felt increasingly alone and isolated with her own pressing fears.

John Johnson recalls two startling examples of these anxieties about which he was uncomprehending at the time. One evening while talking with Elizabeth after they had visited Felicité in hospital the conversation had turned to Viola, John's mother, who was now living alone in Greece and about whose welfare they were both concerned. Then, by some underground connection, Elizabeth confessed to John: 'Sometimes at night I find myself screaming out loud.' John was stunned and unable to comment. In recalling this wretched admission he was reminded of an occurrence which at the time had shocked him similarly in its intensity. Some years before Felicité's illness he had been at dinner with Elizabeth in Halsey Street. 'We had probably both drunk a good quantity, anyway Elizabeth dropped and broke a sugar bowl. It didn't look to me particularly special but nevertheless its breakage provoked in Elizabeth the most terrible reaction. She was absolutely *overcome* with rage and shouted: "Objects are even *more* terrible than people." The shock must have registered on my face because the next day in the bookshop Felicité said rather tentatively, "I understand Elizabeth was a little overwrought last night."'

The following year, Alan Davidson, whose booklet on fish Elizabeth had enthusiastically written about in the *Spectator*, was made Alistair Horne Visiting Fellow at St Antony's College, Oxford in order to finish the book he was working on at the time. (Alan Davidson's growing expertise on fish had resulted in more publications and in 1975 he left the diplomatic service to write full time.) 'The Dean of the college stopped me one day in the corridor and asked me, "In what way do you propose to make manifest to the other members of the college your presence here and the reason for it?"' Taken aback, Alan asked what he would suggest and was told: 'A seminar.' He decided that as there 'wasn't any provision in the university calendar for food history I would remedy it . . .' He asked Elizabeth amongst several others if she would attend. She didn't manage the first two but came to the third where 'She made highly relevant and pointed contributions about the history of cookery books in England. Her attendance helped to give the thing a lot more impetus and the next one was a full-scale symposium.' This was the initiation of the international Oxford Symposium on Food and Cookery, now attended from around the world by some of the more thoughtful writers on the subject.

In the same year, by a circuitous set of circumstances, Alan 'accidentally' founded, with Jill Norman, Elizabeth and Richard Olney (a mutual friend) a publishing company, Prospect Books, and a journal called *Petits Propos Culinaires* (*PPC*), both of which aimed to publish in-depth articles and books on food and its history. Elizabeth wrote several detailed pieces on her reigning preoccupations in the early numbers of *PPC*. These ranged from a disentanglement of the true authorship of the seventeenth-century Countess of Kent's book to '*Banketting Stuff; Concerning Coriander; An Eighteenth Century Kitchen Garden at Christmas*; an article on 'a high-summer fête in the gardens of Versailles for Louis XIV in 1668', partly researched by her niece Sabrina Harcourt-Smith, and more on Elizabeth's researches into ice. In thanking Sabrina for her efforts at the Royal Library at Windsor Elizabeth added that her 'work into the history of ices isn't getting on very fast'. With her thanks came a copy of the relevant *PPC* and the comment: 'an eccentric little publication'.

Elizabeth was ambivalent about the skilfully edited and produced journal, possibly the only publication which would have recognized the importance of her present work. This ambivalence stems from a dilemma which she could not solve. Alan Davidson over-modestly credits Elizabeth's essays as the main reason for *PPC*'s immediate success, whilst the Oxford Symposium also prospered and grew, spawning similar events around the world. Each year 'Elizabeth took a considerable interest in what was going on . . . and felt that the proceedings consituted a major new resource of information about food history. Some of the more recondite contributions particularly struck her,' says Alan. ' "Some little known aspects of Trans-Caucasian Mountain Ram cookery". She thought that one was great . . . a really good subject!'

Alan's irony here obscures the fact that his combined efforts have been instrumental in the increasing recognition of food history as an invaluable and almost unexplored area of social history, to which Elizabeth was now dedicated. Paul Bailey, who met Elizabeth in her last years through their mutual friend Jane Grigson, recalls that by the late 1980s she would say to him, 'I don't want to write recipes any more. God, I can't carry on writing them, I've done all that. The excitement of life now is in tracing the texts.' She was saying, 'I want of find out how these things came into being, who thought of them.'

Ten or so years earlier Elizabeth had met Richard Leech, owner of the Holland Press, publishing sorely needed facsimile editions of rare and out of print bibliographies relating to food and wine. Richard Leech and Elizabeth began collecting material for a series of books on the Stuarts at table and Richard and his then wife's friendship with Elizabeth became a source of scholarly and emotional support to her. Richard Leech told the author, 'Elizabeth was really not interested in food by now you know. She would enjoy a pleasant Middle Eastern restaurant, but really didn't make food. At Halsey Street food was just little bits and pieces, but you were always assured of a *good* glass of wine.'

In about 1982 Elizabeth met Peter Davidson, a young academic at Warwick University, with whom she discussed an edition of Kenelm Digby's cookery book, *The Closet of the Eminently Learned Kenelm Digby Kt. Opened*. Elizabeth would write a lengthy introduction, despite telling Peter that she wished she had had the scholarly training to approach seventeenth-century material with confidence, and that she had stumbled into scholarship in her later years and felt disadvantaged having to move forward so slowly, checking every-thing. 'Yes, she did regard herself as self-taught,' says Paul Bailey. Apropos this preoccupation Peter Davidson remembers a lunch in London with Elizabeth and Jill Norman. Peter Davidson told the author, 'Mrs David asked about Richard Waller, the seventeenth-century Fellow of the Royal Society, and I knew whatever it was and she turned to Jill in rather a proprietorial way and said, "You see, he *knows*, it's his *world*." (Peter Davidson has recently completed the Digby edition with Jane Stevenson for Prospect Books and dedicated the volume to Elizabeth's memory.)

Meanwhile Alan Davidson continued feeding Elizabeth all man-ner of information on unexplored territory, including some crucial research on a variety of subjects for her ices book in the Bodleian Library. 'Elizabeth had a phenomenal memory,' he says, 'she was alert to every detail. She could quote word for word and if she corrected you she was *always* right.' Her work was now of a clearly academic nature and she especially regretted to Peter Davidson, who 'translated quite a lot of Latin here and there', her ignorance of it. Yet until the end of her life she remained ambivalent about the whole academic enterprise. On the one hand she could write irritably to Alan saying that the bibliography for the late Jane Grigson was an editorial mistake because it was 'boring, which Jane never was', and add soon afterwards that she hoped 'no one would even *think* of doing one for me'. Meanwhile her response to other less scholarly members of her profession could be vitriolic if she thought they had got something wrong. She loathed being referred to as 'the doyenne of cookery writers', saying to Paul Bailey, 'Who wants to be the doyenne of *them?*'

In 1979 she was happy to accept an honorary doctorate offered her by the University of Essex. At the same time she was perhaps most proud of being made a Fellow of the Royal Society of Literature in 1982 and the recognition as a writer which this conferred. Grey Gowrie told her that he had used her work for his students at Harvard as examples of how to write. 'She appreciated that her books could be used as pieces of writing. She went beyond the bounds of cooking writing. She had pace and rhythm and could be read well out loud. A feel for the physical world is very good in a writer.' But Elizabeth's dilemma over her increasingly scholarly inclinations was that broadly speaking the milieu in which she had grown up esteemed fine literature above 'bookishness'. The notion that literature should be achieved through apparent effortlessness and insouciance in many ways ran counter to the zeal, precision and analysis necessary for the practice of scholarship.

During the following decade Elizabeth experienced a diminution of that drive and will-power which were necessary for sifting research material in a consistently disciplined manner. She continued to write articles arising from her researches but the greater stamina required to fashion her boundless research into a book, an extended coherent whole, was elusive. She was still her formidable self, with her memory razor-sharp, but, despite having several of the aforementioned friends prepared to carry out primary research for her in various ways, the purpose which had formerly spurred her on was now in decline.

Another of the hazards of ageing, the loss of old friends and relatives, also began to weigh upon her. The painter Lett Haines was first to go, leaving Cedric finally alone apart from their devoted housekeeper Millie. Felicité wrote a letter of commiseration to Maudie O'Malley, a close friend of the duo at Benton End. Acting for so long as the guardian of Elizabeth's interests, Felicité's own persona appeared to many shadowy by comparison with her passionate sister. But those who took the trouble to know her soon discovered that she was anything but a mouse, and possessed of a sense of humour too.

'Oh, Felicité had a real twinkle in her eye,' recalls John Johnson. 'She had that slight smile hovering on her lips. The smile of those who have lived an internal life, have been observers and not always spoken as much as listened.' But Felicité's path had been determined long ago, in part simply by being born Elizabeth's sister, and was confirmed inexorably when she came to live with her. In the following passages to Maudie, Felicité reveals her plight with touching clarity:

'Elizabeth gave me your letter yesterday, for which we both thank you. Am sure she'll write herself before long, but as she's struggling hard with research for next book (or books, am not sure and seems frightfully preoccupied with any number of things) I'm writing in the meantime.

'Wish I could say something constructive about Cedric. I could ... write a great deal on what you said about friends (in inverted commas). Seems to me to be one of the major penalties of having in some way been great or famous ... or in some way of use to the in no way great or gifted ... Exploitation in fact. Poor Cedric ... Terrifying to think of the loneliness of very old age ... I still totter in three mornings a week to the bookshop, but do little work, as I have truly lost my wits, my balance, my strength and much else besides. Apart from that am trying to eke out extra occupation and finance by copy-typing here at home. Never was my favourite occupation ...'

One recalls that during all her years at Halsey Street Felicité had continued to type most of Elizabeth's articles and books. She continues: 'Wish I could get about a bit more . . . I hanker for my one time independence. I sold my beloved bicycle a few days ago, finally admitting it seems implausible I'll ever be able to ride it again. . . . I greatly envy people like yourself who paint, like Elizabeth who can write. In fact I envy of course anyone who is creative and for whom every day is far too short. Altogether I must admit to a feeling of great desolation . . .'

The following year, 1982, brought the death of the Gwynne sisters' brother-in-law Chris Grey. Elizabeth wrote to Maudie: 'Yes, Chris was our doctor and we have always been very close to him, I have known him since I was twenty when Diana first met him. His death is a crushing blow.' Cedric Morris also died that year and Felicité again wrote to Maudie saying, 'I think of him every day, of course, because of his two pictures (one of Wootton) which give me perpetual delight and solace.' Her health showed no improvement and she said she 'appears to be an idle old good for nothing.' . . . In the course of this letter she hopes and prays that Maudie's 'home life is more peaceful again. The hazards of married life would I know have always been too much for me. Have never been strong enough to cope with my own dottiness, let alone a husband's or whatever person I'd have committed myself to.' Further on she says, 'The thing I'd most love to be able to do would be to write – not for publishing or anything like that – but just the ability to spin words together to my own satisfaction.' (From early youth Felicité had in fact written a considerable amount of poetry, but obviously not to her satisfaction.) She concludes 'Meanwhile I type Liza's spectacular scholarship and her skill with words. The gods gave *her* all the genius, and had not a vestige to spare for me. You can paint like an angel . . . miraculous and haunting pictures, for which I'm insanely envious. Think of being able to write music, poems, books. All I've ever been was . . . quite a good bookseller . . .'

During the 1980s the small number of admiring younger people who were welcomed into Elizabeth's life and revived some of her enthusiasm for her remaining years included Michael Day, proprietor of what he calls the Big Cheese Company. Michael is an uncommon man whose air of ingenuousness and wordliness are none the less underscored by a determined optimism and lack of cynicism. His generosity can be outrageous. He is a gossip, he is also one of those who knows how to entertain as well as to listen. And, under the mask of the showman his intuitive sensitivity extends itself to a sympathy with the old. He took on the role of court jester for Elizabeth and thus sometimes lightened her own failing spirit.

I met Felicité first because I used to swap cheese with her for books, and I used to have tea with her and admire her scarves. I was giving a party and I asked her and she asked if she could bring her sister Elizabeth. I didn't know who Elizabeth David was and I hadn't read any of her books . . . I asked her and Bernard Levin to come to lunch. John Clements (his brother wrote *Dad's Army*) was there too, in Leyton's Wine Cellars. She wasn't temperamental then. There were about four people who had a key to her front door and I was one of them. I would leave cheese there. I liked her. She used to call me an imbecile. I used to read books to her in Danish and she would laugh and I would fall over. She would say outrageous things. She came with Jane Grigson to the Crystal Room in the Mayfair. We had a competition . . . who could get the most time spent on them by a famous chef. At Mosimann's he spent about five minutes flattering Elizabeth and then spent two minutes on me. At Nico Ladenis . . . I thought he was a conceited, arrogant man and I said, 'You don't have to buy my cheese.' He wanted Elizabeth to do an introduction to his book and she wouldn't although she did think he was a good chef. Elizabeth could be pretty vicious sometimes.

At the beginning, every fortnight I would go round and we would drink seven or eight glasses of wine. Jeremy (Round) and Lindsey (Bareham) . . . when they got to know her well we would take Elizabeth out together. We were very fond of her. Elizabeth was very observant. She had some Henry Moore prints of sheep on the wall and I took them off the wall and put them under the sofa because I thought I would borrow them. . . . She came back into the room and said, 'Michael, where are those prints?' 'Oh, those prints.' And I had to put them back.

She seriously did cook me an omelette with roquefort in it.

She wasn't cooking by then. Then we stopped this drinking habit, because it was stupid. We'd take her out to eat instead. She would go to sleep at about 2 a.m. and we'd whisper, 'She's asleep' and she would shout at us, 'No I'm not!' and we'd say, 'Bedtime,' and she'd say, 'No it's not!'

Her top books were *Cold Comfort Farm* and *Wind in the Willows*. She had an impressive ability to put away a lot of drink and still come up with a pretty acid line at the end of it. That was a most endearing quality. If she didn't like you she didn't and that was that. Once or twice she got a bit narky with me. But she could be very charming. She wrote a letter of apology to me saying, 'Sorry I behaved so badly.'

She did get grumpy, but she knew she was behaving badly. I think she pushed it as far as she could to see who would back off and who'd stand up to her. Not that many people did. I got on quite well with her in a strange way. People would come to the door . . . fan club, sycophantic people. The eye contact between us said it all. She'd let them go on for about thirty seconds before she'd hit them with some put-down phrase.

She went in for a sort of testing game. She tested Jeremy Round to see if he did actually know about whatever subject he was talking about. Whether the bread was cooked to this degree, the pasta was made like this or like that. And Jeremy would come back three times as fast as Elizabeth. Hardly anyone could do that. If she was impressed by you that was OK. But for me, being a complete philistine . . . someone who enjoyed the fact that I'd never read any of her books . . . it was nice to watch and see them. 'Yes I like him because he *can* answer my question. He *does* know.' And if they *didn't* know what they were talking about they were out. She had little time for people who were fools . . . except me fortunately. ('But you played the floor as the fool didn't you?' 'Yes, but it was the only one I could play,' and he laughed, 'I didn't know anything about cooking.')

A young woman who did know something about cooking was Lindsey Bareham, then writing the restaurant reviews for *Time Out* magazine. With trepidation she had been introduced to Elizabeth one evening by the proprietor of the Lebanese restaurant in Abingdon Road, the Phoenicia. 'Oh, she loved all those handsome waiters, those liquid brown eyes looking down into hers,' recalls Paul Bailey. 'But she loved the food too. She'd say, "Why do we bother with French food? This is just the best thing. You don't gorge yourself, you just pick and choose." We talked about books, writers we both liked, what was in the air. She liked to be entertained and she did drink a lot and she didn't care.'

To Lindsey Bareham's enormous surprise Elizabeth knew and liked her work. Lindsey asked her out to lunch at the Caprice where Martin Lam was then chef. 'We seemed to have so much to talk about we finally left at 4.30 p.m. You couldn't make sloppy remarks with Elizabeth. She concentrated my mind so much, I found her very stimulating company and very damning about food writers of the time. She said they all had "half-baked ideas" – except Jeremy Round. She did feel that she had set a standard, had done a lot of the research that other people made free with. She always had the latest books, would know what everyone was up to. Not many people in the food world came across her but she was keeping a beady eye on *them*. She was aware of the influence she'd had on food writers in a general way.'

Paul Bailey remarks that Elizabeth's 'influence on writers has been circuitous. She had an ego about her talent, but she did believe in manners. She was very much aware that many people went into food writing for all the wrong reasons. And the most wrong was to make a lot of money quickly. The cleverness of the new writers was that they realized that Elizabeth had touched a nerve . . . I feel Elizabeth was one of those writers who was ignorant of her audience. But I don't think she cared. She is one of the few who liked writing and one of the few food writers who has made any impact on *writers*.'

As to the restaurateurs, Lindsey Bareham observes that 'she affected the up and coming restaurateurs, but they gave her credit for it. Martin Lam, Alistair Little, Rowley Leigh, Simon Hopkinson. They were a generation of chefs who appreciated her writing for its own sake as much as the recipes.'

Elizabeth had always gone out to restaurants with friends, but this happened more frequently as she became uninterested or unable to cook herself. One of her favourite chefs, Simon Hopkinson, joined

Terence Conran in opening his restaurant Bibendum in 1986. Among the first friends to take her there were Hugh and Judy Johnson and to everyone's enormous relief she liked it. Terence Conran's concern to have a lift especially to accommodate the difficulty Elizabeth now experienced in walking was repaid, as she returned often.

Lesley O'Malley had continued living in the basement flat at Halsey Street for thirty years but it was clear to her family that Elizabeth no longer made her feel so welcome. With encouragement from Elizabeth, after her retirement Lesley decided to move permanently to her weekend house in Great Missenden in Buckinghamshire. Here she would be closer to her old friend from Cairo, the writer Roald Dahl. She was an entirely loyal friend and made no complaint.

With designs made by Elizabeth's nephew Johnny Grey the basement at Halsey Street would now be converted into another kitchen. It was intended that this large basement 'with better light than the original kitchen upstairs' would be a study-sitting room-kitchen area for winter use. In fact Elizabeth used the upper kitchen much less after this second one was completed.

During early 1984, with Jill Norman as editor, Elizabeth put together her splendid selection of journalism and other more scholarly pieces written over the last forty or so years and entitled, *An Omelette and a Glass of Wine*. While this was in progress, and continuing her life-long habit of spending several weeks of every year out of England, in February Elizabeth was in Uzès in the South of France with Jean Bolland. Here they were staying in the house of an old friend, Elizabeth's doctor Patrick Woodcock, during his absence for the winter. Elizabeth described the beautiful house and her time in Uzès in an article in *An Omelette and a Glass of Wine* entitled 'Confort Anglais, French Fare'. The theme, that it was increasingly preferable to eat French food on picnics or by cooking it oneself at home, had been established in 'Eating out in Provincial France 1967–77', a disillusioned piece on the decline of French restaurants, originally written as an introduction to her revised edition of *French Provincial Cooking* for Michael Joseph in 1977. Rejected as too long – probably also regarded by Michael Joseph as too down-beat and not an encouragement to sales – Elizabeth had first published it in *PPC* before reprinting it in *An Omelette and a Glass of Wine*.

From Uzès Elizabeth wrote to her niece Sabrina, saying that she'd had a wonderful three weeks, with the days passing at devastating speed. In the Saturday market, selling delectable food, she was able to buy at least fifty different cheeses; the bakery sold seven varieties of brown bread; and the pâté in the charcuterie was delicious. But in the big supermarché they sold 'sliced white Mother's Pride type loaves . . . Who buys it . . .'

Near Uzès was Elizabeth's old friend Lawrence Durrell. Jean Bolland's friend Mrs Bain remembers that Jean ' would be instructed to do the cooking, being told, for instance: "Lawrence will be coming for lunch today – we will have . . ." Jean, who was pretty imperturbable, said that she was frequently shaking at the knees by the time she had finished.'

In 1979 Jill Norman had set up her own imprint, now including on its projected list the most prestigious cookery book writers in England: Elizabeth, Jane Grigson, Alan Davidson and Claudia Roden. In January 1984 Jill Norman had negotiated to move her imprint under the auspices of the publishing house John Hale. However, by July, when Elizabeth had just signed the contract for *An Omelette and a Glass of Wine*, disagreements had arisen and Jill was dismissed from Hale. An appeal against unfair dismissal was brought and either through loyalty or her increasing litigiousness, perhaps both, Elizabeth joined the fray on Jill's behalf in the publisher's magazine, the *Bookseller*. Statements had to be retracted and a kind of stalemate was reached through the courts.

The particular ferociousness of Elizabeth's reputation for scorning pretension and inaccuracy arose from a genuine distaste for both. Looking behind Elizabeth's projection of herself, one senses that sometimes this otherwise commendable trait arose from a well-submerged lack of confidence. 'There were so many people she didn't approve of,' says Paul Bailey. 'Elizabeth had very strong opinions. There was a very clear borderline of people she didn't like and she wasn't afraid to say so. She didn't like people who didn't write well: opportunists or entrepreneurs. If she could see someone was being pushy she didn't like them.'

A case in point was *The Foodie Handbook* brought out in 1985 by the journalist Paul Levy with Ann Barr. A frenetic, tongue-in-cheek journalistic mix of fact and fashion, the book traced the rise of the current obsession with food reflected by the coinage of the word 'foodie'. Despite some potentially thought-provoking observations and a collection of mini-biographies of influential figures in the field over the last century or so, the 'facts' are often inaccurate and the several different agendas not all out in the open. On the one hand the reader is apparently beckoned to join the fashionable crowd who 'worship food' and on the other is being sneered at for doing just that.

Elizabeth featured prominently in the book and was incensed at the biographical inaccuracies about herself as well as the general tone. In a long letter about the book to her friend Hugh Johnson she said she believed that Ann Barr had been 'corralled' into it but regarded Levy as an opportunist, calling him 'fraudulent, a climber and pretentious'. She regretted not emulating Derek Cooper on Radio 4's Food Programme, who had told Levy that if he printed anything about him he would sue. Elizabeth had written a biting piece decrying *The Foodie Handbook* in the *Tatler* in response to which she said she had had a number of appreciative letters. She was not an advisable enemy.

An Omelette and a Glass of Wine included the brilliant piece 'John Wesley's Eye', in which Elizabeth had described (with omissions) her first attempts at writing in reaction to the culinary horrors of post-war England. Among the other essays are tributes to some of those who had influenced her, in particular Norman Douglas. In 'Have It Your Own Way' she cites his dictum: 'Do as you please, and send everybody to Hell, and take the consequences. Damned good Rule of Life.' With this Elizabeth was making oblique reference to Charles Gibson Cowan and her projected escape with him to the Greek islands. Norman Douglas's intention had been to 'jolt me out of an entanglement which, as he could see . . . had already become a burden to me. And the gentleman concerned was not very much to his liking.

'"You are leaving with him because you think it your duty . . . Stay here with me. Let him make do without you."

'"I can't, Norman. I have to go."

'"Have it your own way, my dear, have it your own way."

'Had I listened to Norman's advice I should have been saved a deal of trouble. Also, I should not, perhaps, have seen Greece and the islands, not spent the war years working in Alexandria and Cairo, not have married and gone to India, not have returned to England, not become involved in the painful business of learning to write about food and cookery . . . Was he right? . . . Does it matter? I did what I pleased at the time. I took the consequences . . .'

Other essays in *An Omelette and a Glass of Wine* were some of the best from her *Spectator* years. In spite of the illustrations, the book was hugely successful and went quickly into paperback.

Sending a copy to Maudie O'Malley soon after its publication in the autumn, Elizabeth recalled the recent funeral service of her cousin Archie Gordon, which Maudie had been unable to attend. 'Quintin's address splendid. He revealed that Archie's predecessor in the job of producing policicians for broadcasting had been "a very different personage; his name was Guy Burgess". If we hadn't been in Church Q. would have had a big ovation.' Archie, the fifth Marquis of Aberdeen, had been a close friend of Cedric Morris and Lett Haines and Elizabeth tells Maudie: 'I was so sad that when the Cedric and Lett shows opened I couldn't get to either of the parties. At the time I was suffering from a horrible affliction – my legs covered in sores, and I could hardly get my shoes on . . . so I missed all my old friends. I *did* manage to get to the Cedric show in its last week at the Tate. I thought it was splendid, and the catalogue brilliantly done by Richard Morphet.'

Elizabeth's love of painting – she was particular appreciative of still-lifes – was not by any means confined to those with which there was some personal connection. She tells Maudie that the previous evening she had been to a special view of the Fantin Latours, organized by the NACF. Amongst some very beautiful pictures was one of her favourites, a perfectly plain white cup and saucer with spoon. Its companion piece, a little white candlestick, was also there.

Her following had for a number of years extended beyond Europe to the United States and Australia, but she had never visited either country. Hugh Johnson was instrumental in effecting a change. Elizabeth's old friend Gerald Asher was now living in California. Hugh Johnson says of Asher that: 'In the sixties he was the most informative and forward-looking wine merchant in England, import-ing small quantities of then little known bottles into this country.'

445

Asher had left England in 1970 and, with the help of his well-written wine articles for the prestigious American *Gourmet* magazine, established himself as one of the luminaries of the Californian wine trade.

He and Elizabeth remained friends and Asher sent her admirers from the States. Hitherto unsuccessful in persuading her to visit him there, Hugh Johnson swung the balance. 'I thought California an exciting place to be. I told Liz that she must go and visit Gerald. I was sure she'd love it once she got there.' In the spring of 1981 Elizabeth made her first visit. She had long been a friend of James Beard, grand old man of the American culinary world, but under Gerald Asher's wing she was fêted by a new and enthusiastic group. Taken on journeys into the country, on picnics of exquisite preparation, she ate and drank in San Francisco's most interesting restaurants, visited unusual food shops – a Lebanese one particularly seduced her with its powerful aromas of spices, and the apricot paste for summer drinks, evoking memories of Egypt many years before. Other shops were selling beautiful kitchenware, whose inspiration had been Elizabeth's books and Elizabeth David Ltd; and in still others there were the secondhand books she could not live without. Elizabeth liked California, its museums, food, wine, good restaurants; some of these, such as the celebrated Chez Panisse and Zuni, attribute their very existence to the inspiration of her books.

Back in England, in June Elizabeth wrote to Sabrina telling her that her kitchen was now operational again, 'rather too much so, in fact'; she had been repaying hospitality received during her holiday in San Francisco, and the stream of Americans visiting her was set to continue until August.

Nevertheless Elizabeth returned every year to San Francisco to stay with Gerald Asher for a month or more, until 1991 when ill-health made it impossible. One person who appears conspicuously absent from Elizabeth's acquaintanceship in America – and for that matter by mention in her books – is M. F. K. Fisher, the only other writer on food of Elizabeth's generation whose prose was consistently as felicitous, quite a number would say more so. Perhaps professional jealousy prevented Elizabeth from suggesting such a meeting, or Fisher's venerated literary position meant that Elizabeth's friends did not know her, or if the meeting did take place, the two women's respective iconic positions made friendship impossible.

While her sister's opportunities for reviving visits abroad continued, Felicité's life became more constrained as her health continued to deteriorate. At first the cause of her symptoms was in debate, but eventually she was diagnosed with encarditis, inflammation of the nerve-endings of the heart. In March of 1986, when her heart could take no more, she died, leaving Elizabeth alone and desolate. Their niece Sabrina, Felicité's god-daughter and executrix, remembers a frantic journey back from Holland at the end of which she arrived just too late. 'Jean [the housekeeper] and Aunt Liza were there. It was awful. Liza was utterly distraught. She just couldn't cope.' With the help of April Boyes Sabrina tried to organize what had to be done. Felicité was buried in the peaceful little Sussex churchyard close by where their parents, Rupert and Stella, already lay.

Elizabeth wrote after the funeral to Maudie O'Malley: 'Thank you so much for the lovely flowers you sent . . . Poor Felicité, she was so courageous but she had no luck. A recent although short bout of illness looked like leaving her further impaired physically and mentally, and I don't see how she could have coped with much more infirmity so one must accept that her quick end was really merciful, and good for her that she was at home . . . not in hospital.

'I can't quite imagine how I will manage in this house without Felicité. We had shared it for thirty-four years . . . but of course dependent upon each other for so much.' Elizabeth wrote to Alan Davidson, grateful for his condolences, again expressing something of her loss: 'Thank you also for your letter about Felicité. Without her this house is inexpressibly sad.'

Visiting during this period, Lindsey Bareham located the happier facets of 'this house' created by Elizabeth's presence and the setting she had created:

> Lovely things. Books everywhere, pictures, china, glass, wonderful earthenware pots and bowls, wonderful old storecupboards, no mixers anywhere; the kitchen Greek powder blue, the huge kitchen table with that low lamp you kept on knocking into,

she always seemed to have a wind-up timer and an egg-timer on the go. Up the stairs and in Elizabeth's bedroom there were still more books and lovely pictures, and that huge four-poster bed. I don't know how she got in and out of it, it was just *covered* with papers and books, always sprouting yellow stickers. She had steps down from the bed and a tiny fridge next to it. Her dressing-room, her bathroom, her scarves and gloves and blouses hanging everywhere; lovely simple clothes. It was artistic, bohemian. It was also a terribly feminine room. I loved the atmosphere. I went to the house soon after she had died and it was so noticeable that she wasn't there. I have *never* been so struck by a presence as I was by Elizabeth's. It was quite remarkable.

Not long after Felicité's death Elizabeth contracted tuberculosis and was in hospital. Once again friends came to visit, to encourage and restore her. But poor Elizabeth's habit of falling and breaking bones had already established hospital sojourns as a ritual element of her calendar. With lunches in restaurants impossible, some friends would bring picnic lunches to eat with her. One of these was Janet Clarke, a cookery book dealer from whom Elizabeth had bought for several years. Janet's authority on her subject and capacity for warmth endeared her to Elizabeth and professional transactions had developed into friendship. 'Elizabeth always looked lovely sitting up in her white cotton nightgowns. She had her hairdresser come in regularly too. Her appearance *was* important to her. When she kept breaking things in those last years most of the time she wasn't actually ill. She simply had to stay there because she shouldn't walk and move herself about. So she worked and was surrounded by flowers and her books and carried on as normal as possible.' (It was to Janet, confiding in Elizabeth about a painful affair in which the man was married, that Elizabeth had said, 'But the best ones always are my dear. The best ones always are.')

Writing in the spring of 1987 to alter an arrangement to meet Sabrina and Priscilla, necessitated by having to 'go through page designs & pictures, captions etc, for the new edition of *Italian Food*', Elizabeth refers to 'so much time in hospital in the last year'. Indeed a good part of the work on *Italian Food* was done whilst there.

Writing to Sabrina in January of the following year she wonders 'how your Christmas was. Fairly exhausting I expect.' (Sabrina by this time had three growing boys to look after.) Elizabeth continues: '*I* don't do much, other than limp up and down my stairs, and waste a lot of time revising old books, wishing they had been better written in the first place . . . Lots of love Aunt Liza.'

Despite writing several articles and more 'than one learned introduction for others' books since the publication of *An Omelette and a Glass of Wine*, Elizabeth was conscious both that the material in her latest book was not original and that work on her ices book was not progressing with any coherence. Her regrets that her earlier books weren't 'better written in the first place' were understandable, she was reflecting with more than a quarter of a century of writing separating her from them. Elizabeth herself was not always the best judge of where her originality lay. The knowledge that she had not written a new book since *English Bread and Yeast Cookery* must have been galling, particularly during 1987 and 1988 while she made those extended versions of her 'old books', done in the days when her purpose was so much clearer.

With minor revisions to the text, the new editions were produced in large, luxurious format, each one augmented by reproductions of old paintings, much in the way Elizabeth had customarily quoted from other writers to create a *mise-en-scène* for her work. *Mediterranean Food* (with a new introduction), *French Country Cooking* and *Summer Cooking*, through no fault of Elizabeth's, are not very absorbing, however. Their presentation reflects the glossy cookery book as coffee-table-entertainment syndrome, even down to the questionable practice of reproducing the presenting celebrity's signature on the cover. Elizabeth must have balked at this. Despite some good pictures these sleek modern packages were somehow remarkable only for their dampening of the book's original and pervasive spirit: a sense of authority in combination with an irrepressible vitality, freshness and simplicity. Dr Johnson's line from *The Rambler*, 'The love of life is necessary to the vigorous prosecution of any undertaking,' catches something of the essential Elizabeth. It is absent here.

The one exception in these re-editions is *Italian Food*. Writing appreciatively to Alan Davidson in 1988 about a good review in *PPC* of the re-edition of *Italian Food*, Elizabeth was irritated that some other 'critics have been very hostile . . . mainly it would seem, on the grounds that the book has been around a long time and that I have no right to change its image now.' With *Italian Food*, the first of her re-editions, she certainly had changed its image. But here she need not have felt despondent about 'wasting time'. It is a fine book. As well as consolidating all previous revisions, she had added a new introduction, a 'brief new chapter on Italian wines . . . expanded lists of Italian cookery books, of guides to food and wine in Italy, and of relevant reference books'; all these were filled with fascinating commentary. She had enlarged the chapter on ices with interesting aspects of her recent research and, finally, included 'a selection from the accounts written by the scores of English and French visitors to Italy from the end of the fifteen century down to the 1980s'. Since the first publication of *Italian Food* in 1954, Elizabeth's understanding of the cultural significance of travel literature had reached quite a different plane and she cites some of the finest writers. Linked to this (remembering that almost all travellers made their way to Italy for the remains of its Classical past and as the cradle of its resurgence) and in keeping with historians in other fields, throughout the new book Elizabeth's fuller appreciation of the crucial influence the Italian Renaissance also exerted for centuries upon European nations, is abundantly clear.

Italian Food not only has an engrossing text, it is also enhanced by its illustrations. Elizabeth knew she had riches from Italy at her disposal, with the tradition of still-lifes of food reaching as far back as the Romans. After a lapse of centuries, in the late sixteenth century, with painters like Caravaggio, Italy was the first country where still-lifes once again began to appear; not only as details in other paintings, but as a genre of their own. And here Elizabeth gives us a selection of some of the most beautiful of them all: Roman mosaics and frescoes, fifteenth-century miniatures and frescoes, paintings by Caravaggio, Vincenzo Campi, Giovanni Recco, Veronese and the Caracci, and on through the eighteenth and nineteenth centuries until Renato Guttuso in the twentieth. Elizabeth was interested in still-lifes both as works of art and as vital historical records of how things had actually looked. The art historian Michael Helston, who mounted *Painting in Spain in the Later Eighteenth Century* at the National Gallery in 1989, was asked to take Elizabeth round the exhibition. He remembers: 'She was fascinated with the great Luis Melendez. She seemed to have a remarkable knowledge of everything going on in those wonderful still-lifes of food.'

In remaking *Italian Food* Elizabeth was really trying to forge it into a many-layered thing similar to *English Bread and Yeast Cookery*. That was not possible. It was as if she had travelled back almost to where she had begun; from those days with Norman Douglas and her passionate and instinctive response to the ancient in the modern Mediterranean, to this measured and authoritative appreciation permeated by her present absorption in history, and Italy's roots in its ancient Mediterranean past.

In recalling her final years Doreen Thornton describes Elizabeth's sense of isolation: 'Latterly it was so hard. She grew very quiet, didn't speak so much. She was *such* a good friend, but I was getting deaf, and she would whisper on the phone. She *would* quarrel with her best friends and became more and more businesslike with them. People like Renée. Then she became lonely for friends she knew well, though she knew a lot of people. They weren't all real friends. It was awful, she'd ring and say to me, "*Can't* you come up, Doreen?"' (But Doreen lived in Sussex and the trip was as difficult for her as for Elizabeth.)

'The last time I saw her she said to me, "I want to die, Doreen."

'"You can't, Liz, you've got to finish your ice book."

'"I *have* finished it."'

And Doreen did not then know that this was not true. Realizing that Elizabeth was unable to complete it, Jill Norman had come to Halsey Street and taken the manuscript away.

After a stroke Elizabeth died at home on 22 May 1992. At seventy-nine her unquiet spirit was finally laid to rest.

Postscript

ELIZABETH HAD denounced most contemporary writing on food as 'pretentious' and 'precious' and declared that it was never her intention to produce such an effect as she had: 'and I'm not sure that I like it or the intensity and self-consciousness that goes with it.' In the days after her death on 22 May 1992, the obituaries had nevertheless sounded with superlatives in her praise: 'Keeper of the National Palate', The Woman Who Changed the Face of Middle Class Kitchens', 'An Authentic Miracle Worker . . .' In September of that year a memorial service held at St Martin-in-the-Fields brought a mixed gathering of friends, followers and enemies – united at least in their tribute to the significance of Elizabeth's influence.

Elizabeth's will had originally made Felicité the chief beneficiary of her estate, but in the years following her sister's death Elizabeth made successive codicils to the document. To the chagrin of certain other members of her family, with the exception of a few bequests she eventually made over almost her entire estate to her third eldest nephew Stephen Grey, who had gone to live in Australia several years before. Elizabeth's munificence to Stephen Grey extended to the royalties (but not the copyright) on almost all her published books.

Not long before her death Elizabeth gave her favourite painting, Cedric Morris's *The Eggs*, to the Tate Gallery. To the National Portrait Gallery she left the Ambrose McEvoy portrait of her as a girl, the Adrian Daintrey portrait, the drawing by John Ward and the Egyptian portrait photograph of her taken shortly before her marriage. The National Portrait Gallery accepted the photograph and the John Ward but rejected the McEvoy and Daintrey.

Elizabeth stipulated that the Warburg Institute, London University, could choose what they wanted from her large library of culinary and related books. The Warburg was an appropriate resting place in Elizabeth's particular case as its *raison d'être* is the study of the history of the Classical tradition and Mediterranean culture. A number of books went to family and friends. About 2000 other culinary books were bought by the London Guildhall Library, which already houses the greater part of another important cookery library, the late Jane Grigson's. Elizabeth's books are still in store awaiting cataloguing. The task will not be an easy one as most of them were bristling with the yellow Post-it stickers she used for annotations and notes. However, at least the books are together, even if they are not available to the public. April Boyes made a partial card index of Elizabeth's books, but retired from working for her ten or so years before Elizabeth's death, during which time she continued buying books. With no bibliography of her library made before its dispersal, a crucial aspect of Elizabeth's tastes and working methods is sadly lost.

Following the apportioning of spoils from her house, Phillips were instructed by Stephen Grey to auction off the remnants in February 1994. This included the kitchen table (by now famous as her writing desk) as tempting bait, with 200 or so books and other odds and ends to be sold as Elizabeth David memorabilia. Phillips had underestimated the drawing power of their sale. The auction room was large, but not nearly large enough. With no places left even for standing room, over 100 more potential buyers were forced to send in their bids from queues running down the corridors. Members of Elizabeth's family, friends – those left out of the will – and devotees waited in anticipation.

Television and journalists' cameras flashed and whirred and as the sale finally commenced the tension was extraordinary. Despite a rather inadequate catalogue the lots became collectors' items, even before the last one went under the hammer. Phillips had calculated the lots should reach about £20,000 in all. By the end of the afternoon relic-hunters had driven the total up to £45,000. After fierce bidding Prue Leith of Leith's Cookery School was applauded as she won the kitchen-writing table. Wooden spoons in an earthenware jar went for over £300. A scrapbook containing cards from friends such as Lawrence Durrell, and coloured sketches by the illustrator of Elizabeth's earliest books, John Minton, were estimated at £100– £200: it fetched over £800.

The manuscript of the ices book over which Elizabeth had laboured for more than ten years remained unfinished at her death. The task of putting together and editing the notes was completed by her editor and literary executor Jill Norman, who published the book as *The Harvest of The Cold Months* in 1994. It would be reasonable to assume that Elizabeth had hung on to this last book for so long because she was hampered by ill-health. Her illnesses *were* debilitating but above all she had lost her particular sense of intellectual energy and drive. Her objectives were also obscured by having become entangled in the web of scholarship – perhaps antiquarianism is a better description of her late inclinations.

Harvest of the Cold Months charts the history of man's exploitation of the preserving and pleasurable properties of ice. It travels far beyond Elizabeth's initial idea of a history of ices, creams and fruit fools, initiated by her little booklet on syllabubs and fruit fools in 1969. Instead she became fascinated by ice and everything with which it was associated.

Elizabeth describes how ice was first harvested and stored to cool food and drink, then frozen, flavoured to eat as sorbets and ice-creams, eventually recognized as an invaluable preservative and, finally, created artificially. Travel literature is appropriately plundered as a rich source of information, making this book the first social history relating to culinary matters which does so with such thoroughness and authority. Descriptions of the extraordinary early methods of collection and manufacture of natural ice and its uses are exhaustively traced from China through India, Persia and eventually to Europe. By the late sixteenth century wealthy Florentines commonly kept ice stores for snow-chilled wine and beverages. Astounding ice sculptures were regularly incorporated into dazzling spectacles laid out at ceremonial banquets. The ruling Medici family excelled at this, using the talents of gifted artists such as the great sculptor Buontalenti to create unparalleled displays of opulence. This was only one early aspect of a craze which, despite almost unanimous medical condemnation, was to hold Europe in its grip for centuries.

This most perishable and valuable of commodities was transported across land and sea, sometimes thousands of miles, often withstanding attack by thieves. Fortunes were made – spectacularly so by Americans in the nineteenth century – and lost. Late seventeenth-century Europe saw ice commonly used by rich and poor alike. England joined in the vogue relatively late on, but by the end of the eighteenth century rival London confectioners bid to outdo one another in the magnificence of their glacial luxuries.

It is abundantly clear that a great deal of painstaking research went into Elizabeth's final opus, and much of the material is fascinating. There are glimpses of her familiar style – terse, lively and sardonic – but a welter of detail sometimes obscures the narrative and threatens to overwhelm the reader with the worthiness of a doctoral thesis. We witness Elizabeth being overtaken and indulging in the minutiae of scholarship and clearly seeking to be judged on her academic merits. In the light of her increasingly scholarly interests and the reflection of this in her last work, its appeal would, inevitably, have been for a smaller, more specialized audience than her previous work. On the grounds that Elizabeth was entitled to change this was reasonable, even if she did not fully comprehend its effect on her large readership.

The task of editing Elizabeth's manuscript was an unenviable one. The editor's description of the book as comprising essays and the decision to respect the integrity of the original text were praiseworthy.

To live one must eat, and frequently. Food is fuel, but also so much more than fuel. It is custom, routine, conviviality, enjoyment, and is saturated with feeling and association. A cuisine, a way of cooking, is a way of life, and from it springs an abundance of words, metaphors and modes of thought; it is one of the major dimensions of human existence.

Many will consider that Elizabeth, more than any other person during the last 100 years, influenced and altered perceptions of food and culinary practices in England and beyond. Born at the end of La

Belle Epoque, in her early aesthetic education she was immensely privileged, surrounded by a flowering of artistic knowledge and commitment. In her emotional life she was not so fortunate; for all her privilege she was even deprived in some respects – many working-class girls had things much better in their childhood. It was not until her mid-thirties that Elizabeth found her vocation as missionary to the Anglo-Saxon Barbarians, preaching the Gospel of the Mediterranean, of rational hedonism, in lyrical prose of outstanding power and beauty.

Elizabeth continued to develop over several decades, and gradually came to understand that the malaise she had spent so long describing went even deeper than she had thought. But she discovered that there were buried treasures within her own English tradition, if only you were prepared to dig. With this her last message she had fulfilled her great potential, leaving behind a legacy of writing which was at once fine, inspiring and illuminating.

Sources

APART FROM A very small number of essays, publications devoted
to Elizabeth David's life and writings have so far been confined to
journalism. A posthumous selection of her writings, the recent *South
Wind Through the Kitchen: The Best of Elizabeth David* (ed. Jill Norman),
includes some cautious reminiscence from some of those who knew
her. Although it is incorrect to say that Elizabeth never gave
interviews, most of these contain some fundamental inaccuracies – as
she wrote to Hugh Johnson: 'You know Hugh I expect that by the
time you are as old as I am there will be a lot of myths attached to
you, and you'll remember how it's been for me' – and can only be
used with some caution.

In her own writing there is a certain amount of autobiographical
information, but again caution is necessary. Elizabeth was scrupu-
lously accurate when it came to her recipes, but a master at putting
together ambiguous information about herself. Occasionally she was
quite simply inaccurate or she was obscuring the facts.

Her attitude to a biography was similarly unclear; it was
generally believed that she was vehemently against one. However, she
spoke to at least two friends, about them taking on the task, although
it came to nothing. The crux of the matter was really that Elizabeth
(understandably) wanted control over what was said about her as
much as not wanting anything said at all.

The published sources consulted included Elizabeth's articles
spread throughout the many publications for which she wrote. Among
these were *Vogue*, *Harper's Bazaar*, *House and Garden*, the *Spectator*, the
Food and Wine Quarterly, the *Sunday Sketch*, the *Sunday Times*, *Go*, the

Compleat Imbiber, *Harrods News*, *Nova*, *Housewife*, the *Observer*. There were also the little booklets written for Le Creuset and Saccone and Speed, and those published by herself between 1968 and 1969. Other sources were the small number of serious essays devoted to her, family papers, numerous letters to and from Elizabeth, and interviews and correspondence between myself and those who knew her. A bibliography is given at the end of this book which includes some of the texts relating to wider themes than Elizabeth's personal life.

After reflection, in the interests of privacy, but without misrepresenting the essential history of Elizabeth's life, it was decided to omit the occasional name or detail. For want of space other unpublished material, and much from interviews is also, sadly, here left unrecorded. The spelling and punctuation of quoted letters has generally been left as the original.

Bibliography

BOOKS BY ELIZABETH DAVID

FIRST PUBLICATIONS only are listed below. However, with the exception of *An Omelette and a Glass of Wine*, Elizabeth revised and in several cases wrote new introductions for later editions. Most of the publications she wrote for are listed throughout the text.

A Book of Mediterranean Food, John Lehmann, 1950
French Country Cooking, John Lehmann, 1951
Italian Food, Macdonald, 1954
Summer Cooking, Museum Press, 1955
French Provincial Cooking, Michael Joseph, 1960
Spices, Salt and Aromatics in the English Kitchen, Penguin Books, 1970
English Bread and Yeast Cookery, Allen Lane, 1977
An Omelette and a Glass of Wine, Jill Norman at Robert Hale, 1984
Harvest of the Cold Months, Michael Joseph, 1994

Acton, Eliza, *Modern Cookery for Private Families*, Longman, Brown, Green and Longman, 1845
　　　The English Bread Book, 1857; reprinted Southover Press, 1990
Acton, Harold, *More Memoirs of an Aesthete*, Methuen, 1970
Alexander, Michael, *Delhi and Agra*, Macmillan, 1987
Barr, Ann and Levy, Paul, *The Foodie Handbook*, Ebury Press, 1984
Bateman, Michael, *Cooking People*, Leslie Frewin, 1966
Beck, S., Bertholle, L. and Child, Julia, *Mastering the Art of French Cooking*, 1961; Cassell, 1963

459

Bibliography

Bedford, Sybille, *The Sudden View: A Mexican Journey*, Victor Gollancz, 1953

Bitting, Katherine, G., *Gastronomic Bibliography*, 1939; reprinted Holland Press, 1981

Borrow, George, *Lavengro*, 1851; 6th edn, 1900

Boulestin, Marcel, *Simple French Cooking for English Homes*, Heinemann, 1923

> *Having Crossed the Channel*, Heinemann, 1934
> *Myself My Two Countries*, Cassell, 1936

Burnett, John, *Plenty and Want*, Thomas Nelson, 1966

Caesar, Adrian, *Dividing Lines: Poetry, Class and Ideology in the 1930s*, Manchester University Press, 1991

Carpenter, Humphrey, *The Brideshead Generation*, Weidenfeld and Nicolson, 1989

Castelvetro, G. (trans. Gillian Riley), *The Fruit, Herbs and Vegetables of Italy*, Viking, 1989

Chaney Dr Edward, *Quo Vadis? Travel As Education and The Impact of Italy in the Sixteenth Century*, Frank Cass, 1998

Clark, Lady C., *The Cookery Book of Lady Clark of Tillypronie*, 1909; reprinted Southover Press, 1994

Connolly, Cyril, *The Rock Pool*, Obelisk Press, 1936

Conran, Terence, *The Kitchen Book*, Mitchell Beazley, 1977

Cooper, A., *Cairo in the War*, Hamish Hamilton, 1989

Correnti, Pino, *La Gastrononomia nella Storia e nella Vita del Popolo Siciliana*, Milan, 1971

Cowan, Charles Gibson, *Loud Report*, Michael Joseph, 1938

> *The Voyage of the Evelyn Hope*, Cresset Press, 1946

Cuisenier, Jean, *Les Français et La Table*, Editions de la Réunion des Musées Nationaux, 1985

Curnonsky, *Traditional Recipes of the Provinces of France* (trans. and ed. Edwin Lavin), W. H. Allen, 1961

Dale, Frances and Craddock, John, *Around Britain with Bon Viveur*, John Lehmann, 1952

Davidson, Alan and Jane (eds), *Petits Propos Culinaires*, Prospect Books, 1979–1997. See in particular essays on and by E.D.

Davidson, Alan, *Mediterranean Seafood*, Penguin, 1972

A Kipper With My Tea: Selected Food Essays, Macmillan, 1988. See in particular, *An Omelette and a Glass of Wine*

Davies, W. H. *Autobiography of a Super-Tramp*, 1908; reprinted Jonathan Cape, 1921

Dawson, Thomas, *The Good Housewife's Jewell*, London, 1585; reprinted Teatrum Orbis Terrarum, 1977

Dods, Mistress Margaret, *The Cook and Housewife's Manual*, Edinburgh, 1826

Douglas, Norman, *Siren Land*, J. M. Dent, 1911
    Old Calabria, Secker and Warburg, 1915
    South Wind, Secker and Warburg, 1917
    Looking Back, Secker and Warburg, 1933
    Together, 1923, Penguin, 1945
    Late Harvest, Lindsay Drummond, 1946
    Venus in the Kitchen, Heinemann, 1952

Douglas-Home, Jessica, *Violet*, Harvill Press, 1996

Driver, Christopher, *The British at Table 1940–1980*, Chatto and Windus, 1983

Drummond, J. C. and Wilbraham, Anne, *The Englishman's Food*, Jonathan Cape, 1939

Dudley, Georgina, Countess of Dudley, *The Dudley Cookery Book*, Edward Arnold, 1909

Durrell, Lawrence, *The Alexandria Quartet*, (single volume edn.), Faber and Faber, 1962
    Spirit of Place, Letters and Essays on Travel, (ed. Alan G. Thomas), Faber and Faber, 1969

Eliot, T. S. *Selected Essays*, 1932; 3rd edn., Faber and Faber, 1951

Escoffier, A., *Ma Cuisine*, 1934; republished (trans. Vyvyan Holland), Paul Hamlyn, 1965

Farr, Dennis, *English Art 1870–1940*, Oxford, 1978

Fedden, Robin, *Personal Landscape, An Anthology of Exile*, Editions Poetry London, 1945
    Personal Landscape, Turret Books, 1966

Fedden, Romilly, *Food and Other Frailties*, Seeley Service, London, 1948

Fermor, Patrick Leigh, *A Time of Gifts*, John Murray, 1977

Fielding, Xan, *Hide and Seek*, Secker and Warburg, 1954

Fiennes, Celia, *The Journeys of Celia Fiennes* (ed. C. Morris), Cresset Press, 1947

Fisher, M. F. K., *With Bold Knife and Fork*, Chatto and Windus, 1983

Ford, Ford Madox, *A Mirror to France*, Duckworth, 1926
    Provence, J. B. Lippincott, 1935

Freeman, *Sarah, Isabella and Sam: The Story of Mrs. Beeton*, Victor Gollancz, 1977

Fussell, Paul, *Abroad*, Oxford University Press, 1980

Glasse, Hannah, *The Art of Cookery Made Plain and Easy*, London, 1747; 5th edn, 1755

Gray, Patience, and Boyd, Primrose, *Plat du Jour*, Penguin, 1957

Grigson, Jane, *Good Things*, Michael Joseph, 1971
    English Food, Macmillan, 1974

Hartley, Dorothy, *The Countryman's England*, Batsford, 1935
    Food in England, Macdonald, 1954

Heath, Ambrose, *Good Food*, Faber and Faber, 1932
    Kitchen Front Recipes, London, 1941

Holloway, Martin, *Norman Douglas*, Secker and Warburg, 1976

Hope, Annette, *Londoners' Larder*, Mainstream Publishing, 1990

Hutchins, Sheila, *English Recipes and Others*, Methuen, 1967

Jago, William, *The Technology of Breadmaking*, 1911; revised edn, The Northern Publishing Co., 1921

Jenkins, Alan, *The Thirties*, Stein and Day, 1976

Johnson, James, *A Hundred Years Eating*, Gill and Macmillan, 1977

Kent, Countess Elizabeth of, *A True Gentlewoman's Delight*, London, 1653

Kirkland, John, *The Modern Baker and Confectioner and Caterer*, 1907; revised edn (4 vols), Gresham, 1923

Lassalle, George, *The Fish in My Life*, Macmillan, 1989

Lassels, Richard, *The Voyage of Italy: Or a Compleat Journey Through Italy*, Paris, 1670; 2nd edn, London, 1698

Lewis, Lesley, *The Private Life of a Country House*, David and Charles, 1980

Leyel, Mrs C. F., and Hartley, Olga, *The Gentle Art of Cookery*, Chatto and Windus, 1925

Llanover, Lady Augusta, *Good Cookery*, London, 1867

Luke, Sir Harry, *The Tenth Muse*, Putnam, 1954

Lutyens, Mary, *Edwin Lutyens*, John Murray, 1980

Lyall, Archibald, *The Companion Guide to the South of France*, Collins, 1963

Maclean, Virginia, *A Short-Title Catalogue of Household and Cookery Books Published in the English Tongue, 1701–1800*, Prospect Books 1981

Manning, Olivia, *The Levant Trilogy*, single volume edition, Penguin, 1982

Markham, Gervase, *The English Housewife*, London, 1615

May, Robert, *The Accomplisht Cook*, London, 1660

McNeill, F. Marian, *The Scots Kitchen*, Blackie, 1929

Mennell, Stephen, *All Manners of Food*, Blackwell, 1985

Money, James, *Capri: The Enchanted Isle*, Hamish Hamilton, 1986

Montagne, Prosper, *Larousse Gastronomique*, Libraire Larousse, 1938; republished Paul Hamlyn, 1962

Montague, C. E. *Fiery Particles*, in particular the story *Honours Easy*, 1923, Chatto and Windus 1928

Montaigne, Michel de, *The Complete Works of Montaigne, Essays, Travel Journals, Letters* (trans. Donald Frame), Hamish Hamilton, 1965

Morphet, Richard, *Cedric Morris*, Tate Gallery, 1984

Morphy, Countess Marcelle, *Picnic Snacks*, Eldon Press, 1933

Morton, H. V. *A Traveller in Southern Italy*, Methuen, 1969

Orwell, Sonia ed. *The Collected Essays, Journalism and Letters of George Orwell*, Penguin, 1970

Oxford Symposium On Food and Cookery, Proceedings, (ed. Harlan Walker) Prospect Books, 1989–97

Oxford, A. W., *English Cookery Books to the Year 1850*, 1913; reprinted by the Holland Press, 1977

Plat, Sir Hugh, *Delights For Ladies*, London, 1600; republished, Crosby, Lockwood and Son, 1948

Poems from the Desert, George Harrap, 1944

Pomiane, Edouard de, *Cooking With Pomiane*, (trans. Peggy Benton), Bruno Cassirer, 1962

Ranfurly, Countess of, *To War With Whitaker*, Heinemann, 1994

Ray, Cyril, *The Complete Imbiber*, 1956–71, various issues

Ray, Elizabeth (ed., with an intro. by E. David), *The Best of Eliza Acton*, Longman, 1968

Ridley, Ursula, ed. *The Life and Letters of Cecilia Ridley*, The Spredden Press, 1990

Roden, Claudia, *A Book of Middle Eastern Food*, Thomas Nelson, 1968

Root, Waverly, *The Food of Italy*, 1971; reprinted by Vintage Books, 1977

Ross, Janet, *Leaves From Our Tuscan Kitchen*, J. M. Dent, 1908

Rundell, Maria, *A New System of Cookery*, London, 1806

Shand, Moreton, *A Book of Food*, Jonathan Cape, 1927

Simeti, Mary Taylor, *Sicilian Food*, Random Century, 1989

Simon, André, *Food*, Burke Publishing, 1949

    By Request an Autobiography, The Wine and Food Society 1957

Sissons, Michael and French, Philip (eds), *The Age of Austerity*, Hodder, 1963

Sitwell, Osbert, *Left Hand Right Hand*, autobiographical volumes, Macmillan, 1945–48

Smollett, Tobias, *Travels Through France and Italy*, 1771

Spalding, Frances, *British Art Since 1900*, Thames and Hudson, 1986

Spry, Constance and Hume, Rosemary, *The Constance Spry Cookery Book*, J. M. Dent, 1956

Spurling, Hilary, *Elinor Fettiplace's Receipt Book*, Salamander, 1986

Stewart, I. McD.G., *The Struggle For Crete*, Oxford University Press, 1966

Stobart, Tom, *Herbs, Spices and Flavourings*, David and Charles, 1970

Sysonby, Lady Ria, *Lady Sysonby's Cookbook*, Putnam, 1935

Theroux, Paul, *The Pillars of Hercules*, Hamish Hamilton, 1995

Touring Club Italiano, *Guida Gastronomica d'Italia*, 1931; reprinted 1951

Waddell, Helen, *The Wandering Scholars*, Constable, 1927

Waugh, Evelyn, *Officers and Gentlemen*, Chapman and Hall, 1955

Westbury, Lord, *Handlist of Italian Cookery Books*, Leo Olschki, 1963

Wheaton, Barbara Ketcham, *Savouring the Past, the French Kitchen and Table from 1300 to 1789*, Chatto and Windus, 1983

Wheeler, David (ed.), *Convivium*, vol. 1, no. 1, Spring 1993

White, Florence, *Good Things in England*, Jonathan Cape, 1932

White, Gilbert, *Gilbert White's Journals*, Routledge, 1931; reprinted
    David and Charles, 1970
Wickes, George (ed.), *Lawrence Durrell and Henry Miller: A Private
    Correspondence*, Faber and Faber, 1963
Wilson C. Anne, *Food and Drink in Britain*, Constable, 1973
        (ed), 'The Appetite and the Eye' and 'Banqueting Stuffe',
    papers from the 1st and 2nd Leeds Symposia on Food History,
    Edinburgh University Press, 1986 and 1991
Wine and Food Quarterly (ed.) André Simon, subsequently by Hugh
    Johnson, Pamela Vandyke Price, etc.
Withers, Audrey, *Life Span*, Peter Owen, 1994

Index

Index